Thomas Muentzer, a Destroyer of the Godless

THOMAS MÜNTZER.

Thomas Muentzer, a Destroyer of the Godless

The Making of a Sixteenth-Century Religious Revolutionary

Abraham Friesen

UNIVERSITY OF CALIFORNIA PRESS
Berkeley · *Los Angeles* · *Oxford*

University of California Press
Berkeley and Los Angeles, California

University of California Press
Oxford, England

Copyright © 1990 by The Regents of the University of California

Library of Congress Cataloging-in-Publication Data

Friesen, Abraham.
  Thomas Muentzer, a destroyer of the godless : the making of a
sixteenth-century religious revolutionary / Abraham Friesen.
    p.   cm.
  Includes bibliographical references.
  ISBN 0-520-08781-4 (alk. paper)
  1. Münzer, Thomas, 1490 (ca.)–1525.   2. Anabaptists—Germany-
-Biography.   3. Reformation—Germany—Biography.   I. Title.
BX4948.M8F75   1990
284'.3'092—dc20
  [B]   90-32488
                                                                       CIP

Printed in the United States of America

1 2 3 4 5 6 7 8 9

To Eric

Contents

Abbreviations

In citations of multivolume works, the first number given indicates the volume, and the numbers following refer to pages. Line numbers, when supplied, follow the page numbers.

AGBM   *Akten zur Geschichte des Bauernkriegs in Mitteldeutschland*, ed. W. P. Fuchs, 3 vols. Jena, 1942. Reprint: Aalen, 1964.

AE   *Luther's Works*, eds. Jaroslav Pelikan and Helmut T. Lehman, 55 vols. Philadelphia, 1955–1986.

ARG   *Archiv Fuer Reformationsgeschichte.* Guetersloh, 1903–.

Augustine, *Works*   *The Nicene and Post-Nicene Fathers*, ed. Philip Schaff, vols. I–VII. 2nd Series. Reprint: Grand Rapids, 1979.

Bensing/Trillitzsch   Manfred Bensing and Winfried Trillitzsch, "Bernard Dappens 'Articulo . . . contra Lutheranos.' Zur Auseinandersetzung der Jueterboger Franziskaner mit Thomas Muentzer und Franz Guenther 1519," *Jahrbuch fuer Regionalgeschichte*, 2 (1967), 113–147.

CH	*Church History.* Berne, Indiana, 1888–.
CR	*Corpus Reformatorum.* 99 vols. Halle, Berlin and Leipzig, 1834–1982.
Gess, *Akten*	*Akten und Briefe zur Kirchenpolitik Herzog Georgs von Sachsen,* ed. Felician Gess, 2 vols. Leipzig, 1905. Reprint: Cologne & Vienna, 1985.
HJ	*Historisches Jahrbuch.* Munich, 1880–.
HThR	*Harvard Theological Review.* Cambridge, Mass., 1908–.
HZ	*Historische Zeitschrift.* Munich, 1959–.
JdKHB	*Jahrbuch der Kirchlichen Hochschule Berlin.* Berlin, 1963–.
JfRG	*Jahrbuch fuer Regionalgeschichte.* Weimar, 1973–.
JEH	*Journal of Ecclesiastical History.* London, 1950–.
JM&RS	*Journal of Medieval and Renaissance Studies.* Durham, NC, 1971–.
JMS	*Journal of Mennonite Studies.* Winnipeg, 1983–.
JThS	*Journal of Theological Studies.* Oxford, 1899–.
K&D	*Kerygma und Dogma.* Goettingen, 1955–.
LCC	*Library of Christian Classics.* 26 vols. Philadelphia and London, 1953–.
LJ	*Luther Jahrbuch.* Berlin, 1933–.
MQR	*The Mennonite Quarterly Review.* Goshen, Indiana, 1927–.
MSB	*Thomas Muentzer, Schriften und Briefe,* ed. Franz Guenther. Guetersloh, 1968.
Neue Mitteilungen	*Neue Mitteilungen aus dem Gebiet historisch-antiquarischer Forschungen,* ed.

	Carl Eduard Foerstemann. Vol. XII. Halle/ S., 1869.
Neues Urkundenbuch	*Neues Urkundenbuch zur Geschichte der evangelischen Kirchen-Reformation,* ed. Carl Eduard Foerstemann, Hamburg, 1842.
StL	*Dr. Martin Luthers Saemmtliche Schriften,* ed. Johann Georg Walch, 23 vols. St. Louis, 1881–1910.
SCJ	*Sixteenth Century Journal.* Kirksville, MO, 1972–.
ThL	*Theologische Literaturzeitung.* Berlin, 1875–.
WA	*D. Martin Luthers Werke. Kritische Gesamtausgabe.* 61 Vols. Weimar, 1883–.
WABr	*D. Martin Luthers Werke. Briefwechsel.* 18 vols. Weimar, 1930–.
WATr	*D. Martin Luthers Werke. Tischreden.* 6 vols. Weimar, 1912–1921.
ZfG	*Zeitschrift fuer Geschichtswissenschaft.* Berlin: 1953–.
ZfK	*Zeitschrift fuer Kirchengeschichte.* Stuttgart, 1876–.

Acknowledgments

This book has been six years in the making, many more in gestation. It is the ultimate product of an interest in Thomas Muentzer that goes back to a Reformation seminar under Lewis W. Spitz at Stanford University. What began as a fascination with Muentzer historiography gradually, after many years, turned into a preoccupation with the "problem" of Thomas Muentzer. I am grateful that at the very inception of this preoccupation a number of people and institutions provided me with the opportunity to explore solutions in a public forum. Thus, in October 1983, at the invitation of Henry Loewen, Chair in Mennonite Studies at the University of Winnipeg, I delivered three lectures on the relationship of reformers and radicals, one of which dealt with Luther and Muentzer. In early November of the same year, at the invitation of Rexford A. Boda, President of the Canadian Theological Seminary, I delivered, there and at the University of Regina, four lectures, one of which was a revised version of the lecture on Luther and Muentzer. Some two years later, Carl E. Armerding, Principal of Regent College on the campus of the University of British Columbia, invited me to deliver the first in what was to be an annual series of lectures on Anabaptism. At my request he graciously permitted me to inaugurate the series with three lectures on Thomas Muentzer, the very man an older generation of Mennonite scholars sought to excise from the ranks of the "normative" Anabaptists. These opportunities to explore some ideas about

Muentzer forced me to begin formulating, more precisely, some preliminary opinions on the subject.

I have also, from time to time, discussed the themes developed in this study with friends and colleagues—not that the two are mutually exclusive! At first I was met with nearly universal skepticism, even from members of my own family. Gradually, however, I began to win converts. And the skepticism has been most beneficial, forcing me back to the "drawing board," so to speak, time and again. Thus, my colleague, Harold A. Drake, a Eusebius scholar (is there not one in every department?), raised some significant questions about my initial draft of the chapter on Muentzer and Eusebius, leading me into a much more detailed study of the topic than I had initially envisaged. Another colleague, Jeffrey B. Russell, read an initial draft of the first four chapters and offered valuable observations. Peter J. Klassen of the California State University at Fresno and Lewis W. Spitz of Stanford University did the same. Walter Klaassen of Conrad Grebel College, University of Waterloo, read the entire manuscript for content, and my old friend, Victor G. Doerksen of the University of Manitoba, read it for style. To all these, as to my graduate students, especially Jonathan Rainbow and Barry Ryan, who suffered through a seminar in which the chapters on Muentzer were discussed with monotonous regularity, I express my sincere gratitude. I wish also to express my appreciation for the suggestions made by the anonymous readers of the manuscript for the University of California Press—especially the second reader, whose comments have made this a much better book. And the copyeditor's thorough work has considerably improved the style and kept me from a number of errors that had crept into the manuscript. Although I have not accepted every suggestion made, I wish, nevertheless, to express my grateful thanks to all. A scholar must, in the final analysis, make his own mistakes, and I have no doubt made mine. For these I and I alone am responsible.

A Humanities Summer Fellowship from the University of California enabled me to begin preliminary work on this book, and a fellowship from the Center for Mennonite Studies at the University of Winnipeg permitted me to complete it. The great bulk of the work, however, was done on sabbatical leave during the academic year 1983–1984 and in the years following while I was fully engaged in teaching. To both institutions I express my appreciation. Whereas institutional support has been intermittent, that of my wife and son has been continual and unconditional. I wish to acknowledge, with deep gratitude, that support here. Aside from support, my son also suffered—with commendable equanimity—repeated calls for help from a father learning to use a word processor while refusing to read the manual for directions! It is to him that I dedicate this book.

Abraham Friesen

Santa Barbara, California
August 1989

Introduction:
Crossroads at Leipzig

The "supremacy" of the Roman church rests on utterly
worthless decrees of the Roman popes issued within the last
four hundred years.

> —Martin Luther, 1519

Time, the very stuff of which history is made, has a way of modifying or
even reversing the most ingrained of human judgments. What one generation may consider evil another may find beneficent. Thus Thomas
Muentzer of Stolberg in the Harz, born 1489 or 1490,[1] regarded as the
villain of Luther's reformation and nearly universally condemned in the
aftermath of the disastrous defeat of the peasants in 1525,[2] came gradually to be rehabilitated in the wake of the French Revolution.[3] Culminating in the 1841–1843 history of the Peasants' War by Wilhelm Zimmermann,[4] this reinterpretation from a pro-revolutionary perspective found
its way, quite naturally, into that of Friedrich Engels, and through him
into all subsequent Marxist interpretations. Though modified since the
1960s,[5] the latter have left their mark on the work of social historians,
coming together there with a more positive evaluation of Muentzer
from other perspectives following World War II.[6] The older Lutheran
judgment, perhaps in some disarray at the moment, was never totally
vanquished, however. And so one should not be surprised to find that
the rapprochement in Muentzer studies has not pleased everyone.[7]

Perhaps it was the poet's open and unabashed sympathy that elicited
from Heinrich Heine, some ten years before the appearance of Zimmermann's partisan reinterpretation, the observation that if one rose to the
defense of Muentzer (and Heine did, asserting that Muentzer had been
right and Luther wrong), one was forced into opposition to Luther.[8]
The converse is just as valid. The twentieth-century quarrel between

Marxist and non-Marxist has deepened this rift further. Combined with the polemics embedded in the documents of the time, this rift has widened to place historians of the two protagonists even further apart.[9] From these positions they have only recently begun to move closer by seeking to establish the time and place of Muentzer's intellectual transformation and to determine the basis upon which it was founded. To do so is to evaluate better Muentzer's relationship to Luther and understand more fully the motives behind his involvement in the events of those turbulent early years of the Reformation.[10] All the studies devoted to this end, however, have been limited in scope and the majority have been of a systematic rather than historical nature.[11] The present enquiry seeks a larger context and an approach to the problem from an evolutionary perspective. And from the very outset, Luther is the *Gegenspieler,* sometimes lurking in the wings, sometimes strutting the stage of history he so dominated in those years, to frustrate the designs of the man he came to call the "Satan of Allstedt."

In this quest, scholars have begun more and more to concentrate on the period between Muentzer's debate with the Franciscans in Jueterbog of April 1519 and his departure from Zwickau in June 1521 as the critical time in which his intellectual transformation must have taken place. That he underwent such a transformation is not in doubt; its precise nature, however, has yet to be determined.[12] And the questions at issue are essentially the following: Was Muentzer ever really a follower of Luther in the early years of the Reformation, or, like many others, simply caught up in the euphoria of the reformer's opposition to the Catholic Church? If he was a disciple, where, when and under what circumstances did he break with Luther? If not, what was their relationship? Furthermore, what role did Tauler, the Zwickau Prophets, and the Hussites play in all this? Indeed, were there other stimuli, and under what conditions did Muentzer encounter them?

In general, beginning with Zimmermann and culminating in the Marxist interpretation, the attempt has repeatedly been made to free Muentzer from both Luther's influence and that of the Prophets.[13] On the one hand, non-Marxist scholars such as Hans-Juergen Goertz, emphasizing the importance of Tauler's sermons for Muentzer's intellectual development, have tended to diminish the importance of Luther and the Prophets.[14] On the other hand, those who have contended that Muentzer began his Reformation career as a follower of Luther have nearly unanimously argued that he broke with the reformer under the influence of the Zwickau Prophets.[15]

The fact that very little is known about Muentzer's early life makes any generalizations about this period hazardous at best.[16] We do know that he enrolled at the University of Leipzig in 1506 and at the University of Frankfurt an der Oder in 1512. As Guenter Vogler observes, however: "A determination as to how these two universities influenced Muentzer's intellectual development cannot be made since his tracts and correspondence remain silent on the subject, and scholarly study of the two institutions during the time in question has not advanced sufficiently to allow one to reach any conclusions on the matter."[17] Whereas Muentzer does refer to himself as "artium magister et sancte scripture baccalaureus"[18] in an undated letter from Zwickau, where and when he might have acquired these degrees has remained an open question even though some have suggested that he might have received his theological degree at the University of Wittenberg in 1518.[19]

Unlike Luther who was a monk, Muentzer belonged to the ranks of the secular clergy entrusted with the cure of souls. His first public office, however, appears to have been as *praepositus* (provost) of the monastery at Frohse and the second as confessor at the convent of Beuditz. Scholars differ as to the precise time he took up his duties at Frohse.[20] Whatever the date, on 6 March 1514 he was offered a small prebend at St. Martin's Church in Braunschweig which he held until February 1522. Such a prebend would seem to indicate that Muentzer had, by this time, established relationships with influential persons in that city. And, indeed, scholars have pointed to his close ties to citizens well connected with the town council and others in the city involved in trade and commerce.[21] He even appears to have spent some time in that city during 1517, but whether it was before or after Luther posted his 95 Theses is not known. His Braunschweig contacts, in any case, would appear to have been sympathetic to reform. If, as is sometimes contended, Muentzer's being a secular priest influenced his later perception of the plight of the "common man,"[22] it can only have begun to do so later in Zwickau.

Whatever Muentzer's relationship to Braunschweig, he seems not to have left Frohse until after the publication of Luther's Theses. Indeed, it may well be the case that the Theses were the cause of his departure and that he left Frohse to go to Wittenberg where he must have met Luther, Carlstadt, Melanchthon, and Franz Guenther, who was a theological student there until the summer of 1518.[23] Nicholas Hausmann, who later succeeded Muentzer in Zwickau, wrote Frederick the Wise on 13 August 1521 that he had first met Muentzer "at the time that the eminent Dr. Martin Luther began to become famous, whose teaching and notoriety brought me to Wittenberg four years ago."[24] Muentzer may well have reacted in the same manner. Such a period of time spent in Wittenberg would explain why, in April 1519, when Franz Guenther withdrew from the pulpit he had taken over in Jueterbog in late 1518 or early 1519, Muentzer was sent to serve as his replacement. While there he picked up the quarrel with the Franciscans which Guenther had been forced to lay aside. It is in the report on this encounter that we get a first sense of Muentzer's thinking on the matter of Church reform. It has therefore also raised the question of Muentzer's relationship to Luther.

According to Bernhard Dappen, the Franciscan priest who reported to the Bishop of Brandenburg on the matter, Guenther had been cited before the monks because he had preached four things: that one need no longer pray to saints; that one need no longer fast; that one need no longer confess sins to a priest; and that Bohemians were better Christians than were the Germans. At the hearing Guenther and his supporters had taken the attack even further, arguing that Church councils did not represent the entire Church; denying that the pope was the vicar of Christ or that Peter had been head of the Apostles; asserting that conciliar decrees had been passed to satisfy the greed of bishops and that no exceptions could be made to divine law; rejecting the counsels of perfection since everything in the Gospel was commanded; and claiming that God expected every Christian to obey the Gospel and aspire to perfection. To add insult to injury, they had made the outrageous assertion that any simple person who appealed to the authority of Scripture should be accorded greater trust than a pope or council who did not.[25]

Guenther's suspension, voluntary or otherwise, had followed in due course. But in his place had come Thomas Muentzer to continue the assault.[26] In his sermons he had attacked the pope for not calling councils every five years when he was obliged to do so and had argued that the pope should remain head of the Church only as long as the bishops tolerated him. He had attacked the pope on the canonization of saints and criticized Scholastic theologians for arguing from rational premises, all of which, he had said, came from the devil. He had charged that whereas the early Church had appointed holy fathers as bishops, the present Church appointed tyrants. This had led to the Gospel being hidden, *sub scamno,* for some 400 years.[27] Like Guenther before him, Muentzer had also asserted that the Bohemians were better Christians than the Germans.

In 1973, Shinzo Tanaka argued that these "Jueterbog Articles" dem-

onstrated that Muentzer had already begun to distance himself noticeably from both Guenther and his teacher, Luther.[28] His argument is not
convincing, however,[29] if for no other reason than that Guenther
himself—if one can use the argument from silence—in a letter of early
1522 was apparently aware of only one difference between himself and
Muentzer, to whom he wrote after the latter's return from Prague:

> People say that the Bohemians are not moved [by you] but remain in the
> other evangelical camp. This most certainly caused you to flee and I hear you
> are now living in Thuringia. I would very much like to see you again and
> hear you speak personally about your spirit. But beware lest the light, that is
> in you, be darkness. People are spreading all manner of gossip about you. Be
> sober and be vigilant, for your adversary the devil walks about like a roaring
> lion, seeking whom he may devour. I hope you have tested your spirit and
> are not hiding some nonsense [fable] beneath it, but are rather fervent in the
> Spirit of Christ.[30]

Had there been differences between them in Jueterbog, Guenther might
well have addressed them in the above context. But he does not. What
he does address as something new, and that rather forcefully, is
Muentzer's claim to possess the Holy Spirit. This was, apparently, from
Guenther's perspective, the major difference between the old Muentzer
whom he had known in Wittenberg and Jueterbog and the new
Muentzer about whom he was hearing disconcerting tidings. Nor did
Martin Luther, who apparently read Dappen's report, see any substantive differences between his views and those expressed in the "Articles,"
for he came to the defense of his Jueterbog colleagues in a letter of
15 May 1519 to the Franciscans.[31]

The rupture between Luther and Muentzer must therefore have taken
place after the Jueterbog incident. And the key issue to divide them may
well have been Muentzer's claim to possess the Holy Spirit, a claim that
Franz Guenther pointed to in the above letter. When did Muentzer first
indicate that he believed himself to possess the Holy Spirit? The answer
usually given is: under the influence of the Zwickau Prophets.[32] I would
like to suggest an earlier time, however, indeed, a time before his encounter with the Prophets. The indication in Muentzer's correspondence is an
oblique one and comes in his first letter to Luther dated 13 July 1520,
while he was still the substitute for Egranus at St. Catherine's Church in
Zwickau. There, in his conclusion, Muentzer referred to Luther as the
"specimen et lucerna amicorum dei."[33] As we shall see at some length in
the first chapter, the term "friends of God" is repeatedly used by Tauler
and refers to persons who have experienced a conversion through the

power of the Holy Spirit. Whereas Muentzer uses the term with reference to Luther, there can be little doubt that he regarded himself as a "friend of God" by this time as well.

If we are right, Muentzer's intellectual transformation must have taken place between May 1519 and July 1520, perhaps even before he came to Zwickau in May 1520. Without the above argument, Bensing and Trillitzsch, already in 1967, suggested that the Leipzig Disputation must have had something to do with it;[34] others have suggested that his reading while at the secluded convent in Beuditz produced the new perspective in him.[35] In what follows we shall suggest that the critical period of Muentzer's intellectual development occurs in the months before and after June 1519 when Martin Luther and John Eck engaged in the famous Leipzig Disputation. Issues raised at that debate, which Muentzer attended, determined the direction of his reading and study for some time. He came to that meeting, however, just after having immersed himself in the mystical sermons of John Tauler. With this as background, Muentzer heard the two protagonists address such questions as when the Catholic Church had entered upon its path to deformity, whether councils and popes were infallible, and whether Luther was not a Hussite. Because Church history was important in answering the first question, Muentzer ordered a copy of Eusebius's *Church History*. With regard to the second question, the Disputation made it evident that Augustine's opinion was the critical one, and so he ordered a copy of Augustine's sermons and letters. In order to answer the third question, Muentzer ordered a copy of the Acts of the Council of Constance that had tried and condemned John Hus. Muentzer's ordering these books from the Leipzig book dealer Achatius Glov seems obviously to have been a response to the issues raised at Leipzig. Aside from Tauler's sermons, however, scholars have just begun to study what Muentzer read in connection with his intellectual development.[36]

Scholars have known, of course, that Muentzer had been influenced by Tauler. Exactly what form that influence had taken, however, was less clear. They also knew that Luther had read Tauler, had edited the mystical *Eine Deutsche Theologie*, at first in fragmentary form in 1516 and then in complete form in 1518. Was Luther the man who mediated Tauler to Muentzer? If so, were both men influenced in the same way? To clarify the importance of Tauler for each, I therefore begin, in the first chapter, to reconstruct as much as possible this relationship as it might have developed.

Because Muentzer ordered Eusebius's *Church History* from Achatius

Glov immediately after the Leipzig Disputation, it appears to me likely that the problem of the point at which the Roman Catholic Church had become deformed, discussed by Eck and Luther at Leipzig, must have motivated him to turn to his own study of Church history. Whereas Muentzer had earlier accepted Luther's dictum that the Word of God had lain "hidden under a bench" since the Scholastics had become dominant, after reading Eusebius he changed his mind, coming to believe that the deformity had set in much earlier. He quoted Hegesippus, whom he discovered in Eusebius, repeatedly to this effect. When I too took up Eusebius—though I had read him before—I realized that Muentzer must also have taken his view of the pure Apostolic Church from him. This glorified picture of the early Church—this "myth" as Gordon Leff has called it with respect to its medieval polemical use[37]— is of considerable importance for Muentzer's thought.

But the question remained: Why should this Apostolic Church be born anew in Prague in his own day, as Muentzer proclaimed in his *Manifesto* of 1521? The sermons and letters of Augustine, which Muentzer also ordered from Achatius Glov after the Leipzig Disputation, suggested some answers. In his defense of the Catholic Church against the attacks of the Donatists, Augustine had exploited the Parable of the Tares to the fullest. It had served him well in defending the Church as a mixed body of elect and reprobates who would be separated from one another only in "the time of harvest" at the end of the age. Here, then, was the other major source of Muentzer's argument. Eusebius had convinced him that the Apostolic Church had been composed of pure wheat, but it had very early become defiled with tares. These, however, would be removed from her only in the time of harvest. Joachim of Fiore, I became convinced, had not provided Muentzer with his eschatology; Augustine had. But, once again, Luther at Leipzig, along with Tauler's sermons, had been the mediators. Was it the same Augustine who had influenced all three? Was the Augustine who spoke through Tauler the same as the one who confirmed Luther in his theology of the Righteousness of God? The relationships between Tauler and Augustine, between Luther and Augustine, as well as between Muentzer and Augustine all had to be clarified.

From this point on, the chapters are developed more chronologically, though still systematically. The fourth chapter deals with Muentzer's sojourn in Zwickau and especially with his relationship to the Zwickau Prophets. Since my research for the first three chapters convinced me that Muentzer's intellectual perspective had been fully developed before he came to Zwickau, the influence that the Prophets are generally assumed to have exerted upon him could not have been so great—if at all—as scholars since Paul Wappler's 1908 study have held. If this was indeed the case, what had been the relationship between Muentzer and the Prophets?

The fifth chapter deals with Muentzer's *Prague Manifesto* and with his relationship to John Hus. It argues, indeed, that it was Hus, not the radical Taborites, who attracted him to Prague. The sixth and seventh chapters deal with the critical *Auseinandersetzung* between Muentzer and the Wittenberg reformers, especially Luther. Beginning with his observation of 1520 that Luther was the "specimen et lucerna amicorum dei," Muentzer gradually began to doubt Luther's Taulerian credentials, arguing after the Wittenberg Unrest of 1521–1522 that Luther was a man from whom the Holy Spirit had departed. The seventh chapter continues this argument, reinterpreting Muentzer's last letter to Luther of July 1523 in light of Luther's "egregio libro" referred to in that letter by Muentzer. From there the chapter investigates the gradual estrangement of the two in a series of tracts and letters, and it ends with Muentzer's judgment that Luther is just another rational scribe seeking to prevent the establishment of the *futura ecclesia,* the new Apostolic Church, in the same manner that the scribes and Pharisees had attempted to do in Christ's day.

Chapter eight begins with an outline of Muentzer's reform program and then proceeds to define his relationship to Catholic princes whom he called "godless," and to the Lutheran princes whom he called "pious Christian princes." These two sets of relationships must be kept separate from one another because they begin from different events, run different courses and cannot be regarded in any sense as arbitrary. Chapter nine deals with Muentzer's involvement in the Peasants' War in Thuringia. It attempts to delineate the interaction between Muentzer's ideology and the events that led up to the war. Furthermore, the chapter accounts for the ultimate failure of Muentzer's reform program. The last chapter, an epilogue of sorts, seeks to arrive at some modest conclusions concerning this controversial iconoclast.

A. G. Dickens, in his recent historiographical study of the Reformation, has observed: "Historians who exclude theology from their inquiries are usually committing a supreme act of folly, an act even more perverse than the exclusion of individual human motivation from the list of historical causes."[38] In its pursuit of the antecedents of Muentzer's intellectual transformation, this study has largely excluded the social, political, and economic factors and might therefore be criticized by the social historian. Although it has done so to a certain extent out of necessity because of the paucity of any kind of evidence regarding Muentzer's formative years, it has attempted to take these factors into consideration beginning with his stay in Allstedt and proceeding on into the Peasants' War. Nonetheless, its primary focus has remained intellectual and unabashedly so. This is not to say, however, that those other factors are unimportant. To do so would be as extreme an act of folly as the one castigated by Dickens above. No, this study is merely limited by necessary constraints of focus and space. It hopes only to add one more building block to that edifice which will eventually constitute the biography of Thomas Muentzer.

CHAPTER I

John Tauler and the Baptism of the Holy Spirit

Should you find pleasure in reading a pure, solid theology
in the German language very similar to that of [Christian]
antiquity, then procure for yourself, if you can, the sermons
of John Tauler [who belonged to the] Order of Preachers.
What I send you here is an unknown excerpt of his total
work. For I have not found, either in Latin or German, a
more wholesome theology, or one in greater conformity with
the gospel.
            —Luther to Spalatin, 14 December 1516

It would be surprising if the arguments enunciated by Franz Guenther
and Thomas Muentzer in Jueterbog did not represent the thinking in
Wittenberg shortly before the Leipzig Disputation. Luther had begun to
prepare for that debate at least by January 1519. By late February he
had reached the conclusion that the papacy was an institution of man's
devising and that the pope might well be "the Antichrist himself or his
apostle."[1] Seeking an authority for the institution of the papacy, he
studied the Church Fathers and the Church Councils to determine their
role in its creation. The attack on Church Councils in Jueterbog by
Guenther and Muentzer may very possibly be a direct reflection of the
discussions that must have been going on in Wittenberg, especially since
Guenther had left there in late 1518 and Muentzer, according to
Dappen, came to Jueterbog directly from Wittenberg in April.[2] Therefore, when Muentzer departed Jueterbog in late April or early May
1519, he must have done so under the very strong impression that he
and Luther were in full agreement. That he continued to see his relationship to the Wittenberg reformer in this light for some time seems to be
indicated by Han Pelt's letter to him of 25 June 1521.[3]

Because Muentzer had been enrolled at the University of Leipzig, he
must have been quite familiar with the city. This was where Luther and

Eck were to confront each other in late June, and Muentzer must have determined to be present. That he was present is beyond doubt. As there were nearly two months before the debate was to open, Muentzer appears to have spent some time in Orlamuende on the way. It was there that he apparently had an intense encounter with Tauler's mystical theology that was to mark the first and perhaps most important stage in his growing estrangement from Luther, though he may well have thought that by immersing himself in Tauler he was simply following Luther's repeated recommendations.

Whether Muentzer was drawn to a study of Tauler through Luther's mediation cannot be unequivocally ascertained, even though we know that he read the latter's first and second editions of *Eine Deutsche Theologie*.[4] Initially, at least, Luther himself held Tauler's theology in high esteem. He probably encountered Tauler first through the recommendation of Johann Lang in Erfurt to whom he referred in a letter of mid-October 1516 when he wrote "you and your Tauler."[5] That Luther had read Tauler before he completed his lectures on Romans is apparent from a passage in which he commented on Genesis 1:2 which speaks of the Spirit of God moving upon the waters: "Notice," he said there, "that it says 'upon the face of the deep' and not 'upon the deep,' for, as far as we can see, *all seems to go against us when the Holy Spirit comes over us* and is about to do what we ask for. About this endurance and sufferance of God, I refer you to Tauler. He has written in German about this matter and more enlighteningly [*sic*] than anyone else"[6] [italics mine]. Although this is the only direct reference to Tauler in the text itself, it is evident that Luther drew upon him in other passages as well.[7] This is not surprising since most scholars argue that in 1516 while working on those lectures he annotated his copy of Tauler's sermons, which was subsequently found in Lang's possession.[8] Although Tauler's sermons may have struck a responsive chord in Luther here and there, his annotations indicate that they did not influence him in the central core of his teaching, his doctrine of justification. He apparently came to Tauler with that experience, described so vividly in his 1545 retrospective,[9] already in place,[10] or at least well under way.[11] For our purposes that fact is of decisive importance.

Luther had not yet completed his lectures on Romans when he discovered a mystical fragment that he edited on 4 December 1516 as *Eine Deutsche Theologie*.[12] In a brief preface, he observed that, unlike the work of the general run of preachers and teachers, this little booklet did not merely skim the surface "like foam on the water, but has been

drawn from the depths of the Jordan by a true Israelite. . . . To judge
from the content, the material is very similar to that of the illuminated
Doctor Tauler of the Order of Preachers."[13] On 14 December he sent a
copy of his edition to Spalatin, observing: "Should you find pleasure in
reading a pure, solid theology in the German language very similar to
that of [Christian] antiquity, then procure for yourself, if you can, the
sermons of John Tauler of the Order of Preachers. What I send you here
is an unknown excerpt of his total work. For I have not found, either in
Latin or German, a more wholesome theology, or one in greater conformity with the gospel."[14] Whereas in his preface he merely alluded to the
similarity between the theology of the fragment and that of Tauler, in
his letter to Spalatin he declared it an "unknown excerpt" from Tauler's
writing. By the time, however, he came to edit the complete piece in
early June 1518—when Muentzer may have been in the city—he no
longer ascribed it to Tauler, nor did he even mention the latter's name.[15]
Nonetheless, he asserted that he had learned more from this book
"about God, man and all other matters" than from any other book with
the exception of the Bible and the writings of St. Augustine.[16]

Some four months before publishing the second edition of *Eine
Deutsche Theologie,* Luther wrote to Staupitz: "What I have done is that
I follow the theology of Tauler and of that book which you recently gave
to Aurifaber to print [*Eine Deutsche Theologie*]; I teach that men should
trust in nothing save in Jesus alone, and not in their own prayers, or
merits, or works, for we shall not be saved by our own exertions but by
the mercies of God" (Rom. 9:16).[17] It was for this reason, he continued,
that he differed from the Scholastics: "My adversaries excite hatred
against me from the Scholastic doctors, because I prefer the fathers and
the Bible to them."[18] Certainly, he argued, since they disagreed among
themselves he had every right to disagree with them. In a letter to John
Eck of 7 January 1519, he asserted his position even more emphatically:
"I learned more from Tauler alone than from all the other Scholastics."[19]

Exactly what Luther learned from Tauler and *Eine Deutsche Theologie,* however, is difficult to assess. Some things may nonetheless be asserted. First, both in his preface of December 1516 and his letter of the
same month to Spalatin, Luther stresses the pristine, biblical nature of
this theology. Second, between the first and second editions of *Eine
Deutsche Theologie,* Luther's Theses against indulgences were dissemi-
nated far and wide in the realm. Gradually but nevertheless inevitably
this brought the wrath of the theologians and Church officials down
upon his head. They came to suspect him of propounding novel theologi-

cal ideas, so novel in fact as to merit investigation for heresy. Increasingly, it became important to Luther that he not be perceived as standing alone in these beliefs. Thus he repeatedly pointed to the Bible and to Augustine as sources, and now also to Tauler and *Eine Deutsche Theologie*. In the introduction to the 1518 edition of the last piece he remarked, using a phrase Muentzer was to employ repeatedly in Jeuterbog:

> And now I find, first of all, that it is true that some of our highly educated Wittenberg theologians speak disparagingly, as though we intend to start something new, as though [such] people had not existed earlier or in other places. Indeed, there have been others, but God's wrath, aroused because of our sin, has made us unworthy [and incapable] of seeing and hearing this. For it is obvious that such matters [as are contained in this booklet] have not been dealt with in our universities for a long time, with the result that the Holy Word of God has not only languished, *hidden under a bench,* but has nearly been destroyed by moths and dust. Let anyone who wishes read this little book, and then let him say whether our theology is old or new, for this book is certainly not new [italics mine].[20]

This noble little book, Luther continued, though "poor and unadorned as it is in words and human wisdom," was nonetheless—unlike Scholastic theological writings—rich in divine wisdom. That was not surprising, however, for when one contemplated God's wonders, it became obvious "that brilliant and pompous preachers [are] never chosen to spread his words." Was it not written: "*Ex ore infantium,* 'By the mouth of babes and infants,' that is, of those who are inarticulate, 'thou hast chanted thy glory in the best manner?' "[21] Surely God was, once again, using the simple things of this world to confound the wise, in this instance to confound the Scholastics. And so Luther ranged himself with St. Paul, Augustine, Tauler, and the anonymous author of *Eine Deutsche Theologie* against the pompous preachers of Scholasticism. For the same reason he could write Eck that he had learned more from Tauler than all other Scholastics.

When one compares the passages in all his works where Luther specifically referred to Tauler, another pattern emerges. It is a pattern that has to do with the parallels between his own and Tauler's struggles for the faith in which the content is less important than the process. The passage in his lectures on Romans refers to the Holy Spirit coming "over us," and "About this endurance and sufferance of God."[22] In his resolutions of 1518 concerning indulgences, he wrote in a similar vein, though with words much more striking, speaking of "suffering these punishments" that "were so great and so much like hell that no tongue could adequately express them, no pen describe them" as referring to himself.[23] And in his lectures on Genesis he wrote of how God "wants to crucify him, mortify him, and reduce the old man to nothing."[24]

These three passages make it eminently clear that Luther saw his own religious struggle reflected in Tauler's sermons. In all three, Luther emphasized the suffering, the mortification of the spirit—to such a degree in the second passage that Hartmann Grisar some years ago called Luther's language "the language of a sick man."[25] Be that as it may, in all the instances where Luther referred to Tauler, his emphasis was on the process of preparation for God's work in man, not upon the work itself. Never did he use Tauler's words to describe his own experience of faith; that experience and its theological formulation was ultimately to rest on St. Paul,[26] with Augustine as confirmation,[27] not on Tauler.[28]

Although Muentzer must have been in Wittenberg during the time that Luther edited *Eine Deutsche Theologie* and praised Tauler, his relationship to the latter is different. Unlike Luther, he did not mention Tauler by name. Nonetheless, Tauler's influence on Muentzer's intellectual development is more profound. The only reference to Tauler in the extant body of Muentzer's work comes not from the latter's pen but from that of Ursula, a nun at the Beuditz convent where Muentzer was a confessor after the Leipzig Disputation. Dated about a year later, the letter contains an ironic reference to the fact that neither Tauler nor Suso would have taught Muentzer to buy gifts for the "pretty maids" at the local parish fair.[29]

The other reference stems from Kaspar Glatz, the later Lutheran pastor at Orlamuende. Approximately one year after he had published the second edition of *Eine Deutsche Theologie,* Luther sent a copy of Tauler's sermons to Glatz.[30] Its arrival may have coincided with Muentzer's short sojourn there before he left for Leipzig to attend the Disputation. In any case, as the irony of history would have it, in that very copy Glatz noted the impact of Tauler's sermons on Muentzer:

> Through this teaching of Tauler / concerning the Spirit and the abyss of the soul / not well understood / Thomas Muentzer and his followers were led astray. (For he read him constantly as I was told and know first hand) together with a woman who was cook to Master Conrad, priest at Orlamuende, and very well known in Leipzig where she was held to be a saint. From her said Muentzer received not a little help in developing his heresies. He was followed in this by Andreas Carlstadt / who also believed these heresies and was led astray. From Orlamuende they began to spread their heresies / out of jealousy / I fear / for I knew them both very well.[31]

Glatz must have written this comment well after the event, for in 1519, just prior to the Leipzig Disputation when Muentzer was supposed to have visited Orlamuende,[32] there was as yet no reason to assume—given Luther's repeated endorsements of Tauler's sermons—that he considered the latter's theology suspect or that Muentzer and Carlstadt saw themselves as coming into opposition to Luther. On the contrary, Luther's repeated recommendations of Tauler's sermons along with his editions of *Eine Deutsche Theologie* could only have led to the opposite conclusion at the time. Muentzer's presence at Leipzig and Carlstadt's cooperation with Luther until the days of the Wittenberg Unrest in December 1521, and Luther's return from the Wartburg on 6 March 1522, some six months after Muentzer had issued his own call for reform in Prague, could only have confirmed such a conclusion. Although Glatz may have correctly measured the impact of Tauler's sermons on the intellectual development of Thomas Muentzer, there is no need to conclude, as Glatz seems to have done retroactively, that such an influence necessarily led to an immediate rupture between Luther and Muentzer.

Since the copy of Tauler's sermons which Luther annotated came into the possession of Johann Lang of Erfurt, we know that he worked with the 1508 Augsburg edition.[33] From the entry in the Weimar edition of Luther's works, it could appear that the edition Luther read did not contain the ostensible biography of Tauler usually appended to the editions of his sermons published in 1498 and thereafter.[34] An inspection of the volume itself, however, proves such an assumption erroneous.[35] Muentzer appears to have studied Tauler from the same edition.[36] Therefore, they must both have read the so-called *Meisterbuch* or *Historia,* the pseudo-biography of Tauler. And scholars who seek to assess the impact of Tauler's sermons on Muentzer's intellectual development should do so as well.[37]

The *Historia*—as we shall call it—was considered to be genuine until it was discredited by Heinrich Denifle, who contended that it could not have been written by Tauler and, more important, that it had nothing to do with Tauler's life for the following reasons: first, the "Master" in the story could not be identified with Tauler who had not been a "Master of Sacred Scripture" and had never been referred to as such; second, according to the *Historia,* Tauler was supposed to have withdrawn from his public ministry for two years, yet no such hiatus could be discovered in his actual career; third, there was concrete evidence that Tauler had not died where the *Historia* claimed. Furthermore, Denifle continued, the sermons in the *Historia* differed dramatically in style, content, and sophistication from those of Tauler. The sermons contained in the older and longer manuscript versions of the *Historia*—which had been deleted from the last manuscript—especially showed the "Master of Sacred Scripture" violating the sanctity of the confessional and committing other indiscretions that no educated cleric would do. At the same time, the Master's attack on all ranks of the clergy were sweeping and universal, whereas Tauler, although critical at times, was always and in all things submissive to the Church.

Having said this, Denifle proceeded to compare the various manuscript copies of the *Historia*—from the earliest to the latest of 1486—tracing the gradual elimination of those sermons that, from a clerical point of view, were the most troublesome. None of the manuscripts—with the exception of the last, the 1486 copy that served as the basis for the 1498 Leipzig edition—identified the "Master of Sacred Scripture" as Tauler. That one copy did so in the words of the following note appended to it:

> It should be noted that according to the content of the history sketched here a Master of Sacred Scripture of the Order of Preachers preached in a certain city. At a certain point in time, through the eternal providence of God and the guidance of the Holy Ghost, a simple layman came to him and declared the right path to complete truth to him. *It is quite possible (mildiglichen zugleubenn) that this was the blessed and illuminated teacher, Brother Johann Tauler, whose sermons are contained in this book* [italics mine].

Clearly, then, the association of the *Historia* with Tauler's life rested on nothing more than the assumption of the person who prepared the 1486 manuscript. Denifle therefore concluded that the *Historia* had in all probability been written by one Rulman Merswin, a layman, and therefore incorporated all the prejudices of the pious layman against the clerical ranks.[38]

Any impartial reader of Denifle's work is forced, by the evidence and the persuasiveness of the arguments presented, to concede the point. Nonetheless, the English translation of Tauler's sermons made by the Rev. Walter Elliott in 1910 included the *Historia* as a trustworthy preface to the sermons, either openly passing over Denifle's work or ignoring it.[39]

Those who read the pseudo-biography in the sixteenth century did not have the benefit of Denifle's work; hence, they took it to be authentic. Yet, as Denifle pointed out, the tale is tendentious, and there are distinct differences between it and the sermons. In the words of James M. Clark: "It belongs to a special type of devotional tale, in which the characters are usually a priest and a layman, the latter gets the better of the former and shows him the way to true religion. It is all part of what we might call propaganda; the anti–clerical bias [absent for the most part in the sermons] betrays the layman–author. It will be remembered that such a story [also] grew up round the figure of Eckhart."[40] At the same time, in contrast to the sermons which admonish the hearers (readers) to pursue the "counsels of perfection," the *Historia* presents them with a paradigm of the true conversion to the Christian faith—a conversion that takes place in a famous preacher who has had all the benefits of the Church's sacraments, its theological education, and its prerogatives. For Thomas Muentzer, both the paradigm of conversion and the "counsels of perfection" would prove to be important; the former, however, perhaps more than the latter.

Unlike Luther, who came to Tauler's sermons with his conversion and theology of conversion already well under way, Muentzer came to them influenced by Luther's reform movement but inexperienced in the renewal and establishment of his faith. The importance of this fact can be at least partially gleaned from the *Prague Manifesto* where Muentzer informed his audience that he had, "more highly than anyone else, desired to understand how to establish a holy invincible Christian faith."[41] Apparently Luther had not taught him how to do this. For this reason—if we may be permitted a speculation—the *Historia* had such an impact upon him. He was a seeker looking for the *method* by which the Christian faith could be firmly established. And the *Historia* provided him with the paradigm he sought. It is possible, therefore, that pseudo-Tauler was important to Muentzer, first for psychological reasons: it fulfilled a deep-seated need within him which had not been met by Luther. Once he had discovered and experienced it, however, he could "concentrate vehemently on the Truth," as he told the Bohemians in the *Manifesto*.

In his marginal gloss, Glatz referred to two areas in which Tauler had influenced Muentzer's thinking: his understanding of the Holy Spirit and his mystical concept of the abyss of the soul. Although this assessment is undoubtedly valid, it falls short of the whole truth. A comparison of Muentzer's writings with Tauler's sermons suggests at least several other areas of influence. First is Muentzer's emphasis on the *Christfoermigkeit* of the believer. This derives, at least in part, from Tauler's stress on the counsels of perfection and his assumption, at

times explicit, that they apply to all Christians, not only to the profes-
sionally religious.[42] This emphasis is also partially responsible for
Muentzer's growing conviction that Christendom was utterly corrupt
and in desperate need of a fundamental reformation.

No one who has ever read the sketch of Tauler's ostensible conversion in the *Historia* can fail to be struck on the one hand by the negative
attitude toward learning and theology, and on the other by the exaltation of the Holy Spirit.[43] In that account, John Tauler, ostensibly the
"Master of Sacred Scripture," is confronted after one of his sermons on
"the perfect life"—or the Christian life of perfection—by an ordinary
layman who has come to "offer [him] some advice." The Master, at first
skeptical, finally consents to hear the layman's reproach: "Thou art a
great clergyman, and in thy sermon thou hast given a good doctrine; but
thou thyself dost not live up to it."[44] Because of this, "few receive an
increase of the grace of the Holy Ghost from thy preaching."[45] According to the layman, therefore, the Master is a Pharisee who may know the
Word but does not practice it. The result is that his message remains
ineffectual. This life the layman contrasts with the lives of "spirit-filled"
persons as illustrated in the following dialogue about St. Catherine:

> "Tell me, dear sir, how did it happen, that dear St. Catherine, who was
> but a young girl of fourteen years, yet vanquished by her discourse fifty of
> the greatest professors, so that they were ready to die for the truth? Who
> worked that wonder?" Then the Master said, "The Holy Ghost did that."
> And the man said: "Think you not that the Holy Ghost still has that power?"
> The Master answered; "Yes, I believe it firmly." Then the man said, "Why
> then wilt thou not believe, that the same Holy Ghost here and now speaks to
> thee through me, all unworthy as I am and a poor sinner; even as He spoke
> the truth by the mouth of Caiaphas, who was also a sinner."[46]

Persuaded by this argument, the Master places himself under the
tutelage of the layman and in due course learns "to tread the way the
Lord pointed out to the young man, namely, thou must take up thy
cross and follow Jesus Christ, imitating Him in very truth; in all humility and in patience."[47]

For two years the Master suffered trials and tribulations in his preparing to receive the Holy Spirit, until he at last reached the final stage of
utter detachment from the world, his fellow man, and all creatures. In
that state, and deeply repentant of his sins, the Master heard a voice
saying: "Stand fast in thy peace, and trust in God. And remember that
when He was on earth in His human nature, when He cured men of
bodily sickness, He also made them well in their souls."[48] No sooner

were these words spoken than "he lost all sense and reason, and knew not whether he was carried away nor how. But when he came to his senses again, he found a great change had taken place in him. All his interior and his outward faculties were conscious of a new strength; and he was gifted with clear perception of matters that before had been very strange and alien to him."[49]

Because the Master did not know the source of this transformation within him, he sent for his lay mentor who told him the following:

> Dear sir, thou must understand that now for the very first time thou hast found the true, the great grace of God. I say to thee that now for the very first time thou hast been touched by the Most High. And this thou must know: as formerly the letter has somewhat killed thee, so now shall the same make thee alive again. For now thy teaching comes from God the Holy Ghost, whereas before it was from the flesh. Now thou hast the light of the Holy Ghost, received from the grace of God, *and thou hast the Holy Scriptures in thee.* Therefore hast thou now a great advantage, and in the future far more than formerly thou shalt understand the Scriptures; for thou knowest full well that the Scriptures in many places seem to contradict themselves. But now that in the light of the Holy Ghost thou hast received divine grace to possess the holy Scriptures in thyself, so wilt thou understand that all Scripture has the same meaning and is never self-contradictory [italics mine].[50]

If Muentzer did indeed "read him [Tauler] constantly . . . together with a woman who was cook to Master Conrad" and "received not a little help [from her] in developing his heresies," it is probably safe to conclude that he came away believing himself—like pseudo-Tauler—to have experienced the advent of the Holy Spirit in his life. If he was convinced further that the event had transformed him as it was supposed to have transformed Tauler, one should not be too surprised to find that he felt constrained to proclaim, in the opening sentence of his *Prague Manifesto:* "I, Thomas Muentzer, born in Stolberg and at present in Prague, intend, in the place of that dear and holy warrior John Hus, to fill the resounding and versatile trumpets with the new song of praise of the Holy Spirit."[51] Muentzer averred that he had been a sincere seeker after this higher truth all his life, having attempted to determine, much more profoundly than anyone else, "how a holy invincible Christian faith may be established."[52] Pseudo-Tauler's experience provided him with the clear proof that such a faith could be established only by the presence of the Holy Spirit in the believer's life. It was probably for this reason that Muentzer turned almost immediately in the *Manifesto*—after his opening confession of faith—to a criticism of the clergy whom he called "the foremost among the Christians." Repeatedly, he asserted, he had heard them proclaim "the bare Scriptures"; yet while they proclaimed the Word, they "denied that the Spirit of God could communicate [directly] with the people."[53] Such men could not be the right kind of servants of God; rather, they were the ones who had polluted and poisoned the entire Christian Church.[54]

The parallels between the "Master" being led by the layman to conversion and the reception of the Holy Spirit, and Muentzer being led in the same direction by the "woman who was the cook to Master Conrad" while they studied Tauler's experience and his sermons together are intriguing. By means of the transforming work of the Holy Spirit, the "spirit-filled" layman and the "spirit-filled" laywoman lead the educated cleric to an "invincible Christian faith." Had pseudo-Tauler not been "conscious of a new strength" and "gifted with a clear perception of matters that before had been very strange and alien to him"? Had the layman not told him that now he had the "light of the Holy Ghost, received from the grace of God, and . . . the Holy Scriptures"? Muentzer, as we shall see, certainly came to believe as much with regard to himself and believed this possible at least for all other "elect." Hence his advice in the *Manifesto* to the Bohemians to study the Word of God directly from God's own mouth. Were they to do so, he promised, they would quickly realize the extent to which the entire world had been betrayed by the priests. Tauler—or pseudo-Tauler—not Luther, had shown him the way to spiritual renewal.

Although this pseudo-biography of Tauler may have provided Muentzer with the means he sought by which to establish an "invincible Christian faith," he could also have gleaned much the same emphasis from those parts of the sermons where Tauler spoke of the Holy Spirit. The model would not have been so clear, but the emphasis was certainly there.

Reinhard Schwarz, in his study of 1977, has pointed, as I did in 1974, to the centrality of the desire for reform in Muentzer's thought.[55] This desire may have been similar to that of the Taborites, but neither did it derive from them nor did his solution of the problem come from them. Rather, it came from Tauler who continually spoke of the Holy Spirit in terms of its transforming power in the life of the true believer. We have already noted this in the *Historia;* it is equally striking in Tauler's sermons.

Tauler described the work of the Holy Spirit in many places, but especially in a series of sermons dealing with Pentecost. The tone was set earlier, however, in a sermon on the "Pool of Healing." There, speaking with reference to a "true and entire conversion to God" and the healing of those who arrived at the pool before the others after the "stirring of the waters," Tauler compared the latter to the "descent of the Holy Spirit into a man's soul."[56] This resulted, he observed, in the "stirring up with a powerful movement of grace his whole interior life" which "so totally transformed [him] that things which once he loved have now become absolutely tasteless to him. Once he fairly dreaded and strenuously avoided what he now covets with all his heart—to be stripped of all things and to live like a banished man; to retire into inner silence; to be humiliated and to be cast off by all men" (135). In a somewhat later sermon on Matthew 15:21–28, once again with reference to the work of the Holy Spirit, Tauler remarked: "Ah, dear children, this passage of the Gospel shows us the noblest, most profitable, surest and deepest conversion to God that a man can ever experience. And be assured, besides, that any conversion that is not, in some way or other, effected after this manner, will be of little or no benefit, no matter what we may do or leave undone" (194).

That this conversion is not effected by mere theological knowledge becomes very apparent from Tauler's sermons. He called those who pride themselves in such knowledge "scribes and hypocrites" from whom Christ departed (194). "By scribes," Tauler continued, "we mean intellectual men, who value everything according to the standards of their reason and the observation of their senses, and have a great store of this kind of knowledge. At present they are much admired; they discourse with beautiful and stately words. But in the depths of their soul—that interior source of all true science—there is nothing but an empty and barren waste" (194–195). Yet, while they pride themselves on their "inventions," they condemn God's real friends who are guided by "the interior admonitions of God's Spirit" (195). Improvement of life was not to be expected from such persons, for they do not have the transforming power of the Holy Spirit within. According to Tauler, they "glory in learning, in knowledge of doctrine, in their bright understanding, and their talent for speaking. It all lifts them up high and honorable—but it never changes for the better their mode of living, nor leads to good works" (300).

In words anticipating the opening sentence of Erasmus's *Enchiridion*—where the latter declared, "Let this book lead to a theological life rather than theological disputation"—Tauler advised his listeners to avoid such rational and arrogant men:

> Among yourselves as often as you meet together talk about God and about a virtuous life. This does not mean disputations about the Deity or any other such things, nor does it mean subtle reasoning of any kind; for that will only help damn your soul and the souls you draw into such conversations. . . . Avoid subtle and disputatious men, who are the serpents of whom we were lately discoursing. They are externalized men; thou must not draw them into thy sacred interior life. By their means the evil one may manage to entrap thee, taking advantage of thy weaker tendencies. (332)

The Holy Spirit was the only transforming power available to the Christian who through it could recognize evil. "Our Saviour also teaches," Tauler observed in one of his sermons on Pentecost, "that when the Holy Ghost comes He will teach us all things, even future things. This does not mean that we shall be taught beforehand whether the corn harvest will be great or the price high or low; but that He will teach us all that is necessary for a perfect life. He will teach us the secret wisdom of God: that this world is false, our natural lights are misguiding, that the evil spirits are crafty" (281). It is the Holy Spirit, Tauler continued, who "reveals to us our sins as they are in reality." Without the Holy Spirit we cannot recognize the evil in the world, in our midst, or in our selves; indeed, we cannot recognize that we need to be transformed.

Once evil has been recognized and the Christians' lives transformed by the power of the indwelling Holy Spirit, they must then separate themselves from evil. If they do not do so, the Holy Spirit will depart from them. Thus Tauler remarked in his third sermon on Pentecost: "Fly from these Jews, shut yourselves safely away from them, put an end to your dangerous companionship with them, beware of dallying with them, whether by words or deeds; for God's honor and praise is not with them. And if you fail in this, be sure that you will lose the Holy Ghost and forfeit all His gifts" (335–336).

Turning away from all things created, all things exterior, must be followed by turning inward to one's soul. For it is here and here alone that a person can encounter God. One may know the "external, written Word" of God and yet not know God in one's soul. Quoting St. Augustine, who had observed that "What is it to me that the eternal generation of the Word ceaselessly takes place if He is not generated in me? All depends on whether or not he is born in me," Tauler remarked: "Thus it behooves us to speak of this generation, begun and perfected when God the Father utters His Eternal Word in a perfect soul" (75). Not only must the Eternal Word be born anew in each soul, but also the soul is already to a certain extent the abode of God, even though one might not recognize it. Again Tauler quoted Augustine: "O noble soul, O noble creature of God, wherefore goest thou outside thyself in search of Him who is always and most certainly within thee, and through Whom thou art made a partaker of the divine nature? What hast thou to do or why dost thou concern thyself with creatures?" (68).

According to Augustine, the soul has an interior and sacred abyss in which union with God could be effected and in which "the things of time and of this world have no place . . . , but only what is high above them and above all that concerns the body and its activities" (321). This being so, Tauler cited Augustine's advice: "Turn into thyself; there alone shalt thou find God" (250). Or: "O Love, ever burning and never extinguished, how late have I come to know thee! Thou wast within me and I sought thee out of me; thou wast with me and I was not with thee" (257). Thus Tauler could argue that man's soul is "exceedingly close to God and kindred to Him in the soul's deepest depths, hidden in that inner and Divine stillness" (218). That is also where God speaks to man and where "that Word is understood, more plainly or less, in proportion as the interior ear of the soul is turned more or less intently to listen, in proportion as the soul abides in greater or less interior quiet and union of spirit with the Word" (218).

If it is in the soul that the Word is most clearly understood, and God is "the all essential and perfect light" that "shines in the most interior regions of the soul's light" (654), if He is "the light that lighteth every man that cometh into this world, shining upon all, good and bad, as the sun shines upon all creation" (655), then, "If a man were in a dark room, and could open a window wide enough to let his head be thrust out into the sunlight, he would be in the light. So may men open their souls and be presently in God's light" (655). Augustine, whom Tauler quoted yet once again, said as much when he remarked: "Empty thyself if thou wouldst be filled. Go forth, if thou wouldst enter in" (68).

Tauler was very much aware that this view of the soul as the abode of God was not unique to Christian doctrine. Citing Augustine, Tauler remarked:

> This deepest region of the spirit was in a manner known to some of the Gentiles of old; and as they searched its depths, this knowledge caused them to despise all transitory things. Such great philosophers as Proclus and Plato gave a clear account of it to guide others who knew it not. Therefore St. Augustine says that Plato has proclaimed the first part of St. John's gospel,

"In the beginning was the Word," as far as "There was a man sent from God" [vs. 1–5]. But all this the philosopher taught with words of hidden meaning. The same philosopher gained some knowledge of the most holy Trinity. Children, all such things came from the deep recesses of the soul, in which such men as Plato lived, and whose stores of wisdom they had access to. (658; cf. 505)

If the Holy Spirit alone can reveal evil to us, confront evil in the world, transform human beings from this evil to live a "holy invincible Christian faith"—as Muentzer would have it—it is important to understand how the Holy Spirit works in the lives of the "friends." Tauler's answer is equivocal: on the one hand, he stresses the individual's need to prepare for the coming of the Holy Spirit; on the other, he stresses—nearly in Lutheran terms—the exclusive work of the Holy Spirit.

Tauler observed in a sermon that the first step toward the reception of the Holy Spirit is the preparation of one's soul: "As Pentecost day was the festival of the Holy Ghost's being sent to the disciples, so is every day of the year a Pentecost day to each Christian. . . . If he will but thoroughly prepare his soul, the Divine Spirit will enter in with all His graces and gifts" (322). Throughout his sermons, Tauler gave some indication of what is to be subsumed under this preparation. Perhaps most importantly, one must turn from "creatures"—those things exterior to us. Thus he said on one occasion: "Therefore, no man shall be fit to receive Divine grace whose heart is in possession of creatures" (282). Or again: "This beloved Spirit of God is given to each one of us, as often and as much as we are shut off from all creatures and turned wholly to God" (336).

Not only must they who seek to prepare for the coming of the Holy Spirit turn away from all creatures, from all things external, and turn inward toward the abyss of their souls, they must also root out all evil in the garden of their souls. Thus Tauler could say on occasion: "The beginner needs to cut off the gross sinfulness, such as impurity, envy, wrath and pride; also all worldly vanity, and silly amusements, all joy in creatures animate and inanimate. In a word, unless a man shall with a determined spirit and his whole heart turn to God, so that he shall love Him in the depths of his soul and have Him in mind above all things whatsoever, and unless he shall be found thus minded at the end of his days, he shall never come to God" (604). Or, as Tauler observed in another of his Pentecost sermons:

Let every man now prepare for the approaching feast of the Holy Ghost, that he may receive Him with the best possible dispositions, keeping only

God in view. Let each one search his whole way of life with care, considering his interior soul, and whether anything dwells therein that is not God. This preparation will consist of four dipositions [*sic*]: detachment, self-renunciation, the interior spirit, and union with God. (317–319)

Whereas the above passages emphasize our role in preparing for the coming of the Holy Spirit, there are others in Tauler's sermons that clearly state the opposite. For example, he said: "When God speaks all things must keep silence. If God shall rightly work in us, needs must we give Him room to work, and rest passive under His action. Two cannot do the same work in us at the same time; one must stop while the other acts" (464). In another sermon he warned: "But let no man presume to take this high and holy work of God on his own initiative. Rather let him humbly await God's guidance, abandoning himself in all peacefulness and in total detachment to the Divine influence, whenever it may come to him" (240–241). In another, he observed that: "The first and most important preparation must be made by the Holy Ghost Himself, making a proper place for His abode; and that He does by two acts. One is to empty the soul, the other is afterwards to fill it" (329).

This rebirth, Tauler observes, is the one thing in earth that God desires above all else—"that He may find the deep abyss that He has created in man's spirit empty and ready for the perfect work He will do there." Although He has all power in heaven and on earth, "one thing alone is lacking Him, the accomplishment of His holy will in man's soul." The reason is "that a man has his own role to play in the Divine work, and that it is to arise from all things whatsoever that are not God—from all creatures, including himself" (113).

Once, however, one has renounced all "creatures," weeded the "garden" of the soul, and sought God in the abyss of the soul—where God resides—then the work of transformation can begin, then "the Divine birth in the soul of man" can take place (69). For, Tauler observed, "when a man thus clears the ground and makes his soul ready, without a doubt God must fill the void" (86, 251). Since a spiritual vacuum cannot exist—either God or the devil must of necessity be in control of one's life—the very heavens would sooner fall down than the soul remain empty. Therefore, Tauler continued, if we would but be silent, "the Word of the divine birth shall speak" in us and "be heard" (69). In this way one is transformed, for, in the words of Augustine quoted by Tauler: "God became man that I might become God; He became the Son of man that I might become the son of God" (251).

Tauler, however, was not one of those mystics who lose themselves in contemplating God in the abyss of their souls. His stress from the very outset was upon a "conversion," a "transformation," a "rebirth" of the soul, or the "divine birth" within the soul. He repeatedly warned against remaining in a passive state of *Gelassenheit*. We must, he said, "use our spiritual gifts and not enjoy them" (332–333). Similarly, he continued elsewhere, "Just as a copious rain produces a good harvest, so does God will that His gifts shall not be unfruitful—He develops all natural powers of the soul and body, so that He may in due order act by their means for thy sanctification." In the same sermon he even stressed the doing of good works while waiting for the coming of the Holy Spirit: "Again, do not suppose that thou shouldst wait inertly for the Holy Ghost, ceasing to perform thy usual external works of religion, ceasing to observe the rule of life, such as singing and reading thy prayers, serving thy neighbor, and doing works of charity. No, it is not thus that we must wait for the Holy Spirit—supinely letting everything slip away from us" (303). And in this context of the Christian *vita activa*, the more we empty ourselves, the more God can fill us and the more fruitful our Christian lives will be.

Indeed, Tauler went so far as to argue that it is precisely such people who are the "mainstay of the Church," without whom Christendom would collapse (653). He remarked in one of his last sermons that "These are the chosen spirits whose work on earth is divinized; and they are vouchsafed a foretaste of their eternal paradise. *Upon them as a house upon its foundation stands the holy Church; if they were not in Christendom, Christendom could not stand* [italics mine]" (52).

But although these "spirit-filled," transformed persons are the mainstay of the Church and the only reason why Christendom has not fallen, most Christians are not in this category. Indeed, in the very first sermon he observed:

> God's friends—those who seek in all things His glory—can hardly keep back their tears when they behold the hateful tyranny with which these three enemies hold sway over so great a multitude of men, among whom they usurp the place of God. And these souls are to be found in the worldly state of life and in the cloister. To God's friends the eternal destruction of their brethren is a great torture. Their hearts wither away with sorrow as they consider that self-love is so rooted in the world that there are few who love God purely and tend toward Him solely. (720)

Things had come to such a pass in Christendom that, whereas "in former times the pagans tortured God's friends . . . nowadays good appearing Christians persecute those who would closely follow Christ"

(690). Tauler described the wicked state of Christendom in other passages, calling his age a "dangerous time" (566), a "miserable age" (478), and Christendom "the city over which our Lord now weeps" (701), as He once wept over Jerusalem.

The reasons for this state of affairs were apparent on every hand. To be a friend of God, one had to take up the cross, for, said Tauler, "The man who takes up the cross of Christ perfectly is the best man on earth." In his time, however, Tauler complained, no one was willing "to endure any pain at all." People had become "weak–spirited and delicate–natured. The diligence and earnestness of former times have almost disappeared, the fire of love is quenched." Men no longer wished to suffer, for they loved only themselves and sought self in everything; St. Paul had warned about such "last days" as dangerous times in which men would be lovers of themselves (325). This was manifestly the case in his time, Tauler concluded, "for the world is full of misery because men, both of the world and of the clerical state . . . are both openly and secretly striving to defraud one another" (690).

Because men were lovers of themselves, they despised their souls. They sought satisfaction in the externals of life, in created things, in creatures. "Many hearts," he said, "are lost to God by loving creatures, the blindest love and the direst misfortune of the world" (690). If we could only know how angry God was over this, fear would overcome us. But rather than fear God, men joked about it and deemed their disregard of eternal penalties "a mark of honor." "The wounds of Christ would bleed afresh over so awful a deed as shutting out Christ's cross from our souls," Tauler concluded (142). Others, he observed elsewhere, were given to such excesses in eating and drinking—satisfying the cravings of the flesh—that they became like animals, unable to "say so much as a Pater Noster." Holy men, therefore, should take great care in this regard to guard themselves. "But, alas," Tauler complained, "it is now come to such a pass that even some clergymen—and this is the most to be regretted—cannot and will not be content with what suffices even rich worldlings." Such men become spiritually blinded and cannot resist the temptations of the devil. "But how different," he remarked, "are men who have been truly converted" (566).

Because of this preoccupation with the externals of life, men refuse Christ's invitation to his banquet table—as had the king in Matthew 22:4—"the like of this is all too common among us in different classes of people, both secular and religious; for when God calls to perfection, objections and excuses are everywhere heard on the score of worldly

occupations and even of mere slothfulness" (479). These are men of
the senses, not of the spirit, even though they may give us a "show of
religion, confession, and prayer." They are "full of [their] own will,
full, full, full! How few strong characters," Tauler asserted, "do we
meet with, men who subject themselves wholly to God; indeed, the
majority of those who act thus are poor, humble women" (480). Thus
it would appear that "there are whole countries that seem to be
averted from God" (494). We give "a willing ear to the voice of Satan,
[whereas] we are all deaf to the voice of the eternal Word of God
within our souls" (573).

All the while Tauler pointed his accusatory finger at both the clerical
and lay estates. Not often did he draw in the secular rulers specifically,
but when he did, his hand fell heavily upon them as well. Quoting the
passage from St. Paul about wrestling "against principalities and powers, against the rulers of the world of this darkness," Tauler remarked
that Paul is not merely speaking about devils, but also about "the human princes of this world." Although these should be "the very best of
men," they are more often "the very horses that the demons bestride,
causing them to spread disturbance everywhere, and to oppress the
people. They live in pride," Tauler continued, "they usurp power, they
are in many ways wicked men, as is plain to be seen over the whole
earth." Then he returned to the "darkness" and observed:

> What awful darkness over spreads the Christian world, enveloping both
> clergy and laity. We can measure its thickness by the fact that Jews and
> pagans, with all their blindness of heart, live up to their law and their natural
> reason far better than we Christians observe the gospel of Christ, the teach-
> ings of holy faith, and the example of the saints. Our souls are blinded by
> vice, we are full of vanity, and we are preoccupied with thoughts of created
> things. We do not sincerely love God nor regard God in our daily conduct. In
> the end we shall be judged and condemned with the benighted and infidel
> nations. (330)

Although Tauler did not name the theologians of his time, they nonetheless came in for their share of criticism. Few men, he observed, "even
of those whose vocation calls for it, and who show outward signs of
spirituality," empty themselves of their false self-love and seek God in
the inner abyss of the soul (64). "Nobody," he continued, "seems willing to yield to the Holy Spirit's action; everybody must have his own
plan of spiritual life—such is the rule of our perilous times." Rather
than turning to the soul—which is to God, "who is our origin and end,
what the stream is to the fountainhead"—many rely upon their reason,

their "natural light," when it comes to spiritual matters (300). Such people "glory in learning, and their talent for speaking. It all lifts them up high and honorable—it never changes for the better their mode of living, nor leads to good works" (332). Such "subtle and disputatious men," Tauler warned his hearers a little later on, are to be avoided, for they are serpents, "externalized men; thou must not draw them into thy sacred interior life. [For] by their means the evil one may manage to entrap thee" (53). These scribes and Pharisees, who know the letter and ceaselessly run "about looking for something new," also have an "external and showy exercise of religion" (196). It is because of them and the general corruption of Christendom that that same kind of religion "prevails greatly nowadays among all classes" (329).

In contrast to these externalized teachers of God's Word, who may proudly "set out toward perfection by ways of high reasoning—not traveling by this humble road of St. Peter"—every one of whom "will fall into the pit of hell"—turning inward to the abyss of the soul and gradually allowing the Holy Spirit to take control of one's life is done by very few, "even of those whose vocation calls for it" (342). Those who do, however, are richly rewarded, even intellectually, for as Tauler said in quoting Jerome: "All truth that is ever known or ever spoken comes from the Holy Ghost" (82). Not only are the "spirit-filled" persons transformed and therefore enabled to fulfill the high moral demands of Christ, but also they have now tapped the fountainhead of truth. As Tauler remarked: "For all the truth that those teachers who follow reason alone have ever taught, all that such will ever teach till the last day, is nothing in comparison to the wisdom in the depths of the soul" (353).

If this truth "is imparted interiorly," and does not come from reason and books, then it is not surprising to find Tauler seconding the recommendation of St. Francis to his followers "that they should not busy themselves much with books and writings." Even though they might be unlettered, they should not be overly concerned, "but rather be absorbed above all things in striving after the spirit of God, and with pure hearts pray for His holy operation in their souls" (356). For, in the school of the Holy Spirit "the most secret meaning of holy Scripture was imparted to them [the disciples], and the truth of God was revealed nakedly to them, and that in a way wholly incomprehensible to all the doctors in the schools" (353). Quoting St. Gregory, Tauler noted:

> "The Holy Ghost is a marvellous workman. He takes up His abode in a fisherman and makes him a preacher; He takes up His abode in a cruel persecutor and makes him a teacher of nations; He takes up His abode in a

publican and makes him an evangelist." Who is like this master workman? To teach everything that He pleases He requires no time—a single touch and all is taught the soul—nothing more is necessary. (72)

One is reminded of Luther's comment in his preface to the second edition of *Eine Deutsche Theologie:* "*Ex ore infantium. . . .*"

Nor was this internal Word dependent upon the written, the external, Word of God. "You must know," Tauler informed his hearers, "that the Eternal Word is self-begotten in the soul, and that the soul itself, when favored with the Divine generation within it, knows the Eternal Word better than all teachers can describe Him" (350). Thus, even though Tauler quoted the written Word often, the truly enlightened man, the transformed person, has met God in the abyss of the soul where the Holy Spirit teaches more, and more purely, in an instant than the scribes can do in a lifetime. Indeed, the scribes will never arrive at such wisdom since their entire motivation is self, pride and external knowledge.

Frequently Tauler spoke about this internal Word in his sermons surrounding Pentecost, particularly in the context of the Apostles' receiving the Holy Spirit. Only twice, however, did Tauler address the problem of whether the Holy Spirit still works in his day as it worked in the time of the Apostles. In one of these Tauler said: "One might enquire: Why did God prepare the disciples for this privilege and does not thus prepare me and other men, at least in this wonderfully special manner?" (350). He gave two answers: first, because of "God's free choice, by which he prefers some men rather than others for the bestowal of his most familiar love"; second, "some men correspond better with God's invitation and more diligently co-operate with it than others do" (472). In another passage Tauler discussed the spiritual gifts: "In the days of the apostles, the Holy Ghost wrought wonderful things among *His friends* for the proof of the Christian faith, including prophecies; and His final work was the martyrdom of the apostles and their disciples. Miraculous signs are not needed in our days, although it must be confessed that living Christian faith is as little evident in some among us as in pagans and Jews [italics mine]" (281).

There was another reason for this condition, at least indirectly implied by Tauler. In his Pentecost sermons he argued that it was only through the Holy Spirit that one could recognize evil. The Holy Spirit "reveals to us our sins as they are in reality," teaching us "the secret wisdom of God: that this world is false, our natural lights are misguiding, that the evil spirits are crafty" (336). Without the Holy Spirit, one could recognize the evil neither in one's own life nor in the world. Once the Holy Spirit has enlightened the mind and made the evil apparent, however, it is incumbent upon the enlightened that they distance themselves from the evil both in their lives and in the world. Indeed, Tauler argued, if they fail to separate themselves from the world, the Holy Spirit would depart from them. For, he said, "if you fail in this, be sure that you will lose the Holy Ghost and forfeit all His gifts" (332). Was this the real reason why Christendom had fallen into such sinfulness? Repeatedly he warned his listeners to "avoid subtle and disputatious men" (336), to "beware of the hateful Jews, that is to say men who would rob you of God" (227), to "waste no time with self-righteous men, led only by reason's light" (138), to "depart out of the Egypt of this world and out of the bondage of Pharaoh, its king" (227). Using the example of King Solomon, from whom the Holy Spirit had departed, Tauler stated:

> How many men are there not—men of fair appearance spiritually, and with whom God in the beginning worked wonders—who have, nevertheless, finally failed? It was because they did not accept this truth in single-hearted sincerity, but rested upon self, inwardly and outwardly, in mind and body. Look at King Solomon as an example of this; God once spoke familiarly with him. Look at Samson, who received God's message by a holy angel. And upon both of these fell God's wrath and condemnation, because they were not willing to die themselves in spirit and in act, as they ought to have done. (138)

Christians had therefore to be constantly on guard lest they mistake the external, the visible, for the essential.

It is no wonder, then, that though lamenting the wicked state of Christendom with its "shadowy exercise of religion," its few truly "spirit-filled" friends of God, and its attempt to justify "living in Egypt" by practicing only an external religion, Tauler longed for the "former years, when times were not so wicked" (691). Thus he devoted so much time to Pentecost and the reception of the Holy Spirit by the Apostles. Although there are indications that Tauler saw a decline in the Church over the years, these are nowhere systematically developed. His emphasis on conversion by means of the Holy Spirit and his repeated complaints about the decline of Christendom indicate sufficiently that he was not very optimistic about the spiritual quality of his time. Given this situation, it is no wonder that, whereas "in former times the pagans tortured *God's friends* . . . nowadays good appearing Christians persecute those who would closely follow Christ [italics mine]" (690).

It should be apparent even to the most casual observer that these elements of Tauler's thought must have had a major impact upon Muentzer. The central emphasis on the *experience* of conversion through the power of the Holy Spirit, the argument that this was the only way to enable a person to live a "successful" Christian life, that such a person was a "friend of God" in contrast to the rational and learned scribes and Pharisees, that one was enabled to plumb the depths of God's wisdom immediately through the indwelling Holy Spirit, and that all of this took place in the abyss of the human soul without the "written Word," were all to impress Muentzer in profound ways. This was not all, however. Such "friends of God" worked miraculous things in this world; they sustained a corrupt Church; they were the only ones—because they possessed the Holy Spirit—who could distinguish good from evil, the wheat from the tares. Yet even from these the Holy Spirit could depart if they did not keep themselves separated from the world. Over the years the world had infiltrated the Church, and the two had become more and more synonymous with one another. How, then, could such "friends of God" separate themselves from the mass of the Christians being led by those of merely externalized religion, the scribes and Pharisees as Tauler called them? Under the influence of these ideas Muentzer arrived in Leipzig to attend the Disputation between Luther and Eck. He must, therefore, have recalled Tauler's warnings as he viewed these important events of the Reformation.

CHAPTER II:

Eusebius and the Apostolic Church

Those inspired and wonderful men, Christ's apostles, had completely purified their lives and cultivated every spiritual value, but their speech was that of every day. The divine wonder-working power bestowed on them by the Saviour filled them with confidence; and having neither ability nor the desire to present the teachings of the Master with rhetorical subtlety or literary skill, they relied only on demonstrating the divine Spirit working with them, and on the miraculous power of Christ fully operative in them.

—Eusebius, *Church History*

Perhaps Muentzer had accorded Tauler only a first reading in Orla-muende, but he was to return to him and Heinrich Suso after the Leipzig Disputation while at Beuditz. Nevertheless, Tauler—and the *Historia*—must already have served him as a filter for the ideas debated by Luther and Eck. One of the most important of these was the point at which the Church had started down its path to deformity and the relationship this had to Scholastic theology and the displacement of the Word of God.

In the introduction to his June 1518 edition of *Eine Deutsche Theologie,* Luther observed that the "Word of God had languished, hidden under a bench," for some time. Muentzer, as we have seen, repeated the charge in his debate with the Franciscans at Jueterbog in May 1519 asserting, not once but repeatedly, "that the holy Gospel had lain under a bench for more than 400 years."[1] While Luther had not identified a specific period of time in his introduction during which God's Word had been hidden, he did so in his explanation of the 95 Theses of the same year. There he said: "From this you can see how, ever since the scholastic theology—the deceiving theology (for that is the meaning of the word in Greek)—began, the theology of the cross has been abrogated, and everything has been completely turned upside-down"; and in his response to Sylvester Prierias of October 1518 he gave the length of time this had been so as 300 years.[2] On the eve of the Disputation, however, he spoke of the worthless decrees of the popes "issued within the last four hundred years."[3] Since Muentzer may well have spent time in Wittenberg while Luther was preparing for that debate, possessed a copy of Luther's second edition of *Eine Deutsche Theologie,* used a metaphor identical with that of Luther and had read the 95 Theses, he must have absorbed Luther's views on this matter. He even reflected Luther's own ambiguity as to whether the Word of God had "lain under a bench" for 300 or 400 years, for Dappen wrote, in one place, that Muentzer had charged that "the holy Gospel had lain under a bench for three or four hundred years."[4] In any case, this dependence upon Luther would seem to indicate that Muentzer, initially at least, held Luther in high esteem as the restorer of the "Holy Gospel."

This view of Luther came from the great reformer himself. In the introduction to his 1516 fragmentary edition of *Eine Deutsche Theologie,* Luther had referred to the unknown author of that piece as one who had "drawn from the depths of the Jordan" like a true Israelite. In his letter to Spalatin of December 1516, he referred to *Eine Deutsche Theologie* as a "pure, solid theology in the German language very similar to that of [Christian] antiquity." He had, he continued, "not found, either in Latin or German, a more wholesome theology, or one in greater conformity with the gospel." To Staupitz he wrote in February 1518, once again in connection with Tauler and *Eine Deutsche Theologie,* that "my adversaries excite hatred against me from the Scholastic doctors, because I prefer the Fathers and the Bible to them."[5]

Luther drew the lines of demarcation between this biblical, "pure . . . theology . . . very similar to that of [Christian] antiquity," and that of Scholasticism even more sharply in his Heidelberg Disputation of April 1518. There, using terms reminiscent of Tauler's sermons and *Eine Deutsche Theologie,*[6] he spoke of biblical theology as the "theology of the cross," which he contrasted to Scholasticism's "theology of glory": "Ergo in christo crucifixo est vera theologia et cognitio Dei."[7] No wonder he could claim a few months later, in the introduction to his June 1518 edition of *Eine Deutsche Theologie,* that this Word of God had languished under a bench for such a long time.

While the Word of God had been hidden, it was Luther's intention to resurrect it in all its glory. In his reflections on his confrontation with Cardinal Cajetan at Augsburg, he observed that "since the sacred Scriptures are abandoned and the traditions and words of men . . . accepted," the Church was being misled.[8] In another passage he asserted: "The truth of Scripture comes first. After that is accepted, one may determine whether the words of men can be accepted as true."[9] While Jurists could emphasize their traditions, "theologians preserve the purity of the Scriptures."[10] Therefore Scholastic commentary, papal pronouncements, indeed all human accretions had to be swept aside. This argument, which began with his rejection of Aristotle's view of "human righteousness" in his commentary on Romans,[11] culminated in his response to Erasmus's 1524 attack on him. There Luther wrote: "The gold must be rescued from these men, and pure Scripture separated from their dregs and filth, as I have always sought to do, in order that the divine writings may be kept in one place, and their trifles in another."[12]

And the Word of God had indeed been restored. As early as July 1520 he wrote that sacred letters had not been treated with such integrity in a thousand years, indeed that this gift of God conformed very closely to that in the age of the Apostles.[13] He repeated this argument from time to time, and in 1524, wrote to the councilors of the German cities:

> Since knowledge of languages declined, nothing of importance has taken place in Christendom, but many abominations have occurred because of the ignorance of languages. Now, however, since a knowledge of languages has returned, they have brought with them so much light, and are doing such mighty things that the whole world is astonished and forced to admit that we now possess the Gospel in nearly as pure and undefiled a fashion as the Apostles did. Indeed we have it in its earliest purity, much more so even than at the time of Jerome or Augustine.[14]

With this pure Word, he wrote in 1522, he had "opposed indulgences and all papists, but not with force; I only wrote, preached, and used God's Word, and nothing else. That Word," he boasted, "while I slept and drank beer with Melanchthon and Amsdorf, has broken the papacy more than any king or emperor ever broke it."[15]

Although they had the Word of God in as pure or nearly as pure a form as the Apostolic Age had had it, this did not mean for Luther that a new age was dawning for mankind. Instead, it signalled the end of time and God's final judgment. As early as 1522, once again in connection with the recovery of the Word, he also pointed to the pope, together with the Turks, as the Antichrists of the end times.[16] One year later, he remarked: "My desire and hope is that it is the Judgment day. For at this time the signs appear to come together and the whole world seems to be in great turmoil, which can only mean some great change is in the offing. At the same time the light of the Gospel has risen so brightly, which has always been followed by some great change because of the unbelievers."[17] In a sermon of August 1525, just after the Peasants' War, he declared that God would not allow such wickedness to go unpunished, especially since it coincided with "such a rich preaching of the Gospel, and in a clearer fashion even than at the time of the Apostles."[18]

In contrast to most other sixteenth-century thinkers, Luther did not see the history of the Church primarily in terms of decline and revival as the above passages might indicate. Already in his reflections on Augsburg and his meeting with Cajetan he wrote: "I do not wish the power of Scripture to be reduced to mere words, and I reject the folly of certain very simple—minded men who would fix the church of Christ in time and place."[19] Rather, it was the Word of God alone that had permanence, it alone was the absolute norm. People responded to it in faith— greater at some times, lesser at others—but there was no progress here. "The Church," he declared, "is always born and always changed in the succession of the faithful. Now this and now that is the Church, yet always the same."[20] Or again: "Thus the militant Church is one from the beginning of the world; one generation passes, another comes, one after the other the Church succeeds in the same Church."[21] He confirmed this position in his 1520 preface to the Revelation of John.[22]

Even though Luther at times singled out the Apostolic Age as an age in which the light of the Word had shone brightly, he argued that his age had seen the recovery of the purity of that Word at times in nearly an equal, at other times in as great a measure. And while he viewed the Church of the Apostolic Age as a tentative norm, as John Headley has observed,[23] everything had always to be judged by the Word, not by a manifestation of the Word's action in history, even if this were the Apostolic Church. Nonetheless, the idea that the Word was being revived and that this revival would lead to a new era came directly from Luther himself. At first, however, the revival of the pure Word of God was, as we have noted, inextricably tied to his expectation of the Last Judgment.[24]

It was with these emerging views that Luther came to the Leipzig Disputation. Thomas Muentzer, also an ardent seeker after truth as he later described himself, had just been initiated into Tauler's sermons by the "woman who was cook to Master Conrad, priest of Orlamuende," and had found the means by which to establish a "holy invincible Christian faith." He may also have followed Luther in taking Tauler's theology as being "very similar to that of [Christian] antiquity."[25] And like Luther,

he had also argued that the Word of God had been hidden from 300 to
400 years. Perhaps he also made contact with Luther at Leipzig, although
he does not appear to have associated himself openly with the latter's
party.[26] Whatever the case, the debate was to have an impact upon
Muentzer, for it acted as both a confirmation of insights already received
from Luther and a stimulation to pursue other matters.[27]

The major conflicts between Luther and Eck at the debate were the
problem of the "deformity" of the Church and the problem of papal
and conciliar authority and infallibility. Eck posed the problem of papal
supremacy by citing Luther's argument, published about one month
earlier in preparation for the Disputation, that "the 'supremacy' of the
Roman church rests on utterly worthless decrees of the Roman popes
issued within the last four hundred years." These decrees, Luther had
gone on to argue, were opposed "by the text of Sacred Scripture and the
accepted histories of eleven hundred years."[28] The two combatants then
quickly proceeded to the even more important question of the primacy
of the Roman pope within the Church. Eck cited the Fathers he deemed
to support him, whereas Luther countered with his own citations from
the Fathers. Finally, Luther proclaimed the Bible as alone authoritative
and infallible in the Church. He quoted St. Augustine, who had observed in one of his letters to Jerome: "I have learned to bestow this
[sole infallibility] honor on those books alone which are called canonical; the others, however, I read in such a way that no matter how much
they excel in doctrine and holiness, I accept them as true, not on their
own word, but only if they have been able to persuade me from canonical books or acceptable reasoning."[29] In a sermon preached on 29 June
1519 on the famous "Petrine Commission" text of Matthew 16:13–19,
in the Leipzig castle before the beginning of the debate, he had already
said: "This Gospel passage encompasses all of the matters to be discussed in this disputation, for it speaks essentially of two matters: first,
concerning the grace of God and our free will; secondly, concerning the
power of St. Peter and the keys."[30]

Eck was quick to point out to Luther and all the rest present at the
debate that John Hus had been condemned to die at the stake by the
Fathers gathered in council at Constance for the very position Luther
was propounding:

> Among the many dangerous errors for which John Wycliffe was con-
> demned was his assertion that belief in the supremacy of the Roman church
> is not required for salvation. So, too, among the pernicious errors of John
> Hus was his belief that Peter was never head of the holy Catholic church.

And another statement: "There is not a spark of evidence that there must be one head 'ruling the church in spiritual matters' because it has always been associated with the church militant." And he said: "The papal dignity derives from Caesar." And: "The pope's position and appointment emanate from Caesar."[31]

Luther, however, came prepared for the charge. In the same sermon of 29 June he had observed: "Now that the turmoil [over the indulgence scandal] is nearly over, they are beginning to play a new game, and intend, at the forthcoming disputation in Leipzig, to cover up and adorn all earlier outrages and vices while raising others, specifically to accuse me of wishing to defend the Bohemian heresy."[32] Thus, when Eck made his charge, Luther could parry the thrust. At first he argued that he had never been a friend of schism and that the Bohemians had been wrong in theirs.[33] Later he placed himself at least partially on the side of Hus by declaring that "many of the articles of John Hus or the Bohemians are fully Christian and evangelical, which the universal church cannot condemn, as for example the one affirming that there is only one universal church."[34] From this encounter Muentzer may have drawn the same conclusion Luther appeared to draw: John Hus had begun to restore the "pure Word of God" before Luther ever appeared on the scene.[35]

Before proceeding further, we should make one more observation. Muentzer may have been present at the sermon preached by Luther in the Leipzig castle on 29 June just before the opening of the debate. If he was, he would have heard a sermon that could only have reinforced his reading of Tauler and given him occasion to think that Luther, too, was one of the great mystic's disciples. For in that sermon on Matt. 16:13–19 Luther spoke of "the grace of God" giving men "the form of God and deif[ying] him, so that even Scriptures call him 'God' and God's son." There Luther also spoke of "despair" in Taulerian terms as "the best and nearest preparation for grace," a "despair and search for grace [that] should not last only for an hour or a period of time and then cease," but "as long as we live." Therefore, he concluded, "despair of oneself must also continue along with it and false trust in oneself must be left behind."[36]

While in Leipzig, Muentzer contacted Achatius Glov, Melchior Lotter's bookseller. He must have done so because the Leipzig Disputation sparked a renewed interest in him for the history of the Church's development—or, from his perspective, its "deformation"—and in the writings of Augustine, for on 1 January 1520 he wrote Franz Guenther that he was rereading Augustine and returning to many books of history.[37] The books came from Achatius Glov, as Muentzer's letter of 3 January 1520 to Guenther indicates.[38] When he ordered them is not clear, but it may well have been while he was in attendance at the Disputation.[39] Nor is it clear when he received them.

Prior to Leipzig, Luther convinced Muentzer of the fact that the "pure Word of God" had lain hidden under a bench for 300 to 400 years and that he, Luther, was in the process of reviving it. Thomas Muentzer completely affirmed this revival. After Leipzig, Luther added the name of John Hus as one who had preceded him in this attempt to revive the Word. Muentzer may well have drawn the same conclusion. In his mind Hus and Bohemia had become even more important than Luther since Hus had come before him. At the same time, the Disputation raised, once again, the question of when the Church had become deformed. The question of papal primacy as discussed by Luther and Eck during the debate had drawn attention to the early Church, the Church Fathers, and the beginning of the "Roman" Catholic Church. At what point had the process of decline begun? That this question concerned Muentzer becomes evident from his *Prague Manifesto* where he remarked: "I have read hither and yon in the histories of the ancient Fathers and have discovered that, after the death of the disciples of the apostles, the pure virgin church was quickly transformed into a prostitute by the seductive priests. For the priests have always desired to hold the place of honor, as Hegesippus, Eusebius and others confirm."[40]

Muentzer continued studying Tauler's sermons in spite of the fact that his interest in Augustine and Eusebius had been renewed by the Leipzig Disputation. This is made apparent by the letter of the nun Ursula to Muentzer of mid-May 1520. Indeed, she even added Suso's name to that of Tauler.[41] Thus Muentzer was at the same time reading Tauler and the German Mystics while renewing—or beginning anew—his study of Augustine and Eusebius. Whereas the next chapter will pursue the importance of Augustine's sermons and letters for Muentzer's emerging intellectual development, this chapter assesses the impact Eusebius's *Church History* had on it.

Eusebius was available to readers of the sixteenth century in Parisian editions of 1512 and 1518 of the Latin translation of Rufinus.[42] Luther referred to the *Church History* a number of times as did some of the Anabaptists. Although Luther and the Anabaptists varied widely in their perspectives, they used Eusebius in very similar ways, albeit for their own purposes, to illustrate specific points or prove certain contentions. Eusebius did not provide them with the context in which they argued.[43] This is emphatically not so in the case of Muentzer. Here Eusebius provided the context, perhaps the paradigm, of his thought, to a certain extent already suggested by Tauler. The reason why Eusebius played such an important role in Muentzer's thought is that, unlike Luther and the Anabaptists, he had not yet developed a coherent reform program of his own when first reading him; he was still looking for a larger context. The use Muentzer makes of Eusebius is therefore another indication that while Luther provided him with some specific ideas and information, he did not provide him with the larger context of his thought.

It is important to remind ourselves at this juncture of the main outlines of Tauler's thought and their importance for Muentzer, for it is Tauler's influence, not Luther's, which provided him with the key to his understanding of Eusebius. The most important of these was Tauler's emphasis on the role of the Holy Spirit in the life of the individual Christian and in that of the larger Christian Church, as we have outlined it in the previous chapter. With this fresh in his mind, Muentzer had listened to Luther and Eck debate the emerging deformity of the Church, the corrupting influence of the papacy and the importance of the Church Fathers, especially that of Augustine. He became obsessed with the question of when the Church had gone astray. As a result, he began to read far and wide in the Church Fathers, but especially in Eusebius, to find an answer. Whereas Luther in this same search had focused on "the Word" and the extent to which it had shone brightly or had "languished, hidden under a bench," Muentzer sought the "Holy Spirit" and the extent to which it had been, and continued to be, present in each believer and the Church.

The vantage point from which Muentzer viewed the development of the Church, therefore, was totally different from that of Eusebius who became his primary source of information. The latter, as G. A. Williamson has observed, sought to "justify the ways of God to man . . . the overthrow of God's enemies and the triumph of the Church."[44] Muentzer, however, sought the turning point in the Church's development, the point at which the Holy Spirit had departed from it. Eusebius marvelled at the Church's victory under Constantine; Muentzer bewailed its pervasive corruption in his own day. Eusebius saw himself standing on the threshold of the Church's triumph; Muentzer saw himself at the end of the age, indeed in "the time of harvest," when God's judgment was about to overwhelm the Church for its corruption.

From this vantage point, Muentzer's reading of Eusebius must have marked a dramatically new perspective on the development of the Church for him. This is attested by his repeated references—beginning with the *Prague Manifesto*—to certain passages in the *Church History* which dealt with the Apostolic Church and the intrusion of heresies into her midst. In his *Manifesto* he wrote, for example:

> It is a bitter pill for me to swallow that the Christian Church is so downtrodden [corrupt], that God could not plague her any more even if He wished to destroy her. This He will not do, however, with the exception of those thin-shitters who have taught her to pray to Baal. These are more than worthy to be sawn in two, as Daniel says: for they have not practiced the judgments of God. I have read hither and yon in the histories of the old Fathers and I find that, after the death of the disciples of the apostles, the pure, virgin church was quickly transformed into a prostitute by the seductive priests. For the priests have always desired to hold the place of honor, as Hegesippus, Eusebius and others confirm.[45]

He reiterated this in the preface to his *Deutshch-Evangelische Messe*,[46] as well as in his *Fuerstenpredigt*.[47] It would seem, therefore, that while Luther and Tauler may have persuaded Muentzer that the Church was no longer what it had once been—if, indeed, he needed any further persuading at this juncture—his reading of certain passages in Eusebius convinced him that the corruption had set in very early, indeed as early as the middle of the second century.

The three instances where Muentzer refers specifically to the corruption of the Apostolic Church are always in connection with the "Hegesippus passages" in Eusebius's *Church History*.[48] Sometimes he speaks of Hegesippus and Eusebius together, at other times as distinctly separate. Thus, as we have already noted, he says in his *Manifesto:* ". . . as Hegesippus, Eusebius and others confirm." In his *Fuerstenpredigt* he brings the two more closely together, observing: "For Hegesippus and Eusebius say in Book 4:22. . . ." This is an unmistakable reference to a famous passage which Eusebius takes directly from Hegesippus.[49] But in the preface to his *Deutsch-Evangelische Messe* he obviously speaks of two separate and two different books: "Egiosiopus, a trustworthy historian, a disciple of the apostles, in the fifth book of his explanations, and Eusebius in the fourth book of his *Church History* say straight out that the holy bride of Christ remained a virgin until after the death of the disciples of the apostles and thereafter became a lewd prostitute."

The last quotation makes it apparent that Muentzer had not only read Eusebius—through whom alone we know the writings of Hegesippus—

but that he had also read another Hegesippus. This was pseudo-Hegesippus[50] who had, around 371, prepared a rather free translation of the first four books of Josephus's *Jewish War*,[51] and in the fifth book—the one referred to by Muentzer in his *Deutsch-Evangelische Messe*—had translated parts from books five, six, and seven, interspersing these Josephan passages with "appropriate" quotations from the Bible and his own interpolations. Whereas Muentzer read Eusebius in Rufinus's Latin translation from the late fourth or the early fifth century, first printed in Rome around 1476,[52] he must have read pseudo-Hegesippus in the 1510 Paris edition prepared by Faber Stapulensis.[53] Like virtually everyone else throughout the Middle Ages,[54] Muentzer regarded the two Hegesippi as one and the same. This confusion is clearly indicated in the last of the quotations where he referred to his book and called him Egiosiopus.[55] He also referred to him as a "trustworthy historian [and] a disciple of the apostles." Precisely because he believed him to have been a disciple of the Apostles—that is, as one living before the corruption had set in in the Church—Hegesippus was uncorrupted and therefore had authority.

Although it is difficult to determine what impressed him about the fifth book of pseudo-Hegesippus, some general observations may be hazarded. In the first place, this book combines parts of those books of the *Jewish War* which deal with the siege and capture of Jerusalem. Josephus saw this event as the judgment of God on the sins of the Jews.[56] But pseudo-Hegesippus took this one step further, assigning the destruction of the city to the Jews' crucifixion of Christ. For both writers, however, the priests bore the brunt of the responsibility. Here, then, Muentzer may have been confirmed both in his views concerning God's temporal judgment upon a sinful people and in his belief, expressed in the *Manifesto,* that corruption sets in because "the priests have always desired to hold the place of honor," at whatever cost.[57]

With respect to the authentic Hegesippus, whom Muentzer came to know in Eusebius, we have more evidence of influence. In his *Fuerstenpredigt* Muentzer refers specifically to Book 4:22 of the *Church History*. There we read:

> The same author [Hegesippus] sketches the origins of the heresies of his day:
> "When James the Righteous had suffered martyrdom like the Lord and for the same reason, Symeon the son of his uncle Clopas was appointed bishop. He being a cousin of the Lord, it was the universal demand that he should be the second. They used to call the Church a virgin for this reason,

that she had not yet been seduced by listening to nonsense. But Thebutis, because he had not been made bishop, began to seduce her by means of the seven sects (to which he himself belonged) among the people. From this came Simon, and his Simonians, Cleobius and his Cleobienes, Dositheus and his Dositheans, Gorthaeus and his Gorthenes, and the Masbotheans. From these were derived the Menandrianists, Marcionists, Carpocratians, Valentians, Basilidians, and Saturnidians, every man introducing his own opinion in his own particular way. From these in turn came false Christs, false prophets, false apostles, who split the unity of the Church by poisonous suggestions against God and against his Christ."[58]

Muentzer's reference to the Church's prostitution appears to be based on an earlier passage in Book 3:33, where Eusebius wrote, once again after just having quoted directly from Hegesippus:

> In describing the situation at the time Hegesippus goes on to say that until then the Church had remained a virgin, pure and uncorrupted, since those who were trying to corrupt the wholesome standard of the saving message, if such there were, lurked somewhere under the cover of darkness. But when the sacred band of the apostles had in various ways reached the end of their life, and the generation of those privileged to listen with their own ears to the divine wisdom had passed on, then godless error began to take shape, through the deceit of false teachers, who now that none of the apostles was left threw off the mask and attempted to counter the preaching of the truth by preaching the knowledge falsely so called.[59]

It turns out that these two passages—as Hugh Jackson Lawlor pointed out many years ago—belong together.[60] The first two sentences from the passage in Book 4:22, concerning "James the Just" and "Clopas . . . a cousin of the Lord," have no relation whatever to the sentence that follows dealing with the "virgin church." In these first two sentences Eusebius is talking about the Apostolic Succession; in the third, however, about the introduction of heresy. As Lawlor has observed, Eusebius's "scissors and paste" job leaves something to be desired.[61] Nevertheless, for Eusebius there was a necessary connection between Apostolic Succession and orthodoxy. He therefore pieced his Hegesippus together to suit his own purposes. The passages, however, probably fit together in the following sequence:

> Eusebius tells us that Hegesippus, when narrating the events of the times of Trajan and his precedessors, relates "that until the times then present the Church remained a virgin pure and uncorrupted, since those, if there were any in existence, who were seeking to corrupt the sound rule of the saving doctrine were still at the time in obscure darkness somewhere, as it were in hiding. On this account they called the Church a virgin; for it was not yet

corrupt by vain teachings. But Thebutis, because he was not himself made a bishop, begins to corrupt it from the seven heresies among the people—to which he himself belonged. . . . Each [of the heretical teachers] severally and in different ways introduced their several opinions. From these came false Christs, false prophets, false apostles, men who divided the unity of the Church with corrupt words against God and against His Christ."[62]

Now, the Church that Hegesippus here calls "a virgin" was the church at Jerusalem. Eusebius, however, proceeded to make the passage refer to the Universal Church.[63] By so doing, he inadvertently gave the impression—most certainly to Muentzer—that the Church was everywhere being subverted by heresy.

Hegesippus was not an historian. His *Memoranda* (or five books of memoirs—with which Muentzer confused the five books of pseudo-Hegesippus)—were, as Telfer has remarked, "primarily doctrinal and polemical, and only incidentally concerned with history."[64] They were written to demonstrate that heresy was a recent phenomenon and had made inroads only in those regions that no longer possessed a regular episcopal succession to guard and pass on intact the pure deposit of the Apostolic faith. Hegesippus, therefore, appears to have been motivated by his concern to maintain the unity of the Christian Church and what he deemed to be the purity of the Apostolic message. This motive led him to accentuate the importance of the Apostolic Succession and the "virginity" of the Apostolic Church while exaggerating the danger of heresy. The greater the threat of heresy, the greater the reason to emphasize the purity of the Apostolic Church and its message, and to urge their tenacious retention.[65]

Because Eusebius was also desirous of demonstrating the ultimate vindication and triumph of the Church, he too, as Robert Grant has observed, made heresy and persecution worse than they in fact were, for "The worse the heretics or persecutors [were] made to look, the more radiantly the light of the Church [would] shine."[66] Hegesippus also, though not intentionally, depicted a fall from the purity of the Apostolic Church to the contamination of heresies and resulting division. Perhaps, like Socrates Scholasticus, the fifth-century Church historian, he had been motivated to write because of the "vain and subtle disputation [which had] confused and at the same time scattered the apostolic faith of Christianity."[67] At the very least, he seems to have feared that it could come to this. To someone imbued with Muentzer's quest, such statements were only too easily interpreted as evidence that the Apostolic Church had been "a virgin." And since Eusebius himself placed Hegesippus closer to the Apostles than he deserved to be—dating his five books around 130 A.D. rather than 180 A.D. when they were in fact probably written[68]—Muentzer may have come to regard Hegesippus as a more "trustworthy historian" than even Eusebius because he considered the former to be a "disciple of the apostles."[69]

When we add to this the fact that Muentzer read Eusebius in the Latin translation of Rufinus, the question of influence becomes more complicated. As Oulton has observed, Rufinus was careful to "avoid language to which exception might be taken" since he had himself become "suspect of unorthodoxy and singed by the fires of controversy." Because of what many contemporaries considered their Arian overtones, Rufinus modified Eusebius's introduction to his work and completely omitted the tenth book that included the author's Panegyric delivered at the dedication of Tyre cathedral.[70] The first he passed over in silence; the second he justified in the following manner:

> I must point out the course I have taken in reference to the tenth book of this work. As it stands in Greek, it has little to do with the process of events. All but a small part of it is taken up with discussions tending to the praise of particular Bishops, and adds nothing to our knowledge of the facts. I have therefore left out all this superfluous matter; and, whatever in it belonged to genuine history I have added to the ninth book, with which I have made this history close.[71]

In its place, Rufinus added two books of his own, both of which dealt with the problems created in the Church by the Arian heresy.[72]

This emphasis on the internal strife of the Church after the end of the persecutions, combined with Eusebius's own description of the Church just prior to the last great persecution under Diocletian, may well have strengthened the impression Muentzer gained from Hegesippus. Eusebius argued that "increasing freedom transformed our character to arrogance and sloth." Priests began to envy, abuse, and cut each other's throats; they broke into warring factions, "and unspeakable hypocrisy and dissimulation were carried to the limit of wickedness." Even "those of us," Eusebius continued, "who were supposed to be pastors cast off the restraining influence of the fear of God and quarrelled heatedly with each other, engaged solely in swelling the disputes, threats, envy, and mutual hostility and hate, frantically demanding the despotic power they coveted."[73] With the tenth book excised, however, Muentzer would not have read Eusebius's description of how the Church recovered from this time when "through the envy and jealousy of the demon that loves evil, she became by her own free choice a lover of sensuality and evil," and how the "Deity withdrew from her," leaving her "bereft of a protector."[74]

As we have already observed, Muentzer read these passages from the vantage point of his own increasing rejection of the Roman Catholic Church. To this he added Tauler's emphasis on the Holy Spirit, especially his emphasis on the purity of the Christian life of those "friends of God" who had been transformed by the coming of the Holy Spirit. This purity, Tauler had repeatedly insisted, could be retained only by "fleeing Egypt." Mixing with the world, tolerating the tares in one's midst, would force the departure of the Holy Spirit and lead to corruption. When seen in the light of the Hegesippus passages, this tolerance invited the intrusion of "false Christs, false prophets, false apostles" into the Church; as a result, the Holy Spirit was gradually—or perhaps even suddenly—forced out of the Church. Accordingly, Muentzer must later have been struck by Augustine's use of the Parable of the Tares. The Hegesippus passages had convinced him of the "virginity" of the Apostolic Church; Tauler had convinced him that the Holy Spirit would not tolerate tares; but Augustine's interpretation of the Parable was to convince him that, for a time, the tares had to be tolerated. The logical conclusion from these three overlapping convictions was that the Church consisting of wheat and tares could not possess the Holy Spirit. Individuals might continue to do so, but only if they too separated themselves from the world.

Implicit, if not explicit, in Hegesippus's depiction of the early Church as a virgin lay what Gordon Leff has called the "myth of the [pure] Apostolic Church."[75] Eusebius embellished and added to the detailed outlines of this description, for it fitted into his own theme of the importance of the Apostolic Succession.[76] His history, therefore, obviously provided Muentzer with some important aspects of his picture of the Apostolic Church which, in his *Prague Manifesto,* he saw being reborn in Bohemia. How did Eusebius portray this Apostolic Church— and his history is replete with both the term and the concept—and how does Eusebius's assessment compare with Muentzer's?

One of the first things that strikes the reader about Eusebius's portrayal is the way in which the life and Christian ideals of the Apostolic Church had been integrated. Muentzer, who was seeking for a "holy invincible Christian faith," had already found such a faith, worked by the Holy Spirit, in the *Historia* and Tauler's sermons; therefore, he could not but have been struck by the parallels. For Eusebius wrote:

Those inspired and wonderful men, Christ's apostles, had completely purified their lives and cultivated every spiritual virtue, but their speech was that
of every day. The divine wonder-working power bestowed on them by the
Saviour filled them with confidence; and having neither the ability nor the
desire to present the teachings of the Master with rhetorical subtlety or
literary skill, they relied on demonstrating the divine Spirit working with
them, and on the miraculous power of Christ fully operative in them.[77]

Not only had the Apostles been filled with the power of the Spirit.
Eusebius was at pains to portray the Apostolic Church as such as one in
which converts to the faith had sought to bring their life into conformity
with Christ's teachings. He quoted passages from Justin Martyr and
from a report on the Gallic martyrs. Typical among the martyrs was the
statement an ordinary woman made at her execution: "I am a Christian: we do nothing to be ashamed of."[78] Even outsiders like Philo,
Eusebius contended, had written of the early Christians in Alexandria:

> In every house there is a holy chamber called a sanctuary or "monastery"
> where they celebrate in seclusion the mysteries of the sanctified life, bringing
> in nothing—drink, food, or anything else required for bodily needs—but
> laws and inspired oracles spoken by prophets, hymns, and everything else by
> which knowledge and true religion are increased and perfected.... The
> whole period from dawn to dusk is given up to spiritual discipline.[79]

Passages such as these, especially those having to do with Origen and
the martyrs, were strengthened even more by Rufinus in his translation
because he was himself an advocate of the ascetic life. He therefore
added details not known to Eusebius which tended to emphasize the
"principles of a perfect life" and the observance of "an evangelical
simplicity and poverty of life."[80]

Aside from attempting to conform its life to Christian ideals, the
Apostolic Church—a term Eusebius uses over and over again[81]—
manifested a profusion of prophetic gifts,[82] miraculous occurrences,[83]
and many other examples of God's grace and favor, such as revelations,[84] which Rufinus also emphasized.[85] Indeed, Eusebius quoted
Irenaeus who had written:

> So it is that in His name, those who truly are His disciples, having received
> grace from Him, put it to effectual use for the benefit of their fellow-men, in
> proportion to the gift each one has received from Him. Some drive out
> demons really and truly, so that often those cleansed from evil spirits believe
> and become members of the Church; some have foreknowledge of the future,
> visions, and prophetic utterances; others, by the laying on of hands, heal the

sick and restore them to health; and before now, as I said, dead men have actually been raised and have remained with us for many years. In fact, it is impossible to enumerate the gifts which throughout the world the Church has received from God and in the name of Jesus Christ crucified under Pontius Pilate, and every day puts to effectual use for the benefit of the heathen, deceiving no one and making profit out of no one; freely she received from God, and freely she ministers.[86]

According to Eusebius, these gifts were made possible by the presence of the Holy Spirit in the believers of the Apostolic Church. They "relied only on demonstrating the divine Spirit working with them"; they were "utterly devoted to God, and fervent in the spirit."[87] Of one of the martyrs it was written: "He was called the Christians' advocate, but he had in himself the Advocate, the Spirit that filled Zacharias, as he showed by the fullness of his love when he gladly laid down his own life in defence of his brother Christians. For he was and is a true disciple of Christ, following the Lamb wherever he goes."[88] Of others Eusebius said: "they were richly blest by the grace of God, and the Holy Spirit was their counsellor."[89] It would appear, however, that the exercise of the gifts of the Spirit, according to Eusebius, took place only in "fit" Christians, only in "acceptable" persons, whose lives had been so ordered as to conform to the Christian ideal.[90]

This emphasis on the role of the Holy Spirit as the empowering force within the Apostolic Church is of considerable importance in Eusebius's context. He described how, in the early Roman Church, Fabian had been chosen as a bishop by a "miracle of divine and heavenly grace":

> When the brethren had all assembled with the intention of electing a successor to the bishopric and a large number of eminent and distinguished men were in the thoughts of most, Fabian, who was present, came into no one's mind. But suddenly out of the blue a dove fluttered down and perched on his head . . . plainly following the example of the descent upon the Saviour of the Holy Spirit in the form of a dove.[91]

From another description of Novatus by Cornelius of Rome one reads: "And when he recovered [from an illness nearly unto death] he did not receive the other things of which one should partake according to the rule of the Church, in particular the sealing by a bishop. Without receiving these how could he receive the Holy Ghost?"[92] This passage clearly implies that the reception of the Holy Spirit was a phenomenon common to everyone in the Church who had been correctly initiated.

While Tauler had stressed the importance of the role of the Holy Spirit in making a "holy invincible Christian faith" possible in the individual—Mysticism being by its very nature individualistic—Eusebius located that same Holy Spirit in the Apostolic Church. He assumed that this was the way it must always be.[93] And this widespread diffusion of the "gifts of the Spirit" in that Early Church presupposed the *Christfoermigkeit*—to use Muentzer's term—of the members. Thus the critical element in that Early Church was the Holy Spirit. Its presence made possible the integration of faith and life and the profuse diffusion of its gifts. Should it depart, the Church would become deformed. Tauler had argued that it could depart from the individual. Could it also depart from the Church? In any case, whereas the clarity and prominence of "the Word" was the salient element in Luther's description of the Church, for Muentzer it was the Holy Spirit that had been prominently present in the Church at least in the first century and a half. Because Muentzer came to believe that the tares had forced this Holy Spirit out of the Church, a new Apostolic Church had to be—and could be—erected.

But there was even more in Eusebius's description of the Apostolic Church that may have influenced Muentzer. In a number of passages, Eusebius portrayed the early Christians as renouncing their property and holding their goods in common.[94] There Muentzer also read that, as Dionysius of Alexandria had written in a letter to Dionysius of Rome: "he [Novatus] makes light of holy baptism, does away with the faith and confession that precede it, and even when there was some hope that the Holy Spirit would remain or even return to them, he banishes Him completely."[95] But while faith and confession were assumed to have preceded baptism in the Apostolic Church, rebaptism, even of those baptized by heretics, was another matter, as Xystus, Bishop of Rome, indicated in a letter quoted by Eusebius. For he refused to baptize a man again when the latter realized he had not been baptized in the orthodox manner.[96]

Although this Apostolic Church had been attacked by internal enemies like Simon Magus from time to time,

> divine and celestial grace worked with its ministers, [who] by their advent and presence speedily extinguish[ed] the flames of the Evil One before they could spread, and through them humble[d] and pull[ed] down every lofty barrier raised against the knowledge of God. Consequently, neither Simon nor any of his contemporaries managed to form an organized body in those apostolic days, for every attempt was defeated and overpowered by the light of the truth and by the divine Word Himself who had so recently shone from God on men, active in the world and immanent in His own apostles.[97]

But then, as Eusebius, relying on Hegesippus, argued

> when the sacred band of apostles had in various ways reached the end of
> their life, and the generation of those privileged to listen with their ears to the
> divine wisdom had passed on, godless error began to take shape, through the
> deceit of false teachers, who now that none of the apostles was left threw off
> the mask and attempted to counter the preaching of the truth by preaching
> the knowledge falsely so-called.[98]

From passages such as these taken out of Eusebius's larger context
and placed into his own, Muentzer concluded that the early Church had
been filled with true prophets while the post-Apostolic Church had
begun to be subverted from within by false prophets. These, as the early
Christian writer Apollonius seemed to indicate, had been in it for the
money.[99] When such people began to infiltrate the Church, the wheat
came to be mixed with the tares, and the Holy Spirit was forced to
withdraw from it.

Once this picture is clearly in the reader's mind, there can be little
doubt that Muentzer derived his view of the Apostolic Church from a
combination of Tauler and Eusebius, a view confirmed later by his
reading of Augustine. From these writers Muentzer derived three major
arguments: his emphasis on the necessity of the conformity of the believer's life with Christ's teachings, his stress on the legitimacy of
dreams, visions, and prophecy as manifestations of the presence of the
Holy Spirit, and his argument that that same Apostolic Church had
become an adulteress once the false prophets had entered her house.
The amazing thing is how well Tauler's main ideas, expounded largely
for the individual, meshed with Eusebius's depiction of the Apostolic
Church, which he, and Muentzer with him, regarded as the norm by
which all others had to be judged. Perhaps it is this conjunction of
Tauler and Eusebius that leads to the parallels between the individual
and the Church which Hans-Juergen Goertz has termed the "inner and
outer order" in his theology. If it is, Muentzer did not derive it solely
from German Mysticism as Goertz argues.[100]

For the time being, let the following selection from Muentzer's
Fuerstenpredigt suffice as evidence of the foregoing assertions. There he
remarked:

> It is indeed true that Christ, the son of God, and His apostles, yes and
> before Him the holy prophets, established a true and pure Christianity, they
> threw a purified wheat onto the field, which is the precious Word of God
> planted in the hearts of the elect, as Matth. 12, Mark 4, Luke 8, as well as

Ezekiel 36, wrote. But the lazy, careless servants of the same church did not care to continue with this assiduous watchfulness; they sought to satisfy personal desires rather than care for the things of Christ, Philip. 2. Because of this neglect they have allowed the godless, that is the tares, to damage the church by mightily infiltrating it, Psalm 79, where the cornerstone, mentioned here, was still small, of which Isaiah spoke in chpt. 28. He [the cornerstone] had not yet filled the world, but he will shortly fill it completely. For that reason the cornerstone erected in the early years of Christianity was soon rejected by the builders, that is the rulers, Psalm 117 and Luke 20. Thus, I say, that the church begun at that time decayed everywhere and remained in that state until the time of the split kingdom [the Holy Roman Empire], Luke 21 and Daniel 2, Ezra 4. For Hegesippus and Eusebius say in Book 4, Section 22 of their history of the church, that the Christian church remained a virgin only until the time of the death of the disciples of the apostles. Soon thereafter she became an adulteress, as had been predicted by the beloved apostles, 2 Peter 2.[101]

In the same sermon Muentzer argued that it was the rejection of the Holy Spirit by the tares in the Apostolic Church which had precipitated its rapid decline:

Yes, they [the tares] finally even reenacted the passion with Him [the Holy Spirit], after the time when the dear disciples of the apostles died. They held the Spirit of Christ for something to be despised, and do it still, as is written in Psalm 68. They have clearly stolen Him like thieves and murderers, John 10. They have robbed the sheep of Christ of the true voice and have made the crucified Christ into a deceptive, fantastic God.[102]

Without the presence and power of the Holy Spirit, Muentzer continued, it was impossible to tell the wheat from the tares. "Nevertheless they are blind in their folly. Nothing else has misled them, and still continues to mislead them to this very day, than the false belief that, without any reception of the Holy Spirit, who is master of the fear of God, and despising the wisdom of God, they can separate the good from the bad [the wheat from the tares]."[103]

We can now begin to understand Muentzer's proclamation in his *Prague Manifesto* that the new Apostolic Church would arise first in Bohemia and then everywhere else. Only when the Holy Spirit reentered the Church would that new Apostolic Church come into existence. Muentzer intended, therefore, as he proclaimed at the outset of that tract, "to fill the resounding and versatile trumpets with the new song of praise of the Holy Spirit." This Spirit, with the renewed planting of a purified "seed"—the pure Word of God which had begun to come back with Hus and most recently with Luther—would lead to the growing conformity of life and precept. When it did, this would be a sign of the end times. Then the fields would be ripe unto harvest and the tares—because of the renewed presence of the Holy Spirit—could once again be separated.

CHAPTER III:

Augustine and the Parable of the Tares

The Lord's floor [i.e., the Church] is not yet purged—it
cannot be without chaff, be it ours to pray, and to do what in
us lies that we may be good grain.

—Augustine to Maximin, 392

If Tauler persuaded Muentzer of the necessity of being baptized by the Holy Spirit, and Eusebius convinced him that the same Holy Spirit had been expelled from the Apostolic Church by the tares with the death of the disciples of the Apostles, how could a new Apostolic Church be created? The answer would appear obvious: remove the tares from within. At what point in time Muentzer arrived at this conclusion is not apparent. But everything seems to indicate, as we shall argue in the next chapter, that it was before he arrived in Zwickau. If that is the case, then it probably came to him in Beuditz as he was reading Augustine. Muentzer's argument, presented in his *Fuerstenpredigt* in July 1524, that "One must uproot the tares from God's vineyard in the time of harvest,"[1] is not an isolated assertion. It forms, rather, a central theme of his thought.[2] It will be the major contention of this chapter that Muentzer in all probability drew his interpretation of this parable, and that of the Good Seed, primarily from the letters and sermons of St. Augustine, which he read, or to which he returned with a new perspective after the Leipzig Disputation.

The stimulus for his turning, or returning, to the writings of St. Augustine after the Disputation was, it would seem, at least twofold. Undoubtedly, the immediate impetus came from Luther's repeated references to Augustine in his debate with John Eck. But this appeal to the authority of Augustine must have struck a responsive chord in Muentzer, for he had just completed his reading of Tauler's sermons that were to play such a signal role in his intellectual development. He had come face to face with Tauler's many quotations from and references to St. Augustine. Even a cursory count reveals that Tauler cited Augustine nearly more often than all other authors combined and that these citations occur in virtually all the critical instances.[3]

As we noted earlier, in his second edition of *Eine Deutsche Theologie* (1518), Luther had observed that he had learned more from that little book than from any other book with the exception of the Bible and the writings of St. Augustine.[4] Such an observation would seem to indicate that Luther regarded the two—the writings of St. Augustine and the mystical sermons of Tauler—to be mutually reinforcing. We have argued, however, that Luther did not read Tauler and *Eine Deutsche Theologie* in the same way that Muentzer did. Indeed, the former read his own theology into these sources because he had arrived at his own position earlier and independently of them. Nor, as it turns out, did he rely on the same works of Augustine for support that served Tauler's mysticism so well. For Luther, already in his lectures on Romans, was drawn to Augustine's later writings, his anti-Donatist and anti-Pelagian tracts,[5] whereas Tauler drew from his earlier, Neoplatonic works, especially his *Confessions*.[6] This classic of introspection and fount of at least one major strand of Western Christian Mysticism has been described by Peter Brown as a manifesto of the inner world of the Neoplatonists who "provided him [Augustine] with the one, essential tool for any serious autobiography: they gave him a theory of the dynamics of the soul that made sense to his experiences."[7]

It should not be surprising, therefore, that Tauler relied on Augustine—and through him ultimately on the Platonists—for his essential description of the soul. After observing that "many masters, new and old, have treated" of the soul, such as "Albertus Magnus, Master Dietrich, and Master Eckhart," and that some had spoken "of it as a spark of divine fire, others as the inmost depths of the soul, others again as the crown of the soul," Tauler asserted:

> But you must know, dear children, that these masters have experienced in their minds and in their lives the things that they herein treat of; and, furthermore, they have drawn this doctrine from the greatest saints and doctors of holy Church. Even certain teachers before the Lord's birth, as Plato, Aristotle and Proclus, have also diligently studied this subject.[8]

In another passage that refers even more specifically to Plato, Tauler observes: "This deepest region of the spirit was in a manner known to some of the Gentiles of old; and as they searched its depths, the knowledge caused them to despise all transitory things. Such great philosophers as Proclus and Plato gave a clear account of it to guide others who knew it not. Therefore St. Augustine says that Plato has proclaimed the first part of St. John's gospel."[9]

Even though Tauler may have derived his concept of the soul from Master Eckhart, he justified it exclusively with quotations drawn from St. Augustine. Thus, although the concept of the *Abgrund der Seele* may be an expression of German Mysticism, it has its source in Augustine and the Platonists who influenced him. In any case, it is amply evident that Tauler drew heavily from Augustine's *Confessions* and from his early letters and sermons.

Several other aspects of Augustine's thought must be noted before we move on to the Leipzig Disputation and Luther's use of Augustine there. The first is that Augustine's *Confessions* appear to have provided the German Mystics with their archetypal conversion experience. In the first chapter we noted the importance of this experience for both Tauler and Muentzer, as well as the importance of the role the Holy Spirit played in such a conversion. This same transformation took place in Augustine, as he himself described it, brought about, he said, when a "profound reflection had, from the secret depths of [his] soul, drawn together and heaped up all [his] misery before the sight of [his] heart," and a mighty storm arose within him accompanied by a "mighty shower of tears." Weeping bitterly, he withdrew from his friend Alypius, sought solitude under a fig tree, and, "giving free course to [his] tears," asked his God: "How long, Lord? Wilt Thou be angry for ever?" While he was thus distraught, a voice came to him telling him to "take up and read." Restraining "the torrent of [his] tears," he took up the Bible, remembering how Antony had chanced to enter a church while the Divine Word was being read and had been so struck by what he heard that he was "forthwith converted to Thee." He opened and there read: "Not in rioting and drunkenness, not in chambering and wantonness, not in strife and envying; but put ye on the Lord Jesus Christ, and make no provision for the flesh, to fulfil the lusts thereof." No sooner had he read this than "instantly, as the sentence ended,—by a light, as it were, of security infused into my heart,—all the gloom of doubt vanished away." The period of trials was over, and Augustine was so thoroughly converted to God that he could say: "How sweet did it suddenly become to me to be without the delights of trifles! And what at one time I feared to lose, it was now a joy to me to put away. For Thou didst cast them away, and instead of them didst enter in Thyself. . . . Now was my soul free from the gnawing cares of seeking and getting, and of wallowing and exciting the itch of lust."[10] And this transformation, as he never tired of telling his congregation at Hippo, was the sole work of the Holy Spirit. This emphasis upon conversion as the exclusive work of the Holy Spirit was taken up by Tauler and through him found its way into Thomas Muentzer.

Second, Mysticism's emphasis on the various stages of development toward "becoming god-like in retirement," to use Augustine's expression in an early letter to his friend Nebridius,[11] also drew support—if it did not actually derive—from the writings of the young, pre-*Confessions* Augustine. He described the seven stages of this development in his early treatise, *De Quantitate Animae*,[12] and, until he began to read St. Paul differently—that is, from a non-Platonic perspective[13]—around the time of his writing the *Confessions*, his goal was indeed to proceed through these seven stages toward deification.[14]

Ten years later, as Brown argues, "this great hope [of Augustine] had vanished. 'Whoever thinks,' Augustine will then write, 'that in this mortal life a man may so disperse the mists of bodily and carnal imaginings as to possess the unclouded light of changeless truth, and to cleave to it with the unswerving constancy of a spirit wholly estranged from the common ways of life—he understands neither What he seeks, nor who he is who seeks it." He could even suggest toward the end of his life that "St. Paul might still have been 'greatly tainted by sexual desire.' "[15]

This change—signalled, as Brown asserts, by the *Confessions*—is of considerable importance in understanding the slowly emerging antagonism between Thomas Muentzer and Martin Luther. Although Augustine believed at first that his conversion was "successful" in that he thought that he had overcome his evil nature, he later came to hold that the struggle against evil continued as long as one existed in the flesh. This later reading of St. Paul was greatly reinforced by Augustine's experiences as bishop of Hippo: whereas he had earlier spoken of "growing god-like in retirement," he now stressed the alien righteousness of Christ as the means of salvation,[16] the grace of God alone. As Brown observes, the belief that conversions were to be successful had been the prevalent conviction among early Christians.[17] Certainly, it was the one that Muentzer derived from his reading of Tauler and that he found amply confirmed in Eusebius's *Church History*. While there are some indications that Luther himself may have been inclined in this direction early on in his career, already in his lectures on Romans he espoused Augustine's later reading of St. Paul with its emphasis on the alien righteousness of Christ imparted to those of faith. Thus Muentzer's emerging conflict with Luther can, at least in some very important aspects, be viewed as one between the pre-*Confessions* Augustine, transmitted to Muentzer through Tauler and confirmed by his reading of Augustine's letters and sermons, and the post-*Confessions* Augustine, transmitted to Luther through the anti-Donatist and anti-Pelagian writings.

Augustine, then, came to Muentzer through Tauler and later at the Leipzig Disputation. It is important to recall that Muentzer read Tauler just before coming to Leipzig and that he ordered his volumes of Augustine's sermons and letters from Achatius Glov even before he left that city. The repeated references to Augustine by both Luther and Eck at the debate must have impressed him. What role did Augustine play in the famous Disputation?

The main point at issue in Leipzig was Luther's thirteenth thesis, which, in Eck's words, "affirm[ed] that the supremacy of the Roman church rests on utterly worthless decrees of Roman popes issued within the last four hundred years."[18] Almost immediately, however, the questions behind the thesis—whether the Church Militant was rightly ruled by the pope at Rome, Peter's ostensible successor, and whether recognition of him as head of the church temporal was necessary for salvation—became the centerpiece of the discussion. In defense of his position that the pope was head of the Church, Eck began to quote the Church Fathers who appeared to be on his side. Luther countered by citing passages from the Bible and St. Augustine to the effect that Christ alone was the head of the Church. When Eck came back with more citations from the Fathers, it began to become clear to all that Augustine, with his immense prestige in the West, was in fact the critical figure in the debate. Therefore, when Eck quoted from a letter of Augustine's against Donatus in which he had said: "You are Peter, and upon this rock, that is Peter, I shall build my church,"[19] the point appeared made. Although Augustine had explained the passage differently elsewhere, Eck contended that he had never retracted this earlier assertion. Luther, however, countered by arguing that Augustine agreed with him more often than not and finally stated that even "if Augustine and all the fathers had taken Peter to be the rock," he would still oppose them all on the authority of the Apostle Paul or the Bible.[20] He confirmed this position the next day by quoting from Augustine's famous letter to Jerome, already cited in the last chapter.[21] Here was Luther's bottom line, and the authority for his stand on *scriptura sola* was Luther's bottom line, and the authority for his stand on *scriptura sola* was none other than Augustine, whose position on these questions appeared to be ambiguous.

Having encountered Augustine in Tauler and almost immediately again at the Leipzig Disputation, Muentzer ordered the latter's letters and sermons from Achatius Glov in Leipzig.[22] Perhaps Luther's references to Augustine's letter to Jerome at the debate drew him to the letters, and Tauler's sermons drew him to those of Augustine. Whatever the case, the fact that he read these rather than Augustine's treatises is of some importance, as the sequel will show.

In the last chapter we noted the impact Eusebius's *Church History* had on Muentzer, especially the argument that the Apostolic Church had, in Muentzer's words, "remained a virgin until after the death of the disciples of the apostles and thereafter quickly became a lewd prostitute." As a consequence of the influx of false prophets and teachers, then, the Holy Spirit had been forced from the Apostolic Church though not, perhaps, from isolated individuals like Augustine within it. Because of this the Church had lost the power to discern truth from falsehood and, consequently, the ability to separate the wheat from the tares.

Reading Augustine's letters and sermons could only have confirmed Muentzer in the belief that the Church had become deformed in the middle of the second century, for Augustine, in one of his earliest letters, described the corruption of the Church in Africa to his bishop Aurelius.[23] In the letter Augustine did not only complain about the ordinary members: "As to 'strife and deceit,' " he said, "what right have I to speak, seeing that these vices prevail more seriously among our own order than among our congregations?"[24]

He said very much the same thing in a number of sermons from the same period. In one of these on the words contained in the Lord's Prayer: "Forgive us our debts, as we forgive our debtors," he observed: "But still you are saying, Who can do, who has ever done this? May God bring it to effect in your hearts! I know as well as you there are but few who do it; great men they are and spiritual who do so."[25] Although the young Augustine, presbyter at Hippo, was clearly ill at ease with the absence of Christian practice in the congregation, he still hoped to change matters, to reform the people. Under the attack of the Donatists, however, who accused the Catholic Church of tolerating known traditors in its ranks, Augustine defended the Church as an institution containing both the wheat and the tares.[26] Writing to the Donatist Maximin in 392, seeking to resolve the problem of rebaptism of Catholics by

Donatists who had joined their ranks, Augustine remarked: "The Lord's floor [i.e., the Church] is not yet purged—it cannot be without chaff, be it ours to pray, and to do what in us lies that we may be good grain."[27]

In another letter of 395 to his old friend Alypius, Augustine described the revelry that went on in the church at Hippo on the annual feast of the martyrs:

> by the hidden fore-ordination of the Almighty God, that on the fourth holy day that chapter of the Gospel fell to be expounded in ordinary course, in which the words occur: "Give not that which is holy unto dogs, neither cast ye your pearls before swine." I discoursed therefore concerning dogs and swine in such a way as to compel those who clamour with obstinate barking against the divine precepts, and who are given up to the abomination of carnal pleasures, to blush for shame; and followed it up by saying, that they might plainly see how criminal it was to do, under the name of religion, within the walls of the church, that which, if it were practiced by them in their houses, would make it necessary for them to be debarred from that which is holy, and from the privileges which are the pearls of the Church.[28]

Clearly, Augustine was here struggling with the problem of Christian purity on two separate yet related levels. On the first level there was his personal struggle with his own past belief in the perfectibility of the Christian and his subsequent rereading of St. Paul. On the second level there was his struggle with the changing character of the Church in Africa and the Donatist rejection of and attack upon what it had become. The first problem has been dealt with above; Peter Brown shall be our guide through the second.

"The imagination of African Christians of the time of Augustine," Brown argues in his chapter "Ubi Ecclesia," "had become riveted on the idea of the Church." They had thought of the Church "as the preserve of safety and cleanliness in a world ruled by demonic powers" in which the rite of baptism was held to be a "drastic purification." So much was this the case that initiates would wear special sandals for a week afterwards "lest their 'pure' feet touch the earth." They desired the Church to be "morally 'without spot or wrinkle.'" And while they had inscribed the words, " 'This is the door of the Lord' . . . on the lintel of a church in Numidia, 'the righteous shall enter in,' " Augustine observed in his day that "The man who enters . . . is bound to see drunkards, misers, tricksters, gamblers, adulterers, fornicators, people wearing amulets, assiduous clients of sorcerers, astrologers. . . . He must be warned that the same crowds [who] press into the churches on Christian festivals, also fill the theatres on pagan holidays.' "

This "disconcerting double image" of the Church, as Brown calls it, reflected the great changes that had taken place within the Church from Constantine—when Eusebius wrote his *Church History*—to Augustine's day nearly a century later. As Brown observes: "The spread of Christianity in Africa, by indiscriminately filling the churches, had simply washed away the moral landmarks that separated the 'church' from the 'world.' In the conditions of the third century, S. Cyprian could well expect his convert or penitent, to find himself 'among the saints'; Augustine knew only too well that he was just as likely to rub shoulders with the most notorious landgrabber in the neighborhood."[29]

Since 311, this issue divided African Christians, as Brown continues, into Donatists, who defended the purity of the Church, and Catholics, who justified expansion. The former referred to the Church as the " 'true vine,' and like a vine, it had to be drastically pruned." Unworthy bishops, whose official acts they regarded as ineffective, were to be excluded if the Church was to survive as pure. Their continued toleration "threatened the identity of the true Church: it created an anti-church, a sinister *Doppelgaenger*, a 'Church of Judas,' held together by the 'original taint' of its founders."[30]

While the Donatists sought to preserve the Church as "an alternative to the society around them," Augustine reflected the confident attitude of Catholicism that the Church could absorb the world without losing its identity. It rested not so much on the quality of its members as on the " 'objective' promises of God, working out magnificently in history, and on the 'objective' efficacy of its sacraments."[31] The Church's expansion was predetermined, it was inevitable, and Augustine used it as his main argument to confound the Donatists. As it expanded, however, tares overtook it and formed the majority of its members. How could such a Church be holy? Brown remarks that:

> Here the Donatists could appeal to the obvious. If the church was defined as "pure," if it was the only body in which the Holy Spirit resided, how could its members fail to be "pure"? Augustine, however, was a man steeped in Neo-Platonic ways of thought. The whole world appeared to him as a world of "becoming", as a hierarchy of imperfectly-realized forms, which depended for their quality, on "participating" in an Intelligible World of Ideal Forms. This universe was in a state of constant, dynamic tension, in which the imperfect forms of matter strove to "realize" their fixed, ideal structure, grasped by the mind alone. It was the same with Augustine's view of the Church.[32]

In an intriguing sermon that dealt in part with the woman who touched the edge of Christ's garment and was healed of her disease, Augustine discoursed on the nature of the Church in terms of those who merely "pressed" in upon Christ, as the crowd did on that occasion. Interpreting the incident to his congregation, Augustine observed:

> In this case also is His body now, that is, His Church. The faith of the few "touches" it, the throng of the many "press" it. For ye have heard, as being her children, that Christ's body is the Church, and if ye will, ye yourselves are so. This the Apostle says in many places. "For His body's sake, which is the Church," and again, "But ye are the body of Christ, and members in particular." If then we are His body, what His body then suffered in the crowd, that doth His Church suffer now. It is pressed by many, touched by few. The flesh presses it, faith touches it.[33]

Now, he continued, Christians should not "press" the Church; pagans did that. Christ endured those who "pressed" in upon him, but He looked for those who would "touch" Him. Those pagans who "pressed" in on Christ were to be treated gently. But he was speaking to Christians: "in you," he said, "the corruption must be cut out."[34] At present, he continued, Christians were to pray for pagans, not be angry with them. "If very painful feelings excite us," he observed, "it is rather against Christians, it is against our brethren, who will enter into the Church in such a mind, as to have their body there, and their heart anywhere else."[35]

Augustine was aware that, with specific reference to the celebration of the feast of the martyrs, the abuses had entered the Church when it became fashionable to become a Christian. In the letter to Alypius referred to above, he remarked that he had explained to his congregation "the circumstances out of which this custom seems to have necessarily risen in the Church—namely, that when, in the peace which came after such numerous and violent persecutions, crowds of heathen who wished to assume the Christian religion" entered the Church. Because they would not refrain from celebrating "feasts connected with their worship of idols," concessions were made to them "for a time." But things had obviously not changed.[36]

Although in these selections Augustine conceded that the Church contains "chaff," it is also obvious that he desired to bring action into line with profession. In other words, he had not yet given up hope of reforming the Church. We saw him argue that while one had to tolerate the pagans who were "pressing" against the Church, those within were to be dealt with much more harshly, indeed that the corruption had to be cut out. When he came to respond to Donatist charges, his emphasis shifted to a defense of the Church as inevitably containing wheat and tares. This emphasis becomes apparent in his letter to a group of Donatist leaders of 397. There, speaking of the accusations brought against the Catholic Church by the Donatists, Augustine argued that

> in the things which they lay to our charge the blame is due to the chaff or the tares in the Lord's harvest, and the crime does not belong to the good grain; not considering, moreover, that within our unity those only have fellowship with the wicked who take pleasure in their being such, whereas those who are displeased with their wickedness yet cannot correct them,—as they do not presume to root out the tares before the harvest, lest they root out the wheat also,—have fellowship with them, not in their deeds, but in the altar of Christ; so that not only do they avoid being defiled by them, but they deserve commendation and praise according to the word of God, because, in order to prevent the name of Christ from being reproached by odious schism, they tolerate in the interest of unity that which in the interest of righteousness they hate.[37]

He substantiated this argument with numerous examples drawn from the Old Testament and even that of Christ who had tolerated Judas in the midst of His disciples.[38] Schism—"raising altar against altar, and separation from the heritage of Christ now spread, as was so long ago promised, throughout the world"—was the real crime; tolerating the wicked in the Church he now conceived as a positive virtue on the part of the true Christians.[39] No one, he concluded "can erase from heaven the divine decree, no one can efface from earth the Church of God. His decree has promised the whole world, and the Church has filled it; and it includes both bad and good. On earth it loses none but the bad, and into heaven it admits none but the good."[40]

This became the standard argument Augustine used in his response to the Donatist charges.[41] Indeed, in another letter to the Donatists of 402, he wrote: "Your imagination that you are separating yourselves, before the time of harvest, from the tares which are mixed with the wheat, proves that you are only tares. For if you were wheat, you would bear with the tares, and not separate yourselves from that which is growing in Christ's field."[42] The correct criterion for judging which was the true Church, Augustine argued elsewhere, was not whether it contained tares, but whether it was the successor to the Church begun by Christ and his Apostles, which He had promised would spread over the entire world. This argument was used already in 398 in a letter against the Donatists, about whom he wrote: "I thereupon asked him what was the Church within which it was the duty of a man so to live; whether it was the one which, as Sacred Scripture had long foretold, was spread over the whole world, or that one which a small section of Africans, or a small part of Africa, contained?" If this was indeed the true Church that preserved the order of succession established in the most ancient churches throughout the world,[43] how could they justify their separation from that Church and disrupt the unity of Christ?

Thus, while Augustine, from his early Christian-Platonic perspective bemoaned the tares in the Catholic Church—as he saw it especially through his congregation at Hippo—and hoped to reform it, in his defense against the Donatists he came to justify that very same view of the Church and indeed argued that toleration of the tares had been commanded by Christ and was therefore a positive Christian virtue.[44] Whether Muentzer agreed with this as a correct definition of the "true" Church, it could only have confirmed his belief—derived from Hegesippus—that the Church had indeed lost her virginity in the second century. In both Augustine's letters and sermons there was example heaped upon example to persuade him that he had indeed read Eusebius aright in this one crucial instance.

Aside from this use of the Parable of the Tares in his polemic against the Donatists, Augustine also preached a separate sermon on the very passage found in Matthew 13 which contained the Parable. Here Muentzer could have found in concentrated form what he found scattered in various places elsewhere. But he would also have found much more. For here Augustine also addressed himself to the "good seed" of the previous parable, the various kinds of soil upon which this seed fell, a very specific definition of who the tares were and what was to be done with them.

Augustine began the sermon by reminding his congregation of the previous day's parable. In today's parable, he said, the sower had sowed good seed in his field. But while the owner's servants slept, the enemy came at night and sowed tares in the same field. As long as both were only in blade, the two could not be differentiated. Once, however, the fruit began to appear from the plants of the good seed, then the tares also appeared. Offended at this contamination, the servants wanted to root out the tares from the field but were prevented by the owner who told them to "let both grow together until the harvest."

Now Christ had explained this parable, Augustine told his hearers, and had said that He was the sower of the good seed and that the Devil was the sower of the tares. The time of harvest He declared to be the end of the world; His field, the whole world. And then Christ had said: "In the time of harvest I will say to the reapers, Gather ye together first the tares, to burn them, but gather the wheat into my barn." Why, Augustine asked, "are ye so hasty, He says, ye servants full of zeal? Ye see tares among the wheat, ye see evil Christians among the good; and ye wish to root up the evil ones; be quiet, it is not the time of harvest. That time will come, may it only find you wheat. Why do you vex yourselves? Why bear impatiently the mixture of the evil with the good? In the field they may be with you, but they will not be so in the barn."[45]

Thereupon Augustine proceeded to explain that the "wayside," the "stony ground," and the "thorny ground" of the previous day's parable were "the same as these 'tares.' They received only a different name under a different similitude." In parables and similitudes, Augustine explained, "one thing may be called by many names; therefore there is nothing inconsistent in my telling you that that 'wayside,' that 'stony ground,' those 'thorny places,' are bad Christians, and that they too are 'tares.' " Having said this, Augustine again exhorted his hearers to be "good soil" and to bring forth fruit accordingly. All this he said yesterday, he observed, but today he wished to address the tares; "But the sheep are the tares. O evil Christians, O ye, who in filling only press the Church by your evil lives; amend yourselves before the harvest comes."[46] From the tares Augustine turned to the wheat—those Christians whose lives were good and who sighed because they were "few among many, few among very many. The winter will pass away," he promised, "the summer will come; lo! the harvest will soon be here. The angels will come who can make the separation, and who cannot make mistakes." Therefore, the good Christians ought not to concern themselves with the harvest but rather deport themselves in accordance with Christ's advice: "let him that thinketh he standeth, take heed lest he fall." For, Augustine continued, "do you think, my Brethren, that these tares we read of do not get up into this seat? . . . I tell you of a truth, my Beloved, even in these high seats there is both wheat, and tares, and among the laity there is wheat and tares. Let the good tolerate the bad; let the bad change themselves, and imitate the good. Let us all, if it may be so, attain to God; let us through His mercy escape the evil of this world."[47]

It is, of course, significant that Augustine should take a parable Christ had set into the context of the world—that is, the field into which the seed was sown was the world[48]—and place it into the context of the Church. He could do this the more easily because he had already argued that the Church founded by Christ had spread to the whole world; he had defended that Church as necessarily containing both wheat and tares to the Donatists. Nonetheless, there were still enough pagans around in his day, yet these do not figure in his interpretation of the parable at all. Instead of regarding these and other non-Christians as the tares, he argued that "the sheep are the tares," the "evil Christians" in the Church were what Christ had referred to. It was an interpretation ideally suited to the emerging concept of the *corpus christianum* where the lines of demarcation between the temporal and spiritual realms were beginning to cross.

The good seed Christ had interpreted to be His teaching. In his explication to his congregation, Augustine warned his own hearers to be "loth to choke the good seed which is sown in you by my labours, with the lusts and cares of the world."[49] Clearly the pure Word, the Bible, was the good seed. But as we have seen, Muentzer argued—in dependence upon Luther—that this Word of God, this good seed, had lain hidden, languishing under a bench for some four hundred years. Without the good seed being sown, how could there be any wheat at all? It is in this context, then, that Luther's assertion that he had once again freed the pure Word to do its job—and after reading Hus's *De Ecclesia* argued that John Hus had preceded him in this—took on added significance for Thomas Muentzer. The priests' distortion of the Word was responsible for the corruption of Christendom.[50] If only the people could be made aware that God spoke within the abyss of their souls and have this confirmed by the external witness of the purified Word, a renewal of the Church could take place.

Although a renewal might take place, what good would it do if the wheat could not be separated from the tares? Such a separation, however, as Augustine had repeatedly asserted, was to be left to God's angels and would only take place in the time of harvest. That Muentzer regarded "the fields to be white unto harvest" in his own day the *Prague Manifesto* makes clear enough. Might he also have acquired this conviction from Augustine?

The first thing to note is that Muentzer—as will be made much more explicit later on—speaks of the end times exclusively in terms of the Parable of the Tares. He never speaks of it in Joachist terms,[51] and as a consequence I am now persuaded that he knew of what he was speaking when he wrote to Hans Zeiss on 2 December 1523, that although some scoffingly accused him of deriving his teaching from Joachim of Fiore, he had not taken it from him. Rather, it had come to him from on high.[52] He does not speak of it in the terms used by Hans Herrgott. Nor does he see it in the way Martin Luther did, although Luther's very powerful conviction during the early years of the Reformation that he was living in the end time may have helped to convince Muentzer that this was indeed the time of harvest.[53]

Once again, it probably was Augustine who provided him with the context for his thinking about the time of harvest. For in his letters and sermons Augustine spoke of two harvests. In a sermon on Luke 10:2— "The harvest is truly plenteous," words Christ had spoken on sending his Apostles and the seventy-two out to preach—Augustine remarked that this did not refer to the harvest of the Gentiles, for among them nothing had as yet been sown. Instead, "this harvest was among the people of the Jews." It was to this harvest of the Jews that the Lord of the harvest had come; to this harvest He had sent His disciples as reapers. To the Gentiles, however, "He sent not reapers, but sowers. Understand we then that it was harvest among the people of the Jews, sowing time among the people of the Gentiles."[54] The sowers of this first harvest had been Abraham, Isaac, Jacob, Moses, and the prophets. At the Lord's coming this harvest was found to be ripe. Thus Christ had sent out His disciples to reap with the words: "Others have laboured, and ye are entered into their labours." As a consequence, the Gospel had first been preached to the Jews, and those who were wheat had entered into Christ's barn. Those who had refused had been either destroyed or dispersed shortly thereafter. This interpretation may very well have been confirmed for Muentzer by the fifth book of pseudo-Hegesippus.

That first harvest was past, Augustine continued, and they ought now to concentrate on the Gentile harvest—the harvest which they themselves were. Here the seeds had been sown by Christ and His Apostles on all kinds of soil. His hearers, who were the soil, ought to "let the thorns be rooted up, the field prepared, the seed put in, let them grow unto the harvest, let the barn be longed for, not the fire feared." His duty it was to labor in the field; theirs, to receive the admonitions of the Lord faithfully, and together "in Him overcome the world."[55]

If Muentzer took these two harvests as parallel and therefore running similar courses, as Augustine himself seems to have done, and if he accepted Luther's argument that the good seed had not been sown for at least four hundred years, but that now, since Hus and Luther, this good seed was being sown in an increasingly pure fashion—a signal, as Luther had argued, of the end of the world—then we have the context within which Muentzer's thinking on this subject must have taken place. The good seed was being sown, and the Holy Spirit would return to the Church. Influenced by Tauler's sermons, Muentzer had arrived at the conclusion that the entrance of the false prophets into the Apostolic Church had driven the Holy Spirit out and brought on the perversion of the good seed. This had made it impossible to distinguish the wheat from the tares inside the Church. The return of the pure Word of God, and with it the return of the Holy Spirit, would once again make possible the recognition of evil by Christians and consequently would allow them once more to separate the wheat from the tares. The crucial addition to Luther and Augustine here was the role played in the resurrection of the Apostolic Church by the Holy Spirit. This element clearly came to Muentzer from Tauler when he placed the latter into the context provided him by Eusebius and Augustine. Without the discerning power of the Holy Spirit who, in Tauler's words "confronted the evil in the world," that ultimate separation of the wheat from the tares in the time of harvest would not be possible. Perhaps Muentzer saw himself, as his opening line in the *Prague Manifesto* appears to imply, as contributing this last element, this most vital element, the Holy Spirit, to the harvest: "I, Thomas Muentzer, born in Stolberg and at present living in Prague, in the city of that dear and holy warrior John Hus, *intend to fill the resounding and versatile trumpets with the new song of praise of the Holy Spirit*" [italics mine].

There are indications in Augustine's sermons that he, like Thomas Muentzer, longed for the time when the wheat would be separated from the tares. In a sermon on Matthew 20:30, he warned the good Christians not to allow themselves to be sidetracked by the "many Christians in name, and in works ungodly."[56] When a Christian began to live well, he said, began "to be fervent in good works, and to despise the world; in this newness of life he is exposed to the animadversions and contradictions of cold Christians. But if he persevere and get the better of them by his endurance, and faint not in good works; those very same persons who before hindered will now respect him."[57] Clearly, Augustine was concerned by the necessity for the wheat to continue to exist in the Church with the tares until the time of harvest. There was obviously the danger that the much "bad leaven" could spoil the entire body.

While, therefore, they were not to "leave the floor before the time" and were to bear with the chaff on the "floor," in the barn "he will have none of it to bear with." There the winnower will divide the bad from the good. "There will then be a bodily separation too, which a spiritual separation now precedes. In heart be always separated from the bad, in body be united with them for a time, only with caution." Rather than merely be tolerant, however, they were actively to correct "those who belong to you, who in any way appertain to your charge, by admonition, or instruction, by exhortation, or *by threats*[!]. *Do it in whatsoever way ye can*" [italics mine].[58] The injunction of Christ to "have no communication with the unfruitful works of darkness" was therefore to be interpreted not in terms of physical separation, but in terms of rebuking, reproving them. "Find fault with, rebuke, repress them," he advised.[59]

It is not at all clear from Augustine's letters and sermons whether the winnowing process—the separation of the wheat from the tares—was to take place on earth or in heaven. If we are to accept the second, the Gentile harvest, as running parallel with that of the Jews—where Christ and his Apostles were the reapers—then clearly it would also take place on earth, only at the end of the age. If it did, what might such a purified Church have looked like to Augustine? In a sermon on Luke 24:36 he seemed to give an indication of his vision. There, speaking of St. Paul's conversion and his missionary activity, he observed:

> Spread the Gospel: scatter with thy mouth what thou hast conceived in thine heart. Let the nations hear, let the nations believe; let the nations multiply, let the Lord's empurpled spouse spring forth from the blood of the Martyrs. And from her how many have already come, how many members have cleaved to the Head, and cleave to Him still and believe! They were baptized, and others shall be baptized, and after them shall others come. Then I say, at the end of the world shall the stones be joined to the foundation, living stones, holy stones, that at the end the whole edifice may be built by that Church, yea by this very Church which now sings the new song, while the house is in building. For so the Psalm itself says, "When the house was in building after the captivity"; and what says it, "Sing unto the Lord a new song, sing unto the Lord all the earth." How great a house is this! But when does it sing the new song? When it is in building. When is it dedicated? At the end of the world.[60]

Although Augustine seemed to anticipate a continuous development of the Church toward a culmination in the end times when the separation of the wheat from the tares will take place, Muentzer, after immersing himself in Eusebius, clearly did not. The early Church, beginning at Jerusalem and described by Augustine himself as consisting of "burning brands . . . set on fire by the Holy Spirit, when they had all one soul, and one heart to God-ward,"[61] had been led astray by false teachers—those very scribes and Pharisees lacking the Holy Spirit described by Tauler—already in the second century. The Apostolic Church had been pure and filled with the Holy Spirit. However, it had become corrupt, and much earlier than Luther had claimed; now it was being renewed. The evidence was everywhere: but primarily in the preaching of the good seed by Hus and Luther once more and, perhaps even more importantly, by Muentzer's own proclamation of the Holy Spirit. The inner Word in the abyss of the soul was once more in agreement with the purified written Word of God and, as a consequence, the Holy Spirit was beginning to return to the Church. This return would signal the beginning of the separation of the wheat from the tares and allow the new Apostolic Church to emerge in all its purity. Then, perhaps taking another idea from Augustine—who had used the argument of the universality of the Catholic Church as justification for its exclusivity—he asserted that, having begun in Prague, this new Apostolic Church would spread throughout the world.

There are a few other aspects of Augustine's thought as contained in the latter's letters and sermons that may have acted to sharpen Muentzer's theological perspective. His belief in the possibility—nay, inevitability—of the transformation of a person's life as the result of the work of the Holy Spirit cannot but have been confirmed by Augustine's repeated assertions that one had to be "born anew of the Holy Spirit."[62] He documented this over and over again with respect to the coming of the Holy Spirit into the Apostles and the early Church, pointing to the transforming effect this had had on their lives.[63] In one such instance he remarked: "Now in what sort they were converted, how decidedly, and how perfectly, the Acts of the Apostles show. For they sold all that they possessed, and laid the prices of their things at the Apostles' feet; and distribution was made unto every man according as he had need; and no man said that aught was his own, but they had all things common."[64] Here Augustine seems to have regarded the sharing of all possessions in the community of believers as one of the highest evidences of the presence and work of the Holy Spirit! This conjunction of Holy Spirit and "successful" conversion emanating in the community of goods cannot but have influenced Muentzer.

It was equally obvious to Augustine that the Holy Spirit came only to the humble, and that those "who were not aided in their knowledge by the Holy Spirit, and who were obliged to gather floating rumours under the limitations of human infirmity," could not possibly "avoid being misled in regard to very many things."[65] Nonetheless, in his attempt to justify the Church as a mixed society of wheat and tares, he argued that those tares who sat in high places, like his own, were to be listened to, though not followed in their deeds. He spoke of such "scribes" in a sermon, saying: "Such were they whom our Lord Jesus Christ rebukes, because they have the keys of the kingdom of heaven, and 'would neither enter in themselves, nor suffer others to enter in'; in these words finding fault with the Pharisees and Scribes, the teachers of the law of the Jews. Of whom in another place He says, 'Whatsoever they say, do, but do ye not after their works, for they say and do not.' "[66] But, he asked, clearly in response to the Donatist charge that the ministrations of evil men were of no effect, "Whence then did those evil men bring forth good things? 'Because they sat in Moses' seat.' Had He not first said, 'They sit in Moses' seat;' He would never have enjoined that evil men should be heard. For what they brought forth out of the treasure of their own heart, was one thing; another what they gave utterance to out of the seat of Moses, the criers so to say of the judge."[67] Here Muentzer would have drawn the line, for from Tauler and Eusebius he had become convinced that precisely such clerics had driven the Holy Spirit from the Church and had misled the Church, corrupting it until it had become an ugly caricature of its former self.[68]

Yet while Augustine counseled tolerating the tares within the Church—even those sitting "in the seat of Moses"—in his sermons he exhorted his congregation to good works. Those who were "elect," who were "wheat," would be transformed. This world was the arena within which such work was begun, though perhaps not completed. Repeatedly, especially in those sermons and letters in which he spoke of the Parable of the Tares, Augustine exhorted his listeners: "Let the good tolerate the bad; let the bad change themselves, and imitate the good. Let us all, if it may be so, attain to God."[69] These exhortations sound out in his other sermons as well. Indeed, if the Church was in a state of Neoplatonic becoming, then certainly this was also true of its members. Therefore they needed encouragement, exhortation, and even at times threats such as the following: "I do not care whether you expect some well turned phrases today. It is my duty to give you warning in citing the Scriptures. Do not be slow to turn to the Lord, nor delay from day to day, for His wrath shall come when you know not. God knows how I tremble on my bishop's throne when I hear that warning. I cannot be silent; I am forced to preach on it. Filled with fear myself, I fill you with fear."[70]

Augustine may also have influenced Muentzer's view of the importance of sharing all things in common among believers. We have already seen Augustine refer to this practice in the early Church as an expression of "how decidedly, how perfectly" they had been converted. Coming together with Eusebius's emphasis on this practice in the early Church and Tauler's repeated call for the believer to free himself from all "creatures," such an expression could have been important for Muentzer's

own attempts at communal organization later on in Zwickau and
Muehlhausen. At the same time, he encountered Augustine's intense
diatribes against the Donatists' practice of rebaptizing Catholic Christians who joined their ranks. Baptism, Augustine argued again and
again, was effective whether it was done by a Catholic cleric or a
Donatist. In a letter of 397 to some Donatists, he remarked: "What we
dislike in that party is not their bearing with those who are wicked, but
their intolerable wickedness in the matter of schism, of raising altar
against altar, of separating from the heritage of Christ now spread, as
was long promised, throughout the world. We behold with grief and
lamentation peace broken, unity rent asunder, baptism administered a
second time, and contempt poured on the sacraments, which are holy
even when administered and received by the wicked."[71] While they
accepted the baptismal form of one and rejected the other, he observed
in another letter that "baptism belongs neither to the one nor to the
other, but to Him of whom it was said: 'This same is He that baptizeth
with the Holy Ghost.' "[72] It did not matter, therefore, whether one
practiced it on the infant[73] or the catechumen,[74] by the Catholic cleric—
good or bad—or the heretic; the baptism of the Holy Ghost was what
mattered. Under these circumstances rebaptism was certainly of no
avail.

One last matter was probably also of some importance to Muentzer.
In his opposition to the Manichees, who rejected the Old Testament,
Augustine argued for the perfect harmony of the Old and New Testaments.[75] He did this under the auspices of the argument that while the
"process of nature itself and the works of men undergo changes according to the circumstances of the time . . . at the same time, there is nothing mutable in the plan or principle by which these changes are regu-
lated."[76] As a consequence, "there is no variableness with God, though
in the former period of the world's history He enjoined one kind of
offering [he is talking of sacraments], and in the latter period another,
therein ordering the symbolical actions pertaining to the blessed doctrine of the true religion in harmony with the changes of successive
epochs without any change in Himself."[77] This was in basic agreement
with the *Historia* and Eusebius. The former had argued that "now that
in the light of the Holy Ghost thou hast received divine grace to possess
the holy Scriptures in thyself, so wilt thou understand that all Scripture
has the same meaning and is never self-contradictory." The latter had
quoted Hegesippus as saying of the Apostolic Church: "In every line of
bishops and in every city things accord with the preaching of the Law,
the Prophets, and the Lord."[78] The two Testaments, therefore, as

Muentzer repeatedly observed with reference to Luther, had to be reconciled. The Lutherans, he stated to Christoph Meinhard of Eisleben on 30 May 1524, "condemn the Old Testament, dispute learnedly about the role of works in the theology of St. Paul, revile the law in the most extreme manner and still do not understand Paul correctly though they were to burst in the attempt to do so."[79] As far as he was concerned, he declared in his *Protestation:* "the art of God must be demonstrated in the Holy Scriptures through a strict concordance of its total content which is clearly delineated in both testaments."[80]

The impact of Augustine's thought on Thomas Muentzer is therefore both indirect and direct: indirect in that his Neoplatonic-Christian Mysticism and his model of conversion were reflected in Tauler's sermons; direct in that Muentzer must have absorbed Augustine's interpretation of the Parable of the Tares and applied it to what he would come to believe was the "time of harvest." Augustine's emphasis upon a "successful" conversion, a conversion wrought by the work of the Holy Spirit, also came to Muentzer directly through the Church Father's letters and sermons, and that in conjunction with the practice of the community of goods in the Apostolic community. He must also have acted as confirmation of Muentzer's reading of Tauler and Eusebius. But it was Augustine's interpretation of the Parable of the Tares that provided Muentzer with the critical element he needed to complete the puzzle that was to become his interpretation of Church history. Whereas Tauler had taught him the central importance of *experiencing* a conversion through the power of the Holy Spirit in the abyss of the human soul—the only possible means to integrate faith and action—and whereas Eusebius's *Church History* had provided him with the larger ecclesiastical context within which Tauler's argument with respect to the Holy Spirit became applicable to Church history, Augustine provided him—through his interpretation of the Parable of the Tares—with the solution to the problem of reform within the Church. For if the influx of tares into the Church in the mid-second century had forced the Holy Spirit out of the Church, the removal of the tares from within the Church would allow the Holy Spirit to return. And thus the new Apostolic Church could once again come into existence. Here, then, was the solution to Muentzer's problem. But that removal of the tares had been set into the "time of harvest" by Augustine. This eschatological setting was to have revolutionary consequences for Muentzer's involvement in the Peasants' War later on, consequences he could not have foreseen in 1519–1520 when he pieced together the puzzle of Church history.

CHAPTER IV

Zwickau and the Prophets

What they [the Zwickau Prophets] are they themselves will see, Galatians 2. I tremble in divine judgments.
—Muentzer to Luther, 9 July 1523

Having pieced all of the parts of the Church history puzzle together, Muentzer, some time during the first few weeks of May 1520, left the seclusion of the convent at Beuditz and moved to Zwickau where he was to act as temporary replacement for Johannes Wildenauer aus Eger, called Egranus, who had requested a study leave of the town Council. Muentzer, already reputed to be an adherent of the new evangelical movement, was named as his substitute.[1] An Erasmian humanist, Egranus had initially—as so many other humanists in the first flush of reform enthusiasm—become a supporter of Luther. He was a man of culture and the pastor of the Church of St. Mary, the church attended by Zwickau's commercial and ruling elite. The Church of St. Catherine, to which Muentzer would be appointed some six months later, was the church of the poorer and less privileged inhabitants. Like so many other thriving cities of the Empire in the early sixteenth century, Zwickau had its share of economic, social and political tensions. To a certain extent, though not to that Marxist scholars have argued,[2] the two churches were at the opposite poles of these tensions within the city.

Muentzer had used the approximately nine months spent in Beuditz to continue his study of Tauler, to read Heinrich Suso, to immerse himself in the letters and sermons of Augustine, and to discover what he came to believe to be the most important message contained in Eusebius's *Church History*. It was, in all probability, during this time that his views of theology, church history, and reform coalesced into the unique whole we have sought to reconstruct in the foregoing chapters.[3] He must therefore have come to Zwickau, no longer as one in search of a perspective on the currently evolving ecclesiastical turmoil, but as one with a complete program already in hand. It is as such that he encountered the Zwickau Prophets and, later, Egranus himself when the latter returned.

If these are indeed the facts of the case, several things must necessarily follow. First, it must follow that it is highly unlikely that Muentzer could have been influenced in any fundamental manner by the Zwickau Prophets. Yet precisely such an influence, and a remarkably powerful one at that, has often enough been posited by scholars ever since Paul Wappler's near classic *Thomas Muentzer in Zwickau und die "Zwickauer Propheten."* There Wappler wrote:

> The religious views of Storch [chief of the "Prophets"], which he had brought back with him from Bohemia, now gradually gained more and more acceptance with Muentzer. Indeed, Storch's downright startlingly extensive knowledge of the Bible and his remarkable ability to explain one passage of Scripture by means of another filled Muentzer with such amazement, that he did not hesitate to declare openly from the pulpit: Storch was to be "held in higher esteem than all the priests, as the only one who knew his Bible so thoroughly and possessed the [Holy] Spirit to such a high degree."[4]

This assessment of the Zwickau Prophets' influence upon Thomas Muentzer was reiterated in 1975 by Elliger who rejected the Marxist contention that Muentzer was motivated by the plight of the lower classes:

> The man who was so intensely devoted to his spiritual task instead discovered, on closer contact [with his congregation in the Church of St. Catherine], a small Christian community (*Gemeinschaftschristentum*) living quietly on the periphery of the official church which aroused in him a most intense interest, captivated him more and more with its teaching on the Holy Spirit and which finally acquired in him an eloquent advocate.[5]

Now it would not have been the first time in the history of the transmission of ideas that the "wise" or "pious" layman became the instructor of the learned *Magister*, had Storch indeed exercised the kind of influence upon Muentzer postulated by Wappler and Elliger. Precisely such an influence, it was asserted in the *Historia* and long held to be authentic, had been exerted upon the learned Tauler. We ourselves have argued, furthermore, that Master Conrad of Orlamuende's cook had a somewhat similar role in Muentzer's earlier intellectual development as he was led through Tauler's sermons. Although in this latter case the "pious woman" was not the carrier of the ideas, she may have been an intermediary of some kind. No, it is not on the basis of the argument that something of this nature could not happen that we hope to build our case. Rather, we intend to build it on the argument that what Muentzer saw in the Zwickau Prophets confirmed, in some striking ways, his emerging views of what was happening in the world, especially with respect to the birth of the new Apostolic Church in the time of harvest.

Before we do that, however, it is paramount to enquire whether Muentzer expressed some of the ideas we have already ascribed to him in the preceding chapters before he encountered the Prophets, for we must remember that he spent nearly six months in Zwickau before he met them. If he did express them, the case for his intellectual independence from Storch and the Prophets will be considerably enhanced, especially if he propounded them already in the Church of St. Mary, the church of the ruling elite in Zwickau.

Muentzer preached his first sermon in that church on 13 May, the second on Ascension Day, 17 May. No sooner was he installed than he began, in the very first sermons, to attack the monks and clerics. Anticlericalism, of course, was a pervasive sentiment in the sixteenth century, and it should not surprise us to find it in Muentzer. But if he did indeed believe, as we have argued, that the fall of the Church in the mid-second century was due to the self-serving scribes and Pharisees who did not possess the Holy Spirit, that these were in fact the very cause of the Holy Spirit's departure from the Apostolic Church, Muentzer's anticlericalism should have a unique and specific focus. While J. K. Seidemann provides a description of the second sermon delivered by Muentzer on 17 May, it turns out not to be, as might at first appear, a report on that sermon, but rather Muentzer's own subsequent account to Luther.[6] Whether the account is trustworthy, it is all we have.[7]

Whereas the congregation at St. Mary's supported Muentzer, the mendicant orders in Zwickau were outraged at his attack. In the ensuing uproar, the town Council—most of whose members may be assumed to have been Muentzer's parishioners in the Church of St. Mary[8]—wrote to John Duke of Saxony on his behalf, and recommended to Muentzer that he write Luther for support and confirmation. This he did in a letter of 13 July 1520, where he observed that he had chided the "monachos mendicantes, sed universas hypocritas," who dared to declare the souls

> which are not alive, to be alive indeed for a piece of bread, and with their interminable prayers devour the property [houses] of widows by not direct-

ing the dying to faith, for they are intent only on satisfying their insatiable greed. Up to the present, these, whether they be monks or priests, had seduced the church of God. But the laity was also at fault, having neglected to uphold its spiritual leaders with prayers and petitions to God. For this reason the sheep have departed from the Lord and have followed the speculators (innovators). Thus monks, priests and laymen are always joined together in blame; no exception is made, no one is spared. I admonish all in season and out, wherever I have opportunity, in order that they may come to their senses.[9]

If one adds to this letter the passages of the Bible that Muentzer used to support his arguments and that he probably used in the sermon, his intent becomes even more apparent.[10] The first of these passages, Isaiah 19:14, reads; "The Lord hath mingled a perverse spirit in the midst thereof: and they have caused Egypt to err in every work thereof, as a drunken man staggereth in his vomit." This is a clear parallel to the role the tares had played in the Apostolic Church. The second, Ezekiel 13:19, continued the argument: "And will ye pollute me among my people for handfuls of barley and for pieces of bread, to slay the souls that should not die, and to save the souls that should not live, by your lying to my people that hear your lies?" The third passage, Matthew 23:14, sounded a recurring theme in Muentzer's writings: "Woe unto you, scribes and Pharisees, hypocrites! for ye devour widows' houses, and for a pretense make long prayers: therefore ye shall receive the greater damnation." Last, Muentzer cited Isaiah 56:10 which referred to "indolent elect": "His watchmen are blind: they are all ignorant, they are all dumb dogs, they cannot bark; sleeping, lying down, loving to slumber."

While Muentzer might argue that the laity was also at fault for the present predicament of the Church, the passages he drew from the Bible pointed an accusing finger exclusively at the leaders of God's people, at the monks and the priests, the scribes and the Pharisees. These were the ones who knew God's law but did not fulfill it; they were the externalized men, as Tauler had taught, who knew nothing of the abyss of the soul or the role of the Holy Spirit in transforming men. They had intruded human speculations and false teachings into the Church already in the mid-second century, causing it to become a prostitute and forcing the Holy Spirit to flee from it. The blind leaders of "God's flock," they sat in "the seat of Moses." Their time was about to come to an end; therefore they, like the laity, must be brought to repentance. Referring to 2 Timothy 4:2, Muentzer justified the action he had taken by asserting that it was his duty to "Preach the word; be instant in season, out of season; reprove, rebuke, exhort with all long suffering and doctrine."

It is important to note further that in the same letter to Luther, Muentzer referred to the "seduction of God's church" by these clerics.[11] Although not yet expressed with the same fullness as in his later writings, the argument Muentzer derived from the Hegesippus passages in Eusebius is already present. Nor was this the sermon of a man yet to be influenced by the Zwickau Prophets. He had his own program well in hand upon arrival in Zwickau and lost no time in setting about trying to implement it. From Tauler, Eusebius, and Augustine, Muentzer had obviously turned to the Bible and there discovered ample ammunition against the scribes and Pharisees. He used these biblical passages again and again in the future.

From the response to Muentzer's sermons by Tibertius of Weissenfels, the monk who came to the defense of his order and fellow clerics from the pulpit of the Franciscan church in Zwickau, other elements of Muentzer's program began to become visible. Since Muentzer himself reported the full response to Luther, he must have regarded Tibertius as accurate in his attack. The individual points of this response are therefore worthy of being presented here *in extenso*:

1. Christ has died once, in order that He need not die in us. Neither is His sacrament given to us for our consolation, nor may His example be distorted in our attempt to emulate Him; as a consequence of having been given the Mass we no longer need to suffer in the world.

2. The new demagogues [preachers] preach nothing but the Gospel, but that very badly: for they contradict man-made laws, which are to be especially observed. Many of them must be added to the Gospel.

3. One cannot continually live in accordance with the Gospel.

4. If poverty were evangelical, kings would not be allowed to take possession of the world's wealth.

5. If one wishes to set an example of the faith, one can only do so by giving up the world's riches; in that case spiritual pastors as well as the pious must set an example for their sheep in word and deed, as must the princes and kings adhere to such standards of poverty, so that they have no possessions and are absolute beggars.

6. The Gospel does not have as a precept: "If someone smite thee on the right cheek, turn to him the other also." It is the ploy of an heretic boldly to declare himself an adherent of the Church, so that the secular arm will not be invoked [against him].

7. Predestination exists only in the mind. One ought not to base it upon faith, through which we ourselves know ourselves to be safe, but upon works, from which the people must be dissuaded in order that the popula-

tion of Zwickau, which had become dear to him in 24 years, should continue
to burn candles and do other meritorious works.

8. Eternal salvation cannot be called the realm of faith, which is within
us, for it is available only in the future homeland. Here we remain most
uncertain as to our salvation.[12]

Several things, it would appear, may be drawn from these accusations. The first charge sounds nearly like something Luther himself
might have argued against the Catholic view of the Mass as a repeated
sacrifice of Christ. But in all likelihood it is Tibertius's response to
Muentzer's mystically grounded assertion that we must die with Christ
in order that He may be reborn in us. Tauler had quoted Augustine to
this effect. Master Eckhart's message, too, as Gordon Leff has pointed
out, "was a call to empty the soul to let God enter. Only if this had been
done could the Son be born within it and man become one with God."[13]
That this is probably the case, Tibertius's subsequent reference to "suffering" in the first accusation seems to confirm. Christ will not be born
in us unless we suffer His death in us, as the Master of Sacred Learning
had been forced to do in the *Historia* before he was filled with new
strength from above. Tibertius, however, asserted that since the Mass
had been given, "we no longer need to suffer in this world." This first
accusation, then, would seem to be an attack on Muentzer's mystical
theology of regeneration. Muentzer's letter to Luther assumes that Luther was in complete agreement with him, for his closing reads: "In
christo vale, specimen et lucerna amicorum dei!"[14] "Friends of God"
was the term by which Tauler had referred to those who had been
similarly reborn by the Holy Spirit, or within whom the Word, or the
Son, had been born. Not only did Muentzer assume that Luther—
probably because of the latter's repeated references to Tauler and his
description of such suffering—was a person who had experienced such
a rebirth in the abyss of his soul, but also Muentzer referred to him as
the light and example of such people. It can therefore be asserted here
that Muentzer would not have used this term for Luther had he not read
Tauler and absorbed his view of conversion through the Holy Spirit.
Muentzer did not need the Prophets to tell him about the Holy Spirit.

Accusations two and three attack Muentzer's rejection of the *speculatores*, those clerics who had intruded human speculations, innovations,
into the Church, as well as his demand for a "holy invincible Christian
faith." With respect to the former, Tibertius sought to justify the human
additions to the Gospel, as the Council of Constance sought to justify
the withdrawal of the chalice in the Eucharistic service in contrast to the

practice of the primitive Church.[15] Man-made laws, he asserted, were especially to be observed, with many of them having to be added to the Gospel. This may indicate one of two things, or both, with regard to Muentzer's probable assertions. First, it may be a response to Luther's doctrine of *scriptura sola;* indeed, it appears to be so. Second, it may include Muentzer's view of the Apostolic Church in which this Gospel alone had been taught and lived. When man-made laws had been intruded by the false prophets, the Apostolic Church became a prostitute and lost her virginity. It was precisely against John Hus's concept of the primitive Church that the Council of Constance had also responded that "The Primitive Church is the rite, custom, and observance of the church of the faithful, concerning the faith, at the time of the apostles . . . up to Pope Sylvester. What is called the modern church is . . . from Pope Sylvester's time to the present day." Everything in the primitive Church, the Fathers argued, had been done "in a simpler and grosser way than in the modern church." In the modern Church, however, "all things are done more worthily. . . . For the apostles and the other followers omitted what the modern church has fulfilled."[16] Therefore the Gospel was not enough, and the primitive Church was not yet in as perfect a state as it was later to become. Man-made laws, then, had to be added to the Gospel to bring about the increasing perfection of the Church.

Given Tauler's, Eusebius's, and even Augustine's early emphasis upon a "successful conversion," to use Peter Brown's term, and Muentzer's own consequent stress upon a "holy invincible Christian faith," it is little wonder that Tibertius would respond in the third of his accusations that "One cannot continually live in accordance with the Gospel." Obviously, Muentzer must have asserted the contrary, thereby challenging the Church's argument that the vast majority of the Christians, living in that so-called "Christian world," could not live truly Christian lives. Hence, the Church had reasoned, they came under a different set of standards, or obligations, known as *praecepta evangelica.* These moral expectations were those of the Decalogue, also identified with the Natural Law morality, the law written on the conscience of mankind, that St. Paul referred to in the first chapter of Romans. The religious orders, however, were called on to follow the *consilia evangelica,* or counsels of perfection, the higher morality of the Gospels, especially those of the Sermon on the Mount. Since the latter could not be fulfilled in the world, Christ's words, "Come out from among them and be ye separate," became the motto of Monasticism. Like Tauler, Augustine, and Eusebius, Muentzer rejected this solution to the problem. Much like Erasmus, who argued in his *Enchiridion* that too many people believed "that the expression 'world' refer[red] only to those who have embraced the monastic state," while "the Gospels, for the Apostles, and for Augustine, Ambrose, and Jerome, the expression meant the infidel, enemies of the faith and of the Cross of Christ,"[17] Muentzer sought at first to move Christendom in the direction of living in accordance with the counsels of perfection. Erasmus had said as much in a letter to Servatius Rogerus in July 1514: "How much more consonant with Christ's teachings it would be to regard the entire Christian world as a single household, a single monastery as it were, and to think of all men as one's fellow-canons and brethren, to regard the sacrament of baptism as the supreme religious obligation, and to consider not where one lives, but how one lives."[18] It was this same emphasis that led Muentzer to strive to separate the wheat from the tares.

Accusations four and five clearly point in the direction not only of "apostolic poverty," but also of the community of goods among those Christians who had been transformed by the Holy Spirit and had thereby been empowered to live "holy invincible Christian" lives. Too often critics evaluating the problem of the communal ownership of goods and property in Muentzer's thought have focused solely on the passage in his confession where he reportedly remarked: "*Omnia sunt communia* had been an article they had sought to implement, in [accordance with which] goods should be divided according to need as circumstances allowed."[19] When, however, we see this statement and the accusation of Tibertius in the larger context of Tauler's counsels of perfection, of Eusebius's emphasis on the community of goods in the Apostolic Church, of Muentzer's own desire to resurrect that model in the new Apostolic Church, and of Augustine's observation that "having all things common" in Acts resulted from "how decidedly, and how perfectly" they had been converted, then, perhaps, more weight must be given to it. If this had been the case in the Apostolic Church and was the consequence of a "decided" and "perfect" conversion, would not these same conditions have to obtain in the new Apostolic Church? Muentzer must have thought so, just as much as the return of dreams, visions, and prophecies were to be a part of that future church.

What Muentzer may have thought about predestination or the faith "within us," issues raised by accusations seven and eight, is more difficult to determine. Perhaps he stressed the work of the Holy Spirit, the birth of the Word within, while disparaging Catholic "good works" as useless to salvation. Indeed, had he followed Tauler and Augustine at this point, he could well have stressed some form of predestination. He did continue to speak of the "elect" of God in his later writings and, like Tauler, must have conceived of salvation as the work of the Holy Spirit alone.[20] If, like Tauler, Augustine, and those exemplifying the "decided" and "successful" conversions, described by Eusebius, he believed in an experience that one could point to (like the advent of the Holy Spirit whose power could be tangibly felt), then eternal salvation was no longer in doubt, and one did not have to wait to be assured of salvation "in the future homeland," as Tibertius asserted.

Seen from this perspective, then, it is clear that Muentzer began to express views that he would formulate more crisply later in his written work. Perhaps these ideas do not appear so clearly at first because at this point only indirect references to them occur.

When Egranus returned, some six months after Muentzer had arrived in Zwickau, the latter was relieved of his temporary position at St. Mary's and assigned to the Church of St. Catherine. Here he met Nicholas Storch and the so-called Zwickau Prophets. In a contemporary account entitled *A History of Thomas Muentzer* cited by Seidemann, Muentzer's nineteenth-century biographer, the following is recorded:

> ... through the bad conduct of Magister Thomas Muentzer of Stolberg, at that time preacher at St. Catherine's, he drew to himself weavers, who were in turn attracted to him, with whom—rather than with his fellow priests—he preferred to meet in conventicles. This led to the suspicion that Magister Thomas preferred the weavers, especially one by the name of Nicholas Storch, whom he praised in such a fulsome manner from the pulpit as to declare him more worthy of honor than any priest, as a man who knew his Bible inside and out, and who was highly experienced in the Holy Spirit. At the same time he boasted of himself that he, Magister Thomas, knew for a fact that he possessed the Holy Spirit. From this wicked conduct it came that Storch dared, along with Thomas, to preach secretly at these conventicles, as is the custom with the Picards who raise shoemakers or tailors to preach. Thus did Magister Thomas promote this Nicholas Storch; and from the pulpit he proclaimed that laymen must become our prelates and pastors and give an account of the faith, etc.[21]

In light of the preceding four chapters, several aspects of the above report deserve to be accentuated. First, nowhere is it said that Storch influenced Muentzer. What is said is that the two were immediately attracted to one another and that Muentzer uttered some words of rather extravagant praise about Storch from the pulpit. Since both Wappler and Elliger assumed that Muentzer began as Luther's disciple, they were virtually forced to assume, further, that when he appeared to move away from him—and this first became apparent in Zwickau—it was under the influence of the Zwickau Prophets in general and Nicholas Storch in particular. We have, however, already seen only too clearly that while Muentzer may have read some of Luther's writings and read some of the same things that influenced Luther, he read these largely through the inspiration of Tauler and discovered things in them very different from those Luther had. Thus, by the time he came to Zwickau, Muentzer was most certainly no longer, if he ever had been, a close follower of the German Hercules. Indeed, as his first letter to Luther seems to indicate with its reference to Luther as "specimen et lucerna amicorum dei," Muentzer regarded Luther as a fellow disciple of Tauler. And he had good reason to do so.[22] He was, therefore, his own man; neither Luther nor Storch was the decisive factor in his intellectual development.

But why was Muentzer so obviously and so undeniably drawn to the conventiclers, as the above report asserts? The answer lies in three rather revealing statements Muentzer is reported to have made. The first is his remark that Storch knew his Bible inside and out and could explain one part with passages drawn from another. Now Muentzer had himself read in the *Historia* how, when the Master of Sacred Learning had received the Holy Spirit, he had come "to possess the holy Scriptures in thyself, so wilt thou understand that all Scripture has the same meaning and is never self-contradictory." He had read in Tauler's sermons that all truth came from the Holy Ghost, that wisdom drawn from the abyss of the soul was immeasurably more profound than that arrived at by scribes and Pharisees who relied upon their reason but did not possess the Holy Spirit, that even the unlettered could draw on this wisdom through the operation of the Holy Spirit in their souls. For in the *hohe Schule* of the Holy Spirit, Tauler asserted, "the most secret meaning of holy Scriptures was imparted to them [the disciples], and the truth of God was revealed nakedly to them, and that in a way wholly incomprehensible to all the doctors in the schools." Muentzer must have believed he had precisely such a man standing before him in the person of Nicholas Storch: a man unlearned in the knowledge and wisdom of the *hohe Schule*, yet apparently imbued with the wisdom of God, "revealed nakedly" to him.

Whether this observation led to his second assertion—that Storch was highly experienced in the Holy Spirit—or whether Storch imparted this information to him directly, is not of major consequence. What is important is that *Muentzer* was reported to make this assertion about Storch from the pulpit. *Muentzer* was the one who discerned the presence of the Holy Spirit in Storch and proclaimed it to his congregation. *He* was the actor rather than the one acted upon. For his third assertion was that he, Thomas Muentzer, "knew for a fact that he [Muentzer] possessed the Holy Spirit." This does not sound like a man suddenly learning something new, but more like a man finding in others what he believed himself to have experienced. He had encountered the Holy Spirit in Orlamuende while studying Tauler under the guidance of Master Conrad's cook. Now in Zwickau he found others, some of whom had not been educated as he had been.

It was not only their mutual experience of the Holy Spirit that drew Muentzer and the Zwickau Prophets together, however. Storch and his followers must have been visible evidence for Muentzer that the Holy Spirit was returning to the Church. After the Leipzig Disputation, he came to see Hus and Luther as the restorers of the pure seed, the Word of God, to the Church. He called Luther a "friend of God," thereby intimating that he thought Luther had the Holy Spirit. He was undoubtedly aware of at least some of Luther's repeated assertions that they were living in the end times; and he had himself come to believe the same. This must therefore be the time of harvest in which the wheat and the tares would be separated, as Augustine had predicted. He had received the Holy Spirit,[23] and now in Zwickau he met others who claimed as much for themselves. As a consequence, things seemed to be coming together for the establishment of the new Apostolic Church.

Confirmation of the above comes from another portion of the same history not quoted by Elliger, but cited by Wappler who notes that as a consequence of the growth of the conventicles, "a rumor had arisen concerning the *secta Storchiatarum*: for they had increased to such an extent that it was openly reported that they had discussed and actually chosen twelve apostles and seventy-two other disciples." At the same time, as Wappler reports, they began to implement a community of goods in their midst and some of the members began to experience visions and assert that God spoke to them in dreams.[24] The way the story is told, it would appear that these changes came in only after Thomas Muentzer joined their ranks. Perhaps the Prophets were the ones influenced and not Muentzer.[25] More than likely it was Muentzer with his emphasis on the new Apostolic Church who attempted, already in Zwickau, to recreate the twelve apostles and the seventy-two disciples because he believed this to be the "second harvest." Therefore he, like Christ in the first, would send out his own apostles and disciples.[26] They would go into the various regions with his message of the return of the Holy Spirit and form bands committed to this vision, as had taken place in the early Church.

While Muentzer's encounter with the Zwickau Prophets led by Nicholas Storch would appear to have served to confirm him in his views—and we will have to return to that relationship a little later on—these views were challenged in a fundamental fashion one more time before Muentzer turned his back on the city. This time it was the humanist Egranus who, having returned to Zwickau in October of 1520 to resume his duties at St. Mary's, confronted the would-be prophet of the new Apostolic Church.

As early as 16 February, Egranus opened a letter to Muentzer referring to their confrontation before the castle, at which Muentzer had apparently "slanderously attacked" him. Egranus further accused Muentzer of "speaking ill of me in the pub [bei der zech], [and] denouncing me from the pulpit as a devil." Perhaps, Egranus continued, such conduct had been taught him by his spirit, "of whom you boast and whom (as I hear) you have scooped out of the waters"—a clear reference to Muentzer's already repeated assertion that he possessed the Holy Spirit. After a scornful reference to Muentzer's mystical theology of suffering—"You have long wished me the cross"—Egranus informed the latter that he would continue on his way undeterred. In conclusion he remarked that he had written in German "not without cause, since I sense that your spirit is a despiser of all learning and Scripture."[27]

Once again we get a glimpse of certain aspects of Muentzer's theology. There is the unmistakable reference to his assertion that he possessed the Holy Spirit. There is the scornful rejection by Egranus of the mystical assertion that one must experience the suffering of the cross before the rebirth through the Holy Spirit can take place. And lastly, there is Egranus's unmistakable reference to Tauler's assertion—mediated through Muentzer—that the Holy Spirit could impart "the most secret meaning of holy Scripture . . . nakedly" to the unlettered in a way "wholly incomprehensible to all the doctors of the schools."

Although the intervention of the Zwickau Council and Wittenberg, through Johannes Agricola,[28] moderated the public outburst of both parties, the subterranean feud continued. To get away from a confrontation that became increasingly irritating to him, Egranus eventually left Zwickau for Joachimsthal, but not before Muentzer himself had, "in the fog of night," escaped the city in mid-April 1521. In the meantime, however, Muentzer had collected a number of Egranus's theses—which he entitled "Propositiones probi viri d. Egrani"—in the hope of using

them publicly against his theological rival upon the latter's departure.
Unfortunately for him, however, he was unable to do so before he
himself decided that it was the better part of valor to flee the city. As a
consequence, the theses were never published, but discovered later
among his papers. They appear to have been drawn from the sermons
and writings of Egranus, however, and as such have been regarded by
scholars as reflecting his authentic beliefs. Insofar as they are attacks
upon Muentzer's beliefs—and are reported by Muentzer himself—they
may also be assumed to reflect the latter's position accurately.

Since we are here concerned first and foremost with Muentzer's intellectual development, Egranus's theses should command our attention
only insofar as they help to illuminate Muentzer's thought. In this respect, the first seven theses deal with the problem of the human will and
clearly pit the humanist—with his belief in the freedom of the will and
man's consequent ability to choose and perform acts moral and meritorious in the sight of God—against the mystic who believes in the suffering
way of the Cross and the transforming power of the Holy Spirit.
Whereas the first thesis implies the salvation of the "moral pagan," the
second denies that "Christ . . . came into the world in order to teach us
to endure our sufferings with patience and thus follow in His footsteps." The fifth thesis returns to the theme of suffering, asserting that
"Christ's passion was not as bitter as many [foolishly] assert." The sixth
thesis, then, attacks the very core of Muentzer's and Tauler's position
when it asserts that "The forgiveness of sins takes place without any
suffering." It is enough, Egranus asserts, to have the contrition "which
also takes place in robbers." And this contrition "comes out of man's
own powers." Suffering, therefore, as Muentzer must have asserted,
was not something "to be longed for." And temptations of faith were
thus to be rejected as "figments of the human imagination and phan-
tasms of the mind."[29]

What we have here is a clear rejection of the mystical theology of
regeneration Muentzer had absorbed from Tauler. And the perspective
from which the attack comes is that of the humanist. Precisely the
process of suffering that we saw Luther highlight nearly every time he
referred to Tauler is rejected by Egranus as a figment of the imagination.
Nor does one need the Holy Spirit to be able to have a "holy invincible
Christian faith"; contrition and fulfillment of the law came "through
the constancy of their own strength as upright men."

Theses eight through twenty deal primarily with the interpretation
of the Bible. What factors influenced Muentzer's interpretation of the

Bible? We have referred to some of these in the preceding pages; perhaps these should be drawn together at this point in order to see
whether they are the focus of Egranus's attack. The first and most
obvious emphasis to come from Tauler derived from his encouragement
to "be absorbed above all things in striving after the spirit of God
[rather than learning], and with pure hearts pray for his operation in
their souls." Once the Holy Spirit had been acquired—as in the case of
the disciples—"the most secret meaning of holy Scriptures was imparted
to them, and the truth of God was revealed nakedly to them, and that in
a way wholly incomprehensible to all the doctors in the world." Tauler
supported this interpretation with quotations from Augustine, referring
to the "abyss of the soul" as the hidden abode of God. This understanding was confirmed for Muentzer by the picture of the Apostolic Church
he derived from the *Church History* of Eusebius, where the early
Church was portrayed as "Spirit-filled." The "written Word"—the
product of the "spirit-filled disciples"—only came after the outpouring
of the Holy Spirit at Pentecost. The written Word was the manifestation
of the inner reality of the presence of the Spirit, therefore not of primary
but of secondary importance. Indeed, when Eusebius wrote, the canon
had not yet been established, and we have seen even Luther refer to that
history for confirmation that some books were early considered of
doubtful canonicity. The period of Church history, then, that Muentzer
took as the ideal, and that he wished to reestablish in the new Apostolic
Church—the period prior to the second half of the second century—had
been visibly led by the Holy Spirit. It was only later, when the Holy
Spirit had departed the Church "with the death of the disciples of the
Apostles," that the scribes and Pharisees had appeared. They were the
ones who had begun to stress the "written Word" because they no
longer possessed the Holy Spirit. But since the "written Word" was the
product of the Holy Spirit, a true understanding of that Word was
impossible without the Spirit. It was for this reason that the *Historia*
had asserted that, now that the Master of Sacred Learning had received
the Holy Ghost, he possessed the holy Scriptures within himself.

Since the Scriptures had been written by "Spirit-filled" disciples, the
possession of the Spirit was also indispensable for their correct understanding. For scribes and Pharisees, who had only their reason to guide
them, this was clearly impossible. It was also impossible for those "false
teachers" who were in it for the money and therefore perverted the
Word for their own satanic ends. This perspective contained a strong

element of anti-clericalism, for the "Spirit-filled" layman was undoubtedly to be preferred to the scribes and Pharisees.

Contained in the above is also the argument that the contradictions in the Scriptures are only apparent, perceived by those who rely only upon their rational faculties. Once the Holy Spirit has been imparted, one will realize that "all Scripture has the same meaning and is never self-contradictory." If we add to the above Augustine's repeated assertion—in both his letters as well as his sermons, made in reaction to the Manichees who rejected the Old Testament—that the Old and New Testaments were in perfect harmony with one another, Muentzer's witnesses agreed on this point. The two Testaments were therefore to be reconciled. And anyone who possessed the Holy Spirit could easily do so.

With this in mind, it is important to note that Egranus's eighth thesis says that Christians may disregard the Old Testament since it was intended only for the Jews in any case. Such a statement went even beyond Erasmus's repeated assertion that the Old Testament was given to the Jews and could be useful to Christians only if it were interpreted allegorically. Clearly, Egranus would not have concerned himself with this issue—and Muentzer would not have accentuated it in the theses he compiled—had it not been a significant point of conflict between the two preachers. Muentzer must have asserted the essential unity of the two Testaments against Egranus, as he did later against Luther when he declared in his *Protestation:* "the art of God must be demonstrated in the Holy Scriptures through a strict concordance of its total content which is clearly delineated in both testaments."[30]

Thesis nine declares—after having disposed of the Old Testament—that the New Testament is to be understood in its literal, historic sense. This implies—leaving the *sensus spiritualis* aside[31]—that reason, human reason, is all that is needed to interpret the Scriptures. If Egranus did indeed make such an assertion, Muentzer must have regarded him as a scribe and a Pharisee, that is, as a man of "externalized religion" relying only on his rational faculties, yet one who claimed to be a shepherd of Christ's flock even though he did not possess the Holy Spirit. Therefore, he could not possibly interpret the Word of God correctly. Muentzer was to fulminate against such "servants of God" in his later writings, as the cause of all the evils in God's Church here on earth. Certainly, he must have regarded thesis ten as an example of this rationalistic folly when dealing with spiritual matters. There Egranus is supposed to have argued that "Christ, who is the living bread, is not to be asked for in the

Lord's Prayer." It was the daily bread we needed in common with the
Turks and other unbelievers that was intended here. Muentzer must
have interpreted "daily bread" as "living bread," that is, the Holy
Spirit.

In thesis eleven Egranus objected to precisely that form of biblical
exegesis that Muentzer is reported as having lauded so highly in Nicholas Storch: the ability to explain one passage of Scripture by means of
another. In doing so, of course, Storch was assuming "a strict concordance of its [the Bible's] total content"; otherwise, such a method would
be impossible. Muentzer's emphasis must have been on the spiritual
meaning in contrast to the historico-literal meaning championed by
Egranus. The latter wished, therefore, to "guard the integrity [of the
original meaning] so that the author's intended meaning is not distorted
by those [carried in] from other passages."[32]

Theses twelve and thirteen argue that St. Paul is not difficult to understand; the opposite is the case, for "occasionally he speak[s] with reference to the Jews and then the Heathen, none of which pertains to us." In
this fashion Egranus dismissed much of the New Testament as irrelevant
to the Christian, as he had—and does again in thesis thirteen—already
dismissed the Old Testament with its laws, which he now asserted are not
necessary for the recognition of our sins. But Muentzer must have gone
much further, arguing that rather than being "totally freed from the law,"
as Egranus asserted in the first part of thesis fourteen, those who have
been possessed by the Holy Spirit have been enabled to fulfill the law.

Thesis fifteen, with its admonition that "One should not instill a fear
of God in the human heart," seemed clearly to be directed against
Muentzer's assertion—derived primarily from Tauler—that one must
experience all the wrath of God's alienation and the death of the soul
before the Holy Spirit can come and inhabit the soul. This emphasis on
the Holy Spirit—whose work in the human soul is beyond rational
understanding—seems explicitly to be rejected by Egranus in thesis sev-
enteen when he said: "No one is compelled to believe what his intellect
is unable to understand." God has given man a free will—aside from his
reason—and this free will, he asserted in thesis eighteen, even limits
God's omnipotence! No wonder Muentzer singled these theses of
Egranus out for special renunciation. The contrast to his own position
delimited above is nothing less than dramatic. Precisely such a position
as the one espoused by Egranus characterized the rationalistic folly of
the original scribes and Pharisees. Precisely such a position, which rejected the role of the Holy Spirit in the interpretation of the Scriptures

and in the life of the individual believer had been—Muentzer had come
to believe—the cause for the prostitution of the "pure Apostolic
Church." Through such "spiritual guides" the Church had been seduced and deprived of her virginity. These were the *speculatores* he had
spoken of in his very first Zwickau sermons. They were the archenemies
of the Church and had to be destroyed.

It is no wonder, then, that Muentzer quoted Egranus in thesis
twenty-one as having declared that "Only the Apostles possessed the
Holy Spirit. Nor did the rest of mankind need Him because the Church
was firmly established through the labors of the Apostles." This, of
course, was the central issue between the two protagonists. If Egranus
was right, then indeed all Christians had to rely on their own rational
powers, could not be expected to believe "what [the] intellect was unable to understand," would have to rely on "the freedom of [the] will,"
and could not be expected to understand any but the historico-literal
interpretation of the Scriptures. That Muentzer believed Egranus to
hold such a position is made obvious by thesis twenty-two, where
Muentzer had Egranus assert that "In 1000 years no man has possessed
the Holy Spirit, nor has the Church been ruled by Him."[33]

That the role of the Holy Spirit in the believer's and the Church's
corporate life was the crucial issue for Thomas Muentzer is made amply
apparent in his letter of 15 June 1520 to Nicholas Hausmann, some two
months after his departure from Zwickau: Alluding to Isaiah 62:1,
Muentzer wrote; "I intend, most honored brother, for Zion's sake not
to keep silent, not to flatter or support so great a lie, as that which was
uttered, and heard by many citizens, in your parsonage by Egranus—
that man damned in all eternity—who said: 'The Church has not possessed the Holy Spirit since the time of the Apostles.' "[34] Hausmann,
and all who witnessed this, Muentzer continued, were guilty of the same
blasphemy because they had remained silent and not opposed Egranus.
Hausmann, who had come to Zwickau in May 1521, must therefore
have witnessed Egranus make the above statement and had said nothing
to reprove him. Nor is it any accident that Muentzer drew attention to
this particular pronouncement of Egranus, for it lay at the heart of his
concern for the Church.[35] He was not merely concerned about the work
of the Holy Spirit in the individual believer; had this been the case, he
should have singled out Egranus's twenty-second thesis quoted above.
Rather, Muentzer attacked the preceding thesis that only the Apostles
had possessed the Holy Spirit, and that the Church had not possessed
Him since. Nor did it need Him! Precisely such persons, he had been

taught by Hegesippus, relying upon their own natural powers while at
the same time despising the Holy Spirit, had misled the Church in the
first place. Theirs was the most dangerous of blasphemies; they had to
be expunged from the Church. Muentzer would speak out until "her
righteousness would shine out like the dawn, her salvation like a blazing
torch." The Holy Spirit could return to the Church; indeed in this "time
of harvest," it was beginning to return to the Church. Egranus and his
ilk stood in the way, and their blasphemy had to be emphatically rejected. It was this perspective, the antithesis of which Egranus expounded in theses twenty-one and twenty-two—but which lay behind
all the theses Muentzer culled from the former's sermons and writings—
that determined his fundamental attack on Egranus. Since Eusebius had
quoted early Christian writers as observing that these "false prophets"
of the Apostolic Church had been motivated by their greed for money,
he had Egranus say, in thesis twenty-four: "In Chemnitz, where I was
subjected to a binding compulsion [and after lengthy consideration], I
arrived at the conclusion that there was only one spirit worthy of my
acceptance, [that was the spirit] of passionate compulsion for change
and, ultimately, of money." Like all false prophets, who had been led
astray by their "richly endowed rational powers," Egranus, also, had
succumbed to greed. It did not really matter whether this was true or
not; the fact that Egranus was a man of merely "externalized religion"
made it an inescapable and inevitable corollary.

If Muentzer encountered the Zwickau Prophets and Egranus with
his own perspective already well-defined, how do we explain the
similarities between his position and that of the Prophets?[36] In order
to do that, we must return to the sermons of Tauler, for it is in them
that the beginning of the explanation lies. There, in a sermon on
Psalm 91:13, "Thou shalt tread upon the lion and adder: the young
lion and the dragon shalt thou trample under feet," Tauler addressed
"four great delusions, four subtle temptations in the spiritual life."[37]
One of these was the heresy of the Free Spirit from which, as Gordon
Leff has noted, Eckhardt, Tauler, and Suso strove to dissociate themselves.[38] Tauler addressed himself, in part of this sermon, to precisely
this problem:

> And now we are to consider the fourth kind of illusion which affects
> certain men calling themselves contemplatives, who resemble, but yet differ
> from the class we have just been treating. The fourth class consider them-
> selves as mere passive instruments of God, set totally free from all activity of
> their own. God works within them; and they have thereby, so they claim,

more merit than others who do good works and whose personal activity is ever inspired by Divine grace. Although they do nothing, they yet merit reward, so they affirm, and are by no means to be blamed for their inactivity. They live a life of perfect interior rest in God, as they think; and, cultivating a very humble demeanor, they pay no regard to anything whatsoever, and are quite patient with whatever befalls them—as bright souls which are mere instruments of the Divine will. *They have many points of resemblance with men of sound spirituality.* But here is what proves that they are wrong: Whatever they feel themselves interiorly moved to do, whether it be good or bad, they are persuaded is the work of the Holy Ghost. But the Holy Ghost never inspires men to be idle and useless, least of all, to do evil things, nor to do anything against the life and doctrine of Christ and His holy Scriptures. And this demonstrates that such men are under deception. But it is not easy to detect them, for they are cunning in concealing their vagaries. However, they are betrayed by their obstinate self-will. They will rather die than yield the least point of their infatuation. They are greatly opposed to those who tell them that they are not in the way of perfection, for they hold that they are in a most meritorious state. Be assured that all such men are forerunners of anti-Christ, preparing the way for the spread of unbelief and the eternal loss of souls [italics mine].[39]

Tauler was therefore very much aware that the heresy of the Free Spirit had "many points of resemblance with men of sound spirituality." Indeed, as Gordon Leff has observed, "In essentials it sprang from the pantheism latent in Neoplatonism; and to this extent it shared, albeit in a distorted and extreme form, the same sources as that which helped to inspire Meister Eckhart."[40] We should hasten to add that it inspired St. Augustine as well, who played so important a role in justifying Tauler's position. Because these views were attributed to Eckhart by his accusers, Tauler was at pains repeatedly to dissociate himself from them and to base his position firmly on Augustine. Whereas both made union with God the center of their concern, Tauler clearly pinpointed their difference when he argued in the passage above that the Holy Ghost never inspires true Christians to act against the teachings of Scripture. The adherents of the Free Spirit, however, argued that once one had been purified by the presence of the Holy Spirit, all things were lawful—to the pure all things were pure. Therefore, while Tauler constantly sought to express his position in terms acceptable to the Church, the adherents of the Free Spirit felt themselves freed not only from the "normal requirements of the moral order" but from the Church as well.[41]

Furthermore, as Gordon Leff has contended, the heresy of the Free Spirit was characterized by the "obliteration of the difference between

God and man, the infinite and the finite."[42] This was not true of Eckhart or Tauler, neither of whom was Pelagian as were the adherents of the heresy of the Free Spirit. Whereas all these were originally quietistic and individualistic, the Free Spirit adherents, as Howard Kaminsky has pointed out, were, "by the fifteenth century, the strongest representatives of this [Joachist] tradition."[43]

The heresy of the Free Spirit was condemned by Clement V in a bull of 1311 entitled *Ad nostrum*. Issued from the Council of Vienne, it singled out eight propositions as heretical:

1. That a man in this life can attain to such perfection that he is incapable of sinning or surpassing his present degree of grace, since to do so would make him more perfect than Christ;

2. That he no longer needs to fast for he has gained such control over the senses that he can allow them complete freedom;

3. That he is free from all obedience to the Church;

4. That the free in spirit can obtain full blessedness in this life;

5. That every man so blessed does not need the divine light of glory to love God;

6. That the need for virtuous actions belongs to the imperfect man only;

7. That sexual intercourse is not a sin when desired;

8. That there is no obligation to rise before Christ's body in the elevation of the host, or to show him any other signs of respect, since this would entail descending from the heights of contemplation, and so mean imperfection.

Together with Clement's bull *Cum de quibusdam mulieribus* against the Beguines, this document brought the heresy of the Free Spirit into association with the Beguines and Beghards, and, as Leff observes, "from this time onwards the Beguines—and Beghards—came irrevocably to be treated as the source of the heresy of the Free Spirit."[44]

Largely a German phenomenon, the Beguines and Beghards were found most frequently along the Rhine in such cities as Cologne, Strasbourg, Basel, and Constance. Northern France showed some activity as did the Low Countries. It was in the latter, in "Gallia Belgica," that the Beghards were called "Picardi." Here, too, they apparently came to adopt a Joachist eschatology.[45] This is revealed in an Inquisition record of 1411 conducted by Pierre D'Ailly of a Brussels Free Spirit sect known as the "homines intelligentiae." Aside from highlighting the ritualistic sexplay in the group, the report noted:

They say (1) that the time of the Old Law was the time of the Father, and the time of the New Law that of the Son; the present time is that of the Holy Spirit, which they call the time of Elijah. (2) In this time the Scriptures will be reconciled [or, in another version, "removed"], so that (3) those things that were previously regarded as true are now refuted—even the catholic truths that they had used to preach, concerning poverty, continence, and obedience. The opposite of these truths, they say is [to be] preached in this time of the Holy Spirit. (4) [They say] that the preachings and doctrines of the ancient saints and doctors will cease, and new ones will be more easily revealed than it has been up to now, and (5) that the Holy Spirit will illuminate the human mind more clearly than it has up to now, even (6) in the apostles, who had only the outer shell. And they say (7) that the time is at hand in which the Law of the Holy Spirit and of spiritual liberty will be revealed, and (8) then the present Law will cease.[46]

There is some suggestion that the doctrines of the Free Spirit were known in Bohemia by the early fifteenth century,[47] but the first solid evidence of their presence there comes in 1418. As Kaminsky has observed, the "flourishing of the Bohemian reform movement in the early fifteenth century" attracted various groups of heretics, persecuted elsewhere in the realm.[48] According to Laurence of Brezova, a group of forty "Picardi" came to Prague in 1418 with their wives and children. Even though they were well received, they did not join themselves to the Hussite Church; and although they gradually faded into obscurity, they did infect a number of Czechs with their heretical ideas that came to be known as "Pikartism" in Bohemia.

It cannot concern us to pursue the history of the Picards in Bohemia, except to assert that the heresy must have maintained itself there well into the sixteenth century. Its adherents absorbed some Waldensian ideas compatible with their flexible theological perspective.[49] By 1462 these "Bohemian" heresies had spread north even into Zwickau.[50] Perhaps influenced by these ideas, Nicholas Storch had, sometime during the second decade of the sixteenth century, made a trip to Bohemia where it is generally assumed that he became acquainted with and joined a sect known as the Nicolaitans.[51] This was a sect that the contemporary author of *The History of Thomas Muentzer* brought into connection with the Picards.[52] Indeed, they shared many of its doctrines.

What we may have in the encounter between Thomas Muentzer and the Zwickau Prophets—and Nicholas Storch in particular—could then be a confrontation, in the first place, between Tauler with his mysticism emphasizing the role of the Holy Spirit, and the adherents of the Free

Spirit. In their claim to possess the Holy Spirit, both were alike. But they were not alike in the conclusions they drew: the heresy of the Free Spirit leading to libertinism, in contrast to Tauler's and Muentzer's position aiming at a "holy invincible Christian faith" that would lead to the fulfillment of the "doctrine of Christ and His holy Scriptures." Once Muentzer became aware of this—if he did—it could easily have led to a rupture between them. In the second place, they did not see the future in the same way. The Zwickau Prophets, possibly inheriting Joachist concepts of the "Age of the Spirit" from the Picards, were quite different from Muentzer who, combining Eusebius and Augustine, saw the future in terms of the rebirth of the Apostolic Church in the "time of harvest." Third, the Picards rejected the real presence in the Eucharist, indeed, showed no respect for the host at all, whereas Muentzer was the first to translate the Mass into German—ahead even of Luther—making his *Deutsches Kirchenamt* of Easter 1523 the centerpiece of his church services in Allstedt. The other differences, such as baptism, will be dealt with in their appropriate places.

Like Muentzer, who may at first have read the Zwickau Prophets through the eyes of Tauler, Luther and Melanchthon read Thomas Muentzer through the eyes of the Prophets. As a consequence, they missed some of Muentzer's essential concerns while imputing those of the Prophets to him, in spite of the fact that Muentzer was not entirely unknown to Luther or to Melanchthon.[53] This process of misinterpretation may well have begun with the letter of Egranus to Luther of 16 April 1521, just after Muentzer had slipped out of Zwickau. It stated in part:

> Your Thomas—for such he boasts himself to be—has come here to Zwickau and upset everything with his mad shouting and his teachings. The obstinate and brazen nature of the man knows no bounds, for he listens neither to the advice of friends nor the authority of the Scriptures. Rather, relying solely upon his own "spirit," he creates division everywhere. He is a man as though born for schism and heresy. . . . As is his custom, he has, to the shame of an otherwise famous city, drawn to himself, as co-conspirators, primarily by means of the confessional and secret conventicles, known criminal and insurrectionary elements from the lower classes. He has left this poison as his legacy, for his hirelings still spew the same things against all the people of rank, preachers and priests. . . .[54]

It was not until December 1521, during the critical days of the "Wittenberg Unrest" while Luther languished at the Wartburg, that the Zwickau Prophets themselves appeared in Luther's city. There they met with and influenced Carlstadt, Martin Cellarius, Gerhard Westerburg, and Melanchthon.[55] Undecided what to do about them, the latter appealed to Luther at the Wartburg for advice. In his famous letter of 13 January 1522, Luther responded, advising his younger colleague to test their "prophetic spirit"; to enquire—Luther uses obviously mystical terminology—"whether they have experienced spiritual distress and the divine birth, death, and hell"; and not to be too easily persuaded by their arguments for the rejection of infant baptism.[56] The last concern dominates the letter. This fateful conjunction of what Luther considered Carlstadt's precipitous reform attempt with the appearance of the Zwickau Prophets in Wittenberg may have helped to color all of Luther's subsequent views of the "radical" reform measures. Even though he did not mention the Prophets by name in his Invocavit sermons of March 1522, by means of which he recaptured control of the Wittenberg reform movement, he did, on a number of occasions, chide Carlstadt for not taking decisive measures against them.[57] What is more certain is that beginning with the 16 April 1522 letter from Egranus he must have begun to regard the Prophets as emissaries of Muentzer and therefore representatives of his thought.

Toward the end of March 1522, Luther encountered Marcus Stuebner, one of the Prophets at Wittenberg.[58] In May of the same year he visited Zwickau itself. But even before that visit he had written to Spalatin: "Muentzer and his followers have sown dragons in Zwickau, but Egranus is also still sowing. Everywhere the devil is raging and opposes the Gospel."[59] After his visit he wrote again to Spalatin: "I know that the teaching of Thomas [Muentzer] with respect to infant baptism has sunk deep roots, and yet no one seems to be concerned to uproot them. Nevertheless, no impiety or heresy has existed, adhered to more tenaciously by the larger number than this."[60] Clearly, Luther saw Muentzer as the source of this heresy. Whether he was, however, remains very much in doubt. Indeed, there is no mention of adult baptism anywhere in Muentzer's writings, and it is far more likely that the idea came from the Bohemian Picards, influenced by the Waldensians, via Nicholas Storch. This would appear to be confirmed by the letter of 4 September 1522 that Luther wrote to Spalatin, this time observing that "Claus Storch" had visited Wittenberg and captivated Gerhard Westerburg. He said that Storch "had talked of nothing else than infant baptism."[61]

In a "Tabletalk" of August 1531 Luther himself confirmed that this was indeed his understanding of the relationship between Muentzer and the Zwickau Prophets. There he spoke of the Prophets' visits to Wittenberg. The first to attack him, he declared, had been Marcus Stuebner.

Soon thereafter "Nicholas Storch from Zwickau, Stuebner's master, came to me." After this, there "came Muentzer, student of the former two."[62] Had he known the source of Muentzer's thought, Luther must have come to very different conclusions.

From this perspective, then, Luther began to impute ideas and actions to Muentzer that belonged properly to the Picard theology of the Zwickau Prophets, but not to Thomas Muentzer. This would appear to be the case in the passage of his 1533 "Von der Winkelmesse und Pfaffenweihe": "What did that poor man Thomas Muentzer do as he roamed the countryside looking for a nest in which to practice his vices? In Allstedt he confessed to good people that he had been chaplain in a cloister at Halle where he had to perform the early Mass for the nuns. This had often annoyed him so that he had omitted the consecration formula and retained only bread and wine. Apparently he was proud of this and boasted of it in Allstedt, saying: yes, such unconsecrated lordgods—for so he called the host—I have devoured by the hundreds."[63] Now, such a position would not have been alien to the heretics of the Free Spirit, who showed no respect for the host. But Muentzer, though imbued with the "Spiritualist" concepts of a Tauler, would hardly have followed their example. His translation of the Latin Mass and the institution of the *Deutsch-Evangelische Messe* in Allstedt in 1524[64] make Luther's accusation highly suspect.

There are other discrepancies that deserve mention. Wappler, quoting a Johann Schneesing, called Storch an exponent of the most "extreme libertinism." Schneesing, pastor at Freimar, had told Marcus Wagner that Storch "was an unchaste person who . . . when he saw a fine matron or beautiful young lady, would gladly have had his way with her like a lascivious young buck. With gleaming eyes he would say quite openly: Women were created for everyone's flesh and blood [enjoyment] and should be held in common."[65] Once again, this position would fit in with the adherents of the Free Spirit.[66] But even Luther said of Muentzer that he had written him and Melanchthon, complaining of their marriages as little better than prostitution. He taught, Luther said, that a man "may sleep with his wife only when he was assured, through a divine revelation, that a holy child would result from this union; those who did not act accordingly used their wives as prostitutes. As a result, several Zwickau matrons confessed openly, when they had slept with their husbands: this night I have been a prostitute."[67] If Luther was correct, then Muentzer propounded these views already in Zwickau in the midst of the Prophets. The contrast, at least in the above respect, is so glaring between Muentzer and Storch that the two positions are irreconcilable.

Whereas Luther on occasion asserted that Muentzer was the disciple of Storch and imputed all of the latter's positions to him, on other occasions, he asserted that Muentzer had come out from among his own midst. For example, in a "Tabletalk" of 1533 he is recorded as having said: "from Luther [came] Muentzer and the revolutionaries."[68] And in a sermon of 22 September 1538 he remarked that "When Muentzer had departed from the [correct] teaching he became political,"[69] clearly implying that he had at first been one of his followers. But in this assumption Luther was as much in error, as when he assumed that Muentzer had become a disciple of Nicholas Storch and the Zwickau Prophets. At least in regard to the latter, Thomas Muentzer told him so in terms that Luther could hardly have misunderstood.[70]

In a letter to Luther of 9 July 1523, Muentzer characterized his relationship to Storch and the Prophets by citing a passage from Galatians 2. Although not specified, the verse may be the sixth: "As far as those who seemed important—whatever they were makes no difference to me; God does not judge by external appearances—*these men added nothing to my message!*" [italics mine].[71] Nor was his message, he remarked in a letter to Hans Zeiss of 2 December 1523, derived from Joachim of Fiore, even though he regarded the latter's witness as important. His enemies, he observed, ascribed his teachings to the abbot and derided it as an eternal Gospel. But he had not taken his teaching from Joachim, having read him only on Jeremiah;[72] he took it directly from the mouth of God (*vom ausreden Gotis*), as he would prove on the basis of the totality of the Scriptures at the appropriate time.[73]

Although I myself attempted to prove otherwise in 1973,[74] and Richard Bailey returned to the topic several years ago with even more disastrous results,[75] it is Muentzer who is to be believed in this instance as well as in the one regarding his relationship to the Zwickau Prophets. There is no good reason why he should lie to his follower, Hans Zeiss. And, as we have already seen, and shall see even more clearly in subsequent chapters, Muentzer's eschatology was primarily determined by the Parable of the Tares as interpreted by Augustine.

Nonetheless, there may have been Joachists in his midst, the Zwickau Prophets themselves. The Picards, aside from having absorbed Waldensian ideas in Bohemia, had already appropriated a Joachist eschatology. Pierre D'Ailley's inquisitorial report of 1411 on the "homines intelligentiae" would appear to indicate as much.[76] These Joachist ideas were also prevalent among the Taborites[77] and may have been picked up there by Nicholas Storch. There is some evidence, however, to suggest that these ideas were abroad in the region around Zwickau and could have been absorbed there as well. It is clear, of course, that Storch believed strongly in the coming of the new age and even saw himself as its inaugurator.[78] But it was Hans Herrgott who, as a printer and adherent of the Prophets and of Muentzer, wrote a pamphlet in 1526, just after the bloody suppression of the Peasants' War, entitled *Von der Wandlung eines christlichen Lebens.* He personally circulated it in Zwickau and the surrounding region, agitating to keep the revolutionary spirit alive. The opening paragraph of this pamphlet presented the Joachist view of history and was virtually identical with D'Ailley's inquisitorial report:

> *Herrgott:* Three transformations have been seen in history / the first was instituted by God the Father in the Old Testament / the second transformation was instituted by God the Son in the world with the New Testament / the third transformation will be brought about by the Holy Spirit / with this future transformation the world will be changed from the evil in which it finds itself.[79]

> *D'Ailley:* They say (1) that the time of the Old Law was the time of the Father, and the time of the New Law that of the Son; the present time is that of the Holy Spirit, which they call the time of Elijah.[80]

Whereas both of the above divided God's history into the three ages of God the Father, Son, and Holy Ghost, nowhere did Muentzer do so. Instead, he spoke of the birth of the new Apostolic Church in the time of harvest. In order to be reborn, however, the Apostolic Church had to be renewed by the presence of the Holy Spirit.

Although there are similarities, there are also major differences in these eschatological views. Certainly Muentzer did not share the libertinism of Nicholas Storch, his views on infant baptism possibly inherited from the Waldensians, or even his Joachist eschatology. He was right in applying Galatians 2:6 to his relationship with the Zwickau Prophets. He could with equal justification have applied it to his relationship to Joachim of Fiore.

The Zwickau period, then, marks the beginning of the public expression of views Muentzer derived from his reading of Tauler and those other works that he read in response to the issues raised at Leipzig. These views became evident in his very first sermons, not in the Church of St. Catherine attended by the Prophets and the lower classes of Zwickau, but already in the Church of St. Mary attended by Zwickau's ruling elite; in addition, these views were expressed in his letter to Luther of 13 July 1520. They became even more apparent in his *Auseinandersetzung* with Egranus, especially in his argument concerning the important role of the Holy Spirit in the Church. If this is indeed the case, then it must follow that, just as Muentzer was not influenced in any fundamental way by Luther, the Zwickau Prophets cannot have influenced him either, Luther's assumptions to the contrary notwithstanding. Rather, Muentzer stands in the same relationship to the Prophets as the mystical Tauler does to the heretics of the Free Spirit. Such a relationship makes it much easier to explain the rift that obviously came between Muentzer and the Prophets later after his visit to Prague.

CHAPTER V

Prague and the New Apostolic Church

I say that the Church at the time of the apostles was infinitely better ruled than it is now ruled. What deters Christ
from not regulating it better without such monstrous heads as
there have been now, through His true disciples? And see!
now we have no such head and yet Christ does not desist
from regulating His Church.

—John Hus at the Council of Constance

"The Bohemians," Muentzer declared in his debate with the Franciscans at Jueterbog in April 1519, "are better Christians than we are."
Enunciated by Franz Guenther even before Muentzer arrived there, this
argument may go back to the discussions concerning the Eucharist in
Wittenberg prior to the Leipzig Disputation. In any case, it would appear to indicate that Muentzer's quest for a "holy invincible Christian
faith" predated his encounter with Tauler. Yet, while the Bohemians
may have provided Muentzer with a better expression of that faith, it
was Tauler who showed him how to achieve it. When he came to
Leipzig in late June, he was again confronted by the Bohemians, this
time, however, more specifically in the person of John Hus, whose
theology became a central issue in the debate between Luther and Eck.
The reformer's defense of Hus against Eck's accusations of heresy, and
even against the condemnation of the Council of Constance itself, must
have impressed Muentzer. Motivated to find out more about Hus and
Constance, he therefore ordered from Glov, along with the other books
discussed in the earlier chapters of this study, editions of the acts of the
Council of Constance and of its successor at Basel.[1] It is the first of these
that is important in the present context, for there Muentzer must have
discovered Hus both in terms of the accusations levelled against him by
the Council Fathers and in his defense against those charges.

This direct and more concentrated preoccupation with Hus, stimulated by the debate at Leipzig, together with his encounter with the Zwickau Prophets, probably lay at the root of his decision to travel to Bohemia soon after slipping out of Zwickau in mid-April 1521. By late May or early June he had returned, only to embark upon a second trip almost immediately, this time to Prague itself. Whereas the Zwickau Prophets may have sought to turn his interest in the direction of the Taborites or other "left wing" Hussite radicals, the second trip was focused on Prague and John Hus. The opening lines of his *Prague Manifesto* make this apparent: "I, Thomas Muentzer, born in Stolberg and at present residing in Prague, intend, in place of that dear and holy warrior John Hus, to fill the resounding and versatile trumpets with the new song of praise of the Holy Spirit."[2] Muentzer's interest in Hus, then, was not of recent vintage, and was not inspired solely, if at all, by the Zwickau Prophets whom it predated and followed. Indeed, it is quite possible that both trips were motivated by his attraction to Hus and his reform movement rather than by one or the other of the deviant branches which grew out of it.

In any case, Muentzer's interest in Hus is not to be denied. He apparently did not come to Bohemia in order to learn from Hus or the Hussites: once again, the *Prague Manifesto* would seem to make the point. He had come, instead, to proclaim the birth of the New Apostolic Church, just after his attempt to establish it in Zwickau had failed. The obvious question is: why? It is a question that demands an answer before we attempt to determine what drew him to Hus in the first place.

On 15 June 1521 Muentzer wrote three letters that relate to his second trip to Prague. To Nicholas Hausmann, his successor in Zwickau, he wrote that he had already been to Bohemia.[3] To Marcus Stuebner, he wrote to urge their return to Prague, and in this letter he noted that his unrest was caused by the fact that he did not wish to allow Satan to impede their journey.[4] The third letter, that to Michael Gans, as well as the letter to Hausmann, clearly reveals that Muentzer interpreted his return to Bohemia in the light of his awareness of the impending end of the age. Stimulated by Augustine, Tauler, Luther, and the widespread apocalyptic fervor of the early years of the Reformation, Muentzer had apparently begun to study both the Old and New Testaments in order to clarify these issues in his own mind. As a consequence, he seems to have come to link his own persecution, beginning in Zwickau, and possible death with the impending end of the age.[5]

To what extent Luther's citation to Worms and subsequent Imperial ban imposed upon him contributed to his unease remains unclear, but there are some intriguing parallels between their respective situations. At about the time the heavy hand of the emperor descended upon Luther, Muentzer decided to give up the struggle in Zwickau. Did he see his persecution in Zwickau as somehow a part of that larger persecution that seemed to be converging upon Luther and the new reform movement? He knew, of course, what had befallen Hus at Constance. Was he afraid the same would happen to Luther and to him? Did he recall Tauler's remark about how "good appearing Christians" would persecute those who wished closely to follow Christ? In his letter of 13 July 1520 he had addressed Luther as the light and example of such friends of God. Did he consider Hus to be one of these friends of God as well?

In his letter to Hausmann, Muentzer referred to himself as a *servus electorum dei* and asserted that the threat to himself was the result of his preaching the Gospel. Nonetheless, he informed Hausmann, he would not be silenced, as the latter had been. For, he observed with reference to Elijah and the slaying of the priests of Baal:

> St. Paul explains that very passage as follows: "If I were trying to please men I would not be a servant of Christ." I have heard that you, on the contrary, catered not only to the priests, but also sought to placate the council and most powerful magnates after the unrest subsided. You heard Egranus blaspheme and remained silent. In Kirchberg they were very upset that the people who had sworn oaths [to uphold the holy Gospel?] were not quick to contradict him. I intend, most honored brother, for Zion's sake not to keep silent,[6] nor to flatter or support so great a lie, as that which was uttered, and heard by many citizens, in your parsonage by Egranus—that man damned in all eternity—who said: "The Church has not possessed the Holy Spirit since the time of the Apostles."[7]

This determination not to keep silent and to suffer whatever consequences led Muentzer to send his various papers to Michael Gans in Jena for safekeeping. Paraphrasing St. Paul, he wrote Gans: "I hope, if possible, to be all things to all men, until they know the cross and conform themselves to it."[8] This, apparently, was to be the method he hoped to employ in bringing his message of the cross to the Hussites. Did this mean that he intended to begin where John Hus had left off and attempt to lead them—as St. Paul had attempted to lead the Athenians in his sermon on the Areopagus—to the full understanding of the cross he had achieved? St. Paul had begun with the Greek poets, philosophers, and the statue dedicated to the unknown god. Why should not Muentzer begin with Hus and his emphasis on the pure Church of the elect with its many similarities to the primitive Church?[9] In any case, it was imperative to get the message out quickly, for the time of harvest was fast approaching in which the separation of the wheat and the tares would take place.

Therefore, after having chided Hausmann for not openly opposing Egranus, the priests, and the town Council, Muentzer told him: "The time of Antichrist is at hand, as Matthew 24 clearly makes apparent."[10] Now, Matthew 24 contains Christ's answer to His disciples' question: "Tell us, when shall these things ["no stone left unturned"] be, and what shall be the sign of thy coming and of the end of the world?"[11] After mentioning "wars and rumors of wars," nations and kingdoms rising up against one another, famines and earthquakes as signs of the "beginning of birth pains" of the new age, Christ said; "Then shall they deliver you up to be afflicted and shall kill you; and ye shall be hated of all nations for my name's sake." Had this not happened to Hus, and was it not now happening to Luther, and also to Muentzer? To be sure, he spoke of persecution in connection with the fast approaching end of the age. Christ had also said that at that time many would turn from the faith and betray and hate each other, and many false prophets would appear and deceive many people. Because of the increase in wickedness, the love of most would grow cold, but he who stood firm to the end would be saved. Had all this not already transpired according to Muentzer's interpretation of the Church's development? It would seem so, for in that same letter to Hausmann, Muentzer focused on Matthew 24:14: "And this gospel of the kingdom shall be preached in all the world for a witness unto all nations, and then shall come the end." Muentzer paraphrased this verse in the following manner; "With the gospel reigning in all the world and the Lord's word forcing its way in everywhere, then we will recognize the abomination of desolation."[12] Skipping the intervening verses, Muentzer moved directly to verse 36 and continued: "But the reprobates will not believe [that is, that the end of the age is imminent], just as they failed to believe Noah in the days of the flood. [Yet] they all err," he continued, "who say that the last pope [Julius II] was the Antichrist. The same is surely true of the prediction that the fourth beast will rule the whole earth and his reign will be great everywhere."[13] Therefore, although Muentzer concurred with those who believed that the end of the age was fast approaching, he disagreed with those who argued that it had already arrived. The Word, purified by Hus, and now Luther, was just beginning to penetrate all parts of the world. As in the days of Noah, however, this Word would be, and was being, opposed. Hus had died for it; Luther was feeling the hot breath of Imperial persecution; and Muentzer—sincere servant of the elect of

God—sensed he could be next. And this persecution was taking place because Matthew 24 was in the process of being fulfilled. The old age was coming to an end and the world was experiencing the "birth pains" of the new.

Whether Muentzer had encountered Luther's argument—enunciated repeatedly after his reading of Hus's *De Ecclesia*—that the latter had preceded him in attempting to present a purified Word to the world, he seems to have arrived at a very similar conclusion.[14] Since the movement for reform had begun with Hus, and since the Bohemians were already "better Christians than we are," Muentzer may have begun to believe that Prague was the place where the new Apostolic Church would first appear. He asserted as much near the end of his *Prague Manifesto:* "For it is in your land that the new Apostolic Church will rise up, thereafter everywhere [else]."[15] Such a proclamation could hardly have been a spur-of-the-moment utterance. Muentzer had come to Prague with a message.

If this is indeed the case, what was it about Hus's reform program that made it possible for Muentzer to argue in this manner? In the first place, Hus's moral emphasis must obviously have attracted Muentzer, an emphasis that meshed nicely with his own repeated call for a holy invincible Christian faith. Even if we take only the final thirty accusations—with Hus's interlinear glosses—brought against him before the Council, the moral criteria are obvious. There, in passages taken mainly "from the book *De Ecclesia* and certain other smaller treatises," Muentzer would have read the following: "Priests living criminally in any manner whatsoever pollute the priestly power"; or, "No one occupies the place of Christ or Peter [by office or merit] unless he follows Him in morals"; or, "The pope is not the manifest or true successor [by office or merit] of the prince of the apostles, Peter, if he lives in a manner contrary to Peter"; or, "If the pope is wicked, and particularly if he is foreknown, then like the apostle Judas he is a devil, a thief, and a son of perdition, and not the head of the holy Church militant."[16]

Not only do these passages stress morality, they also point to the integral relationship between a moral life and predestination. Only the predestined are, or can be, true shepherds of the Church. Thus in accusation 22 Hus is reputed as having said: "A wicked or foreknown pope or prelate is putatively a shepherd, but actually a thief and a robber [because he is not such according to office and meritorious life, but solely according to office]."[17] To this assertion Thomas Muentzer would have added only that these prelates were such because they had not experienced the advent and transforming work of the Holy Spirit. Therefore they remained men of merely externalized religion, "dividing the Word of God" according to their reason, if at all.

A second aspect of Hus's thought to strike Muentzer as he read through the acts of the Council of Constance was his definition—or implied definition—of the Church. Dependent, as it was, upon Augustine, it must at least in some ways have confirmed Muentzer's own reading of the Church Father's letters and sermons. As Matthew Spinka has observed:

> Hus' "real" heresy was his conception that the *true* Church is limited to the predestinate. Although this charge was always in the forefront of the accusations against him, it was never explicitly formulated or declared heretical, but was regarded as implying Hus' denial of the validity of the Church militant. This latter Church, consisting of both the predestinate and the foreknown, was asserted to be a "true" Church as well. The confusion in applying these two concepts derives from the double meaning with which the term "Church" was employed by the contesting parties. Hus conceded that the Church militant was a "true" Church, meaning thereby the predestinate in its membership. The foreknown were not members of this Church universal, but belonged to the synagogue of Satan. Ultimately, they would be separated from the predestinate as chaff from the wheat. Thus the basic conflict concerned the concept of the Church, as to whether it was an authoritative corporation or a spiritual fellowship.[18]

Spinka goes on to say there is nothing heretical about this concept of the Church, "limited to this aspect of it. It is thoroughly Pauline as well as Augustinian."[19] About Hus's letters, Spinka observes: "They manifest his supreme devotion to the ideal of a church as the body of Christ that exists amid the corruption of secular society 'without spot or wrinkle,' a fellowship of the redeemed, 'unspotted from the world.' "[20] Muentzer, as we have seen and shall see again, strove for the very same kind of Church. And he too had read his Augustine, though combined with Tauler and Eusebius.

This view of the Church—in an even more one–sided manner—was clearly delineated in the accusations brought against Hus at Constance. There, in the passages abstracted from his *De Ecclesia* cited as heretical, Hus was quoted as follows: "There is only one holy universal Church [said in the most essential sense according to Augustine], which is the totality of the predestinate."[21] In the third passage Hus had written: "The foreknown are not part of the Church ["catholic" in the most essential sense], for no part finally falls away from it, since the predestinating love which binds them does not fail."[22] And in the fifth passage he had written: "The foreknown, although sometimes in grace according to present righteousness, nevertheless is never part of the holy Church ["catholic" said in the most essential sense]."[23] Here was the Church, the "wheat" that Augustine had longed to separate from the "tares" and that Muentzer believed to be coming into existence once more after the Apostolic model. While the "foreknown" had forced the Holy Spirit from the Church in the second half of the second century and had come to rule it, persecuting the elect like Eckhart and Hus in the process, all that was about to change.

At this point we arrive at another aspect of Hus's thought Muentzer must have appreciated: his emphasis on the primitive Church as the norm or model.[24] While this emphasis is somewhat muted in the 30 Articles, it does arise more forcefully in other exchanges between Hus and the Council Fathers. In the last of the 30 Articles Hus is recorded as having written:

> 27. There is not a spark of apparent evidence that there should be one head ruling the Church in spiritual matters that should always abide with the Church militant; that is evident, since it is known that the Church has been without a pope for a long time, and now after the condemnation of John XXIII it so stands.
> 28. Christ without such monstrous heads . . . through His true disciples scattered over the circumference of the earth would rule His Church better.
> 29. The apostles and the faithful priests of the Lord had firmly ruled the Church in things necessary to salvation before the papal office . . . was instituted. They would do so if there were no pope—as is highly possible—until the Day of Judgment.[25]

When Hus had been confronted with Article 28 earlier, the Fathers had accused him of trying to play the Prophet. His response was to sharpen the argument in the following manner: "I say that the Church at the time of the apostles was infinitely better ruled than it is now ruled. What deters Christ from regulating it better without such monstrous heads as there have been now, through His true disciples? And see! now we have no such head and yet Christ does not desist from regulating His Church."[26]

While the Articles brought against Hus are vague with respect to the turning point at which this pure primitive Church had gone wrong,[27] in his response to Article 9 he had said:

> "That is what I say: that as far as the outward adornments and the possession of temporal goods of the Church as such, the papal dignity has its origin from Caesar Constantine; and that later emperors also confirmed it,

as is shown in the *Decretum* distinction 96. But as concerns the spiritual administration and office of the spiritual governing of the Church, such dignity originates directly from the Lord Jesus Christ." And the cardinal of Cambrai said: "Nonetheless, at the time of Constantine a general Council was held and there that decree was ascribed to Constantine, on account of his presence and reverence. Why not, therefore, rather say that the preeminence of the pope emanates from the Council rather than from the power of Caesar?" And the Master said: "Because of the Donation, which, as I said, was granted by Caesar."[28]

This was an argument Hus may have derived from Wycliffe, though it was not unique to the latter: Dante, Marsiglio, as well as the Waldensians all made use of it.[29] Even in Hus, however, that same argument does not appear to have impressed Muentzer, for he never so much as mentioned Constantine or the Donation in any of his extant work. The reason for this lies undoubtedly in the fact that Hegesippus had taught him to view the decline and fall of the Church differently. If so, it is one more indication that Muentzer was making his own way through the literature of reform movements past and present. His assertion of independence to Luther with respect to his relationship to the Zwickau Prophets must therefore also apply to his relationship with John Hus.

Before we proceed to a study of Muentzer's *Prague Manifesto*, we would do well to remind ourselves once more of the pervasive Augustinian influence Muentzer had been exposed to. It had come to him through Tauler, the Leipzig Disputation, and a direct reading of Augustine's letters and sermons. And now it also came to him through John Hus's sharp differentiation between the predestined and the merely foreknown, and his definition of the true Church as the Church of the predestined. Combined with the normative character ascribed by Hus to the primitive Church, it came close to Muentzer's own view of the Apostolic Church. The only aspects lacking were Tauler's emphasis on the Holy Spirit, Hegesippus's argument concerning the corruption of the Apostolic Church in the second half of the second century, and the belief that the time of harvest was at hand.

Although Vaclav Husa has argued that Muentzer was invited to Prague by one of the chief lay leaders of the radical Utraquist movement, the knight Burian Sobeck of Kornice,[30] there is no solid evidence upon which to base such an assertion.[31] We do know, from the letter of Hans Pelt to Muentzer of 6 September 1521, that the latter was accompanied by—or had acquired in Prague—"two learned Bohemians who tell the people [translate] the Gospel of Christ into Czech which they hear from your mouth."[32] He may, therefore, have had some initial success in the proclamation of his message. Exactly what that message was, however, can no longer be determined.

Nonetheless, it is probably safe to assume that Muentzer's message did not go beyond the themes he developed in his *Manifesto*. Such manifestos were nothing new in Prague,[33] and Muentzer may have modelled his on those that had preceded him, especially during the turbulent years of the Hussite Revolt. There are three versions of this *Manifesto:* a shorter German version in Muentzer's own hand; a longer German version, probably in the hand of Ambrosius Emmen, Muentzer's famulus,[34] which poses, as Heinrich Boehmer already said some years ago, linguistic problems even the best dictionaries cannot solve;[35] and a Latin version written in Muentzer's hand nearly identical to the longer German version, though somewhat less radical because it was directed toward the educated circles.[36] The longer German version shall serve as our centerpiece.

In the very first sentence of his *Prague Manifesto*, Muentzer does two very significant things: he draws the reader's attention to John Hus, calling him a "holy warrior," and then proclaims his intention to fill the air with "the new song of praise of the Holy Spirit."[37] The two are not unrelated, for Muentzer intends to sound the trumpets with the new song "in the place of" John Hus. Hus would therefore appear to be his point of departure, and the Holy Spirit the most significant addition he intends to bring to the Bohemian reformer's message. This should no longer surprise us. *In his place*, he, Thomas Muentzer, the servant of the elect of God, now proclaimed the power of the Holy Spirit. He had himself experienced this transforming power of the Holy Spirit; he had seen the Zwickau Prophets claim to possess Him, and had confirmed it; he had branded as a great blasphemy Egranus's denial that the Holy Spirit was necessary to the Church; therefore, it was time to speak out "for Zion's sake." And what better place to do this than in Bohemia where, as Matthew Spinka says, John Hus had attempted to establish the ideal or pure Church?[38]

That Muentzer's primary concern lay with the Church of the elect the lines of the *Manifesto* which follow the opening make plain enough: "I bear witness with my whole heart, wherever this letter may be displayed, that I have desperately bewailed the [condition of the] whole Church of the elect, indeed of the whole world. Christ and all the elect," he averred, "who have known me from my youth, confirm this to be so." Now, there is a distinct shift in focus here from anything that we might find in Augustine, Hus, or Luther with regard to the true Church, the Church Triumphant, or the Church of the predestined. It is not only that Muentzer wished to separate the wheat from the tares; the condition of the wheat—the "whole Church of the elect"—is to be bewailed. The reason for this must be found in his view of Church history. According to that view, the Apostolic Church had been a visible church of pure wheat; it had not been invisible! It had possessed the Holy Spirit whose presence in it had been manifested by the invincible faith of its members, the pervasive presence of prophecy, of dreams, and of visions. When the Holy Spirit had been forced out in the middle of the second century, not only could the wheat no longer be distinguished from the tares, but the wheat itself—the very elect—were deprived of the Holy Spirit by unfaithful clerics. It was for this reason that not only the world, but the Church of the elect itself was in such dire straits. Here we understand the massive responsibility Muentzer assigned these men of "merely externalized religion," these scribes and Pharisees, in the corruption, nay the devastation of the Church. Not only, he argued repeatedly, would these men not enter the kingdom of God themselves, but they also kept everyone else, even the elect, out.

Having drawn attention to this pitiful state of the Church, Muentzer proceeded to address the problem of faith, saying: "I give my most solemn pledge that I have desired to understand more intensely and more profoundly than any other person how a holy invincible Christian faith is to be established." Once again, this statement is not unrelated to what has preceded it; indeed, it deals with the very crux of the problem of the Church of the elect—salvation through the work of the Holy Spirit. Only through such an encounter as described by Tauler could such a faith be established. Therefore, Muentzer continued, "I make bold, in all honesty, to say that no pitch-anointed priest, no pseudo-spiritual monk has understood the least little thing about the foundation of faith." This was why such shepherds of God's flock could offer no solace or consolation to troubled seekers. All they could do was burden them further with their man-made rules and regulations.[39] Having said this, Muentzer provided his readers with a number of indicators as to what constituted Christian faith. First, these clerics knew nothing about "the wholesome temptations and that beneficial abyss of the soul in all its emptiness through the providential Spirit." The first reference is clearly to those temptations described by Tauler, and emphasized by Luther virtually every time he mentioned Tauler's name, which, according to mystical thought, preceded the advent of the Holy Spirit that was to take place in the abyss of the soul, first needing to be emptied of all worldly cares and concerns by "the providential Spirit."[40] The clerics were ignorant of all this because "the Spirit of the fear of God, whose sole purpose is to establish the elect thoroughly [in the faith], has not taken possession of them." Here Muentzer not only asserted that none of these clerics—priests, monks or theologians—possesses the Holy Spirit, but also that only the Holy Spirit can "establish the elect thoroughly [in the faith]," that is, create an unshakable faith in them through which they can become followers of the Christ. Without this Holy Spirit, who overwhelms the true believer "in so great a flood"—an inundation the world is incapable of understanding—no one can "hear or understand the living God." Muentzer wished to say it straight out and leave no doubt in anyone's mind about this. "I have heard," he asserted, "no donkey-farting doctor whisper—never mind mention it aloud—even the least little thing concerning the Order (of God and set into all creatures).[41] Even the most distinguished Christians (I mean priests who know everything) have not even had a whiff of what the Whole or the Undivided Perfection consists of, which is a measure equalling the sum of its parts."[42] Often enough, Muentzer complained, he had "heard the bare Scriptures—and that in large doses—from such people," but this was a Scripture that they had maliciously stolen, like so many furtive thieves, from the Bible. Such theft God had no choice but to condemn.

In support of this position Muentzer cited Jeremiah 23:1–4, an instructive passage that not only must have confirmed in Muentzer's mind the above view of the Church's plight, but also have judged those responsible in the most severe manner:

> "Woe to the shepherds who are destroying the *sheep of my pasture!*" declares the Lord. Therefore, this is what the Lord, the God of Israel, says to the shepherds who tend *my people:* "Because you have scattered *my flock* and driven them away and have not bestowed care upon them, I will bestow punishment upon you for the evil you have done," declares the Lord. "I myself will gather the remnant of *my flock* out of all the countries where I have driven them and will bring them back to their pasture, where they will be fruitful and increase in number. I will place shepherds over them who will tend them, and they will no longer be afraid or terrified, nor will any be missing," declares the Lord [italics mine].

It is the "sheep of my pasture" the Lord declares to have been scattered, not the reprobates; it is, in Muentzer's words, "the church of the elect." That Muentzer did in fact identify these two becomes even more apparent about midway through the *Manifesto* where he charged: "Because of this, they [the priests] have scattered the sheep of God so greatly that nowhere any longer can one discern the *face of the church*."[43] The reason for this, he continued, is that "there is no longer anyone present who is able to separate the good [read "elect"], who are unknown, from the large mass [of humanity]."[44] That is to say, no one possesses the Holy Spirit.

This is a clear confirmation of our earlier reading of the way in which Muentzer combined Tauler, Eusebius, and Augustine. The Holy Spirit, absolutely essential to the Church, had been forced out in the second century because of the scribes and Pharisees and false prophets. As a consequence, the elect were scattered "so greatly that nowhere any longer can one discern the face of the Church." Augustine, therefore, had been forced to define the Church as containing both wheat and tares, with the wheat being in the distinct minority. Since very few possessed the Holy Spirit, there was no "understanding of what is pestilential and what is healthy, that is to say, no one is aware that the Church is being destroyed in its very foundations because of these damned people." No one was capable of differentiating good from evil, the elect from the reprobate, and all because "the sheep [the elect] do not know that they must hear the living voice of God." The duty of every true shepherd, Muentzer asserted, "is nothing else than to bring all the sheep to the place where they can be refreshed by [God's] living voice, for it is the art of God that teaches a master, Matthew 23."

It is not surprising that Muentzer referred at this point to Matthew 23, for that chapter, coming as it does just before the chapter dealing with the signs of the end of the age, pronounces a series of "woes" on the scribes and Pharisees. The latter, as verse 2 observes, "sit in the seat of Moses." They are the ones who "bind heavy burdens and grievous to be borne, and lay them on men's shoulders; but they themselves will not move them with one of their fingers." Furthermore, as verse 13 goes on to say, these same scribes and Pharisees "shut up the kingdom of heaven against men: for [they] neither go in [themselves], neither suffer them that are entering to go in." And so the sheep were not being "refreshed by [God's] living voice."

The reason, Muentzer said, why the sheep had not been refreshed for such a long time was "that the elect have, in many respects, become virtually the same as the damned and also virtually swallowed up by them." So much was this the case, he continued, "that nearly the entire world was of the opinion that it was not necessary that Christ had to preach His own Gospel to the elect Himself." He, however, swore that "he who does not hear the right and living Word of God from out of God's own mouth, then bible and babel is nothing but a dead thing." The living Word of God penetrated "to the very heart, mind, bones, marrow, sap, power and strength," and it would run a different course than "our sex-hungry [hodensaeckische = "scrotic"] doctors think." Salvation could come in no other way: "The elect like the damned must be crushed to pieces, and their powers must ebb away from them." Otherwise they would never be able to "hear what God is." But he who received "the Holy Spirit once, in the way he is supposed to, will never again be damned."

It should be obvious that for Muentzer the Holy Spirit is intimately, indeed inseparably, connected with the true Church. Muentzer was no mere Spiritualist, therefore, nor even a "Revolutionary Spiritualist." He was a man obsessed with reestablishing the Apostolic Church he had seen described by Eusebius and found confirmed in the book of Acts.[45] His conviction was that this could be accomplished only by the return of the Holy Spirit—not merely to isolated individuals, as Sebastian Franck had argued in his 1531 letter to John Campanus[46]—but to all God's elect who had been deprived for such a long time.

The scribes and Pharisees had not only stolen "my words everyone from his neighbor," but also deceived the people by claiming to have the Word of God when God had never once spoken to them. They usurped God's words, took the external Word of God—the Bible—but then denied that God's Spirit could communicate with the people. Since this was their attitude, they disdained those who claimed to be "children of God." These were men of insolent dispostions of whom Jeremiah had asked in chapter 23:18: "Who has stood in the counsel of the Lord, and received and heard his word? Who hath marked his word and heard it?" None had heard it, for they were a proud and hardened people upon whom God "intends at this time to pour out his irrevocable wrath because they deny the fundamental healing of faith." Whereas Ezekiel 4:3 had said that they should "form an iron wall [around] the elect to defend them against their opponents and slanderers," these people did nothing but ridicule the Spirit. How could such persons "confirm the Word of God"? Instead of being anointed with the holy oil of the Spirit, they had merely "been smeared with the oil of sinners by Nimrod's pope." Belonging to the damned, they had no business leading God's people. The devil had "destroyed the very foundations of their hearts . . . for without exception none possesses the Holy Spirit." Rather than help, they hindered. Even worse, "they [were] a plague to the people."

Reprobate people like these, Muentzer continued, had been in "the entire world from the beginning." Indeed, they had been "set there to be a plague for the poor people who lack understanding [in matters relating to the Spirit]." Yet as reprobates they had no right to speak for the elect, as St. Paul in Galatians 4:21–31, where he describes two kinds of people, makes plain enough. They were tares who had infiltrated the Church, had become its spokesmen, but who nonetheless denied "the voice of the bridegroom." Accordingly, Muentzer argued:

> This is the true and surest sign that they are nothing but devils. How can they be servants of God, messengers of His Word, when they deny it brazenly with a prostituted mind [cf. Jer. 3:2–3]. For all true priests *are to experience revelations* in order that they may be confirmed in their convictions, I Cor. 14 [:1–5]. But they speak with an obdurate heart that such a thing is impossible. Wherefore it would only be just—since they claim to have devoured the entire Scripture—if they were to be destroyed as though by thunder and lightning, as St. Paul writes in II Cor. 3 where he makes the distinction between the elect and the damned [italics mine].[47]

To such men as these the entire Bible was closed, "locked with the key of David according to Revelation 5 [:1–10]." In Luke 11:52 Christ had said of them that they had "stolen the key" and then "locked the Scriptures shut."[48] How had they locked it shut? By declaring that "God may not speak in person with any man." The Holy Spirit, therefore, was the key to the understanding of the Bible, the key that unlocked its true meaning. This was an interpretation taken directly from Tauler.

Having castigated the "shepherds of [God's] flock" for denying the "living waters" to the elect, Muentzer came to speak on the Parable of the Good Seed. His interpretive guide was clearly Tauler, for he began by saying that "Where the seed falls onto the good soil, that is the hearts [of men] *who are full of the fear of God,* that is then the paper and parchment upon which God writes, not with ink, *but with His living finger, the true and holy Scriptures*" [italics mine].[49] The seed would appear to be the external Word, the Bible, that Hus and Luther had liberated "from under the bench" and that, as he informed Hausmann in his letter of 15 June 1521, was beginning to reign in all the world. The soil was obviously the heart of man. The good soil, however, was the heart "full of the fear of God," or the heart prepared by the Holy Spirit. Once the seed and the Holy Spirit came together in the heart of man, such a heart became the paper or parchment upon which God wrote, "not with ink, but with His living finger, the true and holy Scriptures." Only when this had taken place, could one have a reliable testimony concerning the external Word, the Bible. Only then could one interpret it correctly.

If the seed was indeed the Word of God, purified and raised to prominence once again by Hus and Luther, its public dispersal, its "falling onto the soil," was the indispensable first step in preparing the way for a correct understanding of the Christian faith. But it had to be combined with a heart prepared, emptied, by the Holy Spirit. It had to fall on "good soil," otherwise, it accomplished nothing. If this interpretation is correct, Muentzer must have seen himself, at least at this early stage of the Reformation, as working in harmony with Hus and Luther. The good seed was once again being sown; he was trying to provide the good soil onto which it could fall and bear fruit. For, he continued, there was no surer testimony that could confirm the truth of the Bible "than the living speech of God, when the Father addresses the Son in the human heart." This writing "all the elect, *who exercise their talent,* can read [italics mine]." Luther must have had some sense of this when he observed that Muentzer aspired to something higher than what he preached.[50]

From the above it would appear that Muentzer thought only the elect could "exercise their talent" and become good soil, whereas "the damned would not do so for their hearts are harder than flintstone, which deflects the master's chisel in all eternity. Therefore our dear Lord calls them rocky soil upon which the seed falls, but who produce no fruit, even though they accept the dead Word with joy, with great joy and praise." Thus both the elect and the damned may accept the "bare Scriptures," the external Word, but it bears fruit only if the Holy Spirit prepares the soil in the elect. But it is precisely this Holy Spirit who has been kept from the elect by the scribes and Pharisees. Because the elect are thus deprived, there is hardly any difference between them and the damned at the moment. The Holy Spirit's presence must be added to the seed in the heart of the elect; only then can the Father write the "true and holy Scriptures" in their hearts "with His living finger."[51]

This rocky soil refuses to suffer "any temptations of faith in the Spirit of the fear of the Lord"; the scribes and Pharisees have had "no experiences which they have felt, that could help them in explaining the holy Scriptures"; they become progressively more hardened in their hearts; "they neither wish to, nor can they, empty themselves" since they are repulsed by the Devil who possesses them; and so "they fall away in the time of temptation; they turn away from the Word which has become flesh. The reprobate does not wish in any way to be conformed to Christ in his suffering; he wants to accomplish everything with [mere] honey-sweet thoughts." Such is the nature of the rocky soil and yet they are the priests. Therefore they are already damned; it is no wonder, then, that "they take the right key away and say that such a way [the Holy Spirit] is fantastic and foolish, [that] it is utterly impossible." Since Christ has condemned such priests long ago, "why then should I not also damn them?"[52]

While Muentzer clearly consigned the "shepherds of [God's] flock" to the rocky soil and hence to the damned, he apparently had "no doubts about the [common] people." Or is the insertion wrong? Does he mean here all the people who belong to the flock? In any case, he appears to regard these as the scattered sheep these false shepherds had driven away and "not bestowed [any] care upon." They were the ones who, as Jeremiah had observed, had been led astray by prophets who had "prophesied by Baal" [Jer. 23:13]. These people were the "right, poor and pitiable little band," which had "thirsted for the Word of God! For it is apparent," Muentzer argued

> that no one, or at least very few, know what they should believe and which group they should align themselves with. They desire to know what is right but they do not know what that is of themselves. For they do not know how to act or how to accommodate themselves to the testimony, which the Holy Spirit speaks in their hearts. The reason is that they have been made to fear the Spirit of the fear of God so greatly that the prophecy of Jeremiah has been fulfilled in them: "The children have begged for bread, but there was no one who could have broken it to them."[53]

It would seem, then, that Muentzer saw these other people as belonging to that "Church of the elect" which had been deprived of the Holy Spirit by clerics who did not possess it themselves, could not explain its advent to those who desired to know it, and who ridiculed anyone who considered himself a "child of God." These people had asked for bread, but what had they been given? "There were indeed," Muentzer charged,

> many money-hungry rascals [priests] who threw the papal texts of the Bible, *which they had not experienced,* before the poor, poor people, as one is accustomed to throw bread to the dogs. *But they did not* [indeed, could not because they were rocky soil] *break it to them through the skill of the Holy Spirit, that is, they did not open their minds that they might recognize the Holy Spirit in themselves* [italics mine].[54]

How could they, since they had not experienced it themselves? Even if all of these priests were stacked one on top of the other, Muentzer asserted, they "would not be able to make even one single person understand how to prepare himself for eternal life." Not merely were the blind leading the blind. What was really happening was that the willfully blind were leading astray those who had the potential for experiencing the Holy Spirit if only they could be given the bread "through the skill of the Holy Spirit." It was a perverted world in which the rocky soil prevented the potential growth of faith.

Muentzer attacked the clerics responsible for this perversion:

> What more shall I say? These are the fine lords who spend their time boozing and gorging themselves, enjoying life, seeking night and day how they may nourish these habits and acquire more benefices. They are not like Christ, our loving lord, who compares Himself to a hen who seeks to warm her chicks. Nor do they provide any milk to the disconsolate and abandoned people from the fountain of God's admonitions which never runs dry. *For they have never tried faith.* They are like the storks who gather frogs in the meadows and marshes, thereafter spitting them crudely into the nest of their young. The usurious and tribute–hungry priests are just like that; they devour the dead words of Scripture, thereafter they dump the letter and this unexperienced faith (which is not worth a single louse) into the midst of this upright but poor people. In this way they make certain that no one is sure of his soul's salvation. For these same slaves of Beelzebub bring only one piece from out of the Scriptures to the marketplace. As a consequence, people do not know whether they deserve God's love or His hatred. This poison comes out of that abyss because every whoremongering priest is subject to the most deceitful and most evil lord, the Devil, as the Revelation of John makes plain. *Because of this they have scattered the sheep of God so greatly that nowhere any longer can one discern the face of the Church.* For there is no longer anyone present who is able to separate the good, who are unknown [because they have been denied the Holy Spirit], from the large mass [of humanity]. Nor is there any understanding of what is healthy, that is to say, no one is aware that the Church is being destroyed in its very foundations because of these [already] damned people. For the sheep do not know that they must hear the living voice of God. That is, they must all experience revelations [italics mine].[55]

Whereas these "false prophets," these scribes and Pharisees, had no choice but to act in this fashion, it was "The duty of the shepherd to bring all the sheep to that place where they can all be refreshed by [God's] living voice." Such a refreshment, however, Muentzer continued, had not taken place for a long time because the elect had been deprived of the Holy Spirit. As a consequence, they were now "in many respects virtually indistinguishable from the damned, virtually swallowed up by them." So much was this the case that it was now nearly universally believed that "it was not necessary that Christ had to preach His own Gospel to the elect Himself." Nonetheless, he, Thomas Muentzer, wished to assert and swear by the living God that "he who does not hear the right and living Word of God from out of God's own mouth, then bible and babel is nothing but a dead thing." When God's living voice penetrated a man's consciousness, however, all of this was transformed and man himself changed. This was why there was no other way to be saved. The elect as well as the damned "must be crushed to pieces, and their powers must ebb away from them. Otherwise you will never be able to hear what God is." Once the Holy Spirit had been received, however, a person could never again be damned.

In the meantime, though, "The people are [still] . . . forced to live without true shepherds, for the way to experience faith is never preached to them." Faith is not merely something one grasps with the mind; it must be experienced. But these "Jewish, heretical priests may well say that such a difficult thing [the experience] is not necessary." They assert that one can escape God's anger by doing good works. "Nonetheless they do not learn from all this what God is through experience, what right faith is, what real virtue is, what good works are according to God's entry." As a consequence, things have come to such a pass that it would not be surprising were God to destroy the elect along with the damned, those who had merely suffered the deceptions along with those who had perpetrated them. "For surely our faith is more in accordance with the face of Lucifer and Satan; and is more gross than wood and stone." Other nations, therefore, call our faith a "monkey business," for when they ask us to give an account concerning it, all we can say is that "We have written this and that in our law, when Christ said this, when Paul wrote that . . . indeed [that] Nero-like holy, most hardened pope and pisspot at Rome in the [heart of the] brothel, has ordained this and that great thing." Because we can point only to external matters and *have no experience to show them,* unbelievers suspect that our books have lied. We need *experiences* to confirm them.[56]

Muentzer was convinced that "the Jews and Turks would be happy to hear about our invincible foundation [of faith], even many elect would do so" along with the people. "But," once again, "the Devil's priests screw up their noses and are quick to condemn them, even though they do not possess the right thing themselves, for [like Egranus] they deny that a man can possess it." And so they "speak with mere words." Such a response should, however, be cast into hell along with those who propound it. "For such evasion is madder than madness itself."

This, then, was the pathetic state of the Church of the elect. Was it to continue this way? Did they—his hearers and readers—wish to perpetuate this stupidity? "Does no one feel even a little spark that might light up and catch fire?" he asked. Perhaps mindful of his followers in Zwickau, he answered his own question: "Indeed, there are those who feel it, and I feel it too." It was with a bitterly heavy heart, he continued, "that I have realized that the Christian Church has been so badly trampled under foot that God could not plague her any worse, unless He wished to annihilate her completely." However, Muentzer promised, God would not do this. He would exterminate only "those thin-shitters who have taught her to pray to Baal." They were the ones who deserved to be punished, for they had not practiced "the judgments of God."[57]

How had he reached these conclusions? Having read his Tauler—though he does not tell us this, it is more than a little apparent—he had turned to the "histories of the old [Church] Fathers." In them, he asserted, he had read far and wide, discovering that "after the death of the disciples of the apostles, that the pure virgin church was quickly made into a prostitute by the seductive priests" who had always desired "to sit at the head of the table, all of which and more Hegesippus and Eusebius confirm." When, therefore, the people began to disregard "electing the priests to their positions, it became impossible from the very outset—because of this neglect—to elect a proper council." Consequently, these councils dealt only with petty external matters and "not even once, no, not once did they open their mouths concerning the right and living Word of God."[58]

The past, however, was merely prologue to the future. All these errors had to occur, Muentzer asserted, "in order that the deeds of men—of the elect as well as of the damned—be brought to the light of day; for it is in our time that God will separate the wheat from the tares. Then one will see, as it were in the midday sun, who has misled the Church for such a long time." This separation, as far as Muentzer was concerned, was going to take place here and now, but only in the wake of the return of the Holy Spirit. It was precisely this return that Muentzer had proclaimed in his opening salvo about the "new song of praise of the Holy Spirit" who alone could separate the wheat from the tares. But those who possessed it also received this power. He, Thomas

Muentzer, had received it, and when such possession became wide-spread then, of course, "all of this rascality [would] eventually have to come to light." In the meantime, however, "how ripe [had] the rotten apples become!" Even the elect, denied access to the Holy Spirit, had themselves become mellow! No matter, however, for "The time of harvest [had] arrived!" Since he possessed the Holy Spirit and could discern good from evil, God had hired him into His harvest. In preparation, he had honed his scythe, "for [he had] concentrated vehemently on the truth," and everything about him condemned the reprobates.

Because he had desired to act justly, he had come into the land of his beloved Bohemians. Did Muentzer mean by this that because Hus had first begun to spread abroad a purified seed, the Holy Spirit should also first be proclaimed here? All he asked of the Bohemians was that they "should, with all diligence, seek to study the living Word of God directly from God's own mouth." Were they to do so, they could not help but "realize how the whole world [had] been deceived by the deaf priests [who could not hear the living voice of God]. Help me," he pleaded, "for the sake of Christ's blood, to fight against such powerful enemies of the faith." Were they to do so, he would bring these enemies to shame before their very eyes. "For it is in your land that the new Apostolic Church will rise up," he promised; "thereafter everywhere [else]." The "Church of the elect," submerged for so long by the tares, would once again become visible and be separated. He, in turn, "want[ed] to be ready to answer everyone from the pulpit satisfactorily" when questioned by the people. If he could not prove his mastery of these matters through the Spirit under these circumstances, "then [he] desire[d] to be nothing less than a child of temporal and eternal death." He could give no greater pledge.

Those who refused to heed his warning, Muentzer concluded, had already been delivered over to the Turks who were threatening the entire Balkan region. Nevertheless, as he had told Nicholas Hausmann in his letter of 15 June 1521, the end was not yet. Only after the raging lust of the Turk had been satiated would the real Antichrist begin to rule. But in a little while Christ would "turn the kingdom of this world over to the elect in *secula seculorum.*"

Thomas Muentzer said that he did not wish to pray to a dumb God; he would pray only "to a God who speaks." He would proclaim no "God is dead" theology. After all, he had experienced Him in Orlamuende. There the seed Hus and Luther had sown came together with the good soil of his heart prepared by the Holy Spirit proclaimed to him by Tauler. He had felt God write on the parchment of his heart with living fingers, and he had heard Him speak to His Son in the hidden abyss of his soul. No one could take this from him; *it was his personal experience!* And through that experience he began to understand the true meaning of the written Word. With his scythe sharply honed, he was ready for the great work of the forthcoming harvest.[59] But was the world ready for him?

CHAPTER VI

Estrangement from Luther

The sum of our religion is peace and unanimity, but these
can scarcely stand unless we define as little as possible, and in
many things leave each one free to follow his own judgment,
because there is great obscurity in many matters, and man
suffers from this almost congenital disease that he will not
give in once a controversy has started.

—Erasmus

Whether the Prague authorities, fearing a revival of Taborite radicalism, decided to silence Muentzer,[1] the response to his sermons and *Manifesto* appears to have been somewhat less than overwhelming. And so he turned his back, voluntarily or otherwise, on Prague, returning to Germany in December 1521. Stuebner seems not to have accompanied him, having perhaps left earlier, for on 27 December he arrived in Wittenberg with Nicholas Storch and Thomas Drechsel. Where and why they parted company have remained a mystery.

Instead of going to Wittenberg, Muentzer went to Jena, probably to retrieve the papers he had entrusted to Michael Gans prior to his second trip to Prague. Whether he initiated contact with the monks of St. Peter's in Erfurt from here, the monks, in a letter of late December 1521, invited him to share their monastic tranquility.[2] In spite of the fact that Muentzer may have been in Erfurt in early 1522,[3] he must have declined the monks' invitation. Perhaps it was from Luther's friends in Erfurt that Muentzer first heard of the momentous innovations being introduced in Wittenberg in Luther's absence.

This former monk, so recently the focal point of European attention at Worms, had been in hiding at the Wartburg since late April 1521. Just over a month after arriving there, by 1 June, he had completed a lengthy tract on confession.[4] Probably to thank him for past support,[5] but perhaps also to enlist his protection for the future, Luther dedicated the document to Franz von Sickingen, an Imperial knight of the realm. Among other things, the tract was a frontal attack on the papacy and the Catholic Church. As attacks go, it set the agenda for the Church, forcing her on the defensive. At the same time, in it Luther advocated that believers confess their sins "one to another" in the congregation, that baptism, communion, and celibacy—among other things—all be freed from the coercive jurisdiction of the pope. Undoubtedly, these latter demands reflected the thinking behind the reforms beginning to be introduced in Wittenberg prior to Luther's confrontation with the emperor at Worms. For, already in August of the previous year, Luther had declared to Melanchthon that he would never again celebrate a private Mass. On the affirmative side, he favored the "evangelical" communions certain groups were beginning to introduce in the city. By the end of September, Melanchthon was himself participating in such services, and early the next month the Augustinian monks discontinued private Masses. Some even abandoned their vows. That same month a disputation, presided over by Carlstadt, was held to discuss the Mass. All this concerned Frederick the Wise, but even the commission he created to investigate the innovations, recommended changes. Thus, even though the elector continued to advise caution and, if possible, broad consensus throughout Christendom before implementing any reforms, these continued on apace, not infrequently accompanied by social unrest.[6] It was the latter that especially concerned the elector, for he feared it would give outsiders an excuse to intervene in the internal affairs of his lands.[7] Luther's unexpected appearance in the city on 4 December—and his quite apparent satisfaction with the changes already made[8]—did little to assist the elector.

By mid-December Frederick was convinced that the consensus he had hoped for would not be forthcoming. He therefore ordered all innovations halted and the discussion with other universities renewed. This appears to have caused a split in the ranks of the Wittenberg reformers, with Melanchthon and the rest willing to back down, whereas Carlstadt and Gabriel Zwilling continued to move ahead.[9] Despite the elector's prohibition, therefore, on 22 December, Carlstadt proclaimed that he would celebrate the first public evangelical Mass on 1 January in All Saints Church. Notified of Frederick's displeasure, he decided to perform the Mass on Christmas day instead. In the midst of these rising tensions, the Zwickau Prophets came to town on 27 December, proclaiming the imminent inauguration of the kingdom of God on earth, the illegitimacy of infant baptism, and the direct communication of the

Holy Spirit. Luther, Melanchthon wrote the elector, must be recalled to restore order; things were getting out of hand.[10]

Nevertheless, on 6 January the Augustinian monastery officially permitted any monk to leave who so desired. Those electing to remain would do so under more evangelical conditions. No sooner was this said than images and altars in the cloister chapel were destroyed. To restore order, the Imperial government itself intervened on 20 January, confirming the elector's worst fears. It issued a mandate forbidding all innovations and demanded a restoration of Catholic practices.

The Imperial mandate notwithstanding, the Wittenberg Council promulgated the "Wittenberg Ordinance" only four days later, sanctioning all reforms and transferring monies destined for religious endowments to a common chest in order to fund poor relief. Although quickly forced by the elector's representatives to modify its position, the Council nevertheless refused to back down completely. Caught between an increasingly popular movement and mounting pressure from the Church and the Imperial Governing Council to restore the old religious order, Frederick found himself more and more in an untenable position. At the height of his quandry, on 24 February, Luther wrote the elector what can only be construed as a not very sympathetic letter.[11] In it he congratulated his prince, a notorious collector of relics,[12] on his latest acquisition. Had he not long been collecting relics from every corner of the realm? But now God, having finally heard his prayer, had sent him a "real cross with nails, spears and whips." Congratulating him a second time, Luther told his elector not to fear to stretch out his arms to accept the full force of the piercing nails. His reference was obviously to the social unrest in Wittenberg; such things had to be accepted, he said, if one wished to possess the Word. In conclusion, Luther consoled Frederick with the assurance that this was only the beginning.[13]

Frederick replied on 26 February, opening with a not very happy acknowledgment of his latest "relic." Through John Oswald, one of his counselors, he informed Luther that the Imperial Governing Council in Nuremberg had warned him not to allow the innovations to become ingrained. Indeed, Oswald was to inform Luther that the Council required Frederick to oppose the innovations with force, and, if possible, to assign some able preachers to the task. In response, he had written the Bishop of Meissen, indicating that he would not oppose Luther's preaching such sermons. He even asked Oswald to enquire of Luther whether under these circumstances he intended to return to Wittenberg. The entire letter was couched in very oblique language in order, perhaps, not to make it appear that Frederick was asking Luther to return, since his policy with respect to the *causa Lutheri* had been one of feigning ignorance from the beginning.[14] But if Frederick did not want it to appear that he was protecting Luther, the latter advised Melanchthon, in a letter of 13 July 1521, never to ask permission of the electoral court but always to confront it, as he had done, with the *fait accompli!*[15]

Luther had apparently already determined to return to Wittenberg before he received the elector's instructions on 28 February. Not until 5 March did he respond to Frederick, and then just before reentering Wittenberg. He absolved the elector in advance of anything that might befall him, saying that he was returning to Wittenberg under a higher authority. The tone was totally different from the one in his letter of 24 February, and there was a determination to take hold of matters in Wittenberg once again.[16] In his official account, requested by Frederick for presentation to the authorities in Nuremberg, in justification of why he had returned to Wittenberg, Luther appended a revealing postscript. With reference to his letter of 24 February, he wrote:

> I am not afraid of having my last letter to Your Electoral Grace get out into the public. From now on I do not want to undertake anything of which I would be ashamed should others see me doing it during the day. I was not afraid of rebellion; thus far I have taken it quite lightly, thinking it was directed only against the clergy. Now I am worried, however, that it might also surge against the authorities and, like an epidemic, draw in the clergy as well.[17]

The elector's letter of 26 February, transmitted through John Oswald, must have awakened Luther to the seriousness of the consequences arising out of the Wittenberg reforms. He returned on 6 March, and in the Invocavit sermons of 9–16 March, he undid what had been reformed in his absence.

Two weeks later Thomas Muentzer wrote Melanchthon. To this point Luther had been on the attack, setting his own agenda to which the Catholic Church had to respond. Now came the first extended attack from the Left, by one who had his own agenda and who thought that Luther was, like him, a follower of Tauler.

For a man not present in the city, Muentzer appeared well informed about what was transpiring there. Thus far he had heard only words from the reformers in Wittenberg; these were their first deeds, the first fruits of their new theology. And Muentzer wasted no time in passing judgment on what he saw. He praised Melanchthon: "Hail, Instrument of Christ. I embrace your theology with all my heart, for you have rescued many souls of the elect from the snare of the fowler." He commended the Wittenberg reformers for allowing their clergy to take wives, lest they continue to be bound by the "Roman ghosts." But there his praise ended, for he had somewhat against them.

He reproved them, he said, "in that you continue ignorantly to worship a dumb God, that the elect and the reprobate, because of your ignorance, continue to coexist, that you inwardly repudiate the future church in which the fullness of the knowledge of God will be shed abroad. This your error," Muentzer informed them, "derives, of course, most beloved, completely out of your ignorance of the living Word." Here was Muentzer, the "messenger of Christ" as he termed himself in the salutation, addressing "that Christian man, Philip Melanchthon, Professor of Sacred Scripture." Was he trying to do for Luther and Melanchthon what the "pious layman" had done for John Tauler, "Master of Sacred Scripture"? The latter had been told: "Thou art a great clergyman, and in thy sermon thou hast given a good doctrine; but thou thyself dost not live up to it." Then, just as the "pious layman" had convinced Tauler that he needed the Holy Spirit, Muentzer informed Melanchthon that he continued "ignorantly to worship a dumb God," that his error derived completely out of his "ignorance of the living Word," that is, the Holy Spirit.

The parallels are so striking as nearly to preclude their being accidental. Was this Muentzer, Tauler's disciple, chiding the Wittenberg theologians whom he had earlier counted among the "friends of God?" Had their actions now created doubt in his mind? Were they mere scribes after all, as Tauler had been before the advent of the Holy Spirit, men who possessed a rational understanding of the Word but lacked the power to perform it? Yet Muentzer had said at the outset that they "had rescued *many souls of the elect* from the snare of the fowler [italics mine]," and this could only be done by the Holy Spirit. Had the latter, therefore, merely used their theology? Or had the Wittenberg theologians actually possessed Him at first, at least initially? Whatever the case, Muentzer indicated clearly enough that he now regarded them as being "completely . . . ignorant of the inner Word." They did not now possess the Holy Spirit.

Because of this, they continued to "worship a dumb God." Lacking the Holy Spirit, who provided the elect with the ability to differentiate good from evil, the wheat from the tares, they continued to allow the "elect and the reprobate . . . to coexist." Without the Holy Spirit and

the power to distinguish the elect from the reprobate, what else could
they do but "inwardly repudiate the future church in which the fullness
of the knowledge of God will be shed abroad." For in that new Apostolic Church the wheat would be separated from the tares as it had been
in the original Apostolic Church. But this separation and the "fullness
of the knowledge of God" could come only when the Holy Spirit returned, as Tauler and Eusebius had convinced him. The new Apostolic
Church would be established: what had once been done for the Apostolic Church the Holy Spirit was about to do for the new Apostolic
Church. The Wittenberg theologians should know this.

Having said this, Muentzer gave Melanchthon a healthy dose of
Luther's own Leipzig medicine. "Search the Scriptures," he charged
him, for these very Scriptures that Hus and Luther had liberated "from
under a bench" were now "pressing in upon the world." This had been
foretold in Matthew 24 as a sign of the end of the age, as he had already
informed Nicholas Hausmann. And that Word clearly stated that "man
does not live by bread alone, but by every word that proceeds from the
mouth of God." "From the mouth of God and not out of books are we
to begin," Muentzer chided his correspondent, drawing what for him
was the obvious conclusion from the above passage. He had told the
Bohemians as much in his *Prague Manifesto;* did he have to tell Luther's
partner as well? Had not Luther first directed his attention to Tauler
and *Eine Deutsche Theologie?* Had he not himself repeatedly pointed to
the importance of Tauler's *experience* of the Spirit? And yet Melanchthon did not know that "That which one draws out of books is a
testimony of the true words," not the life-transforming power itself.
Unless that Word was in fact spoken nakedly in the heart, "the word of
man is changed into that of a damned scribe, which, according to Jeremiah 23, is stolen from the holy oracles." Had Luther and Melanchthon, too, merely "stolen" their theology?

In any case, Muentzer, like the "pious layman," also wanted the
Wittenberg theologians to come to an *experience* of the Holy Spirit. He
therefore encouraged them to be "eagerly desirous to become prophetic,
otherwise," he warned them, their "theology [was] not worth a penny."
They should "consider how near God is, rather than how far away."
For God was always more eager to speak than man to listen. Then he
came to what might be hindering them from this complete experience.
"We are full of desires," Muentzer confessed; "this obstructs the finger
of the living God so that He is not able to open up your slate." In other
words, the Wittenberg theologians had not yet fully weeded the garden

of their souls for the advent of the Holy Spirit. And this became clearly visible in their treatment of marriage among the clergy.

"Through your persuasive support of marriage," Muentzer informed Melanchthon, "you nearly force it upon people; under these circumstances it is little else than Satan's brothel, no less injurious to the Church than the most accursed anointed priesthood." Why should this be so? Because they were allowing their passionate desires to impede their sanctification. "How," he enquired, "can the Spirit be poured out on top of your flesh and have the living eloquence of God's power with such a negative attitude? No command," he asserted, "is more binding upon the Christian than our sanctification." The holy invincible Christian faith he had sought from the very beginning was now being imperilled by the new attitude in Wittenberg toward marriage. Not only the faith but also the *futura ecclesia* itself depended upon this sanctification. And it was this Church Muentzer was preeminently concerned with.

Since this was a matter of considerable importance, Muentzer proceeded to instruct the Wittenbergers in the manner marriage was to be conducted in the new Apostolic Church. Sanctification, he observed, "first of all empties our soul according to the will of God, until the soul is no longer able to accept, in any form, the lower passions as its possessor." Because the soul must be freed from these "lower passions," we are to "have wives as though we had them not." Indulging sexual passion at will—even if confined to the marriage bed—hindered the Holy Spirit. Therefore, they were to "Pay what you owe, not as the heathen do, but as those who know that God speaks to you, commands you, admonishes, in order that you know with certainty when you are to pay that which you owe [that is, have sexual intercourse] in order to produce an elect child, so that the fear of God and the spirit of wisdom keep you from those brute passions and you be not devoured by them."

To produce such elect children was important to Muentzer in light of the *futura ecclesia* that would consist only of the elect after the reprobate had been removed from it in the time of harvest. In his *Prague Manifesto* he had spoken of "two kinds of people" with reference to Galatians 4:21–31. There St. Paul had observed "that Abraham had two sons, the one by a bondmaid, the other by a free woman. But he who was of the bond woman" St. Paul had asserted, "was born after the flesh; but he of the free woman was by promise." This was an allegory of the two kinds of covenants, he had continued, with the bond woman having "many more children than she which hath an husband." Then as now, those born of the flesh persecuted those born of the Spirit. Muentzer had used this passage to prove that these two kinds of people had always existed. Now, however, in the time of harvest, the reprobates were to be separated from the elect so that the new Apostolic Church could come into existence. Once established, this *futura ecclesia* should be concerned to promote only elect children, and this could apparently be done only when sexual intercourse was prompted by the Holy Spirit.

After informing Melanchthon that the "vial of the third angel" had already been poured into the sea and that the end times were therefore near, Muentzer returned to the subject of election. "Some," he stated, "are elect, but their minds cannot yet be opened for the above reasons." That is, they had not yet freed their souls from these "lower passions." "As a consequence," he continued, "they still have many works in common with the reprobates, except for the fear of God, which separates them from the others." While two men, he observed, could sleep in the same bed, the work of only one was accepted by God. "Such a work," he pronounced, "surely I discover in you, at the same time however, there are contentions among you concerning the abrogation of the Mass." They belonged to the elect but were not yet conscious of the Holy Spirit, ignorantly still serving a "dumb God." He extolled and commended them that there were "some [among you] who detest the abomination of the papal sacrifice," for, he continued, this opposition was "brought about by the Holy Spirit." And, whereas he had earlier spoken of the *futura ecclesia,* he now told Malanchthon that they were "still involved in . . . error in so far as they do not follow the Apostolic practice as the norm to be imitated." The new Apostolic Church of the *Prague Manifesto* was therefore to be regarded as one and the same with the *futura ecclesia,* for the practices of the Apostolic Church were also to be normative for the Church of the immediate future.

Muentzer followed this up with another implied criticism and some more advice. Had he not regarded Hus and Luther as once again sowing a purified seed? He now appeared to confirm this, saying: "For whoever sows the seed in accordance with God's commands, ought to be ready to harvest." Luther had sown the seed; was he not harvesting? How was one to harvest? Muentzer gave his answer:

> They [the Wittenberg theologians] ought to examine those who have heard the sermon, as long as they have come under the Word, and whoever is able to show some progress in his understanding [some fruit of his understanding]

shall be made known to the congregation and given access to the communion table. For in truth they possess the Holy Spirit, they have been granted the power to recognize the testimonies of God, not the dead ones appropriated out of books, but the promises of the living God.

Had he already been doing this in his Zwickau conventicles? Was this why he had lauded Storch from the pulpit? Whatever the case, improvement in life, in sanctification, was the sign that the Holy Spirit was at work in the elect. Only such should be allowed access to the communion table.

"Our dear Martin," however, as he had made only too apparent in his Invocavit sermons, continued to advocate patience in Wittenberg with respect to those who were not yet prepared to go along with the changes.[18] This meant, of course, that the wheat and the tares would not be separated. To this Muentzer was forced to object. The time for patience and tolerance had ended. Indeed, he informed Melanchthon, "Our dear Martin acts ignorantly, that he does not wish to offend the *parvuli* [the immature], for these *parvuli* have already been damned as 100 year old boys." In other words, those members of the community Luther considered immature Muentzer took to be the reprobates God had already condemned long ago. They had been "born of the bond woman, after the flesh" and would never become elect in any case. Therefore Muentzer understood "not at all why you still think that you have to wait; Christendom truly has no more time to lose. Beloved brethren," he encouraged Melanchthon and others, "multiply, it is time. Wait no longer, summer is at the door." This was not the time to "make friends with the reprobates, for they are the ones who hinder the Word from becoming effective with great power. Do not [even] toady to your princes," Muentzer advised, "otherwise your work will be subverted."

Muentzer's concluding words substantiate the fact that he was primarily concerned for this Church. "If you refuse to cleanse the Church," he informed Melanchthon, "you show your ignorance of the Scriptures and [do not] desire to possess the Holy Spirit." Cleansing the Church of the reprobates was the only way to make sure that the Holy Spirit would return to it. And this cleansing had to take place on a personal level through the sanctification of the individual believer as well as on the corporate level by means of expelling the tares from the Church.[19] Only then would the Holy Spirit return and the *futura ecclesia* be established "in which the fullness of the knowledge of God will be shed abroad." A *purgatio* had to take place. And he commended the Wittenbergers for rejecting the papal version of purgatory, but to "deny that a cleansing is necessary [altogether was] an abomination." Such a cleansing had to take place, and the seven stages of perfection passed through. "Beware!" he warned them, this was a deadly serious business. Should they wish it, he would "open and strengthen the Word of God" in all his writings to them so that they too could grasp the truths he had arrived at. "Be not opposed," he advised them; he had no choice but to do what he was doing. Muentzer was here doing to Luther and Melanchthon what he had just done to Hus: he was adding the Holy Spirit to the Word Luther had liberated. He was indeed aspiring to something higher than Luther had aspired to.

He called the Wittenberg theologians "tender scribes." We have seen him use similar terms in his *Prague Manifesto*. The Wittenberg theologians were still men who understood the Word merely through their reason. There were, nevertheless, signs that the Holy Spirit was at work among them. If only they would go all the way; if only they would prepare their souls completely for the advent of the Holy Spirit; if only they would pursue the life of sanctification and cleanse the Church of the reprobates; if only. . . . They were so close, so "tender," that it would not take much. Nonetheless, they were still ignorant of the "living Word." That ignorance must be done away with, and he, Thomas Muentzer, was only too willing to enlighten them.[20]

This is most decidedly not the letter of an erstwhile disciple of Luther beginning to distance himself from his former mentor. Rather, it is the statement of a man assessing the progress of the reform movement in Wittenberg *from his own perspective* and pronouncing his judgment upon it. It is true, he did feel drawn to the Wittenberg theology, but that was because he at first believed Luther to be a follower of Tauler and a fellow "friend of God." Now that he had had the opportunity to see how the Wittenberg theology was taking shape in the visible reform of the Church, however, he was beginning to have doubts. They had not gone all the way; they were still ignorant of the living Word; they still continued to pray to a "dumb God"; though tender, they were still scribes!

It is not known from where Muentzer wrote the letter to Melanchthon. It may have been from Erfurt, it may have been from elsewhere. Not until 14 July 1522 do we have another letter from him that has a known point of origin. On that date he was in Nordhausen where he stayed but briefly.[21] Next we find him in Halle, possibly at the Church of St. George. By mid-March 1523 he had been forced to leave from there as well.[22] Not until April did he settle for a longer period of time. Then it was in Allstedt.

During this period of over a year, the opposition to Muentzer grew, as his letters of the time indicate. The whole world, he said in the first of these, "thinks that I intend to reject all that which has found universal approbation, and they hold me to be a mad man." He dismissed this reaction to him as the "judgment of the impious" which would not deter him from his God-appointed task. "For," he said, "my mouth will continue to speak the truth hated by the childish, and my lips to curse the enemies of the cross." Once more he averred that he breathed "nothing but the eternal will of God, with which *all the friends of God* must be filled in all the wisdom and knowledge of the Spirit" [italics mine]. This was why the world hated him so. Anyone who had come to the faith, "that is to the belief that he was an elect before the foundation of the world, and has accepted in faith as believable the words of the Lord directed to this end, he cannot be of this world. Instead the world, with malicious hatred, takes him to be a person living on the moon." But this was how it had to be when the Holy Spirit separated a person from the world.[23]

In another letter he wrote—clearly with reference to the reforms being implemented in Wittenberg—that "Our scribes and Pharisees [was there no longer any doubt in his mind?] ought to have gone further in the direction of Jael who killed Sisera, Judges 4, and compared this with the passage in Isaiah 66 and should have sucked and replenished from the riches of his consolation, not ours." Whereas Paul had fed milk to those who were still unable to understand, the Wittenbergers kept them bound in a perpetual state of childishness. A separation had to take place.[24]

In a third letter Muentzer again emphasized that his primary concern was for the Church. Rejecting as a lie the claims of people that he had departed from Christ's teachings, he asserted he was "only and completely concerned to bring the Church, established by Jesus of Nazareth through the predetermination of God, to be correctly understood in its true character by all the impious imposters." It did not matter that some complained that men's minds were made uncertain and confused in the process; "much more dangerous times will face the godless in the near future," he observed obviously in connection with the impending time of harvest. These "puffed up people" who complained "prided themselves on the basis of their own questionable [rational?] conclusions, as though they had been especially singled out by God's grace." Yet they knew as little about the latter as they did of the Milky Way. The elect, on the contrary, read the signs of the times "from the living words, which are infallibly written in [their] heart[s]." This would not change even if God were to extend, as He had in the days of Jonah, some more time to the world. And the elect would continue "to be patient and believe on the words which God has written in their hearts. Believe me," Muentzer concluded, "I have not lied in the least; the divine judgment will truly bring all things to light."

The person to whom these words were addressed must have come from the Lutheran camp, for Muentzer concluded his letter with a reference to the changes made in the Mass, and then retracted, in Wittenberg. He warned him to "keep his tongue in check so that you do not also become a party to that malicious deceit," which was so current among them at the moment. He, Thomas Muentzer, for his part had already "fled the scribes, Pharisees and hypocrites, Matthew 23, [because] their house is desolate, they do not possess the Holy Spirit." He seemed convinced of this because "They seek that which is theirs, not that which is Jesus Christ's."[25] While they had at first still spoken "that one must abrogate the Mass," they were already desirous "to retract that since all the people clamor: right on, right on!" Therefore, whether they were preaching a "good doctrine," they were not living up to it. That was a sure sign that they had remained scribes and Pharisees. They had not been enabled to live a holy invincible Christian life as the result of the transforming power of the Holy Spirit. The Wittenbergers had shown their true colors.[26]

While Muentzer was thus passing judgment on the Wittenberg reforms, the Holy Spirit was, he said, using these trials and tribulations to cleanse and prepare him for the work that lay ahead. He asserted as much to a follower in Halle in a letter of 19 March 1523,[27] but failed to inform us whether God had completed this work in him by the time he was appointed *parochus* in Allstedt. Probably not, for whereas he wrote the above letter on 19 March, by 5 April he was already preaching at the Church of St. John in Allstedt.[28] It was from here on 9 July 1523, that he wrote to Luther for the last time, a conciliatory and respectful letter. Coming as it did a year and some few months after his letter to Melanchthon, this is astonishing. Had something happened to change his mind about the Wittenberg theologians?[29]

The answer to the above question would appear to lie in the first part of Muentzer's letter where he refers to Luther's "egregio libro de facienda confessione."[30] Rather than being a reference to "Ein Sermon

von der Beicht usw., Panzer Nr. 1518, Weller Nr. 2279,"[31] as Guenther
Franz would have it, this can only be a reference to Luther's "Von der
Beicht, ob die der Bapst macht habe zu gepieten,"[32] the tract that Luther
wrote at the Wartburg while still smarting from all the villainy he had
experienced at the hands of ecclesiastical and political authorities, culminating in the Diet of Worms in April 1521.

Not published until late September 1521, the treatise begins with a
reference to the book of Joshua, a reference in which the Catholic
Church is compared to the people of Canaan who were destroyed by the
Israelites at a time they deemed "themselves so firmly seated in their
saddles that no one is able to dislodge them. [So much is this the case]
that I fear that their hardness of heart, their lack of humility, and their
refusal to seek peace, come from God himself in order that, in the end,
they will be destroyed without mercy."[33] Meanwhile, they placed all the
blame upon him, Martin Luther, knowing full well how they had "despised the poor people to this point in their pride." Luther, however,
had often extended the hand of peace to them, had run hither and yon
to answer for his theology, to debate. He had appeared before two
Imperial Diets. But nothing had helped; nowhere had he received justice. On the contrary, he had encountered only malice and coercion. His
life had been threatened lest he recant. "Well then," he remarked,
"when the hour will come when they too will call in vain for peace, I
hope they will recall what they have now deserved." And if they still
refused to change, another would come after Luther who would "teach
them with deeds," not merely with words and letters.[34]

Here, certainly, was language Muentzer understood. These papal
reprobates whose hearts God had hardened were the very scribes and
Pharisees he himself sought to excise from the Church. Had he been
wrong about Luther's Invocavit sermons? Had his judgments been
overly hasty? But there was more, indeed much, much more!

The first point Luther wished to make in the treatise proper was one
Muentzer had been preoccupied with ever since he had put Tauler and
Eusebius together: the intrusion of human teachings into the Church by
"shepherds of the flock" who did not possess the Holy Spirit. Although
Luther did not go as far as Muentzer already had, he did say that in
virtually every verse of Psalm 119 two points were made: first, "that
God wishes to lead, teach, direct and keep us in His way, commands
and laws"; and, second, "that He wishes to guard us against man-made
teachings and laws."[35] Indeed, Christ had himself warned against "false
prophets" in Matthew 7 and the "sour dough" of the Pharisees in

Matthew 16, that was, their "human teaching, which is mere hypocrisy and does not touch the foundation."[36]

Because these man-made laws had spread so widely that they prevailed everywhere, displacing the Scriptures, it had become necessary "to storm against such long-accustomed and deeply-rooted errors with strongly opposing and powerfully dividing passages of Scripture in the hope of exposing their [i.e., papal] unjust intentions and unfair tyranny, and topling them from power so that once again we may teach and learn to avoid, as the poison and death of the devil—whether it be established by pope or bishop, angel or devil—that which God has not commanded."[37]

Nothing was to be added to God's Word. Luther quoted Deuteronomy 4:2,[38] to this effect and reinforced it with Hebrews 2:1–2.[39] He quoted from Isaiah 1 where the writer had chided the people "Your wine is mixed with water, and your silver has turned to tarnish." This could only mean, Luther asserted, that human teachings had been added to God's Word, that tarnish was being sold in place of silver. "Such a thieving crook is the pope," he concluded. And then he observed that Jeremiah had "devoted a whole chapter to such false prophets." The chapter, of course, was 23, one that Muentzer had used to good effect in his *Prague Manifesto*.

Among other things, Luther remarked, Jeremiah had said there that the people were not to "harken unto the words of the prophets," for they "speak a vision of their own heart, and not out of the mouth of the Lord." These prophets, Jeremiah had continued, had not been sent by God, but like the papal church, had preached anyway: not the Word from out of the mouth of God, but human additions. Luther used these passages to argue that "God's Word is too sensitive to suffer any additions; it desires to stand alone, or not at all."

But where was this Word of God to be found? Luther continued:

> "The prophet that hath a dream, let him tell a dream; and he that hath my word, let him speak my word faithfully. What is chaff to the wheat? saith the Lord. Is not my word like a fire? saith the Lord; and like a hammer that breaketh the rock in pieces?" Behold, human teaching is straw, God's Word is fire, how nicely they fit together, and whoever possesses God's Word is to preach it rightly, not transform it into human wisdom. And whoever has a dream, that is a revelation in his sleep, he should stick by that and not make something else out of it. For in Numbers 12 God avows that He reveals His Word in three ways: in dreams, visions and openly in the [human] spirit.[40]

Was this not vintage Muentzer? All one had to do was to read the words, "out of the mouth of God" from Muentzer's Taulerian perspective, and everything else fell into place. Although Luther, one would think, intended it to be read as "the written Word," nowhere did he say so explicitly. What is more, he cited Numbers 12 as confirming that God spoke "in dreams, visions and openly in the spirit." Whatever Luther may have intended, Muentzer must obviously have read this as confirmation for his own position. And Luther unwittingly gave him every excuse for doing so.

In pursuit of this separation of human teaching from the Word which had come from out of the very mouth of God, Luther turned to the New Testament. There, after drawing the reader's attention to Matthew 15:7–3 and Romans 16:17–18, he came to 2 Peter 2:1–2, a passage Muentzer himself used later on.[41] There Peter had said: "But there were false prophets also among the people, even as there shall be false teachers among you, who privily shall bring in damnable heresies. . . . And many shall follow their pernicious ways." Then, turning to passages from Proverbs,[42] where Solomon had warned against the adulteress, Luther observed: "All this was said with reference to the end times, when the devil's church with its man-made laws will deceive the true church of God."[43] Luther returned to this theme of the adulteress church of the end times a few paragraphs later. Insisting, once again, that Solomon, like Christ, had spoken exclusively in parables and similitudes, he continued:

> He [Solomon], indeed, saw that, on the eve of the world's end when the light of the faith had grown dim and the foolish, mad people had all been led astray to trust in external ceremonies and the appearance of holiness, that such people were ripe for this kind of knavery—called human teaching and wisdom—which is so enamored with itself and promises so much, making the path to salvation easy, as is apparent in the church of the pope and to which all these words fit, though to gloss them all here would take too long.[44]

This pope, then, with his church and its man-made laws must be the representative of "Lucifer in hell, who is the father of lies and who has raised up his apostles in Rome in order to deceive and destroy the whole world under the name of Christ, as is now happening."[45] Surely it was for this reason that the proverb had arisen that where God builds a church, the devil builds his chapel next to it. Thus the devil had, throughout the Old Testament, erected altars and other places of worship beside the temple and had raised up false prophets to service them. And in the New Testament, next to the holy Gospel, he had raised up the pope and his sectarian teachings until he alone preached everywhere and the "Gospel lay under the bench."[46] Here, surely, were the reprobates Muentzer had himself so often addressed. And it was obvious from Luther's treatise that it was high time that they be separated from the true Church. For even though he did not speak in terms of the time of harvest, Luther did speak of the church in the end times.

Lucifer's representatives, therefore, had taken over the Church. Yet they asserted that all their teachings—and especially those of the Church councils—had been guided by none other than the Holy Spirit. Nonetheless, Luther charged

> they often contradict one another, stating one thing now and another later, until they became such a confused business that they finally no longer even bothered with Scripture, deciding all things on the basis of their reason. And they did this out of their wicked presumption that the Holy Spirit was with them and would not permit them to err. That being the case, they could do whatever they wished in the councils without fear, without devotion, without understanding, even to the extent of disregarding the faith.

Out of what spirit all this was really done, Luther concluded, "anyone may easily grasp."[47] Indeed, "this scandalous, damned delusion that one was to heed the councils because they had the Holy Ghost—when hardly one out of twenty used the Scriptures and demonstrated the Spirit—was Christendom's greatest misfortune."[48] Since the papists had seen that the first councils had been filled with the Spirit and their decisions accepted as a consequence, they had arrogated the same honor to themselves. That they were thousands of miles removed from the lifestyle and spirit of those early holy council Fathers bothered them not at all. And so they preached their own lies under the semblance of God's truth, and that in His name, paying heed neither to the Gospel nor to the Holy Spirit.[49]

Finally, Luther arrived at confession. This sacrament he now set into the context of the congregation where Christians were to confess their sins "one to another" and to God. The pope, he said, did not like this. Not only were they to confess their sins one to another, they were to forgive one another's sins. By implication at least, Luther appeared to be positing a Church of believers, a Church of wheat, in opposition to the perverted church of the false prophets.[50] The ban, he argued, was to be exercised in a similar fashion, with the sinner being warned at first secretly, then in the presence of several witnesses, and only finally "openly before all the people of the congregation."[51]

Having asserted that the papal church with its false councils had not been led by the Holy Spirit, and that confession, absolution and the ban should be practiced by and in the congregation, Luther came to address the issue of the power of the keys. Citing John 20:22–23, he observed:

> Before Christ gave the command to forgive sins and to bind, He breathed on them [the disciples] and said: "Receive ye the Holy Ghost: Whosoever sins ye remit, they are remitted unto them." Here it is determined that no one can forgive sins unless he possesses the Holy Spirit, for the words are clear and do not lie. It does no good to blubber that this is an article of John Hus or Wycliffe condemned at Constance. It will not do to damn; an answer must be given.[52]

But who had the Holy Spirit, and how could one be certain of it? Luther answered: There was no doubt, he said,

> that no one could loose from or bind sin except he who possessed the Holy Spirit so surely that both you and I would know it, and these present words of Christ convince [us] that it is *none other than the Christian Church, that is, the congregation of all those who believe in Christ:*[53] it alone has the keys, this you must never doubt, and whoever arrogates these keys to himself is a truly cunning *sacrilegus,* church robber, be he pope or anyone else [italics mine].[54]

Because of this, Luther continued, the articles of faith were arranged in such an order that the one concerning forgiveness of sins came after the article concerning "one holy Christian Church" and before the one "I believe in the Holy Ghost" in order that we should understand that there could be no holy Church without the Holy Spirit, and no forgiveness of sins without a holy Church.[55]

To confess one's sins and partake of the sacrament reluctantly or under duress, Luther continued, was worse than committing some grievous public sin. He implied that voluntary compliance out of a grateful heart was the only correct motivation; accordingly

> the pope and his followers should cease and desist from such practices, and instead begin preaching, confronting the people with the danger of, and damage caused by, sin, and God's judgment upon it. . . . Therefore confession ought to remain free, with its good and the damage caused by sin being preached. Whoever came [under these circumstances] would come, those who would not should stay away. In the same manner I should like to praise and counsel virginity and chastity. But I should like them to be free, to force no one away from the married state. Likewise I would preach faith and baptism, force no one to them, but accept all those who freely choose to come. In the same manner I would like to preach the grace of the sacrament of the altar, but leave it free, force no one to it. Similarly praise confession as highly as possible . . . but force no one. Behold, these would truly be papal,

episcopal, spiritual offices. *That is how the apostles and the old fathers did it* [italics mine].[56]

Was Luther suggesting a "free" Church here, a "believer's" Church, in contrast and in opposition to the "Lucifer-papal" Church run by force? He did say that this was "how the Apostles and the old Fathers" had done it. Did he mean to imply by this that, at least in this instance, the apostolic model was normative, as Muentzer had argued in his March 1522 letter to Melanchthon? Or was it merely the logic of Luther's opposition to the universal papal Church that led him to proclaim a "free," a "believer's" Church? Luther came back to these "apostolic ordinances" once more in his discussion of the exclusion from the Church of those who refused to be corrected. There he remarked:

> One must therefore proceed as follows: In every parish or congregation where someone sins openly, is chastised by his brother, then corrected in an orderly fashion in the presence of several witnesses, and lastly before the pastor and the entire congregation openly in the church during communion in accordance with the Gospel, is accused and convicted, if he repents the congregation is to intercede on his behalf with one accord as the Lord here teaches and promises to answer. Should he refuse, he is to be put out of the congregation and no one is to have anything to do with him: that is what the Lord calls "being bound," and that is also the right way to practice the ban. This custom was practiced by the apostles for a long time, thereafter by the bishops, until the abomination in Rome raised its head and all this together with the entire Gospel was trampled under foot.[57]

Muentzer probably read this treatise shortly before he wrote to Luther in early July 1523. One can well imagine his astonishment, especially after reading the last section dealing with the exclusion of the incorrigibly wicked from the "congregation of believers," that Luther should have commended Egranus to him, that he should have expected them to work in harmony. It is in this context that he wrote Luther.

Having arrived at the conclusion that it was useless for him "to aspire to your [Luther's] love," since the latter had been misinformed about him by vicious gossip, Muentzer nevertheless imputed only noble motives to Luther, saying he knew Luther had always, and only, been interested in the common good. Then he came to what for him was the central issue: "Yet to my utter amazement," he said, "you commended this pestilential Egranus to me in your letters." Muentzer, apparently, had never been able to understand this, especially since "this crow [Egranus], whose stinking carcass, though disguised in sumptuous plumage, has never desired [God's] secret righteousness and is actually in the

throes of death." Clearly, Muentzer saw Egranus as much of a reprobate as Luther did the papal Church. And these reprobates, as he had
informed Melanchthon, would never change. Had not Luther said as
much in the above treatise? Had he not said that God had hardened
their hearts, that those who refused to be corrected by the "congregation of believers" should be "put out of the congregation and no one is
to have anything to do with them"? Had he not said that another would
come after him who would deal in deed with these reprobates rather
than mere words, as he had done? Why, then, should Luther have
commended to Muentzer the reprobate Egranus, whose church was in
the throes of death in this time of harvest? "You yourself," he continued, "completely and wittily described his [Egranus's or the reprobates']
lustful lower animal parts in a colorful manner *in your excellent book
concerning how to conduct confession* where such [human] wisdom of
the reprobates is commended to the Church by the Evil One. Therefore
the impious are of no use [to the Church] whatever" [italics mine].
Luther had wanted that man, so lusting for glory, "to unite with me so
that enemies could not rise against you; I, on the other hand, turned
myself, for the glory of God, against him like an immovable wall. I
contradicted him with an upright mind: 'Him that hath an high look
and proud heart will not I suffer.' "

This first part of Muentzer's letter, then, which scholars have ignored, is really the key to the entire missive and can be explained *only* in
the light of Muentzer's reading of Luther's "Von der Beicht." If Luther
was so concerned, as he manifestly appeared to be in opposition to the
papal reprobates, to exclude the wicked from the Church, why had he
commended the reprobate Egranus to Muentzer? Furthermore, why had
he recommended patience in his Invocavit sermons, a patience which
had elicited from Muentzer the words: "Our dear Martin acts ignorantly, that he does not wish to offend the *parvuli,* for these *parvuli* have
already been damned as 100 year old boys"? In that same letter
Muentzer had told Melanchthon that there was "no more time to lose."
This was not the time to "make friends with the reprobates for they are
the ones who hinder the Word from becoming effective with great
power." Had not Luther said as much—and more—with respect to the
papal reprobates?

From Egranus and the reprobates, Muentzer turned to the turmoil in
Zwickau. He deemed it necessary to clear himself of all blame. Everyone, he said, "except some blind officials, knew that I was falsely accused of inciting the Zwickau riot." And then comes the famous passage

nearly all scholars have taken as one of Muentzer's less imaginative excuses. He said: "I was actually taking a bath at the time [the riots broke out], expecting no such thing."[58] Indeed, he continued, had he not objected, "the whole council would have been killed the next day." Nor was he unwilling to render an account of his involvement to all.

From the riot, Muentzer turned to revelations and the role of the Holy Spirit. In light of Luther's treatise, this can no longer be regarded "as the critical issue between himself and Luther."[59] Had Muentzer seen it as such, he would probably not have written in such a conciliatory tone. For had not Luther himself in that treatise legitimized dreams, visions, and revelations with his reference to Numbers 12? Beginning with Jeremiah 23:28–29, Luther had commented: "And whoever has a dream, that is a revelation in his sleep, he should stick by that and not make something else out of it. For in Numbers 12 God avows that He reveals His Word in three ways: in dreams, in visions and openly in the spirit." Therefore, rather than trying to justify these to Luther, *Muentzer appears to be trying to assure Luther that he was in fact using them correctly!* He may have felt that Luther had been misinformed about him in this respect, both by his enemies and by the Zwickau Prophets. And so he assured Luther that he had "never said a word about these to the uninitiated, but clearly refer[red] them all here to my judgment."

He would come back to this subject in a moment; first, however, he intended to set these matters in their proper context. We must, Muentzer asserted,

> recognize the will of God, with which we are to be filled through Christ with wisdom, spiritual insight and infallible understanding concerning God, in all things (as the Apostle says in Colossians [1:9]), and must live in such a manner that we are found to be taught from the mouth of the living God [a Jeremiah passage Luther had himself repeatedly emphasized], in order that we may know with all certainty, that the teachings of Christ have not been concocted by man, but have been truly given to us by the living God in His richness. Indeed, Christ Himself wishes that we should be able to judge concerning His doctrine.[60]

It was not so much the revelations Muentzer was concerned with at this point; it was the will of God and the holy invincible Christian faith created by the experience of the Holy Spirit which enabled man to fulfill that will. It was the living "in such a manner that we are found to be taught by the living God" that was of prime importance, the critical point in his assessment of the Wittenberg reforms. God, he continued in his letter to Luther, "removed that [in us?] which is opposed to Him, for otherwise our beloved anointing (which teaches [us] all things) would be contaminated."[61] Had not John 7:17 said: "If any man will do His will, he shall know the doctrine, whether it be of God, or whether I speak of myself?" This was the reason he had stressed sanctification so strongly in his letter to Melancthon. The power to do God's will came from the transformation worked in the elect by the advent of the Holy Spirit. Only then could true knowledge of doctrine follow; only then could "one judge concerning His doctrine"; only then could one be sure that God spoke "in the Bible and not also in the Koran." Thus, he continued:

> No mortal understands Christ and His teachings fully as truth without doubt, unless his will is conformed to the cross, unless he has suffered the waves and billows of great waters which overwhelm the spirit of the elect completely, totally submerging them in the storm so that they slip and fall backwards calling upon the Master until one's throat is raw, so that a man hopes in hope against hope and seeks the one will of God in the day of visitation after long expectation.[62]

What Muentzer was saying in somewhat convoluted mystical-biblical language is simply this: unless one has experienced a conversion like the one imputed to Tauler in the *Historia* and effected by the Holy Spirit, and as a consequence has "his will conformed to the cross," he will never be able to have any assurance of salvation, any discretionary power to separate God's Word from the word of man, or to "understand Christ and His teachings fully." Once such a transformation has taken place, however, a man possesses the Word of God nakedly within him and can, therefore, judge all things.[63] Then "are his feet marvellously stayed upon a rock and the Lord appears wonderfully from afar, and then he receives credible testimonies from the Lord." Anyone, Muentzer continued, who did not "continually and completely hope for the Lord in humility" would not be able to be in complete agreement with the whole Scriptures. Nor was a man, who gloried in Christ, to be believed unless he had the Holy Spirit. For, according to Romans 8, His Spirit bears witness with our spirit that we are the sons of God.

Muentzer then emphasizes again that a man cannot become a son of God "from above unless he is willing to suffer and be led, every day, like a sheep to the slaughter." Once God has granted assurance, however, "no creature is able to separate him from the living God and the surest testimony of Scripture." Then, trusting completely in that testimony, "divine revelation distinguishes the work of God from the spirit of the

Evil One." Only now does Muentzer return to revelations, only after he had made certain that the whole mystical process of salvation has been understood—that is, that the Holy Spirit has been appropriated and the distinction between "true" revelations and those "emanating from the spirit of the Evil One" can be distinguished. Having established this, he observes that:

> these most upright and personal (though difficult to understand) visions are to be nourished and viewed as a profound mystery from out of the mouth of God, according to 1. Corinthians 2, Isaiah 8: "People should seek a vision from God for themselves, for the living and the dead to the law as much as to the evidence [testimony], etc." He who will despise this, "cursed is their king and their God," etc.[64]

Because only the converted, the "spirit-filled" man, the "friend of God," could distinguish true from false revelations, Muentzer had earlier told Luther that he had never "said a word about these to the uninitiated" and had referred all such phenomena "here to my judgment." Since he possessed the Holy Spirit, he obviously had the power to judge such matters.

"My very dear Patron," Muentzer continued, "you know the name and condition of Thomas." By that he probably meant to say: you know me better than that. "I do not receive ecstasies and visions unless God compels me," he assured Luther; "those that are received I trust only if I see them as the work of God in me. Nor have I invented anything so important, which is a grace given to the perfect man according to the measure of the gift of Christ. Who is worthy of this?" He was not trying to justify visions; he was attempting to persuade Luther—who had himself authenticated them as a means by which God spoke with man— that he was using them properly, indeed scripturally. No one, he assured Luther, "with the exception of those who possess the testimony of Scripture [those who can demonstrate that their revelations conform to those of Scripture], will find support in my presence."[65] Nor would he ignore the warnings in the books of Moses about "praising dreams to the unwise," and that many "are surely led into error through dreams." St. Paul, he asserted, considered "this to be a lesser, rather than a greater, cause of error." Then, citing Micah 3:6, Muentzer observed that those who did not possess "wisdom and the testimony of God, have not deserved to have God visit them at night."[66] Not only was he trying to convince Luther that he was using these revelations in accordance with the teachings of Scripture, Muentzer was also willing to be corrected by Luther's superior testimony in these matters if the latter considered him to be in error. He wished this so that they might "walk the one way in love"! And why not? Luther's "Von der Beicht" had obviously shown Muentzer that he had been hasty in his condemnation of the Wittenberg reforms, that he and Luther were not so far removed from one another in their theological positions, and that Luther was indeed still the "specimen et lucerna amicorum dei."

There remained the problem of the Zwickau Prophets, however. "But you object . . ." Muentzer had Luther say: "what about Marcus and Nicholas?" And Muentzer answered the question he had himself put into Luther's mouth with: "What they are they themselves will see, Galatians 2. I tremble in divine judgments. What they may have told you or communicated to you, I ignore." What can this mean? The reference has been taken by Guenther Franz and others as referring exclusively to Galatians 2:6, and that may be a partial answer, as we also asserted in an earlier chapter. But the reference may in fact have other implications as well.

The Galatians passage deals with Paul's journey to Jerusalem with Barnabas and Titus. Muentzer may well have seen a parallel between Paul's journey and his own to Prague with Marcus Stuebner. Paul says that he made the journey in response to a revelation; did Muentzer do the same, or at least think he did? And did Muentzer's reference: "What they are they themselves will see, Galatians 2," really refer to verse 4? He did not here speak of what the Zwickau Prophets had contributed to his teaching—that was not really the issue at this point. The issue, as he saw it, was "what they are." Apparently, they did not yet wish to recognize what they really were, but, he argued, they themselves would soon see this. What then were they? Perhaps verse 4 gives us the answer. There Paul says: "This matter [i.e., circumcision of the Gentiles] arose, because *some false brothers had infiltrated our ranks* to spy on the freedom we have in Christ Jesus and make us slaves" [italics mine]. Did Muentzer intend to imply to Luther that the Zwickau Prophets were "false brothers?" Had he come to see them as such, as Tauler had come to see the heresy of the Free Spirit? Muentzer followed up the reference to Galatians 2 with the statement: "I tremble in divine judgments." Such a statement, surely, is too strong to apply to verse 6 where St. Paul says: "these men added nothing to my message." If we recall how seriously Muentzer took the matter of separating the human from the divine Word, the tares from the wheat, then perhaps the above interpretation makes the most sense. Certainly, if he had come to see them as "false brothers"—after having praised Nicholas Storch from the pulpit as *also* possessing the Holy Spirit—then he would have been fully justified in saying that he "trembled in divine judgment." Then even he who claimed to possess the Holy Spirit and could discern good from evil had had difficulty in separating the tares from the wheat. This was indeed a dangerous business he had embarked upon.[67] If this view of the matter is correct, it would explain the rupture between Muentzer and the Zwickau Prophets.[68]

Although Luther did not respond directly to him, Muentzer did not have to wait long for an answer. It came from Hans Zeiss, the Allstedt castellan who had apparently visited Luther toward the end of July.[69] Whether he had come on his own or as an emissary, Luther told Zeiss— as he informed Spalatin in a letter of 3 August—"to distance himself from the spirit of the Prophet Muentzer."[70] This must have come as a rude shock to Muentzer who, even though he had already written off the Wittenberg theologians after his letter to Melanchthon of 22 March 1522, had been forced to a reconsideration after reading Luther's "Von der Beicht." Now, after a most conciliatory letter to Luther, Zeiss had been warned to stay away from him. What must Muentzer have thought? Was Luther duplicitous? Did he say one thing against the papists, another to those who wished to correct him?

Surely Luther cannot have missed Muentzer's reference to his "egregio libro de facienda confessione." By now he must have known about Egranus—had he not said in his letter to Spalatin of 5 May 1522 that while Muentzer was sowing dragon seeds in Zwickau, Egranus was also sowing his seeds?[71] He was certainly aware of Muentzer's criticism in the letter to Melanchthon that they were not separating the tares from the wheat in Wittenberg.[72] Yet in "Von der Beicht" he had discussed the use of the ban with regard to the wicked in the Church at some length. And this man had commended Egranus to Muentzer! In his letter to Spalatin, however, there is no mention whatever of all this. All Luther said there is that he hoped Zeiss had in fact already distanced himself from Muentzer. As for himself:

> I, in any case, cannot tolerate this spirit, whoever he may be. He praises me (he writes this himself) in one breath and attacks me in the next, all the while aspiring to something different, something higher. At the same time he employs an absurd jargon and words not found in the holy Scriptures, so that one might believe him to be either drunk or mad. He avoids us, does not wish to meet with us, yet boasts mightily of himself. I have therefore asked the castellan to persuade the man to discuss his teaching with us. Whether he will

be able to do so, I do not know. In any case, our spirit is not the kind to fear a confrontation with, or render an account of, himself to any other spirit, good or evil.[73]

If Luther said something even remotely similar to Zeiss who must have reported it to Muentzer, then Muentzer must have been profoundly disillusioned. The man whom he had called the "example and light of the friends of God," the highest praise a Taulerian could give, had turned out to have feet of clay, to be a scribe and a Pharisee after all. First the Zwickau Prophets had turned out to be "false brothers"; now Luther had revealed himself as a Pharisee. Did Muentzer alone stand against a world hostile to God?

CHAPTER VII

A Faith Different from Luther's

It is my earnest conviction that I preach a Christian faith
that is not in agreement with Luther's, but such a one as is
uniform in the hearts of all the elect on earth.
—Muentzer to Frederick the Wise, 3 August 1524

Word of Luther's brusque rejection must have reached Muentzer by early August 1523 at the latest.[1] With the possible exception of further indirect attempts to bring him to Wittenberg, this was to be Luther's last contact with the man he was soon to call the Satan of Allstedt.[2] Muentzer, as he was repeatedly to do later in writing, must have rejected such a hearing on Luther's turf, however. This may have prompted Spalatin, perhaps at the instigation of Luther, to employ a different approach. For during the early part of November 1523, while the Saxon court spent a few days in Allstedt on its way to the Diet of Nuremberg, the ducal secretary posed, in writing, a number of questions to Muentzer concerning the nature of faith.[3] Had he not already done so, these questions, delivered to Muentzer by Zeiss, must surely have caused the former to study Luther's theology on this matter more closely. That Muentzer had probably not done so before July 1523 may be inferred from his letters discussed in the previous chapter. In the first of these he still asserted that he embraced the Wittenberg theology with all his heart, though he did criticize the Wittenbergers for not fully and immediately implementing it. Similarly, in his July 1523 letter to Luther he spoke of the latter's "excellent book" concerning confession. In that piece Luther had also written at some length about "brotherly admonition" in the Church. None had been forthcoming to Muentzer, however.

Muentzer's tract, *Von dem gedicteten Glauben,* published in early 1524, would appear to be his direct response to Spalatin's questions.

This, however, had been preceded by his *Protestation oder Erbietung*.[4] Though not as centrally as the other, the *Protestation* dealt with the subject of faith. It could therefore be argued that Muentzer was already in the process of clarifying the differences between himself and Luther on this issue before Spalatin's questions were placed before him. If this is the case, then it may well have been Luther's rebuff which served as the catalyst.

The first eight sections of the *Protestation* deal with the rise, corruption, and reformation of the Church. Not until the ninth does Muentzer come to treat faith. The purpose of the tract would therefore seem to be to provide the reader with a comprehensive statement of his position, and we shall have to return to the first half of the *Protestation* in another context. Here, in our pursuit of the evolving relationship between Muentzer and Luther, it is sufficient to point out that Muentzer makes it apparent at the close of the tract that he is addressing the matter of faith in opposition to both Catholics *and* Lutherans. For he wrote: "Through this my undertaking I wish to lead the teachings of the evangelical preachers onto a higher plane [i.e., to an understanding of the role of the Holy Spirit], but I do not wish to despise our backward, slower Roman brothers either."[5] Whether Muentzer meant to imply by this that he still had greater hope for the Evangelicals than for the Catholics, he was not yet attacking Luther.

The *Protestation* confirms the fact that Muentzer had become convinced that a truly successful reformation must rest on a correct understanding of faith, indeed, on a holy invincible Christian faith. Although, as we have seen, he was undoubtedly influenced by Eusebius, the early Christian Augustine, Tauler, and Hus, Muentzer accepted Tauler's definition as correct. Such a faith, as Tauler had already argued, was not widely, if at all, in evidence any longer. Nonetheless, all—even while groping about like blind men—continued to think of themselves as having a healthy faith.[6] Under such circumstances, no reformation would come about unless God Himself first opened the people's eyes, enabling them to recognize their blindness, especially with regard to their fictitious faith and hypocritical works. When confronted with the fact of such a blindness, current scholars—like the scribes confounded by Christ's miraculous cure of the blind man in John 9:29—simply kept asserting the truth of, and their belief in, the "written Word." They refused to recognize that the primary purpose of this written Word was "to kill rather than make . . . alive."[7] This Word had been written,

Muentzer contended, "for us ignorant humans in order that holy faith, like a seed of mustard, should come to everyone as a very bitter thing. . . ." Just because the Church accepted this written Word as an external authority was no reason to reject "any other advent." By this "other advent" Muentzer undoubtedly had in mind the advent of the Holy Spirit and a successful conversion.[8]

"Fictitious faith," then, was an external matter, an intellectual assent to words, a thing of reason and not of experience. It was the rational product of faithless scribes who had not themselves experienced the transforming power of the Holy Spirit. It was an easy faith, for all one had to do was "remember what Christ had said."[9] Such a faith, however, was not enough. "You must suffer and know," Muentzer informed his readers, "how God Himself uproots the weeds, thistles and thorns from your fruitful soil, that is from your heart."[10] Without such an action on God's part, only the "devil and corn-cockles" would thrive there. Even devouring the entire Bible—by which Muentzer probably meant possessing a comprehensive, rational understanding of that book—would not help; instead

> you must suffer the sharp ploughshare. For you will certainly not have faith unless God Himself gives and teaches it to you. Before that can happen to you, dear scribe, the book [Bible] must become closed to you [that is, one must become convinced that the Bible will remain a closed book unless the Holy Spirit opens it]. And neither your reason nor any other creature can open it to your understanding, even though you were to burst in the attempt.[11]

God must divest us of all trust in creatures, even in human reason; He must Himself gird our loins. Once He has done so, once the Holy Spirit has transformed us, then we can proceed to understand the Scriptures on the basis of a "strong comparison of the total spirit of the Bible." Taking a passage here and another there out of this broad context only resulted in our mistaking the side door for the front entrance. Christ had declared such people to be thieves and robbers. Muentzer conceded that one might, on occasion, stumble upon a correct interpretation with the above method, but in every instance it would fall short of the mark. He sought to prove this with the following example: "If one says Christ has accomplished everything Himself, this falls short of the mark. If you do not grasp the Head with the members, how do you expect to follow in His footsteps? I suppose on a nice warm rug or on a satin pillow."[12]

Rather than choosing isolated texts "pleasing to our nature,"

Muentzer urged his readers to choose the "narrow way in which all judgments are studied, not according to human wisdom, but according to the most precious will of God in His living Word [the Holy Spirit], and *experienced* in all kinds of temptations of the faith" [italics mine].[13] Only under such circumstances could faith become firmly established.

Even St. Peter had not understood such a faith at first, Muentzer asserted, for

> though he was grounded on the rock he still had to fail since he was not completely in a right state of mind. His faith did not wane, rather it increased mightily because of this fall; he became better grounded, and not before. Therefore we must recognize in truth that the apostles and all the prophets could not stand with the mere Word of God until all the tares and the audacity of a fictitious faith had been uprooted. And we scholars think it enough to have the Scriptures, that we need not *experience* the power of God, even though Romans 1:[16] clearly tells us that the gospel is the power of God. But this remains hidden to us. Yet I must know whether God or the Devil has spoken this, must have the power—in the abyss of my soul—to discern the works of the one from the other [italics mine].[14]

As Muentzer had repeatedly argued, only the Holy Spirit could provide this power of discernment. Without it, one would continue to be tossed about by every wind of doctrine "as the untested scribes persuade themselves and others."[15] Without the Holy Spirit their speech lacked the power of God. Yet they continued to say, with a brazen forehead, they had "no other faith than the one they have stolen [not experienced] from the Scriptures." It was a fictitious faith concocted by reason in order to make it easy to attain salvation.

It would appear from the foregoing that Luther's exaltation of the Word had become the primary focus of Muentzer's attack. In the *Prague Manifesto* his focus had still been the man-made regulations of the Roman Catholic Church—its "foolish works." This was not unlike Luther's own attack on that Church in his 1521 "Von der Beicht." Although the basis of Muentzer's reasoning did not change, the focus of his attack shifted by the time he came to write the *Protestation*. This becomes even more evident in the following passage:

> It falls far short of the mark if one preaches that faith must justify us and not works. It is an arrogant saying. Thereby our nature is not confronted with *how* a man comes to faith through the work of God, a work man must wait for before—and above—all else. Otherwise faith is not worth a trifle and *according to its effects is completely false* [italics mine].[16]

True faith was invincible; true conversion must be successful. Where this was not the case, faith could not be true. Muentzer had made his judgment of the Wittenberg reforms in his March 1522 letter to Melanchthon on this basis. There he had seen some good, and some not so good, "effects." As a consequence, he had told Melanchthon that some—though by no means all—of their reforms had been the work of the Holy Spirit.

Now, however, Muentzer had reached the conviction that "those who urge on the Gospel praise [this kind of] faith most highly." As a result, natural man thought: "Ah, if nothing more than faith is needed, how easily can one achieve that!"[17] For without a doubt we have all been born of "Christian parents," have never doubted, and intend to stand firm. Yes, indeed, we are all good Christians. But could one be saved so easily? Could one simply "grasp salvation out of the air" and not know—never mind experience—anything about its beginning or end? Did everyone in the world really desire to become "good Evangelicals [merely] with many proud words?" If so, they were being greatly deceived.

Muentzer asserted that those who "chew[ed] their way through this fictitious faith see that the word onto which true faith is hung is not a hundred thousand miles away from them, but they see how it springs from the abyss of the heart, they recognize that it comes from the living God."[18] This was the Word experienced, the living Word, which God Himself spoke in the abyss of the human soul. But before this word could be uttered there, "one must be alert, send all desires on vacation and wait with the greatest effort on such a word and promise of God."[19] When this finally happened, one no longer believed he had heard the word from someone else. Then it did not matter whether the entire world accepted or rejected it. Such a man's inner eye had waited a long, long time "on the Lord and His hands, that is on godly works [i.e., the work of transformation], and thus he finally achieves edification, even to the extent of the full return of the [Holy] Spirit."[20] It was in this way that a man must experience God's immovable mercy.

To accept the external, written Word so lauded by Luther, Muentzer asserted, only made one a beginning Christian. In like manner, one might say, the resurrection of the Word, "from under a bench," by Hus and then Luther made possible the *beginning* of reformation. This was undoubtedly a signal contribution to its inauguration. But for the Word to be truly affirmed, one must first suffer it "at which time there seems to be no consolation in all eternity for our works." When one arrived at such an impasse, one came to believe that one possessed no faith at all.

The central thrust of Muentzer's argument would seem to be that although Hus and Luther had made a good beginning, they had never gone quite far enough. They had resurrected the written Word but had never experienced the inner Word; they possessed a faith based on hearing—a stolen faith—but had never experienced the transforming power of the Holy Spirit; they had begun to reform, but had refused to cleanse the Church of the tares so that the *futura ecclesia* could arise; though tender, they had remained scribes. They had allowed neither the letter to kill nor the Spirit to bring them life. Thus they continued to believe that life could come from the dead letter of the Word.

There follows a description of conversion reminiscent of pseudo-Tauler's in the *Historia*. But there is a difference. Whereas pseudo-Tauler had been guided to the true faith by a pious layman, Muentzer's seeker was forced to struggle with a "faithless" scribe who fobbed off his anguish of soul with the words: "Ah, my dear fellow, you must not concern yourself with such high matters. Just believe in all simplicity and drive these thoughts from you. They are pure fantasy."[21] As a consequence, no true faith existed. The seekers—the elect—were turned away because the scribes were themselves blind. There were no pious laymen around to lead the seekers to conversion and true faith. Unable to enter in themselves, the scribes made sure no one else entered in.

Muentzer must have sent a copy of the *Protestation* to Hans Zeiss, for on 2 December 1523 he wrote the latter: "One thing, dear brother, was forgotten in my answer to that [argument?] that Christ alone has been designated [chosen] to suffer, so that we need not suffer anything since He has truly suffered for our sins." Apparently Muentzer had omitted something in his discussion of salvation in the *Protestation*. He did not wish to deny, he said, that Christ had "truly suffered for our sins." He wished to say, however, that this was not all there was to it, that Christians, too, had to suffer. Muentzer did so by combining the mystical concept of unity in diversity[22] with St. Paul's description of Christ's relationship to the Church in I Cor. 12:12–14: "For as the body is one, and hath many members, and all members of that one body, being many, are one body; so also is Christ. For by one Spirit are we all baptized into one body, whether we be Jews or Gentiles, whether we be bond or free; and have been all made to drink into one Spirit. For the body is not one member, but many." This was so, St. Paul contin-

ued, even though the members of the body differed in their functions.
With this passage in mind, Muentzer explained the Christian's relationship to Christ and his Church:

> Adam is a negative type of Christ; Christ, however, the [positive] oppo-
> site. The disobedience of creation is being restored through the obedience of
> the Word, Who became flesh in nature. Similarly, our human nature, once
> faith has taken root, must decrease in part as it had [already] done in the
> whole Christ as head. Therefore Christ has atoned for all the harm done by
> Adam, in order that all the [various] parts should cling to the whole, as the
> holy messenger of God [St. Paul] clearly states. I fulfill that which the suffer-
> ing Christ has left [behind] to be fulfilled; [for] in the absence of His [physi-
> cal] body, the Church suffers. St. Paul did not wish to suffer for the [whole]
> Church, except as a member, who fulfills [the duties of] his office. We must
> all follow in Christ's footsteps, must all be armed with similar thoughts; no
> gloss will obviate this, [especially] not of those people who think that, by
> means of their reason, they have overcome works righteousness. Such people
> [Luther] have only poisoned the world more with their fictitious faith than
> the others [Catholics] had already done with their foolish works.[23]

The Church, therefore, as Christ's body on earth, had to suffer as the
Head had suffered while He had dwelt on earth. She had to be obedient
just as Christ had been obedient. No gloss could interpret this away.
Therefore, even though Christ had truly "atoned for all the damage
done by Adam," the true Church continued to suffer. In the physical
absence of the Head Who was the Whole, the Church as a whole continued to suffer in its members. It was therefore not enough to say that
Christ had accomplished everything, as Muentzer repeatedly charged in
opposition to Luther.[24] "We must all follow in Christ's footsteps, must
all be armed with similar thoughts." The disciple was not above his
master. It was in this sense that it fell short of the mark to say that
Christ had accomplished everything. It was not that Muentzer denied
that Christ had died for the sins of mankind. To the contrary, he affirmed it. But man had to die as well.

Approximately a week-and-a-half later Muentzer dealt with the same
problem in a letter to Christoph Meinhardt of Eisleben. Christ, he reiterated, "has not come to save us so that we need not suffer . . . the poverty
of our souls." His only office was to "console the poor [in spirit] and to
consign the untested to the tormentor." For whoever did not become
conformed to the Son was a scoundrel and a murderer. Such a person,
desiring to rise rather than die with Christ, could never become a "true
sheep of His pasture." A person must, in all earnestness, endure God's
buffeting, grow daily in knowledge of God, and in truth put off the old

Adam. He should not do as the scribes do, merely sow new patches on torn, old garments.

Even though Muentzer had begun to come to grips with what he conceived to be Luther's theology of salvation, he did not yet deem the time appropriate to "reveal such a writing as this [i.e., the *Protestation*]" to a mad world. He had first, he informed Zeiss, to work out his position "according to all the parts of Scripture"[25] in order not to appear defenseless before the new scribes. This is probably why, from now on, Muentzer listed what he considered to be parallel scriptural passages in the margins of his tracts nearly to the point of the absurd. He intended, it would seem, to oppose Luther's "rational" understanding of the Word with his own "Spirit inspired" exegesis, an exegesis based on the conviction that the Law, the Prophets, and the Gospels spoke with one voice.

The tract *Von dem gedicteten Glauben* followed hard upon the *Protestation*. It too had margins replete with biblical references. The scribes were to be overwhelmed with their own "written Word." Many of the same themes were sounded which Muentzer had already developed in his *Protestation;* but there were others as well. In the earlier sections he dwelt for some time on how difficult it was for the elect, "the friends of God," to arrive at a true faith. Abraham, Moses, indeed "all the Fathers, Patriarchs and especially the Apostles all came to the faith with great difficulty."[26] He talked about how, before the wheat could grow in one's acre, it had to suffer the ploughshare and how the Word had to kill before the Spirit could impart life. From the arrival of faith in the individual, Muentzer turned, in section seven, to the uprooting of false Christians by preachers who had experienced conversion through the Holy Spirit, saying: "these [preachers] have not had the Word of God set in their mouths with honied and deceptive words, but are filled with an ardent and right serious zeal to uproot false Christians, to break, to scatter and destroy all their wicked faith, which they have acquired through hearsay or have stolen out of the books of men like so many malicious thieves."[27] This was the essential problem in Christendom, Muentzer continued—the problem of the tares among the wheat—though everyone refused to recognize it as such.

The first step to reform, then, was to listen to such an earnest preacher who would teach the "elect friends of God" how to arrive at a true faith. There can be no doubt that Muentzer had himself in mind; he had said as much already in the *Prague Manifesto*. For the sheep of God's pasture were being poisoned by rotten fodder; they were being fed a sweet Christ. This was the deadliest of poisons; nevertheless, it had been fed Christendom since early on. "By this means man hopes to become like unto God, though he refuses in every way to be conformed to Christ."[28] And yet Christ had said that His sheep heard His voice and would not follow strangers. Who were the strangers? They were, said Muentzer, anyone who allowed the path to eternal life to become overgrown with weeds, allowed the thorns and thistles to stand, and said: "believe, believe! hold fast, fast with a strong, strong faith, so strong in fact as to enable you to drive stakes into the ground with it."[29]

While Luther's understanding of faith had become the obvious focus of his attack, Muentzer never mentioned Luther by name. Not until Luther openly attacked him in his "Letter to the Dukes of Saxony Concerning the Revolutionary Spirit" did Muentzer respond in kind, and even then not before he had written to Frederick the Wise stating his intentions.

In his "Letter to the Dukes of Saxony," indeed in the very opening sentences, Luther placed Muentzer in the company of those false prophets and erring sects that invariably arose in the wake of the preaching of the pure Word of God—not quite how Muentzer had come to see himself! Therefore now, as in the days of the Apostles, Luther asserted, the devil had begun to oppose the powerful dissemination of God's Word by attacking the believers. Seeing that this failed to stem the spread of Christianity, he was again attempting to subvert it from within. This had to be so, as St. Paul confirmed, in order that true Christians could be made manifest. Then Luther observed:

> Therefore now that the aroused Satan has run about in arid places for some one to three years, seeking though not finding a safe haven, he has settled in Your Lordship's principality and made himself a nest in Allstedt, thinking to attack us while enjoying our peace, protection and privileges. For Duke George's principality, though close by, is altogether too well intentioned and weak for such fearless and invincible spirits as these (as they boast of themselves); they would not be able adequately to demonstrate their undaunted courage and bold opposition there. For this reason he cries ferociously, complaining that he must suffer so much, despite the fact that no one, to this point, has so much as touched him either with pen, mouth or fist. Nonetheless they have concocted this great cross which they suffer. . . .[30]

Having called Muentzer the Satan of Allstedt, Luther proceeded to impugn his claim to possess the Holy Spirit. He was grateful, Luther said, that Muentzer and his followers claimed not to have learned anything from him; instead, like the angels, they spoke directly to God. No one dared doubt this "heavenly voice" of theirs, and yet he had never read or heard of a "more arrogant, proud holy spirit (if it were really He)" than this one.[31] He might be more inclined, Luther continued, to respect this spirit if it would produce other fruit than "the burning of churches, monasteries and images, which the worst rascals on earth can also do, especially where they are secure and have no opposition." Were they to act in this fashion in Dresden, Berlin or Ingolstadt, Luther might have been impressed. But he was not impressed by their claim to possess the Holy Spirit, for St. John's statement—that one was to test the spirits to see if they were of God—had to be applied here. Muentzer's spirit had not yet been tested, nor was Luther convinced by his actions. Moreover, this spirit refused to submit to the kind of testing Luther had been repeatedly forced to undergo before virtually everyone who demanded it.[32] Instead, Muentzer's spirit appeared bent on social revolution.

Luther asserted he could not boast of such high things. His writings showed clearly enough how tentative he had been at the outset of his attack on the papacy. And yet in this poverty of spirit he had accomplished more than this "world-devouring spirit" had even attempted, who, every time danger threatened, avoided a confrontation by fleeing the field of battle. He, in contrast, had been to Leipzig, to Augsburg, to Worms with all their attendant dangers long before he had ever heard of the "spirit of Allstedt." Pursuant to St. Peter's command, he had given answer in humility and gentleness of spirit, to everyone who had asked of him.[33]

If the spirit of Allstedt, Luther continued, was so much higher than his, it ought to have produced better fruit. The spirit he and his followers preached and taught at Wittenberg, Luther asserted, produced the fruits St. Paul spoke of in Galatians 5: love, joy, peace, patience, goodness, steadfastness, gentleness, and moderation. And, in accordance with Romans 8, they taught "that he destroy the works of the flesh and crucify, with Christ, the old Adam with his lusts. . . . In sum, the fruits of our spirit is the fulfillment of the ten commandments."[34] Since the spirit of Allstedt claimed to be superior to theirs, it would have to produce "something higher than love and faith, peace, patience, etc. [Even though St. Paul holds love to be the highest fruit I Cor. 13.], and must do something much better than God has commanded."[35]

This brought Luther to perhaps one of the most important differences between himself and Muentzer. Luther responded to the accusation that Muentzer had levelled against him in his letter to Melanchthon of March 1522, namely that he did not live in accordance with his teachings, by saying of Muentzer and his followers that the spirit in which they speak is not a good one. . . .

> The criticism of one's teaching because of a defective life, however, does not come from the Holy Spirit. For the Holy Spirit censures false doctrine and tolerates the weak in faith and life, as St. Paul teaches in Romans 14 and 15, and elsewhere.[36]

For Muentzer, the Pharisee was someone whose doctrine appeared sound enough but who lacked the power to fulfill what he knew to be right. For Luther, a Pharisee was a person who judged teaching because of an inadequate life. Muentzer, like the early Christian Augustine, believed in a successful Christian conversion. Luther, like the post-*Confessions* Augustine, saw the struggle depicted by Paul in Romans as continuing as long as one remained in this mortal body. From these conflicting positions both made judgments as to the possession of the Holy Spirit by the other: Muentzer arguing that the absence of a successful Christian lifestyle signified the absence of the Holy Spirit; Luther arguing that the Holy Spirit censured false doctrine and tolerated those who were unable to live in accordance with their teachings. From Luther's point of view, therefore, Muentzer's spirit was the spirit of Satan. Muentzer, however, never said this of Luther; he simply asserted that Luther did not yet fully have the Holy Spirit.

Muentzer's first response to Luther's letter to the Dukes of Saxony came in his letter to Frederick the Wise of 3 August 1524. He opened that letter by referring to how the misery of the times demanded "most emphatically that [we] confront and prevent all unbelief." Although this unbelief had "made do . . . with the appearance of a Christian church" until now, there were people abroad who presented it "in the deceptive form of a carnal and fictitious goodness." God had therefore decreed that he, Thomas Muentzer, should, as Ezekiel had said, place himself like an immovable wall "over against a poor, ruined Christendom, which not only stands in need of correction here and there, as some think, but which needs to be completely uprooted."[37] In certain places God had already begun to do this. But Satan did not wish such a radical renewal to take place, and so he was now

> driving the godless scholars [the Wittenberg theologians] to their destruction, as he previously did the monks and priests, for they are revealing themselves in that they, in a most despicable manner, declare the Holy Spirit to be a mockery and label him a devil in many of the elect, as the mendacious Luther now does in his scandalous letter to the Dukes of Saxony, where he

rages in such a furious and hateful manner against me like a haughty tyrant without all brotherly admonition.[38]

To this point, Muentzer had only accused the Wittenbergers of being "ignorant of the living Word"; at the worst, they did not possess it or that it had departed from them. Now, however, they appeared actively in opposition to the Holy Spirit, slandering it and making it a laughing stock. This was a sure sign that they, too, belonged to the reprobates. They were children of the bond woman after all and did not belong to the elect.

Muentzer had recognized the root of the problem in Christendom; he had pinpointed the time when the Holy Spirit had been driven from the Church by the tares. Since that time Christendom had made do with the mere appearance of Christianity; it possessed none of its power through the Spirit. This condition had finally to be opposed in the most forceful manner. Nor would it do merely to patch the old structure; Christendom had to be completely uprooted and a new edifice erected. This is what he—or rather God through him—had begun to do in various places. And just when this was beginning to take place, the new scribes—the godless scholars—were trying to scuttle the Holy Spirit once more, just as they had done in the mid-second century, by preaching another fictitious faith, one perhaps even more damaging than the old. However, in Luther's letter to the Dukes of Saxony, their true identity had been revealed by divulging what they thought of the Holy Spirit: like the tares in the Church of old, they, too, were making a mockery of the Holy Spirit. How could the new Apostolic Church, the *futura ecclesia,* come into being if people like himself, who had *experienced* the transforming work of the Holy Spirit, refused to confront such slander in the strongest of terms? Not only had Luther slandered the Holy Spirit, he had referred to it as a devil in the elect followers of Muentzer, clearly manifesting his inability to discern good from evil.

Once again we are confronted by what Muentzer believed to be the most important element in the reestablishment of the Apostolic Church: the return of the Holy Spirit. Yet the very person he had once called the "light and example of the friends of God" was now making a mockery of the Holy Spirit and labelling Thomas Muentzer, the elect servant of God himself, a devil. It was clear, the Wittenberg theologians would not help to establish the new Apostolic Church. They were merely another variation on the old theme of the scribes and Pharisees.

Little wonder, then, that Luther, in opposition to his own statements in his "Von der Beicht," had now written this scandalous letter to the Dukes of Saxony. He had not answered Muentzer's conciliatory letter of 9 July 1523, had sent his rejection through a third party, had tried to silence him by making him appear for a private hearing in Wittenberg, and now attacked him in an open letter. Was this the action of a Christian? Had this merely been a personal attack, Muentzer wrote Frederick, he would not be inclined to retaliate in kind. This was much more, however: "Because of the offense caused to many pious [people]," he asserted, "who have come to hear my teachings from distant cities and lands, not to answer such charges would be irresponsible."[39] Therefore, he requested that Frederick neither "hinder nor forbid [him] to preach and write" against Luther.

In the meantime Muentzer had reached a most important conclusion. "It is," he informed Frederick, "my earnest conviction that I preach a Christian faith that is not in agreement with Luther's, but such a one as is uniform in the hearts of all the elect on earth." Even were a Turk in their midst, Muentzer continued, "he would still possess the beginning of such a faith, that is the moving of the Holy Spirit, as it is written of Cornelius in Acts 10." The example of Cornelius was particularly significant in Muentzer's context, for Cornelius, a pious Gentile, had been confronted by an angel and told to call for St. Peter who would explain the Christian faith to him. And while Peter was yet speaking, "the Holy Ghost fell on all them which heard the Word." Obviously one of the elect, God had moved in the abyss of Cornelius's heart and prepared him for the reception of the Holy Spirit. The "word" spoken by Peter was merely the witness to what had already been going on in the heart of Cornelius.

Since he preached such a faith as was common to all the elect, Muentzer refused to submit to Luther's judgment. His judges, he asserted, should be drawn from around the world and belong to the elect who knew what he was talking about. That was why, he informed Frederick, he desired "to avoid being interrogated privately," to which the scribes pressed him. In any case, even Christ had told Hanna: "Why ask me, ask those who have heard my teaching." In this fashion Christ directed the godless rulers to the people. If Christ had acted in this manner, why then should he "throw the pearls before swine, who have openly ridiculed and slandered the Holy Spirit?" Had not Christ himself said that they were born of the devil? Should those who mocked the Holy Spirit be the judge of the Holy Spirit? Should the tares judge the wheat? The answer was obvious.[40]

Muentzer enclosed an initial copy of his exposition of the Gospel of Luke in the letter to Frederick the Wise. It was later to be printed in Nuremberg by Hans Herrgott as the *Ausgedrueckte Entbloessung* in October 1524, some three months later. Although somewhat longer than the version sent to the elector, it is not substantially different and belongs to Muentzer's immediate responses to Luther's denunciation in his letter to the Dukes of Saxony.[41]

That letter must have touched a raw nerve in Muentzer, for he was to return to it time and again. On the one hand, he was now certain as to where Luther belonged in the larger scheme of Christian history. This insight must have come as a great disappointment to him. The utter conviction must have set in that he had been as wrong about Luther as he had ever been about the Zwickau Prophets. Did this give rise to self-doubts about his own "discerning power" he claimed through the presence of the Holy Spirit? On the other hand, Luther's attack on his "fearlessness," his penchant for escaping dangerous situations before they reached a climax, must have rankled deep within him, for there was some truth to the accusations. It would do Muentzer no good to respond by trying to detract from Luther's own courageous appearances.[42] For, whatever one might say about Luther's motives, *he had appeared!* But when the chips were down, Muentzer had shaken the dust from his sandals and moved to safer ground. He avoided confrontation with the enemy, except in writing. As Luther charged, Muentzer had many and bold words, but bold deeds were strangely absent.

Since Luther had shown his true colors in his letter to the Dukes of Saxony, and it was now fully obvious where he stood, it was all the more incumbent upon Muentzer to speak out and oppose this purveyor of scandalous denunciations, this slanderer of the Holy Spirit. He intended, he said, to do so "by interpreting the holy Scriptures in the teaching of the Holy Spirit through the comparison of all the secrets and judgments of God."[43] He would oppose their faith in the letter of the Word, which they praised so highly while denying the precious power of God, making Him "a dumb, mad and fantastic God with their fictitious faith."[44] God was not dead; indeed, He was about to come very much alive again. Since no one else would grasp the rudder because of the difficult battle ahead, it had fallen to him to expose the "poisonous damage which had entered so deeply" into Christendom.[45]

Once more, then, Muentzer began with the problem of faith. It had now become the central focus of his attack. Quoting Christ's question in Luke 18:8—"when the Son of man cometh, shall He find faith on earth?"—Muentzer began to discuss the absence of a true faith in his day, saying: "Therefore it is an unspeakably vexing misery that unbelieving persons (as is patently obvious) try to preach the Christian faith to people which they themselves have never discovered, never mind experienced, nor do they know how a believer feels. They think it is very easy to acquire faith, as nearly all of them boastfully declare."[46]

Instead, like the scribes and Pharisees, everyone was talking of a "cheap faith" in contrast to the tested faith of a Gideon. But even Gideon had initially not been willing to heed the voice of the angel, for an "untested faith has at first no other judgment than to be filled with fear. . . . He who believes readily has a frivolous heart. The fear of God, however, makes room for the Holy Spirit in order that the elect may be surrounded by Him Whom the world in its foolishness fears, to the great detriment of its [true] wisdom."[47] And now the emphasis on the role of the Holy Spirit in bringing about a true faith comes forcefully to the fore, as Muentzer wrote:

> Therefore the beginning and the end of this surrounding of the Holy Spirit, who teaches us faith through the pure fear of God, is contained in this Gospel. This creates great astonishment in the impossible work of faith, where the power of the Most High (as Luke describes it in the first and last chapters) completely rejects all fictitious and secret faith most radically. For [such a faith] becomes exposed through the appropriation or passage [of the Holy Spirit] in the abyss of the soul. Paul says: "You must put on Christ," [if that is done] false faith cannot be sustained anywhere. He who has not experienced such an advent [passage], knows absolutely nothing about faith.[48]

In spite of this, the new scribes defended their fictitious faith with their stolen Scripture. When asked how they had arrived at their glorious faith, and why they were not rather Jews or Turks, all they could say was; "Behold, I believe the Scriptures!" Sensing skepticism in the questioner, they became jealous and angry: "O ho, this man denies the Scriptures!" In this fashion they sought to intimidate everyone and refused to satisfy the profound inner longing of the elect, turning them over to the devil. They were doing what Christ had told the godless scribes to do: "Search the Scripture," he had said; "for in them ye think ye have eternal life." Was Christ being ironical? Muentzer appears to have thought so. In any case, in this way the scribes deceived the people so greatly that no one could measure the damage. It is in this context that the accusation came that stood at the heart of Muentzer's concern for these "poor, deprived people." And that concern is not primarily, if at all, economic! Muentzer thus characterized the scribes:

> With all their words and deeds, they make it so that the poor man cannot learn to read because of his struggle to scrape together enough food, and they preach shamelessly that the poor man must allow himself to be exploited by the tyrants. When, therefore, is he supposed to learn to read the Scriptures? Yes [they answer], dear Thomas, you fantasize, the scribes are to read the beautiful books and the peasant is to listen, for faith comes from hearing. Indeed, here they have discovered a fine artifice; for this would set many more—and worse—rascals in the place of priests and monks than have already been there since the beginning of the world. God, however, be blessed that many elect are beginning to recognize the root of unbelief in this fact, even though they have tried to hide it and even today would like to let things grow wild—and so the wheat can begin to grow again.[49]

If this "root of unbelief" was finally to be destroyed, Muentzer continued, then one would have to give up the godless ways of the scribes, for they only used the Scriptures to cover up their shame. They claimed that it gave faith when the "Son of God has said that the Scriptures are a witness." In this way the truth had been kept from the poor masses by "these arrogant babblers," and had been asleep for such a long time. But it must once again be brought to light. "For at the present time," Muentzer asserted, "if a Christian should say, in the midst of the poor masses, that he had learned the Christian faith directly from God Himself, no one would believe him."[50]

Muentzer continued to argue that one could arrive at faith without the Bible—an argument very reminiscent of a similar one in the *Historia*.[51] Thus he asserted that even if one had never heard the Bible, or seen it, one could still, through the correct teaching of the Holy Spirit, have as authentic a Christian faith as all those had had who, without any books, had written the holy Scriptures.[52] It did not seem to bother him that such an assertion blunted somewhat his argument in favor of more time for the "poor masses" to learn to read. Nevertheless, such a faith worked by the Holy Spirit in the abyss of the human soul would be a uniform faith, resting on one's having *experienced* the Holy Spirit, not upon some "rational" interpretation of Scripture. The latter, Muentzer apparently thought, led to conflicting interpretations; the Holy Spirit, however, worked a uniform faith.

In the process of making his case for such a faith, Muentzer attempted to turn the tables on Luther who had accused him of denigrating the Bible by referring to it as "bibble, babble, bubble." Muentzer, in turn, now accused Luther of "turning people, who dare to say anything against them, over to the devil with their hasty judgments, at the same time making a mockery of the Spirit of Christ. Brazenly they dare to cry and write: spirit here, spirit there."[53] They said that one should not begin with the Spirit of Christ in the matter of faith; one should not boast of possessing the Spirit, for anyone who did so must obviously be a false prophet. Instead, it was the Word that was to give faith. But these scribes were all opposed by "Maria and Zacharia, Abraham, Joseph, Moses and all the Patriarchs, who all heeded the movement of the Holy Spirit in the abyss of their souls and never once turned for help to the guidance of the desperate, incompetent godless, of whom Isaiah spoke in chapter 8 verse 12."[54] Whereas such a faith was impossible for the carnal man, with God everything was possible.

Returning once more to the need for a transformation, indeed deification, of man,[55] Muentzer argued that Luther had become so abusive of him precisely because he did not wish to change. Instead, "he intended to retain his lusts, his pride and riches," while still claiming a proven faith. Christ, however, had clearly told His followers in Matthew 6 that they "cannot serve God and Mammon." If they chose the latter, God would leave them empty.[56]

Muentzer interpreted Luther's opposition and that of the rest of the godless as the sure sign that God was once again sending His light into the world. This was apparent by the way in which the rulers acted, making conditions so bad that God would no longer tolerate them.[57] Such evil rulers might be the just recompense for the sins of the people;[58] nonetheless, the underlying cause of the problem in Christendom was the fact that "the precious wisdom of God, the true Christian has been despised and dishonored. And that has happened because those people who do not possess the Holy Spirit, or have the fear of God within them, have been taken into the Church [Christendom]. And these, as is apparent to everyone, must be worshipped by all and sundry."[59] Muentzer emphasized the same point a little later: "The world," he said, "and its froth the scribes, think it the most impossible of things that the lowly shall be exalted and separated from the wicked. Yes, indeed, this is the most serious hindrance. They do not wish to give the text of Matthew 13 any room at all which speaks of the separation of the godless from the elect."[60]

The scribes, Muentzer charged, had imagined that the angels would do the separating at the Last Judgment. They thought they could lead the Holy Spirit around by the nose, for they stated unabashedly that God does not reveal His judgments to anyone. Therefore, they refused to recognize that the angels "were the right messengers (according to Malachai [3:1–5]) to separate the good from the wicked in the future."[61] They asserted instead that no one could know who belonged to the elect or the reprobates. In this fashion their faith gave aid and comfort to the wicked godless. They did indeed say that "The Lord knows His own," but they failed to heed the passage immediately following: "He who seeks the name of God departs from evil."

While Muentzer could stress the successful nature of conversion and the gradual deification of the believer, he did recognize that even the elect sinned. The difference between the elect and the reprobates in this regard, however, was that the conscience of the elect admonished them to flee sin; not so the conscience of the reprobates. The goal of the latter was to satisfy their every desire; therefore, they could never become the enemies of evil. They constantly sought after the good life and the things of this world; they remained bound to the creatures.[62]

These scribes, these tares, these reprobates had devastated God's temples: the external temple of the Church as well as the interior temple in the abyss of the human soul. To recover from this devastation and be raised up once more, the Church would have to cast these usurious evildoers aside, for they were unfit servants. But how were the reprobates to be unseated? The poor, ordinary people, Muentzer asserted, must remember the Holy Spirit and cry—(Romans 8:14: "For as many as are led by the Spirit of God, they are the sons of God.")—and pray and wait for a new John, "a Spirit-filled preacher who has experienced the faith in every way through his unbelief, for he must know how an arch-unbeliever feels, and he must know that the measure of faith accords with the measure of one's desire [for the faith]."[63] That man—did Muentzer need to say it?—was himself.

Muentzer took one last shot at Luther toward the end of the tract. There he accused him of trying to avoid a true reformation by saying: "Indeed, we are all sinners. But Christ did not despise sinners, why then should this pharisaical spirit despise us?" There would never be a Church of pure wheat, Luther seemed to be saying; man would always remain *simul justus et peccator*. He, Muentzer, had warned the Wittenbergers about their fictitious, stolen faith, but they had responded by flaunting their sins in order to excuse and justify themselves.[64] As a result, their teachings failed to bring about any changes: "they are not put into practice and are conducive only to greater libertinism. Thereby they poison the Scriptures for the Holy Spirit. At times one does indeed see them walking on the right path, but not for long. None of their followers becomes better because their teachings have been stolen, Jeremiah 23:[30]."[65] Therefore they also asserted that it did not matter whether their preachers were good or bad; they were still able to dispense the sacraments and preach the Word rightly. And so they continued to justify the godless.

Unless God raised up His servant to oppose these scoundrels, Muentzer continued, the poor people, who so desired to believe, would not come to the true faith. However, the time was now ripe for God to begin to send such servants to His Church so that, at last, a true witness to the faith would see the light of day. Once such a faith wrought by the Holy Spirit had returned, one would once again be able to separate the wheat from the tares, the elect from the godless, in the Church. Such a separation would bring a true Christian Church into existence.[66]

The signs that the time of harvest was at hand when such a separation would take place were everywhere in evidence. It did not matter that all the tares shouted that the harvest was not yet. It was indeed the time of harvest as well as the time of transformation. And Muentzer predicted that this transformation would be even greater than the one at the time of the Apostles. The elect would be gathered from all lands and nations and be far superior to the lazy European Christians. Then the new Apostolic Church would arise, founded upon a faith worked by the Holy Spirit in the abyss of the human soul.[67]

Muentzer's last blast of the trumpet against the monstrous regiment of scribes came in his *Hochverursachte Schutzrede*. Aside from its frontal attack on Luther, it marked, in many ways, the culmination of his struggle to understand Church history, to understand the Church's problems past and present. He saw these problems from the vantage point of the seduction of the Apostolic Church by the tares within. That central problem had been and continued to be the rejection of the Holy Spirit within a Church dominated by the tares. In the early Church the Holy Spirit had been crucified by the false prophets; in his day it was being called a devil by Martin Luther himself.

Muentzer began the tract by mimicking Luther's salutation in his letter to the Dukes of Saxony. He, however, dedicated his piece to Christ, his Lord. He had no sooner made this statement than he turned once more to the topic of Luther and the Holy Spirit. Throughout history, Muentzer began, the Holy Spirit had had the great misfortune of being labelled the worst of devils by the scribes despite the fact that

Christ had possessed it without measure from the beginning, and all the elect had received it from Christ's fullness. There could be no doubt that the Holy Spirit lived in the elect. Indeed, said Muentzer, Christ gave the Holy Spirit to all those who strove to reach Him according to the measure of their faith. Those who did not possess it, those whose spirit had not been granted its invincible testimony, did not belong to Christ.[68]

It was no wonder, therefore, that that glory-seeking scribe, that Doctor Liar, made an ever greater fool of himself. Seeking to cover himself with Christ's holy Scriptures so he would not have to die to self, Luther wished to have nothing to do with Christ even though he acted as though he had achieved the very judgments of the Lord Himself. So audacious had this scribe become that he despised Christ's true Spirit to His very face. Had he not, as the result of his mad jealousy and most bitter hatred, made Muentzer, Christ's chosen instrument, a laughing stock before his derisive and malicious fellows without any just or true cause whatever? Had he not attempted to make Muentzer the object of hatred to those who did not know better, calling him Satan and castigating him with his perverse, slanderous judgments?[69]

To justify this condemnation of Luther, Muentzer drew a clinching witness from the Scriptures. There, in Matthew 10:28, Christ had said that the disciple was not better than the master. Muentzer asked, "therefore, if they called Christ, the innocent prince and redeemer rich in consolation, a beelzebub, how much more will they do to me, Thy unperturbed soldier, after I followed Your voice and spoke out against the ingratiating rascals at Wittenberg[?]"[70] What the scribes and Pharisees had once done to Christ, Luther was now doing to Muentzer.

To make this case, Muentzer portrayed his quarrel with Luther as parallel to Christ's quarrel with the scribes and Pharisees of His day. Christ had stood at the foundation of the Apostolic Church; Muentzer was standing at that of the new Apostolic Church. Both had and were being opposed by similar enemies out to subvert the new Church. Both he and Christ preached the fulfillment of the Law. Thus, Christ had begun with Moses and the Prophets and explained the Law from beginning to end. He had taken human wisdom captive. But since His teachings were so much higher than those of the scribes, and His person so insignificant, they had become angry at Him, calling Him a Samaritan and accusing Him of being possessed by a devil. They judged according to the flesh, however, as was pleasing to the devil and the world he dominated.[71]

Likewise, the godless Wittenberg flesh was doing the same thing to Muentzer now that he had begun to expound the Bible from the beginning and was striving for the purity of God's Law. Muentzer charged that this was especially true since he had begun to proclaim the renewed advent of the Holy Spirit. But without practicing the Law, even the elect would not come to a knowledge of their unbelief. Muentzer therefore set Christ and all His members as fulfillers of the Law. For the will of God had to be accomplished from its very foundations through a study of the Law; otherwise, no one would be able to distinguish between faith and unbelief.[72]

Because Luther did not take his own conversion seriously—claiming that even the true Christian remained a sinner—he also became a justifier of the wicked princes and of the evil of the *status quo*. This was another sign that Luther did not belong to the elect: he did not despise the godless; rather, in order to justify them, he labelled the God-fearing ones as devils and revolutionaries. In this way, by his great consideration for their sins, Luther blinded this scum to their own sins in order to receive from them honor, goods, and the greatest of titles. Like all tares, Egranus included, Luther was consumed by the riches and the glory.

While Luther was ingratiating himself with the princes, he was accusing Muentzer of fomenting revolution. Luther's evidence lay in Muentzer's letter to the miners where he asserted that the "entire community possessed the power of the sword and the key of dissolution."[73] Princes were not lords, but servants of the sword; they were to execute justice, not act as they pleased. This meant, said Muentzer, that the people ought to be involved in making decisions as a check on the lawless tendencies of the princes in accordance with old Germanic custom. Because no one had stepped into the breach on behalf of the needy, the powerful acted as they pleased.

Muentzer went on to attack Luther on a number of other issues, but the essential point had been made: Luther belonged to those reprobates who despised the Holy Spirit. Like the Pharisees of old who had rejected Christ's higher teaching, Luther had rejected Muentzer's teaching of the Holy Spirit. He refused to reform himself; his teachings, therefore, justified the wickedness of the reprobates. To cover his tracks, he ingratiated himself with the powerful of the world, refusing to associate with the despised masses who were being led as sheep to the slaughter. He was quick to judge the weak and the lowly, but he argued that no one was to judge the godless princes. When he did condemn them on occasion, he made sure they did not mind too much, giving them cloisters and churches. He denied the living Word, while perverting Christendom with a fictitious faith. He denied that preachers had to become prophets, as St. Paul had mandated in I Corinthians 14. In Muentzer's view, unless one possessed prophetic powers, one would never be able to judge the true from the false teachers. That Luther did not know the difference between the two was obvious from the fact that he had accused Muentzer of being a devil. This meant either that he had never possessed the Holy Spirit, or that the Holy Spirit had departed from him as from a latter-day Saul.

The parallels that Muentzer set up between himself and Christ in this last tract are striking. And they are not accidental. They point to the larger frame of reference within which Muentzer was operating. The one pole was Christ at the beginning of the Apostolic Church; the other was Muentzer at the advent of the new Apostolic Church. The enemies of both were the same: the scribes and Pharisees, the reprobates, the tares who were out to destroy Christ's vineyard. They belonged to the offspring of the bond woman; they were servants of the devil who were out to keep the Holy Spirit away from the Church. Initially, Christ had vanquished them, and the Apostolic Church had consequently been founded as a Church of pure wheat. But the tares had returned, infiltrating the Church and banishing the Holy Spirit. For years they had dominated the Church, arguing that no one could tell the wheat from the tares. Nor did it matter whether a priest was a wicked person. Now, however, Muentzer, standing in the place of Christ, had begun to proclaim the return of the Holy Spirit and the consequent birth of the new Apostolic Church. But before that Church could be born, it was again attacked by the tares, once more under the guise of a purified Christian doctrine. This attack was no longer in doubt now that Luther had most wickedly slandered the Holy Spirit and labelled him a devil in Thomas Muentzer, God's chosen servant. It is to the second part of this comparison—Muentzer and the birth of the new Apostolic Church— that we must now turn.

CHAPTER VIII

Of Reform, "Godless" and "Pious Christian" Princes

You [the princes] must change and give way before the
Word of God. If you do not do so willingly, you will have to
under duress.

—Luther, "Ermahnung zum Frieden"

Thomas Muentzer's interpretation of Church history is of the first importance for an understanding of his reform program. He said as much
himself in his *Protestation* when he observed: "The damage [done to] an
injudicious world must first be recognized in all its origin, otherwise it
will not be possible for our understanding Father to put aside His
gracious rod of punishment."[1] Only the courageous truth, he asserted,
could free God's elect from the immeasurable damage already done to
Christendom. In order to understand the source of this damage, he had,
as he informed Franz Guenther shortly after the Leipzig Disputation,
turned to the study of Church history.[2] He reiterated this in his *Prague
Manifesto*, saying that he had read far and wide in the "histories of the
old Fathers." There he had discovered that "after the death of the
Apostles, the pure virgin church was quickly made into a prostitute by
the seductive priests."[3] The latter had banished the Holy Spirit from the
Church and then filled it with tares, in the process submerging the elect
to such an extent that no one could any longer distinguish them from
the tares.

It should not surprise us, then, that Muentzer could focus repeatedly,
and nowhere more forcefully than in his *Deutsch-Evangelische Messe,*
on the Parable of the Tares. There, in the opening lines, he asserted that
our Redeemer, Jesus Christ, had "proclaimed all the evils of Christendom in Matthew 13 well before they happened, when He said: 'While
the people slept . . . , the enemy came and sowed tares among the

wheat!' "[4] We have, from time to time, and especially in the third chapter, drawn the reader's attention to the importance of this parable for Muentzer's thought. Here we see it proclaimed once again, this time in splendid isolation, as exemplifying the central problem within Christendom. *All the evils,* Muentzer charges, are derived from the fact that the enemy has sown tares among the wheat in the Church while the people slept. Such a judgment can only signify that Muentzer had rejected the Constantinian/Augustinian view of the Church, even though he saw its downfall as having come a century and a half before Constantine. In the same way that he aspired toward a successful conversion through the work of the Holy Spirit for the individual, Muentzer intended to strive toward the creation of a new Apostolic Church of pure wheat in society.[5] Therefore, the separation of the wheat from the tares was of the greatest importance to him. It was a lesson taught by Christ and repeatedly confirmed in the history of the Church.

Even though Christ had "proclaimed all the evils in Christendom in Matthew 13 well before they happened," He had nevertheless, Muentzer continued, begun a true Christianity. In other words, the Apostolic Church begun by Christ had been the Church of pure wheat. It had become polluted, however, "because of the negligence of the indolent elect,"[6] and this in spite of St. Paul's warning in Acts 20:29 to guard against the ravening wolves that would "enter in among you" after his departure. To make sure that these warnings of Christ and Paul would not be perverted by some scribe's deceptive reasoning, twisting the meaning to suit his own devious purposes and in the process inflict even greater damage upon an already devastated Church, one had to take to hand all the "trustworthy" books of history. From such books, Muentzer declared, it became apparent that the above words of Christ and His chief apostle, as well as those of all the holy prophets concerning the ruined Church, had been more than fulfilled. And he once again cited "Egiosiopus . . . and Eusebius" as his prime witnesses.[7] Combined with the Parable of the Tares, this concept of a pure Apostolic Church is repeated in a number of other places in Muentzer's writings to explain the Church's fall.

If Christ had indeed "proclaimed all the evils of Christendom in Matthew 13 well before they happened," and if Sts. Peter and Paul had also predicted the infiltration of the Church by the tares, warning the early Christians to be on their guard, it had to follow, as Muentzer wrote Melanchthon in March 1522, that the early Church had "contained the apostolic practice as the norm to be imitated."[8] Although this

emphasis on the normative character of the Apostolic Church is nowhere systematically developed in Muentzer's writings, it nonetheless
constitutes a central theme of his reform thought. At various points in
his writings it is combined with the assertion that the holy prophets of
the Old Testament attempted to establish the pure Church. It was this
perspective, as we have seen, that determined Muentzer's very first
sermons in Zwickau and his attempt to establish the new Apostolic
Church, as he was to call it in his *Prague Manifesto*.[9]

If the mixing of the tares with the wheat in the Church was the cause
of "all the evils in Christendom," the solution must be, as Muentzer
never tired of asserting, to separate the wheat from the tares and begin
another "true Christianity." We have argued that he attempted to do so
as early as 1521 in Zwickau.[10] It was from within this context, then,
that Muentzer spoke to Melanchthon in March 1522 concerning the
normative nature of the Apostolic Church.[11] The latter was obviously to
be the model of the *futura ecclesia* in which personal sanctification was
to be practiced and in which the wheat was to be separated from the
tares.[12]

Muentzer pursued this theme in his later writings as well. In his Easter
1523 *Ordnung und Berechnung des Deutschen Ampts zu Allstedt*, he
remarked that he intended for the entire Psalm to be sung in the church
service as it "had been done at the beginning of Christianity through the
pious disciples of the holy Apostles."[13] And in the preface to his *Deutsch-
Evangelische Messe*, he contrasted the practice of the "deceiving, false
priests, monks and nuns," who read the Mass in Latin to an incom-
prehending congregation, with that of the Apostles who had taught their
listeners the clear Word of God.[14] He repeated the same message in his
Protestation, where he observed in the opening paragraph:

> After the omniscient and caring Head of the household made you into pure
> wheat and commanded you to bear fruit from the fertile soil, you have (be it
> miserably lamented to God) come to this that one can hardly tell the differ-
> ence between you [the "elect friends of God" to whom the piece is addressed]
> and the tares.[15]

The reason for this, Muentzer argued, was that the godless, the tares,
had become so prominent

> that that miserable, lamentable sighing in you, because of the very ornate
> masks of the red roses and the corn flowers, as well as of the prickly thistles,
> has been transformed into a displeasing spectre, a most disdainful mockery,
> and virtually rooted out. Yet this fervent sighing and longing to do God's

eternal will is without fail the only sure pathway to a truly apostolic Christianity which flows from the rock of living waters [the Holy Spirit] for the initiation and beginning of the elect. There is no other way to help the poor, miserable, lamentable, needy, insensitive and decadent Christianity than to point the elect [to this apostolic Christianity] with the most ardent desire, work and unstinting effort.[16]

Muentzer dealt with the same theme at even greater length in his *Fuerstenpredigt,* perhaps because he was attempting to persuade the Electoral Saxon princes to turn away from Luther to him. As usual, the passage stands at the very outset of the piece.[17] The mixing of the tares with the wheat had therefore been the cause of the Apostolic Church's downfall; the mixing itself, however, had been caused by an indolent elect. But in what ways had their lack of vigilance manifested itself? The question is important, for if Muentzer did indeed intend to understand the problem "in all its origin" in order to be able to cleanse the Church, the manner in which the tares had infiltrated her had to be understood. Muentzer makes only one specific reference to this problem, but it is a rather lengthy one and appears in his *Protestation.* There, in section 5, he once again encouraged the Church to "recognize who you are and what you were years ago at the time of the Apostles and their disciples, who, with earnest care watched over [the Church] so that the enemy, the adversary of all the pious, would not be able to mix the tares in with wheat." The way the early Church had done this, Muentzer argued, had been to "admit only mature persons; and these, whom they called catechumens, only after lengthy instruction." It was this aspect—instruction—that appears important in Muentzer's context, for he proceeded to argue that during that early period the Church had placed a greater emphasis upon the "inner essence" than upon the external "holy signs." Not unlike Erasmus, Muentzer considered a concentration upon such signs to smack of superstitition. Having made this introduction, he turned to the specific issue of baptism.[18]

At the very outset of his discussion of baptism, Muentzer asserted that none of the books of the Church Fathers said or proved anything "concerning what right baptism is." He therefore challenged all those learned in books, those great students of the "letter," to show him where it "is written in Holy Writ that a single immature [under-aged] child was baptized by Christ and His messengers, or where it is confirmed that our children are to be baptized in the manner now employed." Rather than argue for some other form of water baptism, however, some other form of the "holy sign," Muentzer reversed his field completely: "Indeed, because you boast so highly about it [i.e., water baptism], you will not find that Mary, the mother of God, or the disciples of Christ were baptized with water."[19] The point Muentzer wished to make, as the following paragraph clearly indicates, was that "The true baptism has not been understood, therefore admission to the Church has become a beastly monkey business." In this regard, Muentzer concluded, the scribes had betrayed the poor, pitiful mother, dear Christendom, from the very beginning beyond all measure. Did he mean to imply that at least in this one respect even the Apostolic Church had erred?

If water baptism, any form of water baptism, was the wrong kind of baptism because it diverted attention from the "inner essence" to the "holy signs," what, according to Muentzer, was true baptism? Muentzer began his analysis with John 3:5, a passage, he contended, the scribes had taken out of context. There John had written: "Unless one is born of water and the Spirit, he cannot enter the kingdom of God." No doubt, Muentzer conceded, these words were true; but their real meaning, "together with the harmonious and consistent whole of the Gospel of John, are concealed from poor Christendom." Touting his own spirit-filled exegetical method once again as providing the only correct interpretation of the above passage, Muentzer argued that true godly learning "must be demonstrated out of the holy Scriptures by means of a strict concordance of all its parts," that were clearly delineated in both Testaments. In the present case, all the parts of John's Gospel had to be taken into consideration in order to arrive at the correct interpretation of the above passage. Thus, Muentzer continued:

> Our scribes have not opened their eyes to the genuine truth, under the delusion that John 3 does not fit together with John 7, where the voice of truth says: "If any man thirst, let him come to me and drink. He who believes in me, as the Scripture has said, out of his body shall flow rivers of living water." *This he said of the Holy Spirit, whom the believers will receive in the future.* You see, dear companion, the evangelist interprets himself and speaks of the waters in the manner of the prophets, for the water is the stirring of our spirit in God's spirit, as John himself explains, drawing on Isaiah in John 1 [italics mine].[20]

Clearly, then, it was the baptism in the Holy Spirit, the coming of the Holy Spirit with transforming power into a man's soul, that Thomas Muentzer was concerned with, not the holy signs, the external trappings, whether for infant or adult baptism.[21] Those concerned with the trappings were the scribes whom Tauler had called men of merely externalized religion. The elect friends of God, by contrast, had experienced the inner essence, they had been transformed by the power of the Holy Spirit. Therefore both infant and adult baptism, Muentzer argued, detracted from the inner, the spiritual, the absolutely essential transformation Tauler had himself so often emphasized.[22]

These "heathenish rites and ceremonies," Muentzer asserted, these external holy signs, had seduced the elect. They were therefore an "abomination in the holy place." Through infant baptism "immature children were made into Christians and the catechumens dispensed with." Consequently, Christians had become children, "for then all understanding disappeared from the Church." Then the real baptism was "covered up with that loathsome, hypocritical relationship called 'godfather,' which is much praised with great pomp and clung to as a dog clings to a sausage."[23]

Since Muentzer regarded the inner essence, not the holy signs, as important, he appears to have retained the practice of infant baptism in his Allstedt reforms.[24] In his *Ordnung und Berechnung* of 1523 he wrote:

> *When we baptize a child,* the godparents are admonished by their soul's salvation, to pay attention to what takes place during the baptismal ceremony, so that, when the child has come of age, they are able to explain it to him so that baptism may, with time, come to be *understood* [italics mine].[25]

Again, it would appear to be the *understanding* of the true meaning of baptism Muentzer wished to ensure; he was relatively indifferent to the external symbol. With infant baptism, however, Muentzer retained what he was shortly to criticize in the most severe terms: he kept right on inducting tares into the Church along with the wheat. This seems to have become apparent to him later.[26] How did he intend to resolve this dilemma?

Muentzer's solution must be set within the broader context of two kinds of people St. Paul had described in Galatians 4:21–31, where he had observed that Abraham had had two sons: one by a free woman and one by a bond woman. Muentzer took this statement to mean that whereas some people were of the elect, the rest belonged to the reprobates. The two had been at enmity since the days of Abraham, for those born of the bond woman had persecuted those born of the free. The former would never change; the latter, however, because they were the elect, had the potential of being reborn through the Spirit if only they could be shown the right way. Muentzer attacked the scribes and Pharisees precisely because they scoffed at the possibility of possessing the

Holy Spirit and refused to show, indeed were incapable of showing, the right way to salvation. Consequently, the friends of God were kept from experiencing the transformation of their lives through the power of the Holy Spirit.

Since instruction in this baptism of the Holy Spirit was so important in Muentzer's theological scheme of things, he repeated that only persons who had *experienced* such a transformation themselves ought to serve as preachers. As early as his *Prague Manifesto* he proclaimed: "The people exist without the right kind of shepherds, for they have never been *taught how to experience* the faith" [italics mine].[27] The reason for this failure, he observed in his *Ordnung und Berechnung,* was that the preachers had never experienced it themselves. There, speaking of his liturgical reforms, Muentzer observed:

> Thereupon the entire congregation wishes God's servant a pure spirit (as St. Paul teaches his disciple Timothy, saying): "And with your spirit," in order that the same needy congregation not have a godless man as a minister. For whoever does not possess the Holy Spirit is not a child of God; therefore, how can such a man know anything about the work of God when he has not *experienced* it? If he knows nothing about it how will he instruct others? In this fashion one blind man leads another in ignorance.[28]

He made the same observation in his *Von dem Gedichteten Glauben,*[29] his *Ausgedrueckte Entbloessung,*[30] and his *Hochverursachte Schutzrede.*[31]

Muentzer described this spirit-filled preacher more fully in his *Ausgedrueckte Entbloessung.* There, in a passage where he claimed that Luther's teachings produced no change in his followers, Muentzer compared such preachers to John the Baptist:

> John is a very different preacher, an angel who bears witness to Christ, and who is the prototype of every true preacher. Like John, everyone must have this praise not because of his good works, but because of his earnestness which produces a courageous watchfulness that eventually leads to an alienation from one's passions. This [in turn] allows the powers of the soul to become exposed so that the abyss of the soul, where the Holy Spirit communes with our spirit, may become visible in all its power, Psalm 84. A true preacher must, through such an exposure [of the soul], be driven in wondrous ways from the time of his youth to suppress his own will. That is why John the Baptist, who was declared holy already in his mother's womb, has become the prototype of all [true] preachers. It is from such a foundation that preachers must know Who it is that sends them into the harvest, Matth. 9, John 4, a harvest for which God has honed them like a mighty scythe or sickle from the very beginning of their life.[32] Not everyone is capable of

fulfilling such an office, even though he may have read all the books, for one must first become assured of his own faith, as those were who wrote the Scriptures. Otherwise all we will produce is a discussion [conducted by] thieves and a war of words.[33]

Such a spirit-filled preacher would be able not only to instruct the "scattered sheep of [God's] pasture," which Muentzer obviously considered of critical importance, but also to discern the presence of the Holy Spirit in others.[34] And the sure sign of the Spirit's presence was a person's growing sanctification. Had he not learned as much from pseudo-Tauler's conversion and from Tauler himself? Did he not wait to judge the Wittenberg movement until the first reforms had been made in early 1522? Sanctification and separation, therfore, were the twin pillars upon which Muentzer intended to build the new Apostolic Church. But discerning who was making progress in terms of sanctification and who needed to be separated from the Church could only be done by someone who possessed the Holy Spirit.

There was one other method Muentzer recommended to keep this Church pure once it was formed. That was, as he suggested to Melanchthon in his March 1522 letter, to see to it that members of the Church bear only "elect" children. There, combining the idea of producing elect children with sanctification because the soul had to be freed from the lower passions, Muentzer recommended that the Wittenbergers were to "have wives as though they had them not." Indulging sexual passion at will, even if only in the marriage bed, hindered the Holy Spirit. Therefore, Christians were to

> Pay what you owe, not as the heathen do, but as those who know that God speaks to you, commands you, admonishes, in order that you know with certainty when you are to pay that which you owe [i.e., have sexual intercourse] in order to produce an elect child, so that the fear of God and the spirit of wisdom keep you from those brute passions and you be not devoured by them.[35]

In a *Table Talks* of 1535 Luther drew attention to this passage, observing:

> Once he [Muentzer] wrote to Luther and Melanchthon together: I am pleased that you at Wittenberg attack the pope so strongly, but your prostitute's marriage [Hurrenehe] does not please me! For he taught concerning marriage that a man might only sleep with his wife if he had been convinced by a godly revelation that intercourse would produce an elect child; those who did not act in accordance with this committed prostitution with their wives. Because of this advice a couple of Zwickau matrons were motivated

> to confess openly, after they had slept with their husbands: this night I have been a prostitute.[36]

If Luther's information was correct, Muentzer must have recommended the above approach to childbearing in the *futura ecclesia* already to his congregation in Zwickau, another indication that he had arrived there with all the elements of his program in place. Whatever the case, Muentzer is concerned not so much with practicing the external rite of baptism, as with teaching the elect how to appropriate the Holy Spirit, how to recognize and nurture those who had accepted the Holy Spirit, how to discern and exclude from the Church those who did not possess the Holy Spirit, and how to produce elect children in the Church who would have the potential to possess the Holy Spirit.

From the very outset Muentzer assumed that the vast majority of the people—a very ambiguous term in his usage—given the proper instruction in the way to arrive at a true faith, would accept, thereby demonstrating that they belonged to the elect. As early as his *Prague Manifesto* Muentzer declared:

> But I have no doubts about the [common] people. Oh you right, poor and pitiable little band, how you have thirsted for the Word of God! For it is apparent that no one, or at least very few, know what they should believe and which groups they should align themselves with. They desire to do that which is right but do not know what that is of themselves. For they do not know how to accommodate themselves to the testimony, which the Holy Spirit speaks in their hearts. The reason is that they have been made to fear the Spirit of the fear of God so greatly that the prophecy of Jeremiah has been fulfilled in them: "The children have begged for bread, but there was no one who could have broken it to them." Alas, alas, no one broke it to them. There were indeed many money-hungry rascals [priests] who threw the papal texts of the Bible, which they had not experienced, before the poor, poor people, as one is accustomed to throw bread to the dogs. But they did not break it to them through the skill of the Holy Spirit, that is, *they did not open their minds that they might recognize the Holy Spirit in themselves*. For all of the priests, even if they were thrown onto one big pile, would not be able to make even one single person understand how to prepare himself for eternal life. What more shall I say? [italics mine].[37]

The above passage leaves little doubt that Muentzer like Jeremiah saw the priests, reprobates that they were, as responsible for corruption of the elect. At the same time, he assumed that the common man would be only too eager to accept the right path to salvation if shown the way. Also like Jeremiah, therefore, Muentzer pronounced a "Woe . . . unto the pastors that destroy and scatter the sheep of [God's] pasture!" For "both prophet and priest are profane." As a consequence, the land had come to be filled with adulterers. What was needed under these circumstances, of course, were spirit-filled pastors, priests who had themselves experienced the transformation of their lives through the power of the Holy Spirit. But there were none, and so the flock had been scattered and driven away. Muentzer assumed that the masses would respond eagerly to his message concerning the Holy Spirit.

That Muentzer uses the term "poor people"[38] in the above context rather than in a social, economic, or political context—at least at this early stage of his public activity—is amply confirmed by other passages. In the same treatise, he spoke of the "damned people"—in contrast to the "poor" or "common people,"—as "very prominent damned villains, who have been in the entire world from the beginning, set there to be a plague for the poor people which lack understanding [in spiritual matters]." Since the leaders in the Church were in fact reprobates, they had "no right, either before God or before man, to speak for these people or even claim to do so. . . . Therefore, priests cannot be of any use to the Church, for they deny the voice of the bridegroom."[39] This passage clearly asserts that the people's poverty is spiritual, brought on by the "damned villains"—the priests—who speak for them and deny them access to the Holy Spirit. Economic poverty is not Muentzer's first concern.

In a third passage of the *Manifesto*, Muentzer lamented the deception of the people by the whoremongering priests, servants of the devil, who "devour the dead words of Scripture" and "thereafter . . . dump the letter and this inexperienced faith into the midst of this upright but poor people." In this way they make their salvation uncertain and "scatter the sheep of God so greatly that nowhere any longer can one discern the face of the Church. For there is no longer anyone present who is able to separate the good, who are unknown, from the large mass [of humanity]."[40] In this passage the "poor people" are equated with the "scattered sheep of God," a phrase repeatedly used in Jeremiah 23. Because of these false prophets, the people were forced to live without true shepherds. Once again, the importance of the "earnest servants," the Spirit-filled preachers, becomes apparent in Muentzer's thought.

Since the Church, led and guided by reprobate priests, had arrived at a religion which no longer possessed even the slightest understanding of what constituted the inner essence of Christianity, the common man had placed his faith in the "vain masks" of an externalized religion.[41] Nevertheless, as Muentzer repeatedly argued, this same common man was hungry for the inner essence, for the truth as he had understood it. He must have begun to realize this at least by the time he reached Zwickau, perhaps on being transferred from the Church of St. Mary to that of St. Catherine. For by the time he arrived in Prague, Muentzer proclaimed it in his *Manifesto* as a truth. In both Zwickau and Prague, however, the ruling authorities had thrust themselves between him and the people, forcing him in each instance to depart empty-handed. This obstacle was not found in Allstedt where for a year and some four months, the elect servant of God entered into the midst of the people hungry for the true faith. The results of their meeting must have confirmed Muentzer in his reading of Jeremiah.[42]

GROWING OPPOSITION TO "GODLESS" PRINCES

Muentzer arrived in Allstedt around the beginning of April 1523. The town, relatively small at the time, was located in an enclave belonging to Electoral Saxony already exposed to Protestant ideas before Muentzer's time.[43] The surrounding territory, the bulk of which belonged to George Duke of Saxony, Luther's most bitter opponent, and his vassal Ernest Count of Mansfeld, was almost solidly Catholic. Allstedt was therefore surrounded by hostile territory, and it did not take long for Muentzer to become involved in an extended conflict with both of these Catholic princes, a conflict that was to determine his attitude toward Catholic, or "godless," princes. As we shall see, Muentzer's attitude toward these Catholic princes was very different from the one he was later to adopt toward reformed, "pious Christian" princes. Not only are these different attitudes the product of the ideas he brought with him to Allstedt, but they are determined to a large degree by the very concrete circumstances in which he found himself. It is to these that we turn first.

By Easter 1523, Muentzer's *Ordnung und Berechnung* and *Deutsch-Evangelische Messe* were already in print and presumably in use. For the first time in many years the ordinary parishioner was able to understand what was being transacted in the church service. Instruction and understanding, as we have seen, were Muentzer's primary concerns in the matter of baptism; his opening remarks in the above pieces make apparent that they were also his chief objectives here.[44] Combined with his fiery sermons, Muentzer's German services quickly began to draw people, not only from Allstedt, but also from the surrounding Catholic territories. Ernest Count of Mansfeld appears to have been the first to attempt to inhibit his subjects from attending Muentzer's innovative Allstedt services.[45]

Exactly when the Count ordered the prohibition is not evident. According to Muentzer, it was issued almost immediately after the introduction of his German Mass toward the end of April 1523. In a letter of 4 October 1523, Muentzer informed Frederick the Wise that he had protested the Count's action. That protest must have been ineffective, for on 13 September Muentzer denounced the Count openly from his pulpit.[46]

To explain Muentzer's reaction to this "magisterial" opposition to his preaching and innovative church services, we must keep in mind several things. First, the large number of people responding to these services cannot have been without significance to Muentzer.[47] For some time now in the words of Jeremiah he had been describing the common people as the "scattered sheep of God's pasture," denied access to the living voice of God by priests who, because they belonged to the reprobates and were therefore incapable of having their lives transformed by the power of the Holy Spirit, kept everyone else from this experience as well. Now he, Thomas Muentzer, was once again proclaiming the Holy Spirit and the people were beginning to respond in overwhelming numbers. God had made him, as he informed Frederick the Wise in his letter of 4 October 1523, into an "earnest preacher." He was the new John, the preacher filled with grace, who had experienced all the facets of the faith he was to describe in his exposition of the first chapter of the Gospel of Luke. And the people, the elect who had the potential to experience this transformation of their lives through the advent of the Holy Spirit, were indeed responding.

Second, Muentzer's devastating criticism of the clergy must be recalled in this context. He had called them false prophets because they had subverted the Church and forced the Holy Spirit to depart from it. And just when it seemed that he had finally found a haven—after severe spiritual testing—from which to renew the Church through the "living Word of God," the Catholic princes began to impede the spread of that message. Ernest Count of Mansfeld might have asserted that his objections to Muentzer's innovations were based on a recent Imperial edict.[48] Muentzer, however, saw this action and the similar measures taken by George Duke of Saxony later as opposition to God's Word. What the Catholic Church had done for over a thousand years, the Catholic princes were attempting to do now that the Church was under attack.

Did they not, therefore, belong in the same camp with the scribes and Pharisees? It was precisely this argument that Muentzer raised in his letter to the Count of 22 September 1523. There, in his response to the Count's complaint to Zeiss and the Allstedt Council that he had been denounced from the pulpit, Muentzer wrote:

> Greetings, most noble count. The Electoral Commissioner and Council of Allstedt have shown me your letter, in which you complain that I called you an heretical knave and extortionist. On the whole it is true, and I know for a fact—is it not notorious?—that you have harshly forbidden your subjects by means of a public edict from attending my heretical mass or sermons. I spoke openly in response, and I intend to accuse you before all Christians, *because you were so bold as to forbid the holy Gospel.* And if, which God forbid, you should intend to continue in such madness and mindless prohibition, then I will yet this very day, while the blood still flows in my veins, not only accuse you before Christendom but also write books against you and have them translated into many tongues, calling you a miserable and stupid man to the Turks, Heathen and Jews. You should also know that, in such important and just causes, I do not fear the entire world. Christ Himself cries woe to those who take away the key to the understanding of God, Luke 11. The key to the knowledge of God, however, is the means by which the people are ruled, that they learn to fear God alone, Romans 13. For the fear of God is the beginning of true Christian wisdom. But since you wish to be feared more than God, as I shall demonstrate by means of your actions and edict, you are the one who takes away the key to the knowledge of God and forbids the people to go to church.[49] And you do not provide them with a better way. I intend to continue what I have begun in my services and sermons through the holy Scriptures, even to the most trifling of matters. In order to be able to do this I am willing to put anything that I may possess, including body and soul, on the line. If you are unable to defend yourself against me except by the sword, then, for God's sake, refrain from it. Should you nevertheless determine to do something, be apprised that the conflict will be endless. The prophet says: "There is no wisdom, no insight, no plan that can succeed against the Lord." I, like you, am a servant of God; therefore take it easy, for the whole world must also exercise patience. Do not crack, or the old garment will tear. Should you succeed in turning me over to the oppressor, I shall deal with you a hundred times more severely than Luther dealt with the pope. If you can, wish me well; if not, God will judge. Amen. Given at Allstedt 22 September 1523.
>
> Thomas Muentzer, a destroyer of unbelievers [italics mine].[50]

The Count's action, therefore, was an extension of that of the scribes and Pharisees: he too was attempting to deny the living voice of God to the scattered sheep of God's pasture.

The Count refused to heed Muentzer's warning, however. On 24 September he wrote Frederick the Wise to complain of the treatment he had received at Muentzer's hands because, as he put it, he had "forbidden [his] subjects from attending the sermon and Mass" in Allstedt. His action, he asserted, resulted from his compliance with the most recent Imperial edict which had commanded all subjects to eschew innovations in their religious services. He had not, he maintained, prohibited his subjects from hearing God's Word.[51]

Frederick responded with a letter of 28 September to Hans Zeiss and the Allstedt Council, informing the Council that he had received copies of the exchange between Muentzer and the Count and that he did not approve of Muentzer's actions. But since he was not fully informed as to what had transpired—and even who had appointed Muentzer to his post—he desired a full accounting from Zeiss and the Council. Frederick was not prepared, it seemed, to act one way or another solely on the Count's complaint.[52] The same day he also wrote to the Count of Mansfeld, saying that while he disapproved of what had happened, he was not willing to inhibit the spread of the Gospel. And he would find out about Muentzer and how he had come to Allstedt.[53]

On 4 October Muentzer wrote Frederick himself. The latter's attitude with respect to the spread of the Gospel must by now have been familiar to Muentzer. Perhaps it was for that reason that he felt emboldened to inform the elector that "since almighty God has made me into an earnest preacher, I have cultivated the habit of blowing the versatile and resounding trumpets so that they may reverberate with the zeal of the learning of God."[54] Because the world hated this Word, it also hated him. To the "small, poor and needy flock," however, it was the sweet-smelling savor of life. Fervent zeal for this poor, downtrodden Christendom had consumed him; therefore, he had been persecuted and driven from one place to another without just cause in recent years. All this had led him to the conclusion that the "open proclamation of the pure Word of God" was the only way to save the Church.

Having said this, Muentzer turned to the issue at hand. No sooner, he asserted, had he introduced Psalms and songs of praise into his church service, along with his German Mass, than the Count of Mansfeld had begun—and had continued throughout the summer—to forbid, and attempt to hinder, his subjects from attending these services. This had begun, Muentzer charged, well before the Imperial edict had been issued. By his actions, said Muentzer, the Count was giving cause, both to his own subjects and to the citizens of Allstedt, to revolt.[55] It was not he, Muentzer, who was the cause of unrest; it was the Count.

Muentzer was preaching the "pure Word"; the Count was hindering it. And so he continued:

> Should it come to pass that someone should attempt to stop the spread of the Gospel by means of human laws, Isaiah 29, Matth. 15, and Titus 1, and *at the same time not abide by the letter of the edict while attempting to implement it,* one will only confuse the masses who, according to Romans 13, are to love more than fear their rulers [italics mine].

The princes had not been placed in office to frighten the pious who wished to hear the Gospel. If they did so, the sword would be taken from them and given to the fervent people to the destruction of the godless. Were this to happen, peace would flee from the earth. In closing, Muentzer alluded to the end of the age when Christ would Himself rule, and he appealed to Frederick, under these circumstances, for a fair hearing.[56]

A number of contentious issues in Muentzer's quarrel with the Count of Mansfeld demand further discussion. The first has to do with the date on which the Imperial edict in question went into effect. The second concerns what that edict in fact mandated. And the third touches on whether the Count forbade his subjects from attending Muentzer's services before the edict went into effect.

The edict in question, initially drafted in response to the papal nuncio's address to the Diet of Nuremberg in late 1522, in which the pope insisted that the Diet take action against Luther, was first published for the entire empire on 6 March 1523. To be effective, however, it had to be implemented by the individual local governing authorities. Thus, while Luther appears to have had a copy of the edict in hand by 8 March, Frederick did not promulgate it until 25 May.[57] If Luther was in possession of a copy by early March, it is quite possible that the Count of Mansfeld also had a copy early.[58] If so, he may well have acted upon it as soon as he became aware of Muentzer's activities in Allstedt. Muentzer, however, living within the borders of Electoral Saxony, must have operated on the promulgation date 25 May. Indeed, like others,[59] he may well have read the edict from his pulpit at the behest of the elector himself. If, therefore, the Count did indeed forbid the attendance of his subjects at Muentzer's services shortly after the latter had introduced his German Mass in late April 1523, then, from Muentzer's perspective, the Count was indeed attempting to use the edict retroactively to justify his actions. If, however, the Count of Mansfeld was in possession of a copy of the Imperial edict shortly after it was issued and decided to act upon it with respect to Muentzer's innovations, then he was fully honest in his letter of 24 September to the elector. It is possible, therefore, that both parties believed right to be on their side.

The more important issue, however, is the exact mandate of the edict. Framed essentially by the Lutheran sympathizer, Johann von Schwarzenberg,[60] it was a document ambiguous enough to be acceptable to the majority of the Catholics on the committee charged with drawing it up. From the committee, it went to the larger body where it passed with only minor revisions. The critical passage of that final version proclaimed

> that every elector, prince, prelate, count and other estate in the realm shall, with all possible diligence, so order and decree that all preachers in his territory are justly and equitably advised to avoid everything that might lead to disobedience, dissention and revolt in the holy empire, or that might cause Christians to be led astray [in their faith]. Instead, they are to preach and teach only the holy Gospel and that in accordance with the interpretation of the Scriptures as approved and accepted by the holy Christian Church.[61]

Now, there are manifestly two distinct aspects to the above part of the edict, both of which are important for the quarrel between Muentzer and the Count of Mansfeld. The latter, as his letter of 24 September to Frederick makes apparent enough, concentrated on the first part: Muentzer's liturgical innovations which, according to the Count, were inciting his subjects to disobedience. It was not the "holy Gospel" he was prohibiting; he was trying to prevent "disobedience, dissention and revolt." Muentzer, however, as did Luther in his "Wider die Verkehrer und Faelscher kaiserlichs Mandats," focused his attention on the "preaching and teaching of the holy Gospel," which he believed the Count to be trying to hinder. Whereas he did not go into so great detail as did Luther in his tract, Muentzer's position was not so different in this respect from that of his colleague at Wittenberg.[62] It is important to make the point at this early stage of Muentzer's opposition to the Catholic princes. The similarity can be seen in Luther's tract, where he wrote:

> *One is to preach the Gospel* according to the interpretation of those teachers accepted and approved by the Christian Church. This article they [the Catholics] interpret in such a way as to mean that one is not to preach the Gospel any differently from the way in which the universities, foundations and monasteries with their teachers Thomas, Scotus, and others whom the Roman Catholic Church has approved, teach.
> But we do not find anything in the edict concerning the Roman Catholic Church, nor about Thomas or the universities; rather, it speaks of "the Christian Church." And we should note, in accordance with the plain words,

that it means the oldest teachers, such as Augustine, Cyprian, Hilary and the like even though it is common knowledge that these teachers did not all teach the same things nor even always the correct things. We therefore assert that the Christian Church did not, nor can it, go beyond that which St. Augustine, that special light of the Christian Church, proclaimed and repeatedly asserted when he said: "Only to those holy books, which are called canonical, do I ascribe the honor of believing that their authors were without error; the rest I read in such a way that, no matter how holy or learned, I do not consider them to be right unless they persuade me by means of the Holy Scriptures or clear reason."[63]

Perhaps because of his greater involvement with the edict—it was, after all, addressed to the movement begun by him—Luther recognized nearly immediately the way in which Catholics would seek to interpret it. He, of course, interpreted it differently. On 7 August 1523 he informed the elector, through the latter's emissaries, that if the edict were indeed to be interpreted in a Catholic sense, "he would not follow nor be obedient to it."[64] Others, like Martin Bucer of Strasbourg, interpreted it in an even more positive sense, as "*commanding* that one . . . preach the Gospel in accordance with the teachers accepted by the Christian Church."[65] Johannes Laue, at the time of the edict in Weimar but during the Peasants' War in Muehlhausen with Pfeiffer and Muentzer, said very much the same thing in his 1528 confession: "about the time when the Imperial edict was issued which declared that one was to preach the Gospel clearly and purely."[66] Muentzer appears to have read the edict in the same strongly affirmative sense: that is, that the edict *mandated* the preaching of the holy Gospel. If that is indeed the case, then Ernest of Mansfeld and Duke George, in their oposition to this law of the realm, were quite obviously the cause of revolution, as Muentzer asserted later. They were indeed tyrants, at least from his perspective. From the outset there appear to have been two opposing interpretations of this Imperial edict. Thomas Muentzer came down on the side of Luther, Bucer, and many others supporting Luther's reformation;[67] Ernest of Mansfeld and Duke George came down on the Catholic side.

When Luther spoke of the "perverters and falsifiers" of the edict in the title of his tract, he may well have had Duke George of Saxony uppermost in mind. If so, the Duke's action with respect to his subjects in Sangerhausen proved him right. For on 13 February 1524 the latter forbade his Sangerhausen subjects from attending Muentzer's Allstedt services, issuing the following order to his magistrate in the city:

We have received credible information to the effect that a number of people from your jurisdiction have been going to the sermons in Allstedt. But since the preacher there has dared to teach the common folk many deceptive articles of faith which are opposed to the order and tradition of the holy Christian churches, he has caused the simple to be misled into error and enticed into rebellion. At the same time he has introduced many innovations which deviate from the usage of the holy Christian Church.[68]

Duke George went on to command the official to inform his subjects, under threat of punishment, to stay away from Muentzer's services. "Should you catch anyone violating this order even in the slightest," he wrote, "you must not allow such a person to go unpunished."[69] He said nothing at all about preaching or teaching the "holy Gospel."

Muentzer does not appear to have responded to the Duke's actions with respect to the citizens of Sangerhausen until 15 July 1524.[70] Why it took him so much longer to react in this instance than in that of the Count of Mansfeld is not immediately apparent. Perhaps he was preoccupied with other matters like his escalating quarrel with Luther. Perhaps other things kept him from asserting himself. Whatever the case, he must have been well aware of these events in Sangerhausen, for in that same 11 April report to Frederick, Zeiss and the Allstedt Council wrote: "Who will protect us poor people? *Because of the Gospel* our enemies daily threaten to burn, destroy, displace or take us captive. If we were to complain every time we are threatened, Your Excellency would have no peace night or day" [italics mine].[71] The conflict with the Convent of Naundorf, to which the town of Allstedt paid dues, and the burning of the chapel at Mallerbach on 24 March 1524 must also have taken up some of his time, for, in his confession, he admitted to being present.[72] This was a time in which the Catholic forces in the surrounding regions were out to suppress him and his version of the holy Gospel.

All of these concerns are reflected in his letter of 30 May 1524 to Christoph Meinhard with its exposition of Psalm 18. Aside from once again being a frontal attack on Luther's doctrine of salvation and a justification of his own mystical theology, Muentzer made direct references to the "godless" who were currently giving him so much trouble. He observed "that the godless [might appear to] retain the regiment for ever, but the bridegroom is [in the process of] coming out of his bedchamber with power."[73] By that he meant to imply that Christ was about to arise once more—had he slept since the mid-second century?— and dethrone the godless. He was obviously referring to the Catholic princes who were opposed to the spread of his version of the Gospel in violation of the Imperial edict.

To this point the Count of Mansfeld had been the focal point of

Muentzer's attack on the godless princes. Not until mid-July did he come to the rescue of his Sangerhausen followers with a series of letters, and then only, as he observed in his confession, because Thilo Banse,[74] a sympathetic preacher in that city, had admonished him to write, urging the Christians there to stand by the Gospel and persecute those who opposed it. He remarked further that he had criticized both the Count and the Duke because their subjects had complained to him *"that the Word of God was not being preached to them* and that they were forbidden to attend services [where it was being preached]. Nor would they [the rulers] back down [from this prohibition]" [italics mine].[75] Muentzer advised these people to complain to their overlords. Should nothing come of this, they were to come to his services, for no one was to be kept from hearing the Gospel.[76] We do not know to what extent Muentzer based his argument in the Imperial edict.

Whether Thilo Banse's letter, which is no longer extant, was the real motivation behind Muentzer's three letters to Sangerhausen of 15 July 1524 may be left in abeyance. In the first, addressed to those who already feared God, Muentzer encouraged his followers to stand by his message, to fear God, and to have their faith deepened. To fear God in the proper manner, however, they would have to be freed from the fear of tyrants.[77] He had told the Count of Mansfeld as much earlier. Then, to encourage his followers, he informed them that God, in His goodness, had now

> provided a rich provision, in that more than thirty announcements and leagues of the elect have been made. In every land things are beginning to happen. . . . Do not let your hearts sink, as those tyrants are doing, Numbers 24. It is a just judgment of God that they are so terribly hard of heart, for God intends to tear them up by their roots, as Joshua has declared in chapter 11. Fear God your Lord alone, then your fear will be pure, Psalm 18.[78]

The second letter was addressed to the magistrates in Sangerhausen. Muentzer warned them not to persecute Thilo Banse. It was enough, he charged, that he, Muentzer, had been forced to listen to them all year long, maligning his teaching and forbidding their subjects from attending his services. He would not stand idly by and watch them persecute their own preachers as well. There were, he asserted, no more idolatrous people in the land than they, for one could not at one and the same time forbid the holy Gospel and be a Christian. They had either to accept that Gospel or regard themselves as heathen.

The third letter was addressed to his persecuted followers in that city, presumably those who, as a consequence of Duke George's order, had been—or were being—punished in one fashion or another for their attendance at Muentzer's services.[79] These he informed that Christ had, at His Last Supper, told His disciples how the wicked world would react when "the elect people would begin to recognize the crucified Christ and grasp the true faith." Citing John 16:1—a passage close to Tauler's remark that "nowadays good appearing Christians persecute those who would closely follow Christ"[80]—Muentzer warned his followers that they were, as St. Paul had predicted, entering upon a most dangerous time in which those who sought to follow the Gospel and do what was right would be labelled godless heretics and scoundrels. After once again speaking at some length about his interpretation of salvation, Muentzer reminded his persecuted followers that secular rulers had jurisdiction only over temporal matters and nothing else, as Sts. Peter and Paul affirmed. While subjects were to pay their required dues, the secular rulers were to "have no rule over our souls, for in these matters one must obey God rather than man. Make of that what you will."[81] He told them to fear those who could kill the soul, not those who might kill the body. And they were to suffer persecution as long as God allowed it, *"and until you recognize your own errors"* [italics mine].[82] In other words, Muentzer implied that the elect might act only after they have themselves been fully purified.

The main error Muentzer castigated in his followers was their attachment to material things, the "creatures" defined by mystical theology. He therefore admonished his "beloved brethren" to take an example from the "elect friends of God," how they conducted themselves in time of temptation:

> If you love your possessions then look at dear Job, that holy friend of God, and how *gelassen* he remained. As it is written in the first chapter of his book, when the messenger came and informed him that all his children and all his possessions had been destroyed, he responded with *Gelassenheit* and said cheerfully: "the Lord gave, and the Lord hath taken away."[83]

The holy martyrs of old had done the same. And God loved those suffering in Sangerhausen every bit as much as these. Had He not bought them all with the precious blood of His dear Son, and wished to impart His Holy Spirit to them as well? Indeed, it was so. But before this could happen they too would have to empty themselves of all attachments to "creatures" and stand completely *gelassen* before God.

This imperative Muentzer associated with an impending cataclysm, for his advice to his followers continued with this prediction:

> Therefore I say to you truly . . . the time has come when a bloodbath must come over this hardened world because of its unbelief. When that happens, I know for a fact that all those who were not willing to sacrifice their possessions for God's sake will have to do so for the devil's, and without his thanks. Why do you let yourselves be led around by the nose for so long? For it is well known, and can be easily proven from the Scriptures, that lords and princes, because of the way they are now acting, are not Christian. At the same time, your priests and monks pray to the devil and are even less Christian. Thus all your preachers are hypocrites and worshippers of men. Why then should you still hope? There is little to be hoped for from the princes. Therefore, whoever wishes to fight against the Turk has no need to travel far afield; the Turk is in the land. You, however, should act as I advised you above in order that you may have cause against them and not they against you. So, tell them straight to their face: "Dear lord! St. Paul teaches, saying: 'The Word of God is to be free and not bound.' Why then do you wish to forbid us from hearing it? You did not previously prevent people from running to St. James and to the devil at Heckenbach, you did not prevent them from becoming widows and orphans, or have their money and goods taken out of the country. But now you wish to prevent us from going where we must; you will neither allow us to have [our own] right preachers nor to go elsewhere to hear others. If such are indeed your intentions, I will hold you for a Turk, not a Christian prince or lord." Tell them freely and openly that you will take your stand, that you will fear God alone and not be hypocritical. Should injury come to you as a result, God will Himself stand by you and exact revenge. Do not be hypocritical, for if you are, God will make you so afraid that you will never be able to arrive at truth and will suffer great damage to your soul's salvation. God cannot forsake His elect, even though it may at times appear so, for at the right moment He will take His revenge.[84]

There are a number of aspects to this letter that demand our attention. In the first place, could Muentzer have made it any clearer not only that material possessions were not his primary concern, but that he viewed attachment to them as a positive hindrance to salvation? Second, these possessions will have to be sacrificed in one fashion or another, if not willingly to God, then of necessity to the devil. Third, because of the way the princes had acted since his arrival in Allstedt, Muentzer obviously did not regard them as Christian; therefore, nothing was to be hoped for from them in terms of reform. Though perhaps not so bad in this regard as the monks and priests, they were nonetheless actively opposed to the proclamation of God's Word. Fourth, because of this hardened opposition to himself and his teaching from both the Church and the secular rulers, Muentzer proclaimed that a "bloodbath must come over this hardened world."

This last remark is especially intriguing in light of Muentzer's repeated assertions that the new Apostolic Church was about to be born. That birth was to take place in the time of harvest. He had also said that Christ was about to arise from a long sleep and assert Himself like a mighty warrior. The opposition of the Catholic princes and the hesitancy on the part of the princes of Electoral Saxony to take decisive action as we shall see, however, must have convinced Muentzer by the summer of 1524 that the Gospel would not be preached openly until the princes had been forced to allow it, in spite of the 6 March 1523 Imperial edict. In this bloodbath God would stand only by His elect friends. For, said Muentzer, "God cannot forsake His elect, even though it may at times appear so. At the right moment He will take His revenge." That moment appeared in the offing.

Before we retrace our steps to pick up the strand of Muentzer's relationship with the Dukes of Electoral Saxony, one more thing must be established. From the very outset of our discussion of Muentzer's relationship to the Catholic princes the focal point has been the statement Muentzer quoted from St. Paul in the above letter: "The Word of God is to be free and not bound." This statement came to be inextricably intertwined with the Imperial edict of 6 March 1523. It remained the central issue for Muentzer in this last letter to his imprisoned followers in Sangerhausen as well. Whereas he clearly argued that the princes opposing him were not as unchristian as the monks and priests, he did say they were not Christian. He judged them by their actions, their persistent and inveterate attempts to hinder the preaching of the Gospel, more particularly his reading of the Gospel, in opposition to the clear mandate of the Imperial edict. Therefore, little was to be hoped for from the princes any longer. This is striking in light of what he was to write Hans Zeiss only ten days later with respect to King Josiah and the *Bund* as portrayed in 2 Kings 22 and 23. For there he was to talk of a "modest covenant . . . in which the common man may ally himself with the pious ruler only for the sake of the Gospel." Muentzer was certain that Ernest Count of Mansfeld and George Duke of Saxony did not belong to such pious rulers. But did the Dukes of Electoral Saxony? And how could the elect bring about change if there were no pious rulers?

THE BUND

Muentzer's estrangement from the pro-Catholic princes began with his conflict with the Count of Mansfeld. It centered essentially on the free preaching of and access to the holy Gospel the Imperial edict had apparently mandated. His gradual estrangement from the Dukes of Electoral Saxony appears to have begun with the burning of the chapel at Mallerbach, and concerned itself primarily with the extermination of "idolatrous" priests and their places of worship. To that part of the story we must now turn.

Just outside Allstedt, on the road to Querfurt, stood the small chapel of Mallerbach dedicated to the Virgin Mary. Maintained by the nuns from the nearby Convent of Naundorf, the chapel had become a favorite destination for pilgrims seeking miraculous cures. Those claiming to have been healed hung wax replicas of the appropriate body members on the chapel wall. In his confession Muentzer later remarked: "I preached that the wax images brought to it were an abuse, *a form of idolatry,* and had not been commanded by God" [italics mine]. In that same sermon Muentzer must also have argued (as he was to do later) that such places of idolatry had to be destroyed. In his 22 September 1523 letter to the Count of Mansfeld, he had signed himself "the destroyer of the godless"; here the places of idolatry were coming under attack. The two appear to have been part of the same program.

In his biography of Muentzer, Eric Gritsch argues that the burning of the chapel at Mallerbach on 24 March 1524 was the work of Muentzer's *Bund.*[85] There is reason to believe, however, that Muentzer's *Bund* was already in place in Zwickau.[86] The evidence for this claim comes from Muentzer's letter to Nicholas Hausmann of 15 June 1521. With reference to the "blasphemy" of Egranus concerning the role of the Holy Spirit in the Christian Church, Muentzer wrote: "In Kirchberg they were very upset that the people who had sworn oaths [to uphold the Gospel?] were not quick to contradict him [Egranus]." As we shall see shortly, swearing an oath to defend the Gospel was one of the cardinal tenets of Muentzer's *Bund.* As with so many other aspects of Muentzer's thought, therefore, even his concept of the *Bund* may have been present by the time he came to Zwickau.

Whatever the case, on Palm Sunday, 20 March, some of the "frombds volk," alluded to by Zeiss and the Allstedt Council in their 11 April report to Frederick the Wise, paused on their way home to harass the old caretaker of the chapel. Perhaps because of that, as Muentzer observed in his confession, he had warned the "old man to leave the place." If that is true, Muentzer must, at best, have anticipated what was to come, at worst, have known what was coming because he was actively involved. In any case, the morning after the harassment, several items were found missing from the chapel altar. On the Tuesday following, a small shed

near the chapel went up in flames. As a result, the Naundorf nuns removed the chapel's most valuable artifacts to their convent and, through
a sheriff, instituted a search in Allstedt to recover the stolen items. Then
on Thursday the chapel itself went up in flames. The surrounding forest
that belonged to the elector remained undamaged, for the arsonists exercised due caution in their work.

"I was at Mallerbach," Muentzer confessed later, *"and saw that
people from Allstedt* took a few pictures from the church and later
burned it" [italics mine]. In spite of Muentzer's later confession, the
Allstedt authorities attempted to place the blame for what had happened on the outsiders coming to Muentzer's services. They seem to
have prepared their ground by writing to the authorities in the surrounding regions, enquiring whether they had captured any persons involved
in the burning of the chapel. A number of them wrote letters back, all
dated either 7 or 8 April, indicating that they had indeed held some
persons because of the fire and had recovered a number of stolen
items.[87] With this background, Mayor Rueckert and the Allstedt Council, in their report to the elector of 11 April 1524, sought to place at
least some, if not all, of the blame for the incident on the "frombds
volk" who came to Allstedt on Sundays to hear Muentzer. These, on
their way home, passed through the open chapel (which the abbess and
her provost had already allowed to be partially dismantled) and stole a
bell as well as a few other things. The following Tuesday, 22 March, the
provost sent several of his people to investigate. While searching for the
bell in the basement and attic of the adjacent building with an open
lantern, they probably accidentally set the place on fire. Two days later
a strong wind spread the fire to the chapel, but Zeiss and the town
council did not discover this in time to save the chapel. Therefore in
order to cover up the carelessness of her own people, the abbess now
accused the citizens of Allstedt of setting the building on fire. If she and
the provost, the report continued, could point to anyone in Allstedt
responsible for the fire, let them do so and the Allstedt authorities
would investigate. In this fashion the authors of the report sought to
reject the assertion of the abbess that Allstedt citizens were involved in
the arson.[88]

It could be inferred from Muentzer's confession and the above report
that the Allstedt authorities knew who the criminals were but had no
intention of punishing them or allowing them to be punished by the
Dukes of Electoral Saxony. The abbess of Naundorf, however, would
not let the matter lie. She appealed to the elector, who then ordered his

brother, Duke John, to look into the matter. The latter ordered Zeiss, the mayor, and the Allstedt Council to appear before him in Weimar on 9 May. There he told the Allstedt notables in no uncertain terms to discover the parties responsible for the fires and take them captive within fourteen days.[89]

There was obvious opposition to this course of action within the town,[90] much of it probably instigated by Muentzer and his colleague, Simon Haferitz, pastor at St. Wiprecht's Church. On Sunday, 14 May, Muentzer is reported to have denounced Frederick the Wise publicly from the pulpit as "that old gray-beard, the prince, who has about as much wisdom in his head as I have in my ass." More to the point of the present argument, he was also quoted as saying: "The prince does not understand the Gospel; nor does he accept it. Therefore he is not worthy of it. He wishes to judge matters he himself does not understand."[91] On 17 May the Allstedt authorities wrote Duke John that, aside from Antonius Behr and Hans Boding, who had seen but not recognized several persons involved in the Mallerbach affair, no one knew anything about it. They therefore requested another fourteen to twenty-one days to meet the deadline set them by Duke John.[92]

On 29 May the Allstedt notables wrote Duke John once more to try to divert him from the task at hand by arguing that the issue was not worth creating such a fuss over.[93] A little more than a week later, on 7 June, Duke John received another letter from the "Council and Community" of Allstedt. Obviously written by Muentzer, the letter objected strenuously to the approach that the Electoral princes were taking to the problem. True justice, Muentzer asserted, would not be served by following their procedure:

> But since their [the Naundorf nuns'] appeal has been brought before Your Grace, we poor people have been charged with it [the burning of the chapel]. However, before God we refuse to be held responsible for helping to support and defend the blaspheming of God. Certainly the witness of the holy Scriptures does not require that of us. For it is quite apparent that under the name of Mary, the poor people have unwittingly honored and prayed to the devil at Mallerbach. And now, since that very devil has been destroyed by well-meaning, pious persons, how should we help to catch and imprison them for the sake of that devil? For we know from the witness of the holy Apostle Paul that *Your Grace has been given the sword in order to punish the evildoers and the godless, and to protect and honor the pious* [italics mine].[94]

Even if it impinged upon the rights and prerogatives of the Convent of Naundorf, the destruction of the "devil at Mallerbach" was, for

Muentzer, a pious act. Duke John, therefore, should actively protect the pious perpetrators of this "crime" rather than attempting to prosecute them. Christian magistrates had been given the sword precisely for this purpose. Muentzer made the same point even more emphatically later when he observed: "Because it is now apparent to the whole world *that monks and nuns are idolatrous people,* how can pious Christian princes legitimately defend them?" [italics mine].[95]

We have argued that Muentzer's *Bund* may have been conceived as early as 1521.[96] Its precise origin and its purpose have remained shrouded in darkness, however, and have been the subject of some contention. By July 1524 at the latest, Duke John had become fully aware of its existence.[97] Brought to light by the Mallerbach incident, the formation of the *Bund,* therefore, must lie in the period prior to July 1524. The reasons for its existence are suggested in Muentzer's 7 June 1524 letter to Duke John and the subsequent confession of Jorg Senff. In the first, Muentzer complained about the actions taken by the Convent of Naundorf. In passing he observed that "In spite of being highly provoked by them, we have nevertheless allowed the elector to persuade us to pay them tribute and tithe [zinse und zehenden] which they collect from us without any Christian right or justice in order to be free from any taint of rebellion."[98] This statement would appear to indicate that Muentzer must have recommended against the paying of tribute and tithe to the Convent of Naundorf. Otherwise, the elector would surely not have been in a position to "persuade" them to comply with such customary payments.

The attempt to curtail the payment of dues to ecclesiastical overlords was apparently not limited to Muentzer and Allstedt. Jacob Strauss, a close friend of Muentzer and preacher in Eisenach, appears to have been involved in precisely the same kind of protest. In the introduction to Luther's letter of 25 April 1524 to Strauss, the editors of the Weimar edition of Luther's works wrote:

> The Weimar archives . . . contain a report delivered to Crown Prince John Frederick by Mayor John Oswald and Council Member Henry Weiszensee dated 14 January 1524. . . . According to that report, the Eisenach canons complained to the Duke . . . that they were no longer being paid their rightful dues. Thereupon the Duke commanded the mayor and council to see to it that the monastery receive its dues: he was not willing to allow anyone, even the local canons, to have their property rights or its usufruct in the least infringed upon.[99]

Whether there was any collusion between Strauss and Muentzer to deny local monks and nuns their dues, both incidents appear to have taken place in late 1523 or early 1524. In any event, in the Eisenach case the attitude toward this attempt by the princes of Electoral Saxony is clear; and it must have been exactly the same in Muentzer's case.

Jorg Senff, in his confession of 10 June 1525, singled out such payments as one of the reasons for the creation of the *Bund*. There he observed: "Their convenant had been: to stand by the Gospel, not pay any more tribute [*zins*] to monks and nuns, and to assist in destroying [their property?] and expelling them."[100] If Senff recalled correctly, and the above case of the disputed tithes would appear to support him, then at least one of the issues that prompted the formation of the *Bund* was the payment of tribute and tithes to monks and nuns. The tribute paid by the Allstedt citizens to monks and nuns went to the Convent of Naundorf, about which Muentzer complained in the above letter to Duke John. It is quite possible, therefore, that the two statements refer essentially to the same thing. It was an issue also mentioned in the 11 April 1524 report to Frederick the Wise.[101] If the above is indeed the case, the *Bund* could have been formed well before the burning of the Mallerbach chapel.

On the one hand, this evidence indicates that the *Bund* was directed *against* the Naundorf convent in particular and against monks and nuns in general. The latter were the very people of whom Muentzer, in his letter of 7 June 1524 to Duke John, had said: "it is now apparent to the whole world that monks and nuns are idolatrous people, how can pious Christian princes defend them?" Although pious Christian princes were not to defend monks and nuns, the *Bund* would appear to have been created to expel them and destroy their property, mainly because Muentzer thought them to be idolatrous. Since he considered himself a "destroyer of the godless," the *Bund* may have been his vehicle to justify that title.

On the other hand, the *Bund* was also a defensive organization created to defend the free preaching of the "holy Gospel." Here the context would appear to be Muentzer's confrontation with the Count of Mansfeld, at the latest, and his opposition to Egranus, at the earliest. Jorg Senff, once again, said in his confession that their "covenant had been: to stand by the Gospel. . . ." In his own confession, Muentzer said: "the alliance [*verbuntnus*] was directed against those who persecuted the Gospel."[102] And Claus Rautenzweig later confessed that he understood that the *Bund* intended "that they should all be brothers and love one another like brothers."[103]

These statements agree with what Muentzer himself wrote to Zeiss in a letter of 25 July 1524. There, speaking of the *Bund,* Muentzer asserted that he had preached on the topic "in the recent past."[104] The text for his sermon, he said, had been taken from 2 Kings, 22 and 23. That passage spoke of King Josiah who "did what was right in the sight of the Lord [22:2]." In the eighteenth year of his reign, Hilkiah, the high priest, discovered "the book of the law in the house of the Lord [22:8]." This was read to the king. He thereupon rent his clothes and commanded Hilkiah and others to "enquire of the Lord for me, and for the people, and for all Judah, concerning the words of this book that is found: for great is the wrath of the Lord that is kindled against us, because our fathers have not hearkened unto the words of this book, to do according unto all that is written concerning us [22:13]." Hilkiah and the others enquired of Huldah, the prophetess, as to the will of God. She informed them that God had told her that He would "bring evil upon this place, and upon the inhabitants thereof . . . because they have forsaken me . . . [22:16–17]." But Josiah, the king of Judah, would escape God's wrath because his heart had been tender and he had humbled himself before the Lord. When Josiah heard this, he gathered the elders of Judah and Jerusalem, and

> went up into the house of the Lord, and all the men of Judah and all the inhabitants of Jerusalem with him, and the priests, and the prophets, and all the people, both small and great: and he read in their ears all the words of the book of the covenant which was found in the house of the Lord, to walk after the Lord, and to keep his commandments and his testimonies and his statutes with all their heart and their soul, to perform the words of this covenant that were written in this book. And all the people stood to the covenant [23:2–3].

As a result of this covenant, Josiah ordered the destruction—the burning—of all the artifacts used in the "idolatrous" worship of Baal and the other gods, and "he put down the idolatrous priests . . . [23:4–5]."

The parallels of this story to Muentzer's own must have been striking. To begin with, there was the total corruption of the people of God, of Christendom. This was followed by the recovery of the book of the Law—the resurrection of the Bible through Hus and Luther—which contained God's commandments to His people. King Josiah and all the people of Judah swore an oath "to walk after the Lord," to conform their lives to His commandments. Muentzer wanted his followers to do the same: to defend the "holy Gospel" and to have them "live together as brothers." The affirmative was to be followed by the negative, how-

ever: the destruction of the idolatrous priests and their places of worship. Mallerbach was such a place; therefore, it had to be destroyed.

In that same letter to Zeiss, Muentzer observed that the whole congregation had "stood to the covenant" so that "every elect might enquire
after and protect the witness of God with all his heart and soul."[105] This
was not enough, however, to prepare the elect for the battle to come.
Before they would be ready to spill their blood in the battle against the
truculent opponents of the true faith, they would have to plumb the
depths of the evil that had inundated Christendom.[106] Nor was it
enough merely for the pious people to make such a covenant. Rather,
Muentzer argued,

> a modest covenant of such an order must be made in which the common man
> may ally himself with the pious rulers only for the sake of the Gospel. How-
> ever, if knaves and rogues join it in order to abuse the covenant, one should
> turn them over to the tyrants or treat them according to the circumstances.[107]

Just as in the case of Josiah, the elect, the "whole congregation,"[108]
together with the pious rulers, were to join in a covenant "only for the
sake of the Gospel." The "sake of the Gospel," however, involved two
aspects: first, the defense of the Gospel; second, the destruction of the
idolatrous priests. The Josiah story makes the latter only too obvious. In
a close second to the "idolatrous priests" were those who opposed the
preaching of the Gospel.

Muentzer proceeded to explain the purpose of the *Bund*. No one,
he asserted, should place his trust in the *Bund*; rather, trust was to be
placed in God alone. The sole purpose of the *Bund*, he continued, was
to threaten the godless so they would cease and desist from their
raging [against the elect] until "the elect have had the opportunity to
plumb the depths of God's wisdom and learning with all the witnesses
at their disposal."[109]

But the letter contains one more intriguing problem with respect to
the *Bund*. It is the problem of what to do with those "knaves and
rogues" who may join the *Bund* for their own materialistic (creaturely)
purposes, thereby abusing its intended goal. Such persons should be
turned over to the tyrants or dealt with according to the appropriate
circumstances. Then follows a passage which refers to Matthew 17:24–
47. There St. Peter was asked whether his master, Christ, paid tribute.
He answered: yes. But when he came into the house, Jesus asked him:
"What thinkest thou, Simon? of whom do the kings of the earth take
custom or tribute? of their children, or of strangers?" To this Peter

answered that they took it of strangers. Then Jesus replied: "Then are the children free." Nonetheless, Peter was encouraged to pay for the two of them from the money he would extract from the mouth of a fish, "lest we offend them." With this passage in mind, Muentzer wrote:

> Especially with respect to strangers [the non-elect in the *Bund*] it must be made very clear in the *Bund* that those who entered into the covenant are not permitted to think that they have thereby been freed from paying any tribute to their tyrants, but are to act in accordance with what Christ told Peter in Matthew 17, *so that certain wicked persons not be given an excuse to think that we have made a covenant with one another for the sake of the creatures* [material possessions] [italics mine].[110]

On the one hand, Muentzer recognized that the holy purpose of the *Bund*—defending the Gospel, destroying the godless rulers and the idolatrous priests—could be easily misunderstood. Unfriendly parties might think that they had covenanted together for the sake of material possessions. This he wished to avoid. On the other hand, Muentzer recognized the possibility that even the *Bund* might, perhaps even would, contain tares. Thus he continued:

> When the pious make a *Bund* [covenant], *even though the wicked may also be in it,* the latter will not be able to do whatever they wish, for the upright freedom of the good will allow them to do much less evil than otherwise, in order that the whole group not be condemned. The *Bund* is nothing but a self-defence which cannot be denied anyone in accordance with the natural verdict of all reasonable people [italics mine].[111]

The possibility of the abuse of the *Bund* by the wicked was therefore present, but Muentzer seems to have believed that such an abuse could be held in check. Accordingly, the *Bund* could not be considered as consisting only of the elect; its purpose, Muentzer stated explicitly, was to keep the godless at bay until the wheat, the elect with the potential to receive the Holy Spirit, had the "opportunity to plumb the depths of God's wisdom and learning with all the witnesses at their disposal." In other words, it was a temporary expedient to give Muentzer the time to spread his teachings more widely and to allow the elect who heard him to experience the "conversion through the Holy Spirit" in the abyss of their souls. If Tauler and pseudo-Tauler were to be accorded their due, such a conversion was not something accomplished overnight. The process lasted two years for pseudo-Tauler, and even Muentzer had to undergo a process of cleansing after his Orlamuende experience, as he frequently assured his followers.[112] In any case, the *Bund* was not yet the new Apostolic Church. It was to pave the way for that Church, however. And it had become necessary because of the opposition of Catholic princes like the Count of Mansfeld and George Duke of Saxony.

From its inception, therefore, the *Bund* had both a defensive and an offensive purpose: it was to defend the preaching and teaching of the holy Gospel, at least permitted if not in fact mandated by the Imperial edict of 6 March 1523; and it was a covenant to "put down the idolatrous priests" along with their magisterial supporters who sought to uphold the old idolatrous Catholic practices. These two purposes were enunciated early by Muentzer and his followers. In all of this conflict, however, it was not yet clear where the princes of Electoral Saxony stood. With respect to the Imperial edict, they appeared on the side of the holy Gospel.[113] With respect to "putting down idolatrous priests" and their places of worship, together with the godless princes who protected them, however, their stance was beginning to appear equivocal.

DISAPPOINTMENT IN THE "PIOUS CHRISTIAN" PRINCES

From what has been said thus far about the *Bund*, a number of things have become clear. First, as the Josiah story demonstrated, the elect, the "whole congregation," and the "pious Christian princes" were to work together in defense of the Gospel. But tied to this defense was also the destruction of idolatrous priests. Muentzer, in his 7 June 1524 letter to Duke John, made it apparent that the latter had a modern-day equivalent:

> Therefore we request for God's sake that Your Grace will, as a Christian and praiseworthy prince, consider and take to heart what our Lord God has spoken through the pious Moses in Exodus 23: "You are not to defend the godless." But since the whole world knows that monks and nuns are idolatrous people, how can pious Christian princes legitimately defend them?[114]

True to their founding covenant and the Old Testament example of Josiah, Muentzer and his *Bund* had begun to attack the idolatrous priests. At first they had refused to pay their dues to the Convent of Naundorf, but had allowed the elector to persuade them otherwise. Then they had begun to destroy the idolatrous places of worship, just as Josiah had. But already the electoral princes were coming to the rescue of the monks and nuns. The elector himself had refused to let the pious Christian arsonists go free. Whereas they may have been willing to allow the unhindered spread of the Gospel, they were unwilling to destroy the idolatrous priests and their places of worship.[115]

Under these circumstances, Zeiss found himself in an increasingly difficult position. On the one hand, Muentzer, the Allstedt Council, and the town's citizens were pressuring him not to comply with the 9 May command to ferret out the arsonists; on the other hand, the deadline had been imposed upon him by Duke John. In a letter of 29 May, he pleaded with the Duke not to use force in so unimportant a matter.[116] But the latter remained adamant. And so on 4 June Zeiss arrested Ziliax Knaute, a Council member, and incarcerated him in the electoral castle just outside Allstedt. This was the motivation for Muentzer to write his 7 June letter urging the Duke not to prosecute the pious criminals.

The transcript of the hearing before Duke John in Weimar on 1 August 1524 suggests that Muentzer preached some inflammatory sermons to his congregation during or shortly after this time in which he denounced the Saxon princes and pressed his listeners to join the *Bund*. According to one witness at the hearing, some 300 outsiders joined on the Sunday prior to 13 June. Upon the appeal of the congregation, the Council also joined. Thereupon both groups were joined in the following covenant: "Should the authorities of Mansfeld, and those of other regions, desire to attack those who adhere to the Gospel, they would be willing to sacrifice life and limb for the cause. With regard to other matters, however, such as rents and tributes, they intended to obey their overlords."[117] Once again, the Gospel, ostensibly at least, stood at the center of their concerns.

No wonder, then, that when Zeiss came to the mayor and the Council for help in apprehending the Mallerbach criminals, he was met with nearly unanimous opposition. In a letter of 26 June to the elector, Zeiss reported that he had then asked the mayor up to his castle on 13 June and informed him that he would have to help in apprehending the arsonists. The mayor responded that he could not do so because of the opposition of the Council. The two finally agreed that Zeiss should call on some of the people from the surrounding villages to appear at the castle that evening and then invite the mayor and the Council up to discuss how they might go about implementing Duke John's 9 May ultimatum.[118] When the official invitation from Zeiss came, however, the Council procrastinated, possibly fearing a trap of some kind, and demanded assurances of safe conduct.[119] In the meantime, under the pretext of an imminent attack on the town, Muentzer himself rang the tocsin, calling into action his improvised militia—men and women armed with spears and pitchforks, flails and scythes, some even clad in armor. When the mayor saw them, he attempted to make his way to the castle, but was cut off at the gate. Brought before an aroused and armed citizenry, he was confronted—probably by Muentzer himself—with the by now familiar refrain: "He should indicate unequivocally whether or not he wished to stand by the Gospel."[120] Having limited options, the mayor conceded.

During the night of 13 June, a number of Mansfeld miners and others entered the town because they were concerned that Muentzer and his Allstedt supporters might be in danger "because of the Gospel."[121] The next morning the mayor, the Council, and a few others appeared at the castle. After explaining the presence of the miners and the occurrences of the night before, they informed Zeiss that they had written Duke John "not to punish them so severely for the sake of an idol."[122] They must also have convinced the electoral commissioner to plead their case once more before Duke John in Weimar, for the very next day Zeiss set out for that city. He had to wait until 18 June, however, before he could obtain an audience. Once in, he attempted to persuade the Duke that the situation had become volatile and that he should therefore retreat from his hard-line approach to the problem. He did get the Duke to release Ziliax Knaute, who had already served eight days in the castle stockade, in order to defuse the tension.[123] On 22 June Duke John wrote his brother, informing him of Zeiss's warning and asking what he ought to do under the circumstances.[124] The elector answered on 25 June, telling his brother that he should enquire of Zeiss "whether or not he intended to abide by what he had said in Weimar. Thereupon we will request a report from him, and from the report we will make further decisions."[125] Here the matter rested for the time being, an apparent victory for Muentzer and his followers.

Zeiss's report is dated 26 June. In it, after narrating the course of recent events in Allstedt, the commissioner warned of an impending uprising if the elector did not retreat from his adamant stand and bridle the shrill voices of the nuns of Naundorf. Then he came to Muentzer. The one-time staunch supporter of the Allstedt preacher now suggested that Muentzer be subjected to a public hearing on his teaching before a gathering of scholars. If, under these circumstances, "his teaching were to be found sound and unimpeachable, one should adhere to it; were it to be found worthy of condemnation, he should be admonished and told to move on, in accordance with your best judgment." If this were not done soon, Muentzer's following, which was increasing daily, would reach such proportions that nothing but trouble could come of it. Unless immediate action were taken, Zeiss warned, a revolution was to be feared.[126]

The elector, however, chose not to follow his commissioner's advice. Rather, in his response of 27 June he informed the Council and community of Allstedt: "Since you undoubtedly know who the culprits are that committed such a wanton and outrageous act on the chapel, we command you, by those ties that bind you to us, together with our commissioner at Allstedt and presently here by our command, take them captive." And in the future, in order to avoid electoral displeasure, they were to reject such acts themselves and not allow others to commit them.[127] The use of force, the elector informed them, was misguided in Christian affairs. For if their teaching was of God, "then that, which you think you must suppress with force, will go under of itself, without human intervention, through the grace of God and His power."[128] Frederick had pursued such a policy from the beginning.[129] It was certainly not shared by Muentzer, however.

Whether Zeiss intended for Muentzer to be heard before Luther and the Wittenberg theologians, Luther had himself, as he reported to Spalatin in a letter of 3 August 1523, told Zeiss "to persuade the man to discuss his teaching with us." Now, on 18 June 1524, he wrote Duke John that "the Satan of Allstedt, although he has offered to come before us, has not done so and continues to defy us powerfully from his lair."[130] Muentzer had not yet, Luther continued, been sufficiently humbled to be willing to subject himself to such an experience. Instead, basking in the freedoms Luther had struggled to achieve, Muentzer sat on their dung heap and barked at them. This did not edify Luther. He suggested that Muentzer move over into Duke George's territory in order to put his fearlessness to a real test.[131]

Instead of bringing him before Luther, however, Duke John decided to go to Allstedt himself to hear Muentzer. This came at the very time the influence of Jacob Strauss, through the Weimar court chaplain Wolfgang Stein, was most evident in the Duke's thinking. Stein had come to know Strauss, a personal friend of Muentzer and a preacher at Eisenach. Under Stein's influence Duke John had been persuaded that the Mosaic laws should be implemented in the electoral lands.[132] In his letter of 18 June Luther attempted to convince the Duke that this was not at all necessary. The Duke's son, Crown Prince John Frederick, was concerned enough about this influence to write Luther and thank him for his letter, saying: "I hope to God, however, that I may—with this your letter—at least partially change His Grace's mind."[133] His success, if any, cannot have been immediate, for on 13 July Muentzer appeared before the Duke in the electoral castle near Allstedt to preach his famous sermon on the second chapter of Daniel.

Muentzer's *Fuerstenpredigt* came at a time when he was speaking more and more of a great and impending transformation of the world. In a letter to Duke John of 13 July he observed:

> For I intend to say and write that which is unchanging and can be defended before all people, without regard to the scribes who openly deny the [Holy] Spirit. Should I, however, be inhibited or stopped in this it is to be feared that a marked harm may come to pass since the people have an insatiable hunger for the righteousness of God, indeed, more than I can say.[134]

Two days later he wrote to the prisoners of Sangerhausen that "the time has come when a bloodbath must come over this hardened world because of its unbelief."[135] In a letter to Zeiss on 22 July he warned again of impending strife, and in another of the same day he wrote: "remember that the transformation of the world is now at hand, Daniel 2."[136] On 25 July he wrote Zeiss again, saying: "It is a mighty and great insolence that now, even after the world has already begun to be caught up in a mighty transformation, trust is still being placed in the old usage of the [political] office."[137]

In this conviction Muentzer turned to the second chapter of the Book of Daniel. He had mentioned Daniel as far back as his 15 June 1521 letter to Nicholas Hausmann, but there in connection with Christ's end time predictions in Matthew 24. At the time he had informed Hausmann that "The time of Antichrist is at hand, as Matthew 24 clearly makes apparent"; nevertheless, it was not yet. Focusing on verse 14—"And the gospel of the kingdom will be preached in the whole world as a testimony to all nations, and then the end will come"—Muentzer had remarked: "With the Gospel reigning in all the world and the Lord's word forcing its way in everywhere, then we will recognize the abomination of desolation." Christ had referred to the "abomination of desolation" in verse 15 as a sign of the end time: "When ye therefore shall see the abomination of desolation, spoken of by Daniel the prophet, stand in the holy place. . . . For then shall be great tribulation." If, therefore, Matthew 24 was the chapter that dealt with the disciples' question: "What will be the sign of your coming and the end of the age?" and if this was indeed the time of harvest, then it was time to return to the prophecy of Daniel directly. Muentzer's shift from Matthew 24 to Daniel 2 is therefore probably another indication of the shift from his preoccupation with the prophecy *about* the future to his belief that the *actual time* of the "abomination of desolation" was upon them. The passages from the letters just quoted would appear to confirm this hypothesis, as does the statement, contained in his exposition of the first chapter of the Gospel of Luke, which was sent to Frederick the Wise on 6 August, that "The time of harvest is at hand, Matthew 9. Dear brothers, the tares everywhere cry out that the harvest is not yet. Ah, the traitors betray themselves."

But the sermon is much more. Using the second chapter of Daniel as an interpretive base, it contains the totality of Muentzer's vision for the Church past, present, and future.[138] That chapter deals with Nebuchadnezzar's famous dream of the five kingdoms. The king desired his wise men to tell him the dream itself before interpreting it in order to ensure that they were not fabricating some fairy tale and that their interpretation was correct. Unable to do so, they were all condemned to death. Daniel, a Jew in Babylonian exile, was the only person able to ensure the king on both counts. Nonetheless, he disclaimed any power to divine the dreams of others, saying: "But there is a God in heaven that revealeth secrets, and maketh known to the king Nebuchadnezzar what shall be in the latter days." The chapter, then, has to do with rulers, with dreams and visions, and with "the latter days"—all issues Muentzer was wrestling with at the moment. From his perspective it was a passage ideally suited to interpret the age.

Muentzer's sermon began with the familiar theme of a fallen Christendom, a people of God misled into idolatrous ways, though retaining the outward appearance of Christianity. From the infiltration of the Church by the tares, Muentzer moved on to the Holy Spirit. Nothing, he asserted, was more despised in his day than the spirit of Christ, even though no one could be saved without its assistance. This Holy Spirit had been scorned and crucified after the deaths of the disciples of the Apostles. Having eliminated the Holy Spirit, the scribes and Pharisees asserted that God no longer revealed His secrets through visions or the "Word of His mouth" to His "beloved friends." Inexperienced in the things of the Spirit themselves, they scoffed at those who had experienced God's revelations, saying: "Hey, has God spoken to you lately? Or: Have you questioned the mouth of God recently, or counselled with Him? Do you have the Holy Spirit? This they do with great scorn and mockery."[139] Jeremiah had warned a blinded Israel in his day of the impending Babylonian captivity, but no one had taken him seriously. They, too, had scoffed at the notion that God would deign to warn His people in such a fatherly manner. Nebuchadnezzar had put these scoffers to shame, however, for, even though he served as a scourge of the

elect who had sinned against God, he had accepted God's communication in a dream. The same thing, Muentzer asserted, was happening in
his day.

At this juncture Muentzer turned to his biblical text, centering on
dreams as the means by which God reveals Himself to His people. He
had already addressed this issue in his letter of 9 July 1523, where he
had attempted to persuade Luther that he was using them correctly.
This was his initial concern here as well, saying that "the whole world,
from the very beginning to this day, has been betrayed by the interpreters of dreams, as is written in Deuteronomy 13 and Ecclesiastes 34."[140]
It was for this reason that Nebuchadnezzar had demanded of the interpreters and soothsayers that they tell him his dream before they interpreted it for him. But they had answered that this was impossible. From
their rational perspective, Muentzer said, they could not have answered
otherwise. They had no faith in God, but were godless dissemblers and
sycophants, just as the scribes were in his day. But Jeremiah, in chapters
5 and 8, denied this was the case. What was more, the text said there
had to be men who could communicate with heaven. Yet these soothsayers, these scribes, openly denied that God revealed Himself to man.
They themselves tried to play the Holy Spirit, instructing everyone in the
faith. Whatever their inexperienced reason could not grasp they argued
had to come from the devil. Yet they were not even sure of their own
soul's salvation. Their hearts were hardened, and they themselves unable to distinguish between good and evil since they had no experience
of the Holy Spirit.

Once more Muentzer embarked upon an exposition of his mystical
faith, arguing that the more one tried to grasp God through reason, the
more the Holy Spirit fled from a man. He spoke of how the Word of
God had to arise from the abyss of the soul, how it was within and came
down from God in great wonderment. It was a process that could begin
as early as the sixth or seventh year of life. Those who had not experienced this transformation knew nothing about God even though they
might have devoured a hundred thousand Bibles. From all of this one
could easily guess how far the world was still removed from the true
Christian faith. He proceeded to speak of how God had to remove the
tares from within the heart before one could discern the voice of God in
the abyss of the soul, and how the Holy Spirit could come upon one
only in times of trials and tribulations. Once the Holy Spirit had come,
however, then one received the power of discernment and could distinguish the wheat from the tares, the false dreams that the devil sent from

true dreams that came from God. In this fashion Muentzer answered the question he had himself posed at the outset of his discussion of Nebuchadnezzar's dream.[141]

Correct judgment, therefore, came only with the possession of the Holy Spirit, the key to the ability not only to separate true from false dreams, but also to interpret them correctly. Thus Muentzer argued that God revealed His dreams—as in the case of a Daniel—to His beloved friends in their time of trouble. This had been true of Joseph in the Old Testament even before he came to Egypt, but it was also most certainly true of the time he was called on to interpret Pharaoh's dream. Joseph, Mary's husband in the New Testament, had also been visited by God in a dream in his time of trouble. Even the "beloved Apostles had been forced, with the greatest diligence, to live in expectation of visions, as is clearly described in their histories."[142] Indeed, Muentzer continued, "a proper apostolic, patriarchal and prophetic spirit waits upon such visions which come upon one in times of painful affliction."[143] No wonder, then, that Brother Fatted Swine and Brother Easy Life (Luther), who avoided such afflictions, rejected dreams and visions.

There were exceptions to the above rule, however. Some people, who had not heard the Word of God in the abyss of their souls, had also had visions and dreams. St. Peter, for example, undecided as to what food he could eat and whether he could keep company with Heathen, had been visited by a dream. St. Paul, on the road to Damascus, had received a vision from God. The prophets of old had advised their rulers of God's will by means of visions and dreams, but this advice could be given only by "right preachers." Because of this cloud of witnesses with respect to visions and dreams, the Apostolic Age had taken such things for granted. From this evidence Muentzer concluded:

> that whoever wishes, by reason of his fleshly judgment, to be utterly hostile about visions [and dreams] without any experience of them, rejecting them all, or [again, whoever] wishes to take them all in without distinction (because false dream interpreters have done so much harm to the world through those who think only of their own renown or pleasure)—that surely [either extremist] will have a poor run of it and will hurl himself against the Holy Spirit [of these Last Days (Joel 2:28)]. For God speaks clearly, like this text of Daniel, about the [eschatalogical] transformation of the world. He will prepare it in the Last Days in order that His name may be rightly praised. He will free it of its shame, and will pour out His Holy Spirit over all flesh and our sons and daughters shall prophesy and shall have dreams and visions, etc. For if Christendom is not to become apostolic (Acts 2:16ff.) in the way

anticipated in Joel, why should one preach at all? To what purpose then the Bible with [its] visions?[144]

As a sign that Christendom was in fact once again on the way to becoming apostolic, Muentzer informed his audience "that the Spirit of God is revealing to many elect, pious persons a decisive, inevitable, imminent reformation [accompanied] by great anguish, and it must be carried out to completion"; furthermore, this transformation of the world was inescapable, as Muentzer warned, alluding to Nebuchadnezzar's dream:

> Defend oneself against it as one may, the prophecy of Daniel remains unweakened, even if no one believes it. . . . This passage of Daniel is thus clear as the sun, and the process of ending the fifth monarchy of the world is in full swing.[145]

This impending transformation made relevant once again the example of King Josiah and the Prophet Hilkiah. At the moment, however, the eels and the snakes were still in bed together—the eels being the secular rulers and the snakes being the papists and all wicked clerics. It is clear that Muentzer had in mind the attempt by the Count of Mansfeld and George Duke of Saxony, together with the idolatrous Catholic monks and nuns, to suppress his message. It was important, therefore, that rulers should receive their judgments "directly from the mouth of God" and not allow themselves to be led astray by idolatrous priests. For the "stone made without hands," which had remained small during the Apostolic Age, but which had now become great, was about to crush the fifth monarchy. Indeed, Christ the stone had now become so powerful that should other princes wish to persecute pious rulers for defending the Gospel, the former would be driven out by their own people. Muentzer was obviously convinced that his teaching had taken a powerful hold among the people, for he told the princes that "the poor laity and the peasants see it much more clearly than you."[146]

This was a clarion call to the "pious Christian" Saxon princes to take up the initiative in the holy cause of the Gospel. Under such circumstances, as Muentzer informed Zeiss in his letter of 25 July on the *Bund*, "a modest covenant of such an order must be made in which the common man may ally himself with the pious ruler only for the sake of the Gospel." In the covenant, the true prophet—like an Hilkiah—would also play an important role. Indeed, Muentzer was about to proclaim himself as the "new Daniel" who alone could help lead so severely a damaged Christendom out of its trouble, who alone "must arise and interpret your vision for you, and . . . as Moses teaches (Deut. 20:2), must go in front of the army," reconciling the angered princes with an enraged people.[147]

At this point Muentzer became critical of Luther's interpretation of the princes' role in a Christian society. The latter, seeking to separate the temporal from the spiritual realm, philosophy from theology, had argued that princes ruled only the secular realm. Muentzer, having already stated a number of times that the new conditions just emerging—the impending transformation of the world—required a new view of the role of the political office, now informed Duke John that Luther had made a fool of him when he had told him that "in respect of your office you are a heathen people," that their only function was to keep the peace.[148] This was not so, Muentzer declared, and the example of Josiah, the elect king, and others proved it; for God stood by those rulers who defended the honor of God's name. This meant that it was the pious Christian prince's responsibility to act as Josiah had: "to remove and separate the wicked who hinder the Gospel."[149] In pursuit of this godly goal they were never to doubt but that God would destroy their opponents who sought to persecute them. *They* were to act, not let God's Word alone do it, in accordance with Christ's command given in Luke 19:27: "Take mine enemies and strangle them before mine eyes. Why? Ah! because they ruin Christ's government for him and in addition want to defend their rascality under the guise of Christian faith and ruin the whole world with their insidious subterfuge."[150] Muentzer followed this with another thinly veiled attack on what he believed to be Luther's conception of faith, the faith of the scribes and Pharisees, which taught: do as I say but not as I do. Words, however, were not enough; faith had to be tested in the fire. Therefore, if the Ernestine princes wished to be "true governors, you must begin government at the roots, and, as Christ commanded, drive his enemies from the elect. Beloved, don't give us any hollow jokes about how the power of God should do it without the help of the sword, otherwise it may rust in its scabbard."[151]

The physical separation of the tares from the wheat—indeed, the extermination of the tares—now became the focal point of Muentzer's sermon. We have already seen how important the Parable of the Tares was in his program of reform, and how the separation of the tares from the wheat had come to be tied in his mind to the time of harvest. That time had now arrived. Therefore it was no longer merely a matter of separating the tares from the wheat in order to create the new Apostolic Church that could coexist with the tares in the world. It was now a

matter of Christ's kingdom being established, of the ultimate, eschatalogical separation of the tares from the wheat. Therefore a more radical
approach appeared necessary, inspired by the example of Josiah and
other Old Testament rulers. Muentzer began now actively wooing the
pious Christian princes to help in the extermination of the idolatrous
priests and their godless supporters.

To that end Muentzer quoted Christ's statement contained in John
15, combining, in his own way, verses 2 and 6: "Every tree that does not
bear fruit shall be uprooted and thrown into the fire." Therefore, said
Muentzer: "do not let the evildoers, who turn us away from God, live
any longer; for a godless man has no right to live if he hinders the
pious."[152] He quoted from Deuteronomy 7, where God had said
through Moses: "You are a holy people. You shall have no compassion
on the godless. Destroy their altars! Break down their images and burn
them, so that my anger is not kindled against you."[153] These words of
the Old Testament, Muentzer declared, were "crystal clear words which
must stand in all eternity." Nor had Christ abrogated them; indeed, He
wished them fulfilled. If this were so, why had the Apostles not acted
accordingly? After all, according to Muentzer, they were the ones who
had preeminently brought word and deed together. His answer was that
St. Peter had been "a fearful man." St. Paul, however, had spoken
severely against idolatry in Acts 7. Had he been able to do as he wished
in Athens, he would, according to the trustworthy historical accounts,
have torn down the idols as the martyrs were to do later. Therefore,
Muentzer concluded, the failure of holy men like St. Peter was no excuse
to allow the godless to do as they pleased. Since everyone confessed
God's name, all should be called upon to do one of two things: either
deny the Christian faith, or put away their idols. Luther's suggestion—
and that of the elector—to let the Word alone do it without the help of
the elect was insufficient. Just as the Israelites had to conquer the Promised Land by means of the sword, even though God was on their side,
the sword was necessary to destroy the godless, as Romans 13 made
clear. That this destruction be done in a proper and seemly manner, it
was necessary that their "dear fathers," the pious Christian princes,
who confessed Christ with them, do it. Were they to disobey, the sword
would be taken from them, for then they would merely be confessing
Christ with their mouth while denying Him with their actions. They
would be no better than pseudo-Tauler before his conversion.

Such princes, Muentzer argued, should tell the enemies of the Gospel
that if they wished to be spiritual but continued in their opposition to

the [true] wisdom of God—Muentzer meant the mystical experience of the Holy Spirit—they ought to be put out of the way. If they were not in opposition to God's revelation, he, like the pious Daniel before him, would request leniency for them. Otherwise, they were to be slain without mercy, as Josiah, Cyrus, Daniel, and Elijah had destroyed the priests of Baal.

Why was all this necessary? Muentzer gave his answer: "otherwise," he declared, "the Christian Church will not be able to return to its origin."[154] Here, once again, Muentzer's central concern to *reestablish* the Apostolic Church, or to establish the new Apostolic Church he had first openly proclaimed in his *Prague Manifesto,* can be seen. That Apostolic Church had been prostituted by the tares which had infiltrated it in the second century. It was for this reason he had asserted in his *Deutsch-Evangelische Messe* that Christ had "proclaimed all the evils of Christendom in Matthew 13 [the Parable of the Tares] well before they happened." Little wonder, then, that Muentzer followed his statement about the Christian Church returning to its apostolic origin by saying: "One must uproot the tares from God's vineyard *in the time of harvest.* Then the beautiful red wheat will acquire substantial and permanent roots and grow as it ought. *The angels,* however, who sharpen their sickles for this purpose, *are the earnest servants of God who execute the wrath* of divine wisdom" [italics mine].[155]

Muentzer had described the fall of the Apostolic Church in the introduction to his sermon; here, at its close, he prescribed the cure. The Parable of the Tares lay at the center of both: the coming of the tares had been the cause of its fall; their removal was its cure. Thus, after the deaths of the disciples of the Apostles the tares had infiltrated the Church, ultimately crucifying the Holy Spirit itself and destroying the Church's purity as well as robbing it of its living voice. And that living voice had been the key to the understanding of things divine. To correct this condition, the tares had to be excised from the Church. Once that happened, the Church could once again become apostolic. Such a separation would in any event take place in the time of harvest, and it would be accomplished—not by the Word alone—but by the Word and the "earnest servants of God," of whom Muentzer was the leader.

Muentzer's discussion of the new Apostolic Church had, from the very outset in 1520, been set into an apocalyptic context because of his appropriation of Augustine's prediction that the separation of the wheat from the tares would not take place until the time of harvest. To what extent such a separation would involve a violent upheaval of one kind or another is not clearly enunciated by Muentzer, at least not early on. After he came to Allstedt, however, in April 1523, the opposition of Catholic princes, such as the Count of Mansfeld and George Duke of Saxony, convinced him that such a cleansing of the Church would not be easy. Without the unhindered spread of the holy Gospel and the elimination of idolatrous priests and their places of worship, it might in fact not happen. While the princes of Electoral Saxony had allowed the holy Gospel to be preached, they were apparently unwilling to remove the idolatrous priests from their churches. This had to be changed. They had to be convinced of the necessity of a radical cleansing.

There is a kind of dialectic that runs through the entire sermon. On the one hand, Muentzer proclaimed that the tares will be uprooted from God's vineyard in the time of harvest. On the other hand, he declared the earnest servants of God to be the executioners of divine wrath. Under these circumstances it was critical that this earnest servant know precisely when the time of harvest would be. For that reason, Muentzer had to go to great lengths to persuade Duke John that he was their man. Like Daniel, he too could interpret dreams, for the Holy Spirit had also come over him in great wonderment. He too had suffered persecution, having been forced to move from place to place after leaving Zwickau in April 1521. Because of this he too could tell true from false dreams and interpret their meaning. And he knew for a fact "that the Spirit of God had already revealed to many elect, pious people an important and invincible future reformation, which is badly needed and will have to come to pass."[156]

Muentzer's *Sermon Before the Princes* is a masterpiece. It brought together his view of Church history, his mystical theology of regeneration, his eschatology, his emphasis on the Holy Spirit, and his prescription for reforming the political-ecclesiastical situation he found himself in. Hegesippus and Eusebius are given their due; Tauler once again comes into his own; and Augustine's interpretation of the Parable of the Tares stands at the center of the entire edifice. He had indeed synthesized and meshed all the various pieces of his ideology into a coherent whole.

Report had it that Muentzer came away from the castle pleased with his performance.[157] Given what we have said about his emerging views in the first six chapters, one can hardly imagine how he might have improved upon his presentation. Nor was the Duke opposed to his program. And even though the elector had written Duke John on 9 July to ascertain whether or not Muentzer had acquired his own printer—and if he had, not to allow him to publish anything the Duke had not himself seen or sent the elector for inspection—the sermon was printed within two days.[158] On the day the sermon was delivered, Muentzer promised the Duke in a letter that he would not print anything without his permission. The Duke must also have asked Muentzer whether he would be willing to give an account of his theology before the Wittenberg theologians. Muentzer had given the same reply earlier: "If you desire that I be examined before those of Wittenberg alone," he wrote in the above letter, "that I am not willing to do. I want the Romans, Turks and Heathen to be present."[159]

Whatever Muentzer's emotions when he left the castle after the sermon, he was not diverted from what he considered the task at hand. Within the next two days he wrote three letters to his followers and their overlords in Sangerhausen. He must also have written to Carlstadt and the church in Orlamuende during this time, inviting them to join the *Bund* in its actions against the idolatrous priests and their secular supporters. The church in Orlamuende, however, in a letter of July 1524, wrote back:

> Do you wish to be armed against your enemies, then clothe yourself with the strong crossbow and the invincible armor of the faith, of which St. Paul writes in Ephesians 6. Then you shall overcome your enemies with integrity and put them to shame, so that they will not be able to hurt a single hair on your head. You write that we should join you, make a league or covenant with you, citing the example of Josiah in 2 Kings 22–23, who made a covenant with God and His people. In the same place, however, we find that when the book of the law was brought to Josiah he made a covenant with the Lord that he would walk in His ways, treasure His statutes, commands and ceremonies in his heart with all the power at his command, and resurrect the words of the covenant contained in that book of laws. *And the people were witnesses of this covenant.* That is, the king and the people together made a covenant with God. For, had Josiah made a covenant with God and the people, he would have had a divided loyalty, trying to serve both God and the people. But Christ says that no man can serve two masters. Therefore, dear brother, were we to join ourselves to you we would no longer be free Christians, for we would be tied to the people. This would really raise a hue and cry against the Gospel and discredit it. The tyrants would love it, saying: these boast in the one God, but now they join in a covenant with one another [clearly demonstrating] that their God is not powerful enough to protect them. They just want to create their own sects, unrest and revolution [italics mine].[160]

It is evident from this response that Muentzer must have, as he did in his letter to Zeiss of 25 July, touted the example of Josiah to justify the offensive measures he and his *Bund* were about to implement against the idolatrous priests and their princely supporters. But why should he have reached out to Carlstadt and the people of Orlamuende at this particular time when he had just made such a strong appeal for support before Duke John on 13 July? The answer may lie in the fact that there was no immediate or affirmative response to the appeal in his sermon from the Duke. He may also have begun to sense that the support he had thus far been able to count on from Zeiss was beginning to wane. For, whether he knew it or not, Zeiss had written to Spalatin on 20 July that it was "high time to deal with this matter through a hearing, for if nothing is done *contemptus principum* will be at hand, and it is to be feared that the masses will come together, as he has openly prophesied. That will lead to such a revolutionary state of affairs in the region as has never before been seen."[161] Two days later, Muentzer wrote Zeiss two letters concerning some troubling information he had received from Wychart about how Zeiss had told him: "If the magistrate from Sangerhausen, or any other place, were to come to Allstedt [seeking runaway subjects] one would have to turn them over to him."[162]

Muentzer had, as we have seen, written three letters to Sangerhausen on 15 July warning the magistrates and encouraging his persecuted followers. About the same time the Sangerhausen authorities wrote Duke George that some of his subjects in the city were defying his orders to stay away from Muentzer's services even though they had already been punished. Others said that they would go where the Word of God was being preached regardless of the consequences. Rulers, in any case, they asserted, had power only over externals, not over their souls. And if the authorities in Sangerhausen would not tolerate them, they would sell their property and move elsewhere.[163] Many of them apparently fulfilled their threat, for on 2 August, Duke George wrote to Sangerhausen telling his magistrate that if the wives and children of those who had left remained attached to their men, their property was to be confiscated. And if any of the departed returned, they were to be incarcerated.[164] These people, persecuted for their faith, Zeiss was now willing to turn over to the Sangerhausen authorities, should they so require! Muentzer was outraged.

Muentzer informed Zeiss that his response to Wychart had been: "One might do this [i.e., turn their subjects over to the lords] if the rulers did not act against the Christian faith. Now, however, since they not only acted against the faith but also against their subjects' natural rights [the natural law], one should strangle them like so many mad dogs."[165] One could not, he continued, make friends of such tyrants at the expense of the persecuted who were fleeing them. Under these circumstances the old view of the ruler's office no longer pertained. For, Muentzer continued, "it is quite apparent that they have no regard whatever for the Christian faith. Therefore their power has also come to an end; it will shortly be turned over to the common people."[166] In the process, Muentzer once more named Frederick von Witzleben, who had openly attacked his own subjects in Schoenwerde, as a classic example of such intolerable rulers who inevitably caused revolutions by their actions.

The same day Muentzer wrote a second letter to Zeiss, perhaps because he feared he might have been too outspoken in the first. Zeiss was himself under increasing pressure to settle matters in Allstedt once and for all. Under these conditions, since he had already repeatedly requested that Muentzer be subjected to an examination on his theology, Zeiss may have become somewhat cool toward Muentzer. In the less passionate second letter, Muentzer stated that, although he could not change his opinion about the enemies of the Christian faith, he would not, nor had he ever, incited the common man against "pious magistrates."[167] Certainly, he had no intention of embittering the people against all and sundry; they were to act with discrimination and wisdom according to the circumstances. Zeiss should stick with him in any case because the transformation of the world was at hand.[168] Three days later, Muentzer sent Zeiss the letter in which he justified the existence of the *Bund* with Josiah as the clinching example. Muentzer must have come to believe that the time for action on his part had come, irrespective of what Zeiss or Duke John might do.

Apparently, Zeiss was no longer impressed. On 28 July he wrote directly to the elector stating that he had recently requested that Muentzer be examined as to his theology. Were that not to happen soon, he warned, an uprising was sure to occur. He pointed out that Muentzer was using the attack by Frederick von Witzleben on his own people, the persecution of his followers in Sangerhausen, as justification for an increasingly embittered attack on godless princes. Quite openly he advocated that the people should join in a *Bund* against such princes who opposed the Gospel. And in a sermon of 24 July he had publicly justified such action as in accordance with God's will, advocating drawing the sword against any prince who would draw his sword against them. This had so aroused the inhabitants of Allstedt that the Sunday following a near riot had occurred. He had also promised his followers that one of them "would kill ten thousand," and informed them of a dream "one of the elect" had had in which all the princes, the tyrants who opposed the Gospel, had appeared frightened and cowardly. They were therefore to be confident, "for the transformation [of the world] was near at hand . . . yet every prince seemed to be opposed."[169] The only exception to the above, Zeiss went on to record Muentzer's words, were the Dukes of Electoral Saxony. They, Muentzer had conceded, "permit the preaching of the Gospel, but do not wish to do anything else"—undoubtedly a reference to their unwillingness to destroy the idolatrous priests and their places of worship.[170]

On 28 July Zeiss sent a copy of Muentzer's 25 July letter on the *Bund* to Duke John. Whether it was this letter, or the above letter of Zeiss, that finally moved him to action, Duke John immediately ordered Zeiss to bring Muentzer, the mayor, and several representatives of the Council before him on 1 August. There Muentzer was interrogated first and separately from the rest. He was asked to answer three charges: first, that he had advocated the establishment of a league of the people "against the godless, as he called them"; second, that he had justified such a covenant with the Scriptures, though the Duke thought this impossible; and third, that he had spoken slanderously of the elector. Muentzer answered that he had never spoken such slander, but that he did believe that they were entitled to make a covenant to assure their being able to hear the Gospel without interference. And he would be willing to give an account of his faith before a "neutral Christian congregation."

From the mayor and representatives of the Council, Duke John gained a fairly comprehensive picture of the sequence of events in Allstedt during the last few months. He also learned about the *Bund* in a much more comprehensive manner. According to the transcript of the hearing, the Duke claimed to have been unaware of the nature and extent of the *Bund*. Once informed, however, he demanded that the mayor and the Council reject such an organization; the citizens and the Council were to be informed accordingly. For they knew full well that "the Elector and His Grace had never kept their subjects from hearing the Gospel. All they asked was that it be preached correctly. Therefore Allstedt had no reason for such a league."[171]

Muentzer, on the other hand, was told to abandon the *Bund*, to take care what he did in the future, and to await, in Allstedt, further instructions from the Saxon princes. Although Muentzer did not say much in response, the mayor and the representatives of the Council tried to place all the blame on their preacher. They were simple, ignorant folk, they said, and what they had done had been instigated by Muentzer. They asked the Duke to send a note to the Council, expressing his wishes, in order to strengthen their voice.[172] This he did, reminding the Council and citizens of their promise made to him at Weimar. As a result of that and subsequent reports, the Duke continued, it was now apparent that they had entered into forbidden agreements with outsiders. These they were to reject and obediently do everything the Duke and his electoral brother laid upon the commissioner and the mayor.[173]

On 3 August Muentzer was called to the electoral castle. There he was confronted by Zeiss, the mayor and a chastened Council. Zeiss informed him that his printer would have to go, that he would no longer be allowed to preach revolt or advocate an alliance against the godless, and that the Mallerbach arsonists would have to be taken captive. Muentzer was visibly shaken by the news, especially since Luther had just sent his infamous letter to the Saxon princes concerning the revolutionary spirit in Allstedt into the world for all to read. He demanded that he be at least allowed to respond to Luther, but was told once again that his printer had to go. He responded in anger: "If the Dukes of Saxony wish to tie my hands in this way and not allow me to answer Luther in my hour of need, then I will do the worst I can against them."[174] When informed that the Council felt obligated to report his outburst to the elector, Muentzer attempted to modify what he had just said, conceding that at times his emotions got the better of him. The Council, however, remained adamant. It also made him promise not to leave the town until his position and theology had been fully clarified.

Although the mayor and the Council had been forced to take a hard line against Muentzer, they nonetheless requested the elector to allow Muentzer an opportunity to answer Luther. Nor did they wish him to be condemned without a hearing. The differences between Muentzer and Luther, they said, needed to be clarified, for there were many people who clung to Muentzer's teachings. In any case, he should not be allowed to leave Allstedt without a hearing; otherwise, his followers would remain true to him and not be disabused of his teachings.[175]

On that same day Muentzer wrote the elector once more. At the heart of his concern lay Luther's "scandalous letter," which the latter had published without all "brotherly admonition." Luther, Muentzer said, despised the Holy Spirit and preached a faith different from his. He went on to speak once more of the advent of the true faith, of the scribes and Pharisees, and of an increasingly frustrated common man. Looking to the Ernestine princes for help, Muentzer argued that the elector had been given a greater portion of perspicuity by God than had others.

Were the elector to abuse this, however, it would be said of him: "Behold, this is a man who did not wish to take God as his protector, but rather placed his trust in worldly wealth." It was for this reason, Muentzer explained, that he had sent the elector his exposition of the first chapter of the Gospel of Luke and an instruction—possibly the 25 July letter to Zeiss concerning the *Bund*—on how one might, in a godly manner, deal with a future revolt.[176]

On 9 August Frederick the Wise himself wrote Zeiss, the mayor, and the Allstedt Council. He had taken cognizance, he said, of the threat, and he ordered Muentzer to remain in Allstedt until the matter could finally be disposed of. It was now easy to see, he continued, where Muentzer's teaching was coming from since an uprising was to be feared if he were not given a speedy hearing. For, the elector argued, "where a teaching is righteous and from God, one will not threaten anyone with an [opposition] league, revolt or bloodbath. Rather, one will give the honor and praise to God's Word and His Spirit, which is powerful enough to turn aside these and other troubles."[177] The same day the elector himself wrote Zeiss, warning him against defending Muentzer any longer, as he had repeatedly done in the past.[178] And two days later he wrote his brother, telling him to inform Zeiss, the mayor, and the Council to dismiss Muentzer, for they had never presented him for the position in Allstedt in the first place. The Council had simply appointed him on a provisional basis. He reiterated that they had never attempted to prevent the preaching of the holy Gospel; they had merely wanted it taught correctly.[179]

By the time the elector had made his decisions, however, Muentzer had once again, as Zeiss put it in a letter to Frederick of 24 August, "left Allstedt in the night by climbing over the [town] wall."[180] This must have taken place on the night of 7 August. Recognizing that his support had eroded, that Zeiss, the mayor, and the Council were increasingly in opposition to him, and that the Dukes of Ernestine Saxony were intent on putting an end to his activity in Allstedt, Muentzer once more chose escape as the better part of valor. His attack on Luther's conduct at the Diet of Worms was beginning to sound ever more hollow.

CHAPTER IX

The Time of Harvest

The time of harvest has come, Matthew 9, even though,
dear brothers, the tares everywhere shout that it is not yet.
—Muentzer, *Ausgedrueckte Entbloessung*

THE FREE IMPERIAL CITY OF MUEHLHAUSEN

Thomas Muentzer, Zeiss informed the elector on 24 August 1524, had broken his promise and left Allstedt, slipping over the town wall in the dead of night. In a short note left behind, he had indicated that his absence would only be temporary.[1] But on 15 August he had written from Muehlhausen, taking his permanent leave.[2]

Aside from these letters delivered to their destinations, Muentzer drafted two others that apparently were never sent.[3] They are nevertheless important in assessing the reasons for his departure from the town in which he had experienced his greatest successes. The first, filled with a bitterness in virtually every line, was directed to those in authority, and it referred to Duke John as that "poor, stupid man" before whom the Allstedt notables had grovelled when the time of testing had come upon them: the very men who had desired to hear about the *Bund* from him, but had then opposed it with all their power; men who had enquired about the righteousness of God and the ways of His covenant from him as though they took great pleasure in it, yet had nailed him to the cross at the hearing in Weimar and again three days later at another in the Allstedt castle. As Judas Iscariot had betrayed Christ, so Nicel Rueckert, Hans Bosse, and Hans Reichart had betrayed him to the princes, openly confessing as much to him later on.[4] To add insult to injury, they now held Muentzer's teaching to be that of the devil.[5]

Whereas the above draft appears directed to the Allstedt Council and magistrates, the second was addressed to the people. In a sense, however, it was but another attack on those in power, for it observed that as Christendom began to depart from the false religion, the authorities had become fearful. Reacting in a fashion typical of the godless, they had begun to suspect revolution in the rustling of every leaf. Even his letter to Orlamuende, Muentzer reported, had brought a response "that made the fear of humans so appealing it was marvellous to behold." The people of Allstedt were no different, for they had become so fearful as to "deny the covenant of God, which you call the Old and New Testament." If they desired to do this, he could not stop them, for they knew full well that his writings had not been directed against [all] rulers, only against the insolent tyrants.[6]

In the letter Muentzer did send to Allstedt on 15 August, he once more spoke of the tyrants, the godless princes, who, under the seeming authority of their offices, kept the people from accepting the holy Gospel. It was these he had attacked. However, he had also been given cause to attack those who had given aid and comfort to the enemies of the Gospel. Although Muentzer does not name any of these enemies, he must have had Luther and the princes of Electoral Saxony in mind. He could have done no less, he continued, for he had merely told the princes that "one Christian was not to sacrifice another so miserably on the butcher's block." If the mighty potentates (*grossen Hansen*) would not change their ways, the rule ought to be taken from them. What was he to do if, once he had informed Christendom, it remained too fearful to do anything about this state of affairs? Should he have remained silent and allowed his enemies to have their way with him? Never! The fear of God in him, as opposed to the fear of man in them, would not allow him to do so. The authorities, however, had been so filled with the fear of man that, when they were reminded of the oaths taken to their princes, they had become immobilized. They had not been *gelassen;* they had desired only to avoid tribulation; they had been hypocritical. In order for the world to be reformed, however, it would have to suffer much more profoundly. They should know this. Fearing man more than God, they had proven themselves incapable of suffering.

Was Muentzer beginning to doubt the great eagerness of the people to hear and accept his message? Perhaps not yet, since, in closing, he requested that his German Mass and other liturgical works be sent to Muehlhausen, "for the people are willing to accept this."[7] His faith in pious Christian princes, however, may well have been more deeply shaken.

In the above letters, Muentzer appears preoccupied with the causes for the failure of the Allstedt people in their time of testing. It was a failure that ran the gamut from Zeiss, the mayor, and the town Council, to the people themselves. Even though his most severe condemnation fell on those in authority, the commons had also shown themselves wanting. In the final analysis, it had been their fear of the princes of Electoral Saxony that had immobilized them. Time and again Muentzer had warned against precisely such a fear of earthly powers. To give but a few examples: In his very first letter to Ernest Count of Mansfeld he suggested that "since you wish to be feared more than God, as I shall demonstrate by means of your actions and edict, you are the one who takes away the knowledge of God and forbids people to go to church." Later he warned his persecuted followers in Sangerhausen that, in order to be in a position to fear God properly, they would first have to be freed from their fear of tyrants who sought to impede the teaching of the holy Gospel. And the above letters to his erstwhile supporters in Allstedt clearly show that Muentzer believed such a fear now also to have been induced by the pious Christian princes, for they had come to the aid and protection of the godless. Indeed, the letters make apparent that Muentzer saw the problem as a conflict between the oath taken to God in his *Bund* and the oath taken by the people to their temporal lords—in this case, Frederick the Wise and Duke John. The latter, instead of helping to uproot the tares in society like Josiah, had repeatedly come to the aid of the wicked. In the first draft, just after referring to Hans Reichart as a Judas, Muentzer observed "that such apostate Christians regard their oaths to the princes as more important than the covenant made with God." In the second he charged that the people had become so fearful as to "deny the covenant with God." And in the last he remarked that the people of Allstedt, when reminded by the Saxon princes of their oaths, had become so filled with fear that they were incapable of action.

The oath taken to their temporal overlords, such an integral aspect of medieval society, stood in conflict with the oath the people had taken to God when they joined Muentzer's *Bund*. Such a conflict appeared inevitable in the case of the godless overlords, though even here perhaps not irrevocably so. For Muentzer had said that he only opposed those godless princes who actively impeded the spread of the holy Gospel. Such an opposition should not in any case have come from the pious Christian princes. Yet in Allstedt, these very pious Christian princes, who repeatedly asserted that they had given the holy Gospel free reign, had come to the aid of the idolatrous monks and nuns. Eventually, these princes had even challenged the legitimacy of the covenant made in the *Bund* with God himself, arguing that it stood in conflict with the oath taken by both magistrates and commoners to the rulers of Electoral Saxony. Therefore, for such a conflict not to exist, Muentzer had to find a place where no princes, neither the godless ones nor the pious Christian, would be able to exercise any authority whatever. That could only be a free imperial city of the realm. Muehlhausen was one of two such cities in Thuringia; Nordhausen was the other. That Muentzer was very much aware of this factor would seem to be indicated in his letter written from Muehlhausen to Nordhausen on 15 August 1524, the very day he informed his Allstedt followers he would not be back.[8] That letter began: "Most beloved in the Lord, since you are our neighbors *and with us subject to the empire.* . . ." [italics mine].[9] Perhaps here he could preach the holy Gospel unimpeded as the Imperial edict of 6 March 1523 had mandated. This consideration may well have played a significant role in Muentzer's decision to transfer the locus of his activity from Allstedt to Muehlhausen, a city that, although under the protection of the Dukes of Albertine and Ernestine Saxony, was not under their jurisdiction.[10]

This is not to say that other factors may not also have entered into Muentzer's decision to move to Muehlhausen. One of these may have been the fact that the free imperial city was already in the throes of a political and religious upheaval. Another may have been Heinrich Pfeiffer's presence in the city. And there may have been a fourth factor. In his confession of 19–21 February 1527, a certain Thomas Spiegel is reported to have said that Hans Hut had told him that, in case of trouble, they were to flee to one of two sanctuary cities: either Muehlhausen in Thuringia or Muehlhausen in Switzerland.[11] Hut may have derived this idea from his association with Muentzer and Pfeiffer in Muehlhausen,[12] for he was a signatory to the *Bund*[13] and an eyewitness to the Battle of Frankenhausen. In any case, by 15 August Muentzer was in Muehlhausen. That fact alone indicates two things: first, that Muentzer probably went to Muehlhausen directly from Allstedt; second, that his going there was neither accidental nor coincidental.

By the time Muentzer arrived in Muehlhausen, the city was already in some turmoil. The principal catalyst was a runaway monk and native of the city. Some time in early 1523, Heinrich Pfeiffer left the monastery in nearby Reifenstein and returned to Muehlhausen where he began to preach "the Gospel and to scold the priests, monks and nuns," as the *Muehlhausen Chronicle* put it.[14] From this report of Pfeiffer's preaching, it might well appear that his scolding priests, monks, and nuns was tantamount to preaching the Gospel. Pfeiffer's message found a receptive audience among those both inside and outside the city. This aroused the attention of the Council, but because "the commons [*Gemeine*] clung to him and commanded him to preach," it did not dare to take any action against Pfeiffer. Nonetheless, when ever greater numbers came to hear him, the Council on 1 April 1523 cited him to appear before it. Pfeiffer, in turn, demanded a safe conduct. When this was denied him, he stepped to the pulpit of St. Mary's Church and said: "Whoever wishes to stand by the Word of God and assist in upholding it should lift up two fingers."[15] Whether this statement was inspired by the Imperial edict, everyone responded, went home to get their weapons, returned to the church, and elected eight men to represent their interests before the Council. These eight elected representatives once again demanded a safe conduct for Pfeiffer, but the Council refused to negotiate.

On the night of 8 June a riot broke out in the city during which threats against the authorities were overheard. On Tuesday, 7 July, while the Council was in session, the tocsin was sounded by one of Pfeiffer's accomplices. This brought armed citizens as well as many outsiders from the Eichsfeld into the city. Together they gathered before the city hall, issued death threats against members of the Council, and fired a few shots. Finally, however, the eight men elected to represent Pfeiffer's faction were sequestered in a local monastery with the Council members until all differences could be resolved. In the meantime, the mob broke into and plundered the local monasteries and priests' residences. Not until 24 August, however, did the Council take action. Then, asserting that it was not opposed to the preaching of God's Word but wished only to "avoid great misfortune and danger," the Council requested that Pfeiffer and Matthes, his right-hand man, be dismissed from the city.[16] In a subsequent letter to Duke John complaining of his dismissal,[17] Pfeiffer wrote that because he had "preached the living Word of God, it [the Council] forced me out and sent me away, unexamined and unconquered."[18]

The issues Pfeiffer raised bear a striking resemblance to those we have encountered in Muentzer's Allstedt.[19] While it would be unwarranted to attempt to establish a causal relationship on the basis of these similarities, the possibility of such a connection should at least be posited. There is first the attack on "priests, monks and nuns," in itself not highly unusual. In the second place, the request to "stand by the Word of God" and to raise two fingers as an affirmative sign was the same oath and sign used in Muentzer's Allstedt. Third, there is the attack on the monasteries and priests in the city, though no overt mention of their "idolatry" appears in the documents. Last, there is Pfeiffer's assertion, after his dismissal, that he had only preached the "living Word of God," a phrase repeatedly used by Muentzer to differentiate his "Word of God" from that of the scribe, Luther.[20] Similarities abound, certainly; causal relationship, however, cannot be established.[21] But though the latter may not have existed, it would appear that Muentzer must, at the very least, have been well informed about events in Muehlhausen when he decided to direct his steps there after stealing out of Allstedt on 7–8 August.

In early 1524 Pfeiffer returned to Muehlhausen surreptitiously, without the Council's knowledge or consent. Almost immediately he again began preaching to the populace with great success, but once again trouble broke out on 3 March over the words of a preacher in the Marienkirche and shortly thereafter over the robbery of a church and the destruction of a number of pictures. The perpetrators later justified their action on the basis of "Christian zeal"; they objected that "it [the picture of Christ] had been an idol."[22] They had not desired to spark a revolt. Some five months later, before 15 August, Muentzer came to the city. Pfeiffer seems not to have objected to Muentzer's relatively more famous, or notorious, presence. That fact alone may indicate that the similarities between them were more than coincidental.

MUENTZER AND PFEIFFER

By 27 August the Muehlhausen Council wrote Wolfgang Stein, asking whether Muentzer had left Allstedt in the good graces of the princes of Electoral Saxony. The reason for their enquiry was that no sooner had Muentzer entered the city than he began to preach with great success to the masses.[23] Obviously, the Muehlhausen Council appeared intimidated once again. And by the time Luther's letter, written on 21 August,[24] reached Muehlhausen, warning all about the Satan of Allstedt, it was apparently too late for the Council to take preventive action against Muentzer.[25]

The *Muehlhausen Chronicle* leaves little doubt that Muentzer and Pfeiffer immediately began to work together. It would appear, however, that Pfeiffer remained the public person while Muentzer provided the ideas behind the actions taken.[26] From the report of Sittich von Berlepsch, Duke George's magistrate in Langensalza, Muentzer is supposed to have preached that the citizens of Muehlhausen "need not obey any authorities, need not pay any rents or dues, and are to persecute and expel everyone belonging to the clerical state."[27] How are these assertions to be interpreted? Perhaps Berlepsch, speaking from his Catholic position, believed Muentzer to be opposed to all princes, all authority.[28] Such an interpretation of the first assertion attributed to Muentzer would have been in error, however, as we have repeatedly seen and as Muentzer himself protested as late as his 15 August letter to Allstedt. Yet it is possible, because of its status as a "free imperial city," that Muentzer did indeed argue that Muehlhausen was under no one's authority.[29] If so, it would strengthen our hypothesis that Muentzer came to Muehlhausen precisely because he wished to get away from the meddling interference of the princes, both Catholic and Lutheran.

Berlepsch's third assertion—that the citizens of Muehlhausen were "to persecute and expel everyone belonging to the clerical state"—is clearly in character. The second, however, is of some interest. In Allstedt, Muentzer, like Strauss in Eisenach, had been forced to retreat from his intention to deny "dues and rents" to clerical institutions because of the elector's opposition. At that time, Muentzer appears to have rationalized his retreat from the original position by citing the passage from Matthew 17:24–47 where Christ advised Peter to pay taxes "lest we offend them," even though, as "children," they were supposedly free. Now, however, under more favorable political circumstances, with the direct power of the elector removed, Muentzer appears to have reverted to his earlier position. Here, too, it would seem that the absence of any *obirkeyt* in the form of princely authority was playing into Muentzer's hands.

Sittich von Berlepsch received his information from the two mayors of Muehlhausen, Rodemann and Wettich, who had escaped the city on 20 September and sought sanctuary in Langensalza. This had been granted them in the name of Duke George. Together with some members of the Muehlhausen Council who fled the city a few days later, they informed Berlepsch that, some eight days earlier [18 September], the commons, probably at the instigation of Muentzer and Pfeiffer, had attacked "the city's churches and monasteries, smashing altarpieces, removing tables and altarcloths, and destroying the reliquaries."[30] If one can trust the letter of Berlepsch, it was at this point that Muentzer made his demands. In conjunction with this attack, the commons threatened to disobey the Council's orders unless they conformed to the Word of God. On Monday, 19 September, the arrest of a drunken reveller, who had impugned the honor of Mayor Rodemann at a wedding feast, set off a chain of events that led to the flight of both mayors from the city the next morning.[31] On that same evening (19 September) Muentzer and Pfeiffer led some 200 of their supporters outside the city where they marched to a wayside chapel, about a half mile away. There, according to Gottfried Seebass, Muentzer had everyone present sign his name to a list supporting an "eternal covenant or league."[32] They had departed the city carrying a red cross and a drawn sword, and, as Berlepsch reported, "practiced their drills until the city once again allowed those from Muehlhausen and their companions to reenter."[33] Further rioting occurred upon their return, causing another ten members of the Council to flee the city. Having cowed the Council, the commons presented those who remained with eleven demands, the most important of which were: 1) that a new Council be elected, one that would act in the fear of the Lord;[34] 2) that justice should be meted out to rich and poor alike in accordance with God's Word; 3) that the Council be permanent, that is, have no time limit placed upon its tenure; 4) that this godly regime enforce right and punish evil under threat of capital punishment; 5) that the members of the Council, should they be in need, have that need supplied so as not to be tempted by greed or avarice. Everything was to be accomplished in accordance with God's Word; there were to be no exceptions.[35]

There can be little doubt that Muentzer's hand was behind these articles.[36] While there is no mention made of separating the wheat from the tares in order to create the new Apostolic Church, there are enough indications that the godly regime envisaged would at the very least act to suppress evil and punish evildoers. The city and all its official acts were to be ordered in accordance with God's Word alone. Much like the *Bund*—which was to make possible the reception of Muentzer's message by the people, to provide them with an opportunity to plumb its depths while removing them from the fear of godless princes—these measures were designed to impose a godly rule upon everyone in Muehlhausen so that the wicked would be held in check and the elect given an opportunity to consider and accept Muentzer's teachings. It would therefore appear that Muentzer was attempting, in both instances, to come to grips with his opposition and the political context in which he found himself. While his goal remained constant, his approach had of necessity to accommodate itself to a changed set of political circumstances. This was a problem Muentzer may not have foreseen when he began his reform activity: beginning with a general principle of reform, he was gradually forced to take cognizance of his opposition and his social and political context. In the meantime, however, the great eschatalogical transformation was drawing closer. In the ultimate sense it would separate the wheat from the tares.

On 21 September the citizens of Muehlhausen gathered in their respective wards to discuss the situation, but could not reach a consensus. The next day Muentzer addressed them in an open letter. Although he had written the people of Allstedt earlier that those of Muehlhausen were willing to accept his liturgical works, Muentzer must still have harbored some doubts as to how his message was being received by the inhabitants of the free imperial city. Thus, on 3 September, in a letter to his famulus, Ambrosius Emmen, Muentzer wrote: "The people in Muehlhausen are slow, indeed somewhat ignorant, though not without cause from God so that nature's reason not bar access to the Gospel."[37] At the same time, the events of the recent past had moved so rapidly as to overwhelm the people. Under these circumstances, as Muentzer observed in his letter, he was driven to give them counsel. Their indecision, he charged, was prompted by their fear of man. And yet, he continued, it was apparent enough from the Council's actions that "You have become fully aware of its wicked ways, because it calls the Word of God heresy and determines not to accept it; rather, it wishes to sacrifice the servants of the Word on the cross."[38] Therefore, the people of Muehlhausen should publish the villainous deeds of their Council so that everyone would recognize and acclaim their Christian forbearance. He would assist them in this in order to discredit the godless who had fled the city. For, Muentzer concluded with a bravado that must have sounded hollow, "the common man (God be praised) is accepting the truth nearly everywhere."[39]

The Eleven Articles had been directed to both the Council and the surrounding villages. On Saturday, 24 September, however, the peasants from these surrounding villages assembled just outside the city and decided to rebuke the commons for their "unchristian" behavior. Were they not to change their ways, the peasants threatened, they would be forced to seek other overlords. The very next day, toward evening, the inhabitants of the village of Bollstedt, southeast of the city, were warned that their village would be set on fire. By six o'clock the next morning it was ablaze, and a large quantity of grain was lost.[40] The Council sought to help, but just before it could do so received a message that prompted it to close all the gates and summon its supporters to the city hall. Probably in response to this summons, Pfeiffer's parishioners from the Church of St. Nicholas raised a crucifix, paraded it through the city, calling on all who wished to "stand by the passion and Word of our Lord" to gather at his church. There they took control of the Felchta gate, intending to keep it open by force of arms. But the Council, with reinforcements from the surrounding villages, had the gate closed and kept it closed until Tuesday, in spite of the opposition's attempt to storm it. When Pfeiffer and his followers were allowed back in on Tuesday, the Council, which had just elected two new mayors in place of Rodemann and Wettich, demanded a new oath of allegiance from everyone in the city. Muentzer must have seen his old nemesis arise once more: in opposition to their allegiance to the "passion and Word of our Lord," some of their Muehlhausen followers had once again chosen allegiance to the temporal authorities. The Council then proceeded to enquire of the wards what they wished done under the circumstances. These decided that Muentzer and Pfeiffer would have to leave the city, and the Council so ordered. Some of their supporters left with them.[41]

DISMISSAL FROM MUEHLHAUSEN

We noted earlier that Muentzer and Pfeiffer, together with some 200 followers, had spent the night of 19 September at a wayside chapel outside of Muehlhausen. Here, apparently, everyone present signed a list supporting an "eternal covenant or league."[42] Whether this was different from Muentzer's earlier lists of those who swore an oath to uphold the *Bund* is not clear. The fact that each individual signed his name, rather than merely have it recorded by a scribe like Hans Reichart, may indicate that Muentzer wished to bind the participants more closely to this covenant. In any case, among the names inscribed on the list was that of one "Hans von Bibra," generally assumed to have been Hans Hut.[43] When Muentzer was forced out of Muehlhausen at the end of September 1524, by Hut's own confession Muentzer spent a night at his home. Here the latter entrusted Hut with the manuscript of his *Ausgedruecke Entbloessung*. Composed between 13 July and 1 August, a shorter version had already been sent to Weimar for approval.[44] Hut, apparently accompanied by Pfeiffer, took the manuscript to Nuremberg where it was printed by Hans Herrgott and his associates in all probability prior to 24 October.[45] The publication resulted in Pfeiffer's almost immediate expulsion from the city; Hut, however, was treated more leniently. The Council detained him until it received an official assessment of Muentzer's tract. Then it confiscated the 400 copies in Hut's possession—100 copies had already been sent to Augsburg[46]—reimbursed him for his expenses, returned his Bible to him, and sent him on his way.

Muentzer arrived in Nuremberg later, possibly in early or mid-December. Here Hieronymous Hoelzel printed his *Hochverursachte Schutzrede* before 17 December. In opposition to Georg Baering, Seebass believes that Muentzer's stay in Nuremberg was of short duration. He, too, however, argues that Muentzer must have met with Hans Denck during this time and exerted an influence upon him, though Seebass does not hold it to have been so powerful as Baering had postulated.[47]

Whatever the relationship between Muentzer and Denck, the former remained well in the background while in Nuremberg. In a letter to Christoph Meinhard of late November or early December 1524, Muentzer wrote:

> I could have made a fine sport with the people of Nuremberg had I cared to stir up sedition, a charge brought against me by a lying world. Instead I will make my enemies so cowardly with mere words that they will not be able to deny it. Many from Nuremberg encouraged me to preach; but I assured them I had not come for that purpose; [I wished] rather to answer my enemies through the printed word.[48]

But was this the only reason for his coming to Nuremberg?

In early September 1524, Conrad Grebel, Zwingli's former disciple, wrote letters to Muentzer, Carlstadt, and possibly Luther.[49] Whereas there is no evidence of a response from Luther, the letters addressed to Muentzer appear to have been sent by messenger to Allstedt. By early September, however, Muentzer was already in Muehlhausen, and by the time the messenger arrived there, he was probably already expelled from the city. As a consequence, the messenger returned the letters to Zurich where, after Grebel's death in the summer of 1526, they came into the hands of Vadian who preserved them. The letter to Carlstadt, however, reached its intended destination. In response, Carlstadt sent Gerhard Westerburg, his brother-in-law, to Zurich in mid-October to meet with the Swiss Brethren. In late October, Westerburg and Felix Mantz arrived in Basel with a number of Carlstadt's tracts. The re-

corded evidence indicates that Mantz sought to assist Carlstadt in publishing these tracts in the city.[50] Martin Cellarius, influenced by the
Zwickau Prophets—as Carlstadt and certainly Westerburg appear to
have been—also came to Zurich in October.[51] Rumor even had it that
Nicholas Storch was to be in Strasbourg in December.[52] Yet Muentzer
came south to meet neither members of the group around Grebel and
Mantz, nor the others mentioned above.

It is known that Muentzer was in Basel where he met and dined with
Oecolampadius. His confession informs us that

> In the Klettgau and Hegau next to Basel he presented a number of proposi-
> tions on how, according to the Gospel, one ought to rule. From these other
> articles were derived. They [the local people] would gladly have taken him to
> themselves, but he declined with thanks. He had not caused the uprising
> there, for it had already been well underway. Oecolampadius and Hugwald
> had told him where to go to preach to the people. This he had done, saying
> that where there were godless rulers there would also be a godless people. [In
> such places] a cleansing would have to take place.[53]

Hans Denck, a former student of Oecolampadius, may have directed
Muentzer to Basel and its reformer. In a subsequent letter to Pirk-
heimer, Oecolampadius asserted he had not recognized his guest at
first; only later, when Muentzer had denounced Luther, did he realize
who he was. Nonetheless, the two seem to have carried on an amicable
discussion on such topics as baptism, Muentzer's mystical theology of
the cross, communion, temporal rulers and the rule of Christ.[54] By
now, however, Muentzer's central concern was "how one ought to
rule according to the Gospel." His past experiences must have convinced him that if this problem were not resolved, a solution to all the
others would never be found. He made the point in his confession
when he observed: "where there [are] godless rulers there [will] also be
a godless people." In other words, godless rulers—perhaps even pious
Christian rulers—were hindering his reformation. In a passage of his
Fuerstenpredigt he even blamed the rulers for the failure of the early
Church to grow: "For that reason the cornerstone erected in the early
years of Christianity was soon rejected by the builders, *that is the
rulers*. . . ." [italics mine].[55] It should not surprise us that Muentzer
increasingly placed the blame for the failure of his reformation upon
the rulers. His experiences with Ernest Count of Mansfeld, George
Duke of Saxony, the Dukes of Electoral Saxony, and the magistrates
and Council of the free imperial city of Muehlhausen had all contributed to this conclusion. Whereas the common man appeared only too

eager to accept his teachings, that acceptance had repeatedly been frustrated by those in power.

In his confession Muentzer reported that Oecolampadius had directed him to the center of unrest in the Swiss-German border lands. There he had addressed the insurrectionists on the subject of rulers. Although the articles on "how one ought to rule according to the Gospel" have not survived, it is widely assumed that they may have formed the basis for the Constitutional Draft, later found among Balthasar Hubmaier's papers by John Fabri,[56] and for the Letter of Articles of the Black Forest peasant army.[57]

RETURN AND REFORM

Whatever Muentzer's relationship to the South German peasant movement may have been—and the question is as yet by no means resolved—his primary concern may well have been with developments in Thuringia.[58] Nevertheless, whereas Pfeiffer appears to have returned to Muehlhausen's environs on his own, Muentzer did not. For, according to the later confession of one Paul Pompe of Muehlhausen, the return of Muentzer and Pfeiffer was engineered by Claus Ernst and Facius Grempeler who wanted the "new government" inaugurated. By "new government" they appear to have had in mind the implementation of the Eleven Articles presented to the Muehlhausen Council just before Muentzer and Pfeiffer were expelled in late September. Together with a number of other persons—some confessions include those of the Eight—they met at Pfeiffer's former church, the Church of St. Nicholas, and there decided to bring Muentzer and Pfeiffer back into the city.[59] According to a letter from Zeiss to Spalatin of 22 February 1525, Pfeiffer had already returned to Muehlhausen's environs by this time, staying with supporters in one of the nearby villages. From here he had made forays to the outskirts of the city, attempting to rally his supporters within. When this came to the attention of the Council, it sought to force him away. In the process, however, it fell afoul of Pfeiffer's radicalized followers in the city and caused a near riot.[60] And so, on 13 December, Pfeiffer was apparently allowed back into the city.[61] In the meantime, Muentzer must have been on his way to Basel. Where it was that word reached him that he was wanted back in Muehlhausen—if, indeed it did reach him—is not known. In any case, it took until mid-February before he returned, for in his letter of 22 February to Spalatin,[62] Zeiss wrote: "I have also been told for a fact that Thomas Muentzer, who has returned to Muehlhausen, not only wants to be a preacher but is also striving to become secretary to, and gain a position on, the council itself."[63]

A faction within the city, therefore, not only wanted Pfeiffer and Muentzer back, but also hoped to implement the Eleven Articles demanded in late September 1524. By early January at the latest, the Eight, together with four preachers and support from the commons, forced the Council to adopt the articles. Then, under the watchful eyes of the preachers, the Council was forced "to remove all the articles therein [the laws of the city?] which could not be reconciled with their interpretation of the Bible and the Gospel, and in their place put ordinances on how civil and criminal matters were to be handled in the future."[64] About the same time another offensive against Muehlhausen's monks and nuns was instigated. Shortly after Christmas 1524 the Council confiscated their possessions and then expelled them.[65] By late January or early February, Sittich von Berlepsch—on orders from Duke George—began to attempt to rally Muehlhausen's princely neighbors against the city, while the Duke himself sought to enlist the aid of the elector, Muehlhausen's other "protector"; but the latter, always cautious to a fault and now near death, declined to be a party to such action.[66] Thus, by the time Muentzer returned to Muehlhausen, internal as well as external matters were coming to a head.

If we are to believe Zeiss, Muentzer sought not only to "be a preacher" upon his return, but also "to become secretary to the council and gain a position on the council itself."[67] Given the threat of external intervention, the Muehlhausen Council's repeated failure to make a decisive break with the old order, and Muentzer's contention that a real reformation would not take place so long as there were godless rulers, Muentzer may well have concluded that even the implementation of the Eleven Articles would not be enough to bring about a change in the Council's policy. He may, therefore, have desired to go one step further: to become—like Zwingli under similar circumstances later in Zurich—a member of the Council and its secretary. Perhaps from such a position of power he would finally have a measure of political control in his own hands and could see to it that the Eleven Articles would be enforced. If, under these conditions, the common man still did not accept his teachings, however, Muentzer might well run out of excuses for the failure of his reformation to take hold. He might then have to put the blame on the common man himself. Or, and this would have been the more traumatic experience, he might have to admit that he had not, after all, received his revelations "directly from the mouth of God."

According to the *Muehlhausen Chronicle*, Muentzer became preacher of the Church of St. Mary on 28 February 1525 by a kind of coup.[68] Nearly immediately, as Sittich von Berlepsch reported to Duke George, he and Pfeiffer made a proposal to abolish "idolatry" completely in the city. Proclaiming from their pulpits that "the Word of God, praise be to the Lord, has now been clearly and purely proclaimed to you, so that the idolatry in the form of images and altars has been removed from your churches," the people had now to take the next step in order to ensure their salvation, namely, the removal of these images from their homes. At the same time, they were to give up the pewter plates hanging on their walls, their jewelry, their silver vessels, and their cash. So long as they clung to these things, they were told, "the Spirit of God would not dwell in them."[69] Once again we come face to face with what to Muentzer were the two essential ingredients of a successful reformation: the clear preaching of the pure Word of God, which Muentzer asserted had already happened, and the coming of the Holy Spirit, which apparently had not yet taken place and which depended upon their being freed from the external things they still clung to.

The above report raises the intriguing and oft-discussed question of whether Muentzer and Pfeiffer attempted to institute some form of community of goods in Muehlhausen. Put in the above context—and Berlepsch appears to be a reliable witness who was apparently kept well informed about developments in Muehlhausen by people from that city—the demand that the people give up the visible marks of their wealth is reminiscent of Tauler's admonition to free oneself from attachment to all creatures, all things external. The assertion that attachment to things external kept Muentzer's followers from possessing the Holy Spirit rings true. Muentzer had encountered this assertion repeatedly in Tauler; in Eusebius he had read where the early Christians had renounced their property in order to hold their goods in common;[70] and Augustine, speaking of how the Apostles had been "born anew of the Holy Spirit," had asserted:

> Now in what sort they were converted, how decidedly, and how perfectly, the Acts of the Apostles show. "For they sold all they possessed, and laid the prices of their things at the Apostles' feet; and distribution was made unto every man according as he had need; and no man said that aught was his own, but they had all things common."[71]

It is this passage in Acts Muentzer undoubtedly had in mind when he is reported as having said in his confession: "*Omnia sunt communia* had

been an article of theirs which they had hoped to implement by giving to
each according to his need as occasion allowed."[72]

There is an indirect confirmation of the above from the community
at Erich that wrote Muentzer on 11 May 1525:

> Grace and peace in Christ Jesus, beloved brother in the Lord. We have
> received your second letter [not extant], written from Ammern, of 10 May,
> have understood it and give you to understand, out of brotherly love, that we
> have taken the valuables of the church we could acquire and have divided
> them among the upright but poor saints according to their need, one like the
> other, in our congregation. As much as we have been able and God has
> granted us, we have attempted to establish a Christian order, to allow the
> Word of God and Christ's Last Supper to be observed; this we did not wish
> to keep from you. . . .[73]

It would seem that the Church at Erich would not have written
Muentzer such a letter had he not encouraged them to implement these
reforms.

With the exception of Jakob Hoppe of Bollstedt, the confessions of
Muehlhausen participants in the Peasants' War do not seem to have
focused on the issue. Even that of Hoppe puts the concept of the community of goods in terms of the general demands of the peasants.[74] Perhaps
the reason for this lies in the fact that the peasants' agenda was not that
of Muentzer. The authorities, however, must have believed—as did
Melanchthon[75]—that Muentzer had indeed asserted "that all goods
should be common," for they enquired of at least some of the participants whether or not this had been the case.[76] And in his 1 March 1532
letter to Philip of Hesse, Eberhard von der Tann wrote, concerning
Melchior Rinck, whom he associated most closely with Muentzer and
Pfeiffer: "[Rinck tried to institute] a fictitious equality and community
of all people and goods here on earth, in a fashion similar to what
Christians believe will pertain in the future life."[77]

If Melanchthon and the ruling authorities saw Muentzer's attempt to
institute an equality of goods as a revolutionary move, it should be
apparent by now that Muentzer did not. Coming from Tauler, he more
than likely understood it to be the only way of making possible the
reception of the Holy Spirit by his followers, of ensuring, as Augustine
had said, a decided and perfect conversion. But did his followers understand it in the same way? The letter from Erich would seem to indicate
that at least some of them did. But the peasants do not appear to have
done so. For them it probably meant what it did for Melanchthon and

the princes: at least, the abolition of long-standing social and economic inequities; at worst, an incentive to revolt.

EXTERNAL THREATS AND INTERNAL FACTIONS

While encouraging his followers to turn their precious things in to the Muehlhausen authorities, Muentzer and Pfeiffer apparently also began to recommend arming the people against the growing threat of external princely intervention. According to Sittich von Berlepsch, a mustering of the troops, together with their field artillery, was held outside of Muehlhausen on 9 March. From Muentzer's perspective, therefore, there appear to have been two major threats to the success of his movement: on the one hand, there was the internal threat posed by his own followers who appeared to continue to cling to their material possessions, thus keeping the Holy Spirit at arm's length; on the other hand, there was the growing external threat posed by George Duke of Saxony who had, at least since the first of the year, tried to organize a princely coalition against Muehlhausen, not least of all because he saw Muentzer and Pfeiffer as the instigators of the unrest in the entire region. With time, these two threats merged, for in the process of attacking monasteries and castles, the goal on the part of Muentzer's followers was material plunder, not spiritual sacrifice. It may well be, therefore, that the social revolution Muenzter became involved in destroyed—at least from his own perspective—the spiritual revolution he had been working for since 1520.

Whatever the case, a mustering of the forces took place on 9 March. The would-be troops practiced their drills, loaded and fired their weapons. Afterwards Muentzer rode among them, preaching as he went. Among other things, he told them that he had already suffered much for the sake of the Word he had proclaimed to them, and that the emperor and many princes would very much like to keep it from them. However, they would no longer be able to do so, for "in a short time they will be driven away by their own people." Having said this, Muentzer asked those among them who intended to abide by and die for this Word, to swear an oath to that effect by raising their hand with one finger pointed in the air. Those who did not wish to do so should leave the field. The captain of the troops challenged him, however, saying: "Citizens, I do not believe there is anyone so foolish that he would not want to stand by the Word of God. That being the case, there is no need to swear an oath." But Muentzer insisted that an oath be taken. Whereupon the captain rejoined: "Dear citizens, have you not already sworn enough oaths? If not, just swear another basket full and hang it around your neck." Then, separating the temporal from the spiritual realm, perhaps in unconscious Lutheran fashion, he suggested that the church, not the open field, was the proper forum for a sermon. The motley army, consequently, refused to swear another oath, and Muentzer and Pfeiffer returned to the city chagrined. According to some present, the latter had hoped to separate their Muehlhausen opponents from the troops, but had been thwarted by the captain.[78]

If the story is true—and it appears confirmed in cryptic fashion by the *Muehlhausen Chronicle*[79]—it is apparent that Muentzer never really had full control even of the Muehlhausen movement. Although he appears—like Zwingli—to have become chaplain of the troops, he could not control the military leaders. Perhaps in order to get greater control he, together with Pfeiffer, demanded a seat on the Council. To determine the will of the people in this matter, all citizens were ordered to come to the Church of St. Mary on 16 March. There Pfeiffer informed the audience from the pulpit that the existing Council had ordered a new Council to be elected. The mayor contradicted him, however, saying that *since the people wished it* they would allow the new Council to be elected. Thereupon all citizens were asked specifically whether they desired such a new Council. The vote being tabulated, Pfeiffer announced that those who favored a new Council outnumbered those who did not by a margin of three to one.[80]

The very next day the old Council members were stripped of their power; this was handed over to the preachers and the Eight. Thereupon an "Eternal Council" was elected. Whether it was Muentzer's verdict, Dr. Johann von Ottera pronounced publicly that " 'He hath put down the mighty from their seats, and exalted them of low degree.' What a marvellous God He is!"[81] The exultation was somewhat premature, for the battle had just been joined.

About the time Muentzer and Pfeiffer were attempting to consolidate their power over the internal politics of Muehlhausen, the external threat began to grow. On 3 March the Erfurt Council wrote to Muehlhausen, bemoaning the fact that the "dismissed and rebellious people had been reinstated to preach," and recommending that the "cause and source of such revolutionary activity . . . be once more torn up by its roots"; on 5 March the Muehlhausen Council rejected the demands of Duke George and Philip of Hesse that Wettich and Rodemann, the two mayors who had left on 20 September, be reinstated in their former positions.[82] In response, Duke George wrote Philip on 10 March, recommending that after notifying the Imperial government they withdraw their protection from Muehlhausen.[83] On 20 March, the very day Wettich and Rodemann sought permission to settle on the lands of Duke George, the Muehlhausen Council justified its expulsion of the families of the two former mayors by saying that the entire population had desired it.[84]

By mid-April Philip of Hesse and Duke George had concluded that,

> if Muehlhausen were not to be punished, the uprising in the vicinity could not be contained because Muehlhausen is its source and cause, and therefore all unrest and revolt flows from this fountain. . . . [Were they to be joined by the Franconian peasants, also in open revolt, they would be even stronger.] Therefore it is His Highness's final recommendation that, because of her revolutionary activity, the city of Muehlhausen be attacked and punished, or at least be forced into an agreement favorable to the princes and their honor.[85]

Only a few day later, Sittich von Berlepsch informed Duke George that now might be the most opportune moment for an attack on Muehlhausen, since it was without money and the new Council most inept.[86] On 20 April, even Frederick the Wise instructed his counsellors to inform the representatives of Sondershausen and Muehlhausen that they were to cease plundering monasteries and were to reinstate the former mayors and Council. They were to stop attempting to rouse the countryside to revolt and were to remove Muentzer from their midst. Should the city not comply, her representatives were to be told that she would be opposed most forcefully.[87]

Under these circumstances Muentzer may have begun to reach out to former friends and allies in order to consolidate his power in Muehlhausen even more. Some time in the first half of March he wrote to his former Allstedt followers, indicating that he had information that they now regretted their earlier apostasy—an apparent reference to the troubles that had caused his departure. They might yet, he told them, escape the upcoming flood about to inundate the "false prophets and their Nimrod" if they would confess their past failure and, like Abraham, begin to put their faith into action.[88] Although this was not yet an open invitation to join him in any action against the princes, it may well have been an attempt to rebuild bridges.

Internally, meanwhile, Muentzer was still trying to firm up his support by getting people to make a solemn commitment to the Gospel. On 17 April, Sittich von Berlepsch reported that Muentzer had had a banner made, some thirty-odd yards in length. On it was depicted a rainbow, under which was written *Verbum domini maneat in aeternum,* and: "This is the sign of God's eternal covenant; those who wish to join this covenant must step under it [the banner]." The banner was kept beside his pulpit in the Church of St. Mary, and some said that he intended to take it with him into battle. About two thousand outsiders were yet to be brought into the covenant, he asserted.[89] We are not informed whether this proved to be a more successful approach than the one he had used on 9 March to try to get the mustered troops to swear an oath to uphold God's Word.

In a report of 22 April, Berlepsch expressed the fear that Muentzer would use the banner to rally not only supporters in Muehlhausen, but also those in the surrounding region. Were this to happen, he continued, "the common man in this surrounding territory would, to a man, rise with him. Without God's help it would be difficult to oppose such a multitude. . . ."[90] On 24 April he informed the Duke that Muentzer had at least 1,500 names inscribed on his list of sworn supporters.[91]

In the midst of this activity, a debate somewhat out of character with the impending events—at least so it would appear at first glance—took place in Muehlhausen. Sittich von Berlepsch wrote the Duke concerning it:

> A trustworthy citizen of Muehlhausen has informed me that a peasant from Wittenberg has come to Muehlhausen in order, as the peasant stated, to chastize Muentzer, that is to overcome his opinions with the Scripture. Should he fail in this, they [the people of Muehlhausen] were to take his life with the sword or however else they wished. Muentzer, however, was not to be harmed in any way, even were he to be vanquished.[92]

Although some persons in Muehlhausen felt that such a debate should not take place, Berlepsch went on to report that it had nonetheless been arranged for that very day in the Church of St. Mary where Muentzer was the preacher.

What, one may well ask, would a Lutheran peasant wish to debate with Thomas Muentzer? The *Muehlhausen Chronicle* gave a credible answer. It recorded, first, that the debate did indeed take place in the Church of St. Mary on Monday, 24 April 1525, "before all the people." The peasant had come, the *Chronicle* continued, "to debate Muentzer and Pfeiffer concerning the question of Cornelius in Acts 10: whether every man had then [the time of the Apostles] received the Holy Spirit, and whether or not everyone still had the Holy Spirit."[93] The debate apparently began at eleven o'clock and lasted until three in the afternoon. One wonders exactly what was said. The *Chronicle* merely records that whereas one person laughed at the peasant and mocked him, another took his side. In the end, however, the peasant had to be escorted from the Church; otherwise, as the *Chronicle* put it, "he would not have escaped with his life."[94]

Of course, some people in Muehlhausen suspected Luther of putting the peasant up to such a stunt.[95] Whether this was the case, the peasant had focused on a biblical passage that was, apparently, of some consequence to Thomas Muentzer. This can be seen from the latter's response to Frederick the Wise concerning Luther's blistering attack in his "Letter to the Princes of Saxony Concerning the Revolutionary Spirit." There Muentzer observed:

> Finally, it is my earnest conviction that I preach a Christian faith that has nothing in common with Luther's. In accordance with Psalm 67, it is a faith that is uniform and found in the hearts of all the elect on earth. For, were even a Turk to be present, he would still possess the beginning of the same faith, that is the moving of the Holy Spirit, as it is written of Cornelius in Acts 10. . . .[96]

Perhaps it was from this letter, written on 3 August 1524, that Luther and the peasant were made aware of Muentzer's use of Acts 10. It is not without significance that the peasant should challenge Muentzer on precisely this topic and this particular passage. For whether "every man had then received the Holy Spirit, and whether or not everyone still had—[or could possess]—the Holy Spirit" was of critical importance to Muentzer. Precisely this conscious indwelling of the Holy Spirit in his followers had been Muentzer's goal for some time now.[97]

THE TURNING POINT

The date 24 April 1525 seems to have been a fateful one in that other, revolutionary, sense for Muentzer as well, for on that very day an uprising of the common man took place in Langensalza.[98] Muentzer and Pfeiffer do not appear to have been informed of this event until 26 April. According to the *Chronicle*, they were about to muster their troops under Muentzer's banner outside the city on that day when word reached them of the Langensalza uprising. Immediately they set out to offer their support, appearing before the gates of the town with anywhere from 400 to 500 men, a few of them on horseback.[99] Muentzer's banner was prominently displayed in their midst.[100] The *christliche gemeyne* of Salza declined their offer of help, however, stating in a cryptic note that they would "work things out amongst ourselves for peace."[101] Apparently, they were interested neither in Muentzer's and Pfeiffer's help, nor even in their brand of revolution, for on 15 October 1529, Hans Ziegler, a native of Salza, confessed that the insurgents had demanded the acceptance of the Twelve Articles by the Council and that the Word of God be preached "as it was in the Elector's lands."[102] Clearly, this was a reference to Luther's rather than Muentzer's interpretation.[103]

Nevertheless, the uprising in Salza appears to have been the signal for others to revolt on their own behalf, some of them joining the Muehlhausen troops outside the gates of Salza. It may have had the same effect upon Muentzer, for on that day—or one day later—Muentzer wrote another letter to Allstedt.[104] Although the message it contained was not new, it did have an altogether new sense of urgency. He told them that they must stand *gelassen* before God; otherwise, He could not reveal Himself to them. Unless they did this, any sacrifice they made would be in vain. Nor were they any longer to "flatter the perverse dandies, the godless villains"; rather, they were to fear God and begin to fight His battle. They were to encourage one another "not to despise the witness of God"; otherwise, they would all perish. This advice, however, was a mere prologue to the news that "All Germany, France and Italy are alive; the Master intends to have His sport; the villains must be sacrificed. During the Easter week alone," Muentzer asserted, "four churches were destroyed in Fulda; the peasants—three thousand strong and growing daily—have risen in the Klettgau and the Hegau of the Black Forest."[105] His only concern, he said, was that the "foolish folk" would enter "into some perverse agreement" because they did not recognize the depth of the damage done to Christendom, a reference to the expulsion of the Holy Spirit from the Church by the tares. If they had not yet recognized this damage, it must follow that they had not yet received the Holy Spirit.

Muentzer then makes an assertion that the context of this impending struggle has never fitted well with his image as a great revolutionary organizer. "If there are only three of you," he stated, "who stand *gelassen* in God, seeking only to glorify His name and [vindicate] His honor, you will not fear a hundred thousand men." How did he mean this? Three such men among many, or only three against a hundred thousand? Perhaps the former, in the same way that Tauler had argued that it was the *amici dei* who sustained the Church full of tares and kept it from collapsing. He must have believed that God would work in extraordinary ways in men who had emptied themselves of "creatures animate and inanimate" and allowed themselves to be filled by the Holy Spirit. He knew himself to be such a person; how many more were needed?[106]

This issue aside for the moment, his sense of urgency now came clearly to the fore. Whether it was the uprising in the Black Forest or the revolution in his own back yard,[107] Muentzer urged his former Allstedt followers to seize hold of the moment, not to feel pity for the godless, though the latter might plead for mercy. They were to arouse the villagers, especially the miners. Repeatedly he urged them to be "up and at them," for the time was ripe. They were to strike while the iron was hot, to hammer on the princely anvils, to destroy their castles. For while the godless princes continued to exist, it would be impossible for them to be free of the fear of men. Nor would they be able to understand God's ways while these princes were in power. "Up and at them," he reiterated, "while it is day. God is going before you, therefore follow! *All of this is described in Matthew 24*, Ezekiel 34, Daniel 74, Revelation 6, and explained in Romans 13" [italics mine]. They were not to fear, for this was God's war, not theirs. If only they remained unafraid, they would see how God would help.[108]

This letter and Salza's rejection of Muentzer's and Pfeiffer's help pose a number of problems that merit discussion at this point. First, were Muentzer and Pfeiffer in agreement on all aspects of the goals and strategy of the revolutionary movement? Second, to what extent was Muentzer involved with Pfeiffer on the Eichsfeld? And third, to what extent was this movement spontaneous and haphazard? Let us begin with the relationship of Muentzer to Pfeiffer.

In his letter to the Council of Nuremberg of early June 1525, George Duke of Saxony wrote that Muentzer had been "especially happy" upon hearing of Pfeiffer's capture.[109] This should not come as a surprise since Muentzer refers to Pfeiffer, in a letter to the Muehlhausen Council of 8 May 1525, as a "Judas."[110] This evidence stands in marked contrast to the apparent cooperation between the two men until the end of April 1525. Something must have come between them, but what it was has remained elusive. Perhaps it was their differing orientations, both intellectual and geographical.[111]

One of the first things Muentzer did after 26 April, the day he was informed about the Salza uprising, was to write the above letter to his erstwhile followers in Allstedt. His concerns in the uprising were obviously more than local: he saw the impending struggle as God's war; he argued it had already been described in Matthew 24. The local events were merely the harbinger of what was to come. He wanted to prepare his followers for this ultimate struggle by making certain they knew how to appropriate the Holy Spirit. And, as we shall yet have occasion to note, he was still much more concerned with Heldrungen and his old nemesis, Ernest Count of Mansfeld, than he was with events on the Eichsfeld. He sent letters to Merxleben, Frankenhausen, Schmalkalden, Sondershausen, Eisenach, Erfurt, with a few to more local destinations. He had obviously kept informed about the more global nature of the uprising, even if his observation that "All Germany, France and Italy are alive," was an exaggeration.

Pfeiffer, on the other hand, had always had a more local orientation. He was from Muehlhausen, had entered the nearby monastery in Reifenstein, and when he left there, returned to his native city. As a former monk at Reifenstein, Pfeiffer retained close ties to the Eichsfeld, to which Reifenstein belonged, and initally attempted to establish himself there; when he did come to Muehlhausen, he became a preacher in the Church of St. Nicholas, located in a suburb of the city which faced in the direction of the Eichsfeld.[112] Pfeiffer was the first to return to Muehlhausen after he and Muentzer were expelled in late September 1524, staying with supporters outside of Muehlhausen until he had rallied sufficient support within to risk returning.[113] If the confession of Bastian Ruediger of Muehlhausen can be trusted, it was Pfeiffer who, when trouble began, rallied the Eichsfeld peasants by writing letters to them, enlisting their support.[114] When it came to communicating with the Franconian peasants, Pfeiffer *and* Muentzer are said to have sent the letters.[115]

The makeup of their following in Muehlhausen also indicates that Pfeiffer had closer ties to the Eichsfeld than did Muentzer. From a number of different sources it is apparent that many—if not most—of these came from the region surrounding Muehlhausen. For example, in his last letter—the letter to the citizens of Muehlhausen of 17 May 1525—Muentzer wrote: "For I know that the majority of you in Muehlhausen never adhered to this selfish revolutionary uprising, and would very much have preferred to hinder it."[116] The counsellors of Elector John, Duke George, and Philip of Hesse, sent to determine what penalty Muehlhausen should be assessed after the war, wrote in their report:

It is quite apparent that the Council and magistrates [of Muehlhausen], with respect to the actions of Muentzer and Pfeiffer, never approved, indeed, to the extent they were able, tried to hinder and deter them. As a result, some of these were forced to flee the city, leaving their families behind, to their financial loss. It is equally apparent that these authorities and the pious citizens of the city were overwhelmed by the inhabitants of the suburbs and surrounding villages, forced to allow Muentzer and Pfeiffer to preach and undertake other unjust actions.[117]

They asserted that few from Muehlhausen had followed Pfeiffer and Muentzer into battle. Those within the city who did support them appear to have come from the poorer elements. Zeiss agreed with this account in his letter of 22 February to Spalatin, as did Sittich von Berlepsch in his report of 17 April to Duke George.[118]

Having said this, one should also remind the reader of Salza's rejection of the help proferred by Muentzer and Pfeiffer. This does not speak well for even the latter's influence over the revolution in the Eichsfeld. The Salza leaders had responded by saying that they would "work things out amongst ourselves for peace."[119] And Hans Ziegler, a native of Salza, confessed that the insurgents there had demanded that the Council accept the Twelve Articles, and that the Word of God be preached "as it was in the Elector's lands," an apparent preference for Luther's theology.[120] Furthermore, as one peruses the documents relevant to the peasant uprising in Thuringia, the references to these Twelve Articles are surprisingly frequent,[121] indicating, it would seem, that Muentzer's influence was relatively limited. In this respect, the only other city where certain individuals appear even to have contemplated the possibility of establishing an Eternal Council after the Muehlhausen model was Nordhausen.[122]

If Salza rejected Muentzer's and Pfeiffer's proferred help because it wished to solve its own problems and had its own goals, the same may well have been true of other towns and villages of the Eichsfeld. Indeed, a reading of Jordan's article on Muentzer's and Pfeiffer's activity there makes it apparent that in virtually every revolutionary action undertaken, the locals rose in revolt spontaneously before the forces under Muentzer and Pfeiffer made their appearance. These forces may have set fire to monasteries and castles, but only after they had already been ransacked by local revolutionaries.[123]

It is important, in the above context, to take another look at Muentzer's so-called "Christian league." What kind of an organization

was it? Or was it an organization at all? How effective was it in binding
Muentzer's followers to him and his cause? And who could belong?

It is possible that the importance of this "Christian league" has been
exaggerated.[124] It may even be that the term is a misnomer. Influenced
perhaps overly much by Friedrich Engels's argument that these were
really revolutionary cells preparing the way for a general uprising of the
peasantry, many scholars have ascribed a greater revolutionary importance to the league than the facts warrant. Whatever revolutionary
activity Muentzer may have been involved in prior to his stay in
Allstedt,[125] his description of the *Bund* in his letter to Zeiss of 25 July
1525 clearly places the discussion into the context of the defense of the
Gospel and the destruction of idolatry. The covenant—and it is basi-
cally a covenant rather than a league, according to the Old Testament
passage cited—was made between God, on the one hand, and Josiah the
king, the elders and prophets, "and all the people, both small and
great," on the other. All of them covenanted "to walk after the Lord,
and to keep His commandments and His statutes with all their heart
and their soul, to perform the words of this covenant that were written
in this book." The reverse side of this positive aspect was the destruction of idolatry and the places of idolatrous worship. Similarly, "to
stand by the Gospel" was obviously the main purpose of Muentzer's
Bund. The other was clearly the destruction of "monks and nuns [who]
are idolatrous people" and their places of worship.

What we know of the staying power of the commitments made by
the covenanters, however, does not speak well for the success of
Muentzer's *Bund*. The first crucial test may have come as early as
Egranus's "blasphemy" in the presence of Nicholas Hausmann and,
apparently, people in Zwickau who had sworn to uphold the Word of
God. It failed again in Allstedt, as we have seen. As Muentzer complained in the letters sent back to that city after his departure, no one
had remained true to the covenant sworn. The same thing happened
repeatedly in Muehlhausen. Whenever it came to hard choices between
the *visible* power of the temporal authorities and their new allegiance to
a *higher* authority (Muentzer's Gospel), the latter always seemed to fail.
Nor does it appear that there was anything particularly secretive about
the oath-taking ceremonies. Most of them were quite public, as was the
last attempt by Muentzer to extract an oath from the troops mustered
outside Muehlhausen on 9 March 1525. Even the banner Muentzer
created as a visible sign of the covenant, openly displayed in his church,
did not seem to solve this problem of the disintegrating covenant when

it came under attack by the temporal authorities. This was—as the captain rightly saw—no way to run an army or foment a revolution.

Who could belong to Muentzer's *Bund?* The covenant, of course, was to be made between the elect—those who had the potential to possess the Holy Spirit—and the "pious rulers," and that "only for the sake of the Gospel." Muentzer was well aware, however, that "knaves and rogues [might] join it in order to abuse the covenant." Their purpose would undoubtedly be to exploit the *Bund* for their own selfish material ends. He sought to avoid this, but said nonetheless: "When the pious make a *Bund, even though the wicked may also be in it,* the latter will not be able to do whatever they wish, for the upright freedom of the good will allow them to do much less evil than otherwise, in order that the whole group not be condemned" [italics mine].[126] It should be quite clear, therefore, that unless Muentzer changed his mind later on—and there appears to be no evidence to this effect—the *Bund* did not include only the elect. Even if the *Bund* had consisted only of the elect, the vast majority of the latter had not yet—as Muentzer repeatedly complained—allowed the Holy Spirit to rule their lives. Such an elect, as he had stated as early as the *Prague Manifesto,* had, "in many respects, become virtually the same as the damned and also virtually swallowed up by them."[127] Under these circumstances Muentzer seems to have assumed that the *Bund*—like the corrupt Medieval Church—would be carried by the *amici dei,* those elect who had been filled with the Holy Spirit. He used this argument in his 26 April letter to his Allstedt followers. It would be logical to assume, therefore, that he did indeed believe himself, as one of the elect filled with the Holy Spirit, able to "catch all the bullets of the enemy in the sleeve of his coat" at Frankenhausen. Once again, this may not have been good military strategy, but it is not inconceivable given Muentzer's theology!

If the above comes close to the truth, the *Bund* as a religious and political organization—not to speak of a military organization—had major weaknesses. By Muentzer's own admission, it consisted of at least three different types of persons: first, the few elect who had appropriated the Holy Spirit; second, those elect who had not yet done so, probably the vast majority; third, the "strangers," the reprobates, the "knaves and rogues," who were in it for obviously material reasons. If the elect who had not yet been filled with the Holy Spirit had "become virtually the same as the damned," how could such a group achieve Muentzer's high spiritual goals? Was failure not inevitable?

Add to this one other factor. According to the *Muehlhausen Chronicle,* when troops under Muentzer and Pfeiffer departed Langensalza to plunder their way across the Eichsfeld, they were met by locals already with "eight or nine wagon loads of plunder" that they had "liberated" from the Eichsfeld cloisters. When they encountered the Muehlhausen faction, Muentzer "praised them as Christian brothers and accepted them as such. He immediately got on a horse and began preaching to them in the open field. After the sermon, he divided the plunder between the rascals from Muehlhausen and the Eichsfeld."[128] This may not have been an isolated incident. But how, one may well ask, does this reported activity mesh with Muentzer's demand that his followers in Muehl- hausen give up the visible marks of their wealth, or his assertions that material plunder was not the goal of his *Bund*, and that the reprobates in his *Bund*—whose goal was material gain—would be held in check by the upright in it? Was Muentzer not undermining his own basic tenet here? As one of the elect who claimed to possess the Holy Spirit, was he not aiding and abetting the victory of the reprobates among the revolu- tionaries? Why would Muentzer not only allow but also aid the politi- cal, material revolution to swallow up his spiritual revolution? Had he not become his own worst enemy? But back to the course of events.

ON THE EVE OF BATTLE

When Langensalza refused entrance to the Muehlhausen troops un- der Muentzer and Pfeiffer, negotiations were carried on with Pfeiffer.[129] From Salza, the troops moved on to Homburg where they plundered the monastery.[130] The next day, 27 April, they traveled to Goermar where they set up camp on the St. Nicholas churchyard. On 28 April they proceeded to Schlotheim where they sacked the convent and plundered the residence of Rudolph von Hopfgarten, whose wife had just recently given birth. Their goal, however, seems to have been the monastery at Volkenroda, on which—according to Sittich von Berlepsch—Pfeiffer had had his eye since early January.[131] From there they returned to Goermar to divide the spoils. While they were doing so, they were joined by the Eichsfelders with eight or nine wagon loads of their own plunder.[132] As we have seen, Muentzer welcomed them, called them "Christian brothers," preached to them and divided the spoils between the Muehlhausen and Eichsfeld participants.[133] This action—as we have just argued—contrasts so sharply with virtually everything we know about Muentzer's attitude toward material things that perhaps all we can possibly say about it is that—if it is true—it must have been done in order to try and establish his authority among people who, over a long period of time, had become attached to Heinrich Pfeiffer as their leader and spiritual guide. Although he was the one who did most of the preaching, Muentzer seems never to have been able to transfer the allegiance of Pfeiffer's followers to himself.

The very next day, 29 April, Muentzer wrote to the people of Frankenhausen in an apparent response to their appeal for help. Muentzer assured them that "not only will we send you such a small group [some 200 troops], but many more; indeed all, all of our people who desire to come to your aid. . . ."[134] Muentzer's response would appear to indicate that his interests lay to the east, with events transpiring there, rather than with the meanderings on the Eichsfeld. But it also seems to indicate that he thought he could convince the people of Muehlhausen and the Eichsfeld to come to the aid of those at Frankenhausen.

Muentzer's letter was written from Goermar. Early the same morning the two contingents set out for Ebeleben. There they plundered the castle of Apel von Ebeleben,[135] drank his wine and fished his streams, stormed the convent at Marksussra and ransacked the castle at Almenhausen. The plunder was taken to Muehlhausen. Their work done, they held counsel before breaking camp in order to determine the next order of business. According to the *Muehlhausen Chronicle*, Muentzer must have recommended proceeding to Heldrungen,[136] Ernest Count of Mansfeld's castle, increasingly mentioned by the nobles as the center of their defense.[137] No sooner had Muentzer done so than a number of the Eichsfeld contingent urgently requested that they all remain on the Eichsfeld until the local nobility had been eradicated completely. While the *Muehlhausen Chronicle* gave a general account of this request, other accounts are more specific, one indeed saying: "Hans Gebbeln, captain of the Wuerbis [troops], together with his followers, fell on their knees before Pfeiffer at Ebeleben and begged that, for God's sake, he should march on the Eichsfeld."[138] As a consequence, the Muehlhausen forces remained on the Eichsfeld, although perhaps not as a unit, as the *Muehlhausen Chronicle* asserts.[139] The later report on this entire matter by the city of Muehlhausen stated specifically that on 2 May Pfeiffer led *his* supporters onto the Eichsfeld, and that "Later on, Muentzer, too, marched to the Eichsfeld with his followers."[140] It would therefore appear that Muentzer was outmaneuvered by Pfeiffer. In order to maintain his hold on at least part of their following, Muentzer's larger ambitions had—at least temporarily—to be sacrificed on the altar of what Engels once called *Lokalborniertheit,* local self–interest.

It is clear from Jordan's account that it was Pfeiffer's decision to complete the revolutionary task on the Eichsfeld before moving on to Heldrungen. Not that he was opposed to the latter; the Eichsfeld merely held priority in his thinking.[141] This was not the case for Muentzer however, who must have felt compelled to rejoin Pfeiffer's followers on the Eichsfeld. If the 1530 report of the city of Muehlhausen is to be trusted, and if the *Muehlhausen Chronicle* is right, then Muentzer renewed his attempt to head the combined forces in the direction of Heldrungen as soon as he had rejoined Pfeiffer's contingent. For, according to Pfeiffer, Muentzer informed the combined forces on 2 May that "he had been told in a dream that he was to march in the direction of the rising sun [Frankenhausen/Heldrungen]."[142] Not everyone believed his vision, however.

Although some reports have Muentzer on the way to Frankenhausen as early as 4 May, this cannot have been the case, for on 4 May he wrote to Guenther Count of Schwarzburg from Duderstadt.[143] As late as 9 May, he was still writing letters from Muehlhausen; by 12 May, however, he was most certainly in Frankenhausen.[144] After leaving the Eichsfeld around 6 May, Muentzer must have returned to Muehlhausen for a few days before departing for Frankenhausen.

Before returning to Muehlhausen, Muentzer appears to have enlisted a number of nobles in the rebel cause. In a letter of 7 May to Frederick the Wise, Zeiss wrote about the activities of the Muehlhausen forces:

> They traversed the Eichsfeld for eight days, wrecking and burning the homes of a number of nobles, and taking whatever they found. They brought the Count von Schwarzburg and Ernest Count of Hohnstein into their *Bund*. It is said that the [Count] of Stolberg has also been forced to swear [loyalty] to them, to remove all burdens and stand by them and the Gospel. They have to come to him [Muentzer] on foot, deny their titles and dignities, and allow themselves to be called brothers.[145]

On 25 April the Council and city of Arnstadt presented Guenther Count of Schwarzburg with 27 articles whose acceptance they deemed essential for the retention of peace; that very day, the Count accepted the articles, and the city renewed its allegiance to him.[146] Other dependencies of the Count followed suit.[147] On 30 April the Count wrote Wilhelm Count of Henneberg that he had ordered his castellan to accept unconditionally all the articles, and on 1 May he signed the document, ordering that the measures requested be implemented.[148] The same day he informed Botho Count of Stolberg of what he had done, and on

4 May Botho signed a similar agreement with his subjects, informing Duke George that he had done so because his subjects were in open rebellion against him and he feared that, any day, "Muentzer will march with his army against me to Stolberg, as he has threatened."[149] Thus, by the time Ernest Count of Mansfeld wrote Duke George on 5 May on this subject, he must have had some knowledge about these events.[150]

On 7 July 1525, a little over a month and a half after the Battle of Frankenhausen, all but the Count of Gleichen were taken to task by Duke George.[151] The latter accused them of joining the rebel cause and of negotiating terms with Muentzer. Although the original articles themselves, except for Botho of Stolberg's letter to Duke George, do not mention Muentzer's name, Botho, like Zeiss, singled out Muentzer as the man before whom the nobles did their obeisance: "Henry Count of Schwarzburg did not come to our aid either, but allowed his son Guenther to join the army at Frankenhausen, and pledge his allegiance to them; that not enough, he himself went to Ebeleben and pledged his loyalty to Muentzer."[152] George levelled the same charge against the Count of Hohnstein and the Count of Stolberg.[153] In all these documents, Pfeiffer is not mentioned by name even though virtually everywhere else he and Muentzer appear as an inseparable twosome.

That Muentzer was indeed the man with whom these nobles dealt is indicated in several places in his own correspondence. In a letter to the Count of Schwarzburg dated 4 May 1525, the very day on which the Count signed the agreement with his subjects, Muentzer wrote—obviously in response to the Count's decision to conclude a pact with him:

> The eternal, unwavering favor of God be with you, most beloved brother. Our brothers have received your letter and have taken Kurt von Tutcheroda, Heinrich Hack, Christoph von Aldendorff and Balthasar von Bendeleben [all, apparently nobles under the Count's jurisdiction] into our *Bund*, have promised them Christian freedom and not to harm or burden them unduly. *This I have done personally in my own hand.* This action, however, depends on whether or not it is the case that they have not hindered the righteousness of God and have not persecuted the preachers [italics mine].[154]

On 7 May Muentzer wrote to the "Christian brothers of Schmalkalden" calling Ernest Count of Hohnstein and Guenther of Schwarzburg "brothers," indicating, in all probability, that they too had joined his *Bund*.[155] And on the very eve of the battle, 12 May, Guenther of Schwarzburg wrote to Muentzer, referring to him as "my beloved Christian brother, the gentleman Thomas Muentzer." He said he would gladly come with him to Frankenhausen, but problems throughout his lands prevented him from doing so.[156]

The number of nobles who joined Muentzer's *Bund* is not the important point; nor is it important that some of them may have joined out of fear. What is important, however, is that in spite of everything Muentzer had said about nobles and princes, they were not necessarily excluded from the *Bund*. Muentzer did not conceive of the struggle as a class conflict, but as one between good and evil.

The explanation for the acceptance of nobles into Muentzer's *Bund*, of course, lies in the archetypal model of the covenant used by Muentzer: the covenant made between King Josiah and all the people of Israel. This was not a covenant directed against rulers; it was directed against idolatry and those who practiced it. Indeed, Muentzer had argued in his 25 July 1525 letter to Zeiss that "a modest covenant of such an order *must* be made in which the common man may ally himself with the *pious* ruler only for the sake of the Gospel." This was the ideal, and Muentzer never lost sight of it. However, in his day rulers like Ernest Count of Mansfeld and George Duke of Saxony actively opposed the Gospel. Even "pious Christian" princes like John Duke of Saxony and Frederick the Wise, although willing to allow the Gospel free reign— albeit Luther's version of the Gospel—refused to silence the idolators or remove the places where idolatry was practiced. Instead, they sought to silence Muentzer. Under these circumstances not only the "godless" princes, but also the "pious Christian" princes became hindrances to the establishment of the Gospel and had to be removed. This did not mean, however, that all princes were the enemy. And the inclusion of any nobles on Muentzer's side simply affirms Muentzer's understanding of the Old Testament model.

With specific reference to the obligation of "pious Christian" princes, there is striking confirmation of Muentzer's views—which, by the way, were shared by Augustine![157]—from a most unlikely source. In a letter to Frederick the Wise dated 1 May 1525, the very eve of his death and the revolution, Georg Spalatin wrote:

> Would to God that Your Electoral Highness, together with your brother, would issue—to the glory of God, and the sooner the better—a directive to all chapters, monasteries and clerics in your principality, [to the effect] that Your Princely Highnesses have been moved by important considerations and by Your Christian and other obligations, to remind them to order their church services in accordance with the Word of God, and to retain only those ceremonies which can be justified by the Holy Gospel, so that you may be exempt

from both temporal and eternal blame. For Your Princely Highnesses wish to unburden your consciences in these matters. By doing this one might hope not only to quiet the present unrest, but also to ensure your eternal bliss. *For I fear that the prime cause of this uprising stems from the fact that the Word of God is being hindered and that we do not wish to depose priests, monks and nuns and* [abolish] *their idolatrous and blasphemous church services, which princes and other rulers are obligated to abolish in accordance with God's command in Deuteronomy the 7th chapter* [italics mine].[158]

Was this a concession to Muentzer's point of view, or had Spalatin arrived at this conclusion on his own?

Muentzer probably returned to Muehlhausen on 6 or 7 May. On the latter date he wrote to the "Christian brothers" at Schmalkalden who were beginning to fear princely offensive activity. And, indeed, on 11 May Philipp of Hesse moved into Eisenach, just north of Schmalkalden, with his troops in preparation for his and Duke George's confrontation with the rebel peasants. In the letter Muentzer informed his Schmalkalden allies about his "brothers" Ernest of Honstein and Guenther of Schwarzburg, saying that he was being delayed because they needed his help. The Schmalkalden "brothers" were not to fear, however, but to be of good cheer and sing: "Though a hundred thousand foes surround me, I shall not be afraid."[159] Perhaps part of Muentzer's bravado hid his own mounting misgivings, for on the very next day he wrote to the Muehlhausen Council—presumably the Eternal Council of his own devising—that "Satan [still] has a great many things to do." He would very much, Muentzer continued, like to hinder the common good, and do this through his own vessels. Such seditious knaves should be hauled before the present authorities and threatened with punishment if they continued to undermine the city and its fathers. Should they pay no heed, the multitude was to punish them. They were to be of good courage, Muentzer concluded: "When the Judas will be revealed, his [punishment] will already have been decided upon. We ask, if at all possible, that this [matter] be earnestly discussed by the entire community before we leave."[160]

Who was this Judas? Was it Pfeiffer, as some scholars have assumed? If so, how was he undermining the common good? By not doing what Muentzer wished? In another letter of the same day to the Council at Sondershausen, Muentzer speaks of another person who should be judged—this time by them. Such people were not to be indulged.[161] Perhaps Muentzer was merely concerned with the purity of the revolutionary movement. Whatever the case, all was not well within.

On 9 May Muentzer wrote his "brothers" in Eisenach. It was yet
another letter encouraging those in revolt. He told them that "God has
[now] singularly moved the whole world to recognize godly wisdom,
and it [the world] has demonstrated this in a most earnest fashion in its
action against the tyrants, for as Daniel makes clear in the 7th chapter,
power shall be given to the common people, and, as Revelation 11
observes, the kingdoms of this world shall become subject to Christ."
These passages, Muentzer continued, undermined the false gloss of
those who, like Luther, would justify godless tyrants. The latter were in
fact and in deed being deposed. It was as clear as day, therefore, that
God, being favorably disposed, was allowing His own to punish their
opponents "only with respect to their property, by means of which they
have hindered the kingdom and righteousness of God from the beginning, as Christ Himself proves through convincing proofs in Matthew 6.
[For], how could it ever be possible that the common man, preoccupied
as he is with eking out a meager existence, should, under these conditions, accept the pure Word of God with a willing heart?"[162] Is this not
a tacit concession that the common man had not yet accepted the "pure
Word of God"? And was the fact that the rebellious peasants were
plundering castles and monasteries really a sign that "God had singularly moved the whole world to recognize godly wisdom"? Perhaps
these statements reveal another reason why Muentzer was willing to
divide the plunder among his followers. Or was Muentzer merely ratio-
nalizing the indiscriminate plunder of the revolutionaries? Indeed, he
had been arguing fairly consistently that the common man everywhere
was accepting the truth. But they were being hindered by the godless
princes. After being expelled from Muehlhausen, he observed that
where godless princes were in control there would also be a godless
people. Now, however, the material aspect began to enter the picture.
Because of the wealth of the nobles and the Church, the common man
did not have enough to live on. He was forced to eke out an existence
under great hardship. Given these conditions, how could he accept the
pure Word of God with a willing heart? How could he find time to
consider profoundly what Muentzer had been saying? And without
having done so, how could he appropriate the Holy Spirit? Or was
Muentzer merely grasping at straws to explain why the common man
was not accepting his teaching? Whatever the case, this justification of
the plundering is difficult, if not impossible, to reconcile with his call
only a few weeks earlier to the people of Muehlhausen to give up the

visible marks of their wealth in order to make possible their receiving the Holy Spirit.

In the meantime, Zeiss was keeping Frederick the Wise informed of Muentzer's activity in particular and the peasant revolt in general. On 1 May, he informed Frederick that half of Allstedt's inhabitants had left in response to Muentzer's letter.[163] A day later he wrote again, saying that only 15 to 20 remained and that they were being threatened by those who had left to join the rebels.[164] People everywhere, he argued, were ready to rise up; not even Luther, who was seeking to stem the tide of revolt in Albrecht of Mansfeld's lands, was having any luck.[165] In his region, the convent of Naundorf appeared especially threatened. Nor was Zeiss himself overly eager to come to the nuns' aid; he did so only after the abbess wrote to Spalatin on 3 May, complaining of Zeiss's inaction, and he was told in no uncertain terms by Frederick's representative on 6 May to come to their aid.[166] It is somewhat ironic that just shortly after Spalatin had written the letter in which he argued that rulers were obligated—according to Deuteronomy 7—not only to promote the preaching of the Word but also to destroy the places of idolatry and those who practiced it, Frederick the Wise—undoubtedly as a consequence of the Abbess of Naundorf's letter to Spalatin himself on 3 May—once more came to the defense of the abbess and the rights of her convent.

Whether Zeiss's reluctance stemmed from his adherence to Muentzer's teachings, it is manifest that he was playing a somewhat duplicitous game with Frederick the Wise. On 5 May he wrote to the same Christoph Meinhard, who was on friendly terms with Muentzer, that what "God, Mary and all the prophets have said about how the mighty will be deposed and those of mean estate raised up," was being fulfilled. God was finally taking the oppression of the downtrodden into account and beginning to liberate them. Zeiss would never have spoken in such a manner to the elector or Duke John. Nor did he tell them, as he did Meinhard, that

Muentzer is not a rebel leader nor a leader of the peasant army, as they say. He is no more than a preacher of those from Muehlhausen. Now, there are many preachers among the rebels who preach the Gospel in accordance with Luther's interpretation. Nor do they pay Muentzer any particular attention, in spite of the fact that he thrusts himself into the midst of the uprising with his letters. Some of them, indeed, are of the opinion that if he had not seen that others had initiated this matter, he would in all likelihood have kept quiet.[167]

Only two days later, however, Zeiss wrote Frederick the Wise that the "Muehlhausen rebels are especially dangerous," and to Spalatin he wrote on the same day that:

> no government has any authority here; all are in great disrepute. Muentzer and Pfeiffer in Muehlhausen are rebel leaders and captains in their own army. As such, they storm and plunder everywhere. They have anywhere from 15,000 to 50,000 troops—accounts vary. Be that as it may, it is a mournful spectacle to see that, although there are supposed to be many princes in the land, not one has unsheathed his sword in his own defence.[168]

Although the above flatly contradicted his letter to Meinhard and he may well, therefore, have been sympathetic to the rebel cause, Zeiss was nevertheless the representative of the elector, whose interests he was obligated to protect. In that capacity he sent his brother on 6 May to plead the elector's case with the rebel forces gathering at Frankenhausen. The brother asked whether the peasants had threatened to kill all those who had chosen to remain at home. Then he told them that they ought not to be in revolt against Frederick because the latter had allowed "the Gospel to be preached openly in every part of his principality, especially in this district, so that even those who were driven out by their lords because of the Gospel could find sanctuary. . . ."[169] The rebel leaders responded to the first question by saying that they had no policy of threatening those who chose not to join them. They had not organized in order to try to force anyone to the Christian faith; they merely opposed those "who fought against it [the faith] and did not wish to allow it to be preached freely." They also knew that Frederick had been the first to accept the Gospel and allow it free rein, nor did they intend to harm his principality in any fashion whatever.[170] As they made apparent in their letter of the same day to Ernest of Mansfeld, it was the Count whom they opposed. Among other things, they accused him of "acting in opposition to God and his Gospel . . . [and of having driven his subjects] away from Christ and His holy Word."[171] In a letter to Muehlhausen of 7 May requesting military assistance, they named Duke George and Ernest of Mansfeld, the "tyrant of Heldrungen," as rulers to whom they were opposed. These were the only two specifically mentioned.[172] They were also the two Muentzer most strongly opposed.

THE SWORD OF GIDEON

On 5 May Ernest Count of Mansfeld informed Albrecht and his brothers that the Frankenhausen forces had plundered the Count's castle at Artern and the residences of some of his vassals, taking two of his servants—Matern von Gehofen and George Buchner—captive while attacking and torturing others. And now they were threatening him.[173] He appealed for help, but they told him not to rely on them because the "Counts of Schwarzburg, Stolberg, and Hohnstein and Gleichen, together with the greater part of the nobility have been captured by the peasants and forced to swear loyalty to them." At the same time, the danger posed by the miners—the very miners Muentzer had asked his Allstedt followers to arouse—was too great for them to leave unattended.[174] Others begged off as well.

Not long thereafter, however, Zeiss informed Frederick the Wise that "the miners—as well as the peasants and townspeople—in the district of Mansfeld have informed Albrecht Count of Mansfeld that if he will remove the grievances they have against him, they will remain loyal to him."[175] Whether Luther had anything to do with this pending resolution of the conflict is not apparent. What we do know from Luther's letter of 4 or 5 May 1525 to Johann Ruehel, counsel to Albrecht of Mansfeld, is that Albrecht, unlike Ernest who remained a staunch Catholic, had joined the Lutheran cause. In his letter, Luther encouraged Ruehel not "to soften My Gracious Lord Count Albrecht in the matter [the peasant uprising], but allow His Grace to continue as he has begun." Luther does not mention any peasant grievances, but he does disparage the professed good will of the peasants—declaring them all to be Muentzerites—and argues that Albrecht, according to Romans 13, has not been entrusted with the sword in vain.[176]

Through his brother, Hans Zeiss had appealed to the peasant army gathered at Frankenhausen on the elector's behalf on 6 May. On 10 May Albrecht of Mansfeld appealed on his own behalf. As the opening lines indicate, Albrecht had at least some aspects of his Lutheran theology well in hand. He informed the peasants that there were two kingdoms: that of God and that of the world. "God's kingdom," he said, "is ruled by the Spirit; in it nothing pertains except faith, suffering, love and the welfare of one's neighbor. Every kind of uprising or revolt is forbidden in it, and it is completely separated from the kingdom of the world. The worldly kingdom, however, is ruled by the magistrates in accordance with God's ordinances, to ensure peace for the good and punishment for the wicked." He then proceeded to tell the peasants that the Gospel obligated them to obedience, and he would like to see them avoid God's punishment for the action they appeared to be contemplating. Since they had some grievances that had driven them to take such drastic action against their rulers, he was willing—and he hoped other rulers would do the same—to listen to their complaints and seek to reconcile their differences.[177] He had nothing to say of the ruler's obligations to his subjects. Nonetheless, it is a fairly remarkable letter for a noble, demonstrating—unless it was written by Johann Ruehel, Luther's friend—as keen an understanding of Luther's teachings as Duke George demonstrated on the Catholic side.[178]

Albrecht may have been emboldened to make this proposal to the rebels gathered at Frankenhausen because of the success of his negotiations with the Mansfeld miners and other of his subjects. Because of this agreement, the miners, some 300 of whom had sworn allegiance to Muentzer's *Bund* about a year before, broke their oaths and remained at home, in spite of Muentzer's letter to Allstedt of 26 April 1525 encouraging his followers to arouse the countryside, especially the miners themselves. Muentzer cannot have been edified by either this development or Albrecht's letter seeking to convince the peasants at Frankenhausen to choose discussion over confrontation, for the peasants at Frankenhausen responded favorably to Albrecht's proposal. Indeed, they suggested a place of meeting and mutual safe conducts.[179] Not so Thomas Muentzer.

Ernest of Mansfeld's situation was different. A loyal Catholic and vassal of Duke George, he and others, who—as he put it in a report to Duke George—"unlike many other counts and some nobles, have chosen to join the unchristian rebels and regard their oaths made to the peasants more important than the pledges made to their territorial lords," had sworn to risk life and limb in defense of their rights and lands. On 2 May he wrote the peasants at Frankenhausen, requesting the courtesy of being informed if and when they decided to attack him so he could prepare to defend himself; in their answer, the peasant leaders told the Count that since not everyone had yet arrived in Frankenhausen, no decision as to their course of action had been reached.[180] On 4 May, however, the latter invaded his city of Artern, caused him 8,000 Gulden worth of damage, and his vassals 4,000. In the process, they took two of his servants captive, returning to Frankenhausen with them. Thereupon he sent the rebels a second letter. On 6 May the peasant leaders responded, listing their many grievances against what they called an unchristian tyrant.[181] Ernest, in turn, urged Duke George to come with all speed to his aid in order to punish the rebels at Frankenhausen.[182] There was not even the slightest hint of any willingness on the Count's part to compromise.

On 7 May the peasants at Frankenhausen wrote to Muehlhausen requesting aid in their quarrel with the "tyrant of Heldrungen and Duke George."[183] The rebels may well have assumed, from the way in which nobles were capitulating to the demands of the peasants, that their strength lay in numbers and that a large enough number might intimidate even Duke George and Ernest of Mansfeld. If this is so, they were mistaken. The two remained steadfast in their determination to oppose the peasants whatever the consequence. The Frankenhausen rebels must have begun to sense this, for in their letter of 7 May to Muehlhausen they said that if help was not forthcoming, "a great deal of Christian blood will be spilled and the holy Gospel severely damaged."[184]

The appeal was discussed in Muehlhausen on 8 or 9 May, a discussion that apparently took place under the conviction that the "princes intend to overwhelm the forces at Frankenhausen."[185] On 9 May the authorities in Muehlhausen issued a call to come to the aid of their beleaguered brothers in Frankenhausen. They were told it was their sacred duty to do so because of the oath they had sworn in the *Bund*.[186] The number of those responding to the call was not overwhelming, and from this day on, Muentzer began to sign his letters with the appendage, "with the sword of Gideon."[187] The first letter so signed was to his supporters in Eisenach; it would appear, therefore, that the term was not necessarily a threatening one. It may imply the sword of justice, but it may also be symbolic of the few stalwart men who chose to follow him—the chosen Gideon—the man filled with the Spirit of God. Like the few *amici dei* of the Middle Ages who, according to Tauler, had sustained a corrupt Church, Muentzer, the elect friend of God, with a few chosen followers would vanquish the godless enemy in this, God's war.

By 12 May, as his letters to the Counts of Mansfeld indicate, Muentzer had arrived in Frankenhausen. There he must have learned of Albrecht's offer of conciliation and Ernest's attempts to intimidate his army of God. He must also almost immediately have been informed of the latter's servants being held captive there. The following day the rebels received a letter from Duke John's counselors at Weimar, encouraging them not to proceed hastily in the case of the captives. It appears this advice came as a response to the peasants' appeal to Duke John, whose brother Frederick had just died on 5 May, for help in their quarrel with Ernest of Mansfeld. The Duke's counselors informed the rebels, however, that John, as an elector of the Holy Roman Empire, was obligated to abide by the laws of the realm. In any case, Count

Ernest was not the elector's vassal, but the vassal of Duke George and the emperor.[188]

From a later report of these events by the city of Frankenhausen—a most tendentious one—it would appear that Duke John's letter reached the peasant leaders before the trial and execution of the captives.[189] If that is the case, and if representatives of the Frankenhausen contingent did indeed plead with Muentzer not summarily to execute the prisoners after their kangaroo court conviction, then Muentzer's action in this matter appears much more one of open defiance not only of the Count, but of Duke John as well. It also manifests a rift between Muentzer's party and those from Frankenhausen, a rift we have already noted in other matters. In any case, the above report asserted that no sooner had Muentzer and his forces arrived in Frankenhausen than a public forum was held in the public square before the city gate. There the captives were brought before him. In the presence of several thousand men, Muentzer called out, asking whether anyone wished to bring a charge against the prisoners. Several men stepped forward: one—N. Kronest from Reinstorff—accused Matern von Gehofen; the other—K. Voypel from Artern—accused Steffan Harttenstein. It was at this juncture, the Frankenhausen authorities later claimed, that they appealed to Muentzer not to proceed with the execution but to follow Duke John's counsel. The accusations against the prisoners had been so gruesome, however, that this appeal for restraint had not prevailed, and the captives were executed by the sword.[190]

According to Ruehel, Muentzer later told Duke George—when asked what had moved him to such action—that not his, but God's justice, had determined it.[191] In his confession Muentzer is reported to have said: "He had spoken the verdict over Matern von Gehofen and the other servants of Count Ernest out of the mouth of the people [*gemeyne*], and consented to it, doing so out of fear."[192] What kind of fear? Certainly not fear of Ernest of Mansfeld, as a later version of the confession has it.[193] For if this were the case, we would have to discount all of Muentzer's letters to the Count—and to others—as pure bombast. Did he mean fear of, or respect for, the verdict of this army gathered to execute the sentence of God over His enemies? He did tell Duke George that it had not been his, but God's verdict. In any case, by this action Muentzer in effect burned his bridges behind him; he must therefore have been confident that God would give them the victory. Or did he fear the loss of any authority he might still have had among the revolutionaries?

He had come to Frankenhausen carrying the "sword of Gideon." In the past he had repeatedly told his followers not to fear the godless. Even if they were only three elect against a hundred thousand reprobates, they were not to fear. This was, after all, God's war. It had been described and foretold in Matthew 24. Like Gideon of old, therefore, who had brought only three hundred chosen men to Jericho, numbers were not important; they, too, would cause the walls to fall and the godless rulers to flee. And so "with the sword of Gideon" on 12 May Muentzer wrote two letters before the battle: one to the Catholic Ernest Count of Mansfeld, the other to the Lutheran Albrecht Count of Mansfeld—one to the godless tyrant, the other to a misguided "pious Christian" ruler.

Muentzer's relationship with Ernest, as we have seen, went back at least to the beginning of September 1523; he wrote Albrecht, however, for the first time on 12 May 1525. He reminded Ernest—if, indeed, the latter needed a reminder—that he had formerly been pastor at Allstedt. Again he admonished him to put an end to his tyrannical raging and no longer tempt the wrath of God. He charged him with having begun to martyr Christians, with having called Christianity foolishness, with having attempted to destroy it. Who, Muentzer wanted to know, had made Ernest a ruler of the people that God had purchased with His precious blood anyway? The Count, Muentzer asserted, would have to prove himself a Christian, and he would have to do so before the "Christian brotherhood" at Frankenhausen, who would provide him with a safe conduct. In their midst he would have to apologize for his obvious tyranny, confess who had told him it was right and proper to conduct himself like a wicked heathen, maltreating Christians so miserably in the name of Christ. Should he refuse to appear, Muentzer promised to denounce the Count to the ends of the earth so that every brother would as happily shed his blood as that of a Turk. Like the tare that he was, he would be persecuted and uprooted; people would be more eager to kill him than they had formerly been to acquire indulgences.

Yet Muentzer held out little hope that Ernest could or would meet these conditions, for, he said: "God has hardened your heart as he did those of the Pharaohs and other kings whom he intended to destroy, Joshua 5 and 11. . . . In short, you have been marked for destruction by the mighty power of God." Nevertheless, in order that Ernest know that God had charged the people in this matter, Muentzer told him that God had commanded he be deposed, for he was of no use whatever to Christendom. In fact, he was a harmful enemy of the "friends of God." God had commanded that such people be destroyed.[194]

To Albrecht he wrote in a somewhat more restrained tone. He left no doubt, however, that he considered Albrecht a spokesman for Lutheranism. It was a pity, he told him, that he abused the Pauline Epistles so miserably in order to justify wicked rulers. Unlike Ernest, Muentzer did not accuse Albrecht of being a tyrannical ruler; he accused him rather of seeking to aid, to justify, reprobate rulers. Did Albrecht not realize, Muentzer chided, that God could raise up even ignorant people in His wrath to depose tyrants? Had Christ's mother, inspired by the Holy Spirit, not said of his kind that "He hath put down the mighty from their seats, and exalted them of low degree (whom you despise)?" Could Albrecht not find in his Lutheran grits and Wittenberg soup—to use Muentzer's figurative language—what Ezekiel had foretold in chapter 37? Had he not been able to taste, in his Martinian peasant dung, what the same prophet had said in chapter 39, and how God had ordered the birds of the heavens to devour the flesh of rulers and the dumb beasts to drink their blood, Revelation 18 and 19? Did he think God was more concerned about his welfare than that of His own people? Albrecht wished, Muentzer continued, under the name of Christ, to be a heathen, to cover himself with St. Paul. But they would not allow him to get away with this.

Like Ernest, Albrecht, too, was invited to appear before the "Christian brothers" gathered at Frankenhausen. He was to appear in recognition of the power which God had transferred to the people, and in order to give an account of his faith. Were he to do so, they were willing to accept him in their midst as a common brother. If not, they would oppose him as they opposed any other archenemy of the Christian faith.[195]

These two letters are replete with themes out of Muentzer's past. Ernest is referred to as a tare about to be uprooted at the time of harvest. Like all reprobates, he had been hardened in his heart by God Himself. As such, he did not even possess the potential to be filled with the Holy Spirit. And so he had been marked for destruction, for he was useless to Christendom; he was an active destroyer of the "friends of God." Since this was God's war, what chance for success could Ernest have? The battle about to commence was therefore the consummation of history—and Muentzer, who had predicted these events, was ready to mount the ramparts and utter the cry of victory.

Albrecht, however, may have been an elect or may at least have had that potential, but he had been misled by the scribe Luther. It was because of him that "pious Christian" princes refused to abolish idolatry and the "idolatrous priests, monks and nuns." To be sure, they said they gave the holy Gospel free rein, but continually came to the aid of the reprobates and the idolatrous clergy. Luther justified such action by the argument that the ruler's office was a "pagan," a secular office.

Although Muentzer signed these letters "with the sword of Gideon," he had not yet stopped trying to influence people. Perhaps numbers were important to him after all, and so on 13 May, two days before the battle, he wrote to Erfurt, attempting to enlist support in the upcoming armageddon.[196] He had seen with what joy the Erfurt people had turned to the truth, he said; however, they were allowing gluttonous Lutheran mush eaters to weaken their resolve with their besmirched charity. St. Paul had spoken of such debauched people, and how in the present age they would put on a good and holy outward appearance, all the while striving with might and main against the power of God. They were no longer to heed such sycophants but were to join the common Christians in the battle against the evil tyrants. They were to help in any way they could.

Once again Muentzer cited the passages about the birds of heaven and the beasts of the field devouring the tyrants; once again he said that power had been given to the people; once more he said that God desired to free them from the tyrants. Nearly every passage of Scripture, he argued, testified to the fact "that creation must become free before the pure Word of God can grow on earth." Only a few weeks earlier he had asserted that the economic hardships kept the common man from accepting the Gospel. Now, however, they had to become politically free, and with them all creation.[197] Apparently the "pure wheat" he was sowing had not yet born much fruit.

THE BATTLE

Needless to say, Ernest and Albrecht, Counts of Mansfeld refused to submit themselves to Muentzer's judgment. And the citizens of Erfurt chose the better part of valor and remained well within their city walls. The following day, Sunday 14 May, George Duke of Saxony, Philipp of Hesse, and Henry Duke of Braunschweig, together with their vassals, appeared before Frankenhausen with approximately 2,500 cavalry and 4,000 infantry. On Monday the princely forces moved into position before the city, only to discover that the peasants had positioned themselves on top of a mountain where they awaited the enemy. When the princes appeared at the foot of the mountain, the peasants sent a note to them: "We have not come here in order to injure anyone, 2 John, but in order to receive divine justice. Nor are we here to spill blood. If you agree with us, we will not do anything to you."[198]

The princes, however, had not come to engage in a friendly exchange of views or to deal away their privileges. They had come, they replied, to punish the blasphemers with the sword entrusted to their care by God. Nonetheless, out of Christian charity and because they believed many of the peasants to have been misled, they had decided the following: If the false prophet, Thomas Muentzer, together with his personal followers, were turned over to them, and if the peasants surrendered unconditionally, they might temper their judgment against them accordingly.[199]

According to Philipp of Hesse's report to the Archbishop of Trier, the peasants were slow to respond.[200] One can imagine the kind of uproar a demand of this nature must have occasioned. For it came after Muentzer had preached to the gathered throng for at least several days, according to Hut's confession, the last being the very day of the battle. Hut said Muentzer had told the peasants that

> God almighty was about to cleanse the world [of tares?] and had taken power away from the rulers and given it to their subjects. As a result, they [the rulers] would be weakened, as was already the case, and they would begin to beg. The peasants were not to believe them, however, because they would not keep faith with their subjects. God was on the side of the peasants. Now the latter carried a banner with them upon which was painted a rainbow. This, Muentzer had said, symbolized God's covenant. And after Muentzer had preached to the peasants in the above manner for three days in a row, a rainbow had appeared in the sky and was seen around the sun. Muentzer had drawn attention to it, consoling the peasants and saying: you see the rainbow, the sign of the covenant; God is on your side. Therefore they were to go heartily into battle and be brave. And he, Hut, had also seen the rainbow.[201]

Hut's report has the ring of truth about it. For some time Muentzer had kept the banner beside his pulpit in the Church of St. Mary. Under the rainbow portrayed on it were the words: "This is the sign of God's eternal covenant; those who wish to join this covenant must step under it." The banner had been carried with the troops onto the Eichsfeld. Muentzer must obviously now have brought it along to Frankenhausen; he had earlier said that he intended to take it into battle. It would have been quite in keeping, then, to bring it along from Muehlhausen, perhaps with the three hundred or so who had answered the call when they were told—probably by Muentzer himself—that it was their sacred duty to do so because of the oath they had sworn in the *Bund*.

Now they were in Frankenhausen: the elect, like Muentzer, who knew they possessed the Holy Spirit. Three such people, he had asserted on numerous occasions, would defeat a hundred thousand. Then there were those who had sworn an oath to the *Bund;* obviously, not all of these had come to do battle. The miners from Mansfeld were notably absent. These belonged to the core of the committed. Hans Hut was one of them; therefore, he must have known what the banner signified and what the covenant implied. But did they all possess the Holy Spirit? And then there were those who had never sworn and, like the captain of the Muehlhausen forces, regarded oath-taking as a waste of time. It is also clear that the forces gathered at Frankenhausen had much less violent goals than did Muentzer. They were there to intimidate Duke George and Count Ernest into granting them the same "divine justice" other nobles had been forced or persuaded to grant in the last several weeks. It was Muentzer who entered with the conviction that this was the apocalyptic struggle foretold in Matthew 24. He was the one who talked about uprooting the tares in the time of harvest. He was the one who preached to the peasant forces about the covenant made with God. And as he did so, pointing to the banner that signified that they were doing battle for the "Word of God which remains in all eternity," a rainbow appeared in the sky. What better celestial confirmation could Muentzer have hoped for?

Having his covenant so dramatically confirmed before the whole peasant army can only have emboldened an already bombastically inclined Muentzer. Under these conditions it is not at all inconceivable that he boasted he would "catch all the bullets of the enemy in the sleeve of his coat."[202] According to the account sent Luther by Johann Ruehel on 26 May, Muentzer also promised the rebels that Heldrungen would be destroyed. When they finally arrived there, everyone in the castle, even the stones, would give way before them.[203] Whether these reports are true, there can be little doubt that Muentzer believed God was going to fight their battle for them in supernatural ways.

Given such a heady atmosphere—or did the peasants really believe all of this?—it is not inconceivable that the peasants marched into battle singing "Come Holy Spirit, Noble Lord." According to Ruehel, the first shots of the enemy fell short, and Muentzer is supposed to have shouted: "Did I not tell you no bullet would harm you?" The next volley of bullets, however, penetrated their ranks; then everyone broke and ran for cover, trying to find sanctuary within the town walls below.[204] When this happened, where was Muentzer? Did he flee immediately as well? Reports on the battle variously state that between 4,000 and 8,000 peasants were slaughtered, with only about 600 taken captive.[205] Why was not Muentzer found among the vast majority who were killed? How was he able to make his way to safety within the city? Was he leading the charge or shouting encouragement from the rear? And if he was not leading the charge, did he really believe what he had been telling his followers: that this was God's war and that He would fight for them?

Zwingli died at the Battle of Kappell; Muentzer, according to the information sent Luther by Ruehel, was found hiding in bed in the attic of a house just inside the city gate. Since he was one of the few to escape the field of battle, he must have been in the forefront of those who fled. That can only mean that he brought up the rear of those who went into battle. The words had come much more easily than had appropriately brave actions. Zeiss probably knew him better than most: he asserted that Muentzer had thrust himself into the midst of the turmoil with his letters; had others not started the revolt, he would have stayed out of it. He was ready to preach at a moment's notice; confrontation with the power of the princes found him cowering in bed. Words, words, words—as Petrarch wrote Cola di Rienzo—Muentzer brought them only words. But deeds, as he had himself pointed out to Melanchthon in his March 1522 letter, were the sign of the presence of the Holy Spirit. What had gone wrong? Had his dreams and visions betrayed him? Had he misjudged "the time of harvest"? Or did the fault lie with his followers? Had they pressed the struggle for the wrong reasons? And even if they had, was Muentzer free of all blame? When the slaughter began, Muentzer must have realized that, for one reason or another, things had gone very wrong. What were the options he had as to the reasons? Was he a false prophet as Luther was quick to assert, or had someone subverted God's plans? Could the latter even be the case? Did he have any options at all?

When Muentzer was discovered in the bed of an attic, he at first feigned illness, trying to give the impression that he was unaware of what had just transpired. In his pouch, however, was Albrecht Count of Mansfeld's letter of 10 May to the peasants. From this his captors deduced his true identity, though he at first attempted to deny it. Was he not willing to take responsibility for his actions? Were these not, after all, God's actions? And where was now the sword of Gideon? The walls had indeed come crashing down, but they were not the walls of Jericho.

And so Muentzer was taken to Duke George who must have delighted in his capture.

CONFESSION AND RETRACTION?

Duke George and Philipp of Hesse began to interrogate Muentzer on the spot. They wanted to know why he had had Count Ernest's servants executed; they wished to know how he had arrived at the conclusion that a prince should have no more than eight horses, a count no more than four. According to Ruehel, Philipp engaged him in a theological discussion—the "pious Christian" prince with the prophet himself—the Duke drawing on the New Testament, Muentzer citing the Old. In the end, however, he was turned over to his archenemy, Ernest Count of Mansfeld, and granted his long-standing wish of going to Heldrungen. He arrived in chains, however, not in victory, and the people and the stones did not give way before him.

Before he was taken to Heldrungen, Muentzer was interrogated more systematically. His confession is dated 16 May, the very day after the battle. He made a second confession on the same day under torture. There are really no startling revelations in either, nor do they reveal any sense of guilt or remorse on Muentzer's part. There is no admission of error. Certain contemporaries believed him to have retracted, whereas others could not be persuaded of this.

On 18 May, Philipp of Hesse wrote to the Swabian League about the Battle of Frankenhausen. In a note appended to the letter he remarked:

> We do not wish to hide from you the fact that we have captured Thomas Muentzer, who has led the people of these parts so badly astray, moving them to rebellion, and have taken him in chains to Heldrungen. He has revoked his own sermons and made a confession. It would be useful for all rebellious subjects to take note of it.[206]

In his first letter concerning events surrounding the battle, Ruehel wrote Luther on 21 May:

> Now that the jig is up, the above-mentioned Thomas Muentzer—and the satan within him—obviously in order to deceive the godless tyrants, has renounced all his errors, taken the sacrament in one form and confessed his adherence to the faith which the Church holds and has held since the beginning, thus proving himself totally papistical in his last days, as you will see from the enclosed document.[207]

George Duke of Saxony, Ernest of Mansfeld, an executioner, and a scribe were the only ones present at Muentzer's second interrogation made under torture. In his letter to the mayor and the Council of Nuremberg of mid-June 1525, Duke George wrote that

> Muentzer has confessed his errors and has expressed regret for his part in spilling so much blood, but especially because he fell away from obedience to the Christian [read Catholic] Church. He has been absolved, has stated that he desires only the unity of the Christian Church, and because of that has taken the holy sacrament in the form of bread alone.[208]

The above opinions rested on a document issued by the Leipzig court, dated 17 May 1525. It claimed that a meeting had taken place between Muentzer and a number of nobles at Heldrungen in which the former had recanted. It stated that Muentzer had asked to be forgiven for having preached against the nobility, that he had retracted his false opinions concerning the holy sacrament, and that he had been wrong to preach revolt against the Church in such a seductive manner. He now wished to be found holding to what the Church had always held, and still continued to hold, and he hoped to die in that faith as a reconciled member.[209]

It would appear that it was this report that Ruehel sent Luther on 23 May. While Philipp of Hesse and George Duke of Saxony obviously believed the recantation genuine, Ruehel suggested that Muentzer was trying to deceive the "godless tyrants." Others have suggested that Duke George had his own reasons for putting out such a report.[210] In any case, Luther was not satisfied and requested, in a letter of 23 May, that Ruehel find out "how he [Muentzer] was discovered and taken prisoner, how he conducted himself [in captivity], for it is useful to know how that proud spirit acted."[211] In his response of 26 May, Ruehel sent Luther a copy of Muentzer's confession given on 16 May and a copy of his letter written to Muehlhausen dated 17 May. About the letter Ruehel observed: "Although our opponents interpret this document as a retraction, to me it appears essentially a justification of everything he did; he puts the entire blame on the peasants, saying that because they sought to satisfy their selfish desires, their cause failed and they suffered punishment." Let them say what they will, Ruehel continued, Muentzer was a desperate man.[212] Luther agreed. In his letter to Ruehel of 30 May 1525, he wrote that:

> Thomas Muentzer was not asked the right questions; I would have caused him to have been questioned quite differently. As it is, his confession is

nothing less than a devilish, hardened justification of his ambitions. For he does not confess to having done anything evil; it appalls me. I had not thought it possible that a man's heart could be so deeply hardened.[213]

Did Muentzer show contrition? Did he admit to the dissemination of errors? Did he take communion and the Last Rights in the Catholic tradition? Did he return to the teachings which the Church had always held? Or was the report of these things fabricated by the Leipzig court of Duke George? To be sure, the two confessions demonstrate nothing of the kind, and Ruehel and Luther were fully justified in their skepticism. And if the report coming out of Leipzig—or Heldrungen—on 17 May is to be believed, then one is justified in assuming that Muentzer's letter of the same day and from the same place to the city of Muehlhausen should manifest at least some of that contrition, some of that justification of the Roman Catholic Church with its faith and rituals. But does it?

The opening of the letter makes it apparent that Muentzer recognized he was facing death. If he did recant on the same day in order to move the princes to mercy, as Ruehel suggested, he at least did not seem to have thought himself successful:

> Since it has pleased God that I shall depart this world in the true knowledge of God's name and with a renewed recognition of a number of abuses accepted by the people—who did not understand me but [rather] sought only to satisfy their own desires, which only leads to the destruction of God's truth—I am quite content that God has led matters to such a conclusion. [This affair], like all His other accomplished works, must not be judged according to their outward appearance, but according to a true judgment. John chapter 7. Therefore, be not angry at my death, which is taking place for the benefit of the good and the unwise.[214]

Thus far certainly no sense of remorse. Indeed the blame for the failure, as Ruehel pointed out, is laid squarely at the feet of the mass of the rebellious participants. How many times had he told them to seek only God's interests, fear Him alone, eschew the things of this world, and cleanse their souls of all creatures so that they could be filled with the Holy Spirit? But they had not understood him and had continued to seek the fulfillment of their own desires. He had promised them failure in advance if they persevered in their old ways, and now he reiterated to them those very reasons for their failure. He was not at fault; they were. Nor should they judge what had happened by mere outward appearance—by the fact that they had lost the battle—but by the truth that he had long ago taught them. No remorse here; no recantation. Rather, a blaming of the peasants for not having understood him and a suggestion that the appearance of defeat was misleading.

But there is more. He warned the people of Muehlhausen to be wary of people like those from Frankenhausen, for "these events undoubtedly transpired because everyone sought to satisfy their own desires rather than seek the justification of Christendom." They were therefore to discern the difference and not make the same mistake in their own case.[215] The mistakes at Frankenhausen and this misunderstanding of his message had led to the killing of over 4,000 men. They were to seek the righteousness of God so that the same thing would not happen to them. For, said Muentzer,

> I have often enough warned you that God's punishment—undertaken by the rulers—cannot be avoided unless you recognize the damage [done to Christendom]. He who recognizes this damage can avoid the punishment. Therefore be on friendly terms with everyone and do not anger the rulers any longer, as many have done for selfish reasons. With that I commend you to the grace of God and His Spirit.[216]

He knew, Muentzer continued, that the majority of the people of Muehlhausen had never supported "this selfish revolution," but had always sought to hinder it. In order that the innocent among them—as had happened to the innocent at Frankenhausen—not also get into trouble, they were not to join the rebellious forces at this point but to seek mercy from the princes, in hopes that they would grant it. He concluded the letter by saying that he had said all this in order to remove a heavy burden from his soul and in order that they not participate in any future rebellion. He did not want any more innocent blood to be spilled.[217] Ten days later his own blood was spilled.

This letter was written on the very day Muentzer is supposed to have recanted, but there is absolutely no indication in it of anything of the kind. He referred to what he had taught them in order to demonstrate to them that his warnings had proven valid. He complained that he was not correctly understood, that the revolutionaries continued to seek selfish ends rather than God's righteousness. He told them not to judge by outward appearances, not to have anything more to do with cowards like those from Frankenhausen, not to oppose the rulers any longer. There is a curious exception to the latter admonition, however. They are not to oppose the rulers "unless one has understood the damage [done to Christendom]." He had mentioned this damage many times: it was the damage done to the Church when the tares had infiltrated it in the middle of the second century and forced the Holy Spirit to leave. It was in this connection he had repeatedly cited the Hegesippus passage found in Eusebius. He had told his followers in Allstedt in late April 1525 that he feared "the foolish folk would enter into some perverse agreement [with the enemy] because they did not recognize the damage."[218] If they did not recognize, or understand, this damage, it had to follow that they did not possess the Holy Spirit. Without Him, failure was inevitable. Did Muentzer finally recognize that the "common man" was not really eager to accept his teaching? Toward the end he was beginning to look in different directions for the cause of this failure. At one point he saw it in the fact that they did not have enough leisure time.[219] Then again he saw it in their lack of material possessions.[220] Previously the blame had always fallen on the "godless tyrants"; now, however, for the first time he put the blame on the common man: he, too—like all the rest—was motivated by gross selfishness.

The one thing Muentzer regretted was the massive spilling of blood. Perhaps it was this Duke George referred to. But it had nothing to do with his teaching. The letter to Muehlhausen can only be seen—as Ruehel and Luther saw it—as a justification of Muentzer's whole perspective. The blame for the failure lay elsewhere. Written on the same day as his recantation touted by Duke George, the letter stands as a negation of that ostensible retraction. Did he then also take communion in the Catholic manner, allow himself to be absolved, and return to the faith of the Catholic Church? Only if Duke George misinterpreted Muentzer's acts because he did not understand his theological perspective.

The striking thing about this letter is that it contains virtually nothing about Muentzer himself. No mention is made of his boast that if there were only three *amici dei* in their midst they would not fear a hundred thousand foes. And he had stated this more than once. There was not a word about how princes had become cowardly and how he would defeat them with mere words. He made no mention of the covenant— the *Bund*—or the rainbow that he had thought just prior to going into battle so dramatically confirmed it.[221] He conveniently omitted to tell them that he had said this was God's war, foretold in Matthew 24. And if he had told the peasants that the bullets would not harm them, but would be turned back upon the princes themselves, he avoided any mention of that too.[222] Did the outcome of his prophecies all hinge upon the people? Was he not at least a little to blame? Had he not deluded himself into believing that he had received all of this "directly from the mouth of God," as he had written Zeiss? He was sorry so much blood had been spilled, but was it not he who was responsible?

After writing this letter, Muentzer had another ten days to dwell on these questions and on exactly what his responsibility in this tragedy was. There is no evidence to suggest that he changed his mind.

Conclusion

If success is the criterion by which we are to judge Thomas Muentzer, a criterion applied by Luther to argue that Muentzer had proven himself a false prophet, then we must render a negative judgment. If, as Wilhelm Zimmermann and most Marxist historians have argued, failure was inevitable because Muentzer was centuries ahead of his time, we might render a more positive judgment. Indeed, judgments of Muentzer have become more positive since World War II. But as the historiography of Muentzer demonstrates, judgments of this sort are hazardous at best and reflect more on the judge than on the object of judgment. It behooves us, therefore, to be satisfied with some modest conclusions.

The first conclusion this study entitles us to draw, I believe, is that Thomas Muentzer was, throughout, his own man. He was never a "Martinian," even though he was influenced by what Luther had to say about Tauler and *Eine Deutsche Theologie*. Nor did he come under the influence of the Zwickau Prophets. Beginning with Tauler, and moving on to Eusebius, Augustine, and John Hus under the impact of the Leipzig Disputation, Muentzer developed his own unique perspective on the problems of the Church, Christian society, and reform. This perspective, together with his assumption that Luther was himself a disciple of Tauler and German Mysticism, determined his relationship to the reformer.

Second, this study, I think, entitles us to conclude that Muentzer was, at least until Luther's letter to the princes of Saxony, open to a reconciliation with the Reformer, though on his own terms. It was Luther who, in the summer of 1523, disdained the hand proffered in friendship and turned more and more vociferously against a former ally. The relationship between the two is, in any event, an interesting study in the growth and development of alienation and conflict.[1]

Third, Muentzer cannot, I think, be held responsible for the nature of the sources he used to construct his intellectual edifice, though it should be said that he might have avoided some pitfalls had he developed the same emphasis on *sola scriptura* Luther had developed at this time. For it was not until 1879 that the *Historia* was proven spurious, and only in recent years has the critical work on Eusebius's *Church History* and other sources Muentzer used begun. The art of historical criticism was in its infancy in his day, but then again, had Muentzer lived in a later age, his conviction—had he maintained it—that he had derived everything "directly from the mouth of God" might have led him to disregard, if not denigrate, such "rational" scribes of higher criticism in any case.

A fourth conclusion must relate to Muentzer the revolutionary.[2] In his development as a revolutionary we can discern three main stages. First, it is, of course, difficult to say how Muentzer might have applied the ideas he developed in 1519–1520, had he not encountered the opposition of the Catholic Count Ernest of Mansfeld in the context of the Imperial edict of 6 March 1523. Nonetheless, one cannot do justice to Muentzer's involvement in the events leading up to the Peasants' War by ignoring the political context and emphasizing only the intellectual influences.[3] He operated within a very specific context, and the ambiguous Imperial edict was a major factor in his opposition to Ernest of Mansfeld. In this attitude he was no different from a host of other reformers, Luther included, who regarded as tyrants those Catholic princes who opposed the preaching of the "holy Gospel" mandated by the edict. That such preaching was mandated by the Imperial decree gives credence to the charge. Had Muentzer stopped at this point, he would hardly have aroused the serious opposition of his Protestant contemporaries. Indeed, in this opposition to the Catholic Church and its princely supporters, there was great similarity, as we have seen, between him and Luther.

The second stage of his development as a revolutionary is marked by his desire to go beyond the mere defense of the "holy Gospel." He sought, on the basis of the Old Testament story of King Josiah, to exterminate, remove, or at the very least suppress the "idolatrous monks and nuns." This led him clearly beyond what Luther and Frederick were willing to do. In this respect, however, he was no different from the late Augustine who used, as we have seen, the same Old Testament passage to make precisely the same argument. From Augustine the Catholic Church itself, which had been exterminating its opponents for centuries, had derived its argument. Only now the tables were turned on the clergy, for they had become the tares to be rooted out of the wheat field. Even Spalatin conceded to the elector on the eve of the peasant uprising that had they suppressed the Catholic Church in their region rather than "letting the Word of God do it alone," the peasants would not have risen in revolt. Indeed, the peasants' argument that they were not opposed to the princes of Electoral Saxony but only to those who undermined the "holy Gospel," gives weight to Spalatin's and Muentzer's position.

What puts Muentzer clearly out of touch with most of his contemporaries, however, is his conviction that, in this "time of harvest," the godless must be destroyed. It is this conviction that constitutes the third element in his road to revolution. For in the midst of the peasant uprising this conviction becomes a self-fulfilling prophecy, providing him with the opportunity to separate the wheat from the tares. This third element, it appears to me, is the critical one, although the second could as easily have brought him—as it did the peasants—into conflict with the Catholic princes. There are, then, stages in Muentzer's development as a revolutionary, and we cannot simply speak of a "theology of revolution," at least not in his case.

In all this, Muentzer's primary concern, as he asserted from time to time, was the purity of the Church. In this objective, he reflected a pervasive sixteenth-century preoccupation. Perhaps he pursued that goal with more passion than compassion. Certainly he did not share Erasmus's pacifism or that of the Swiss Brethren. Indeed, he intended to be a "destroyer of the godless." This notwithstanding, the intellectual edifice Muentzer constructed, clearly the work of a creative individual, reflects an amazingly agile mind. In an age that witnessed the revival of so many literary sources of Classical and Christian antiquity, Thomas Muentzer, not unlike contemporary Christian Humanists, sought to synthesize opposing viewpoints; in his case, however, that attempt had an essentially mystical orientation. Was that orientation the fatal flaw in his intellectual armor? Are mysticism and revolution at all compatible?

However one may respond to these questions, there can be no doubt that Thomas Muentzer aroused the passions of his day and has continued to do so. Over the years he has also attracted the interest of other mystics and revolutionaries. From time to time, even scholars turn their attention to him, never more so than in this the five-hundredth anniversary of his birth. May they be forgiven this opportunism.

Notes

INTRODUCTION: CROSSROADS AT LEIPZIG

1. See the discussion of Muentzer's birthdate by Siegfried Braeuer, "Zu Muentzer's Geburtsjahr," LJ 36 (1969): 80–83.

2. See Max Steinmetz, *Das Muentzerbild von Martin Luther bis Friedrich Engels* (Berlin, 1971), and the response by Gottfried Maron, "Thomas Muentzer in der Sicht Martin Luthers," JdKHB 12 (1975): 71–85, who rejects Steinmetz's charge that Luther's pronouncements on Muentzer constitute a classic case of "Legendenbildung und bewuszten Geschichtsfaelschung." Others, however, like Ludwig Fischer, ed., *Die lutherischen Pamphlete gegen Thomas Muentzer* (Tuebingen, 1976), have accepted the validity of Steinmetz's accusation.

3. See Abraham Friesen, *Reformation and Utopia: The Marxist Interpretation of the Reformation and Its Antecedents* (Wiesbaden, 1974), 115–145.

4. On Zimmermann, see Abraham Friesen, "Wilhelm Zimmermann and the Nemesis of History," *German Studies Review* 4, no. 2 (1981): 195–236.

5. See Friesen, *Reformation and Utopia*, 147–239.

6. See, for example, Bernhard Lohse, "Auf dem Wege zu einem neuen Muentzer–Bild," *Luther* 41, no. 3 (1970): 120–132.

7. See especially Erwin Muehlhaupt, "Die betrogene Forelle," *Luther* 44, no. 1 (1973): 29–35, and his "Martin Luther oder Thomas Muentzer,—Wer ist der rechte Prophet?" *Luther* 45, no. 2 (1974): 55–71.

8. Heinrich Heine, "Franzoesische Zustaende," *Werke und Briefe*, 4 (Berlin, 1960), 516.

9. See Abraham Friesen, "Philip Melanchthon (1497–1560), Wilhelm Zimmermann (1807–1878) and the Dilemma of Muentzer Historiography" CH, 43 (1974): 164–182, especially the concluding observations.

10. Even Max Steinmetz, the dean of Marxist Reformation historians, has written: ". . . die moeglichst umfassende Kenntnis der Buecher, die Muentzer

273

besass oder gelesen hat, die Erforschung der Bibliotheken, die er benutzt haben koennte. Alles das koennte von grosser Bedeutung sein fuer die Erforschung seiner geistigen Entwicklung." "Thomas Muentzer und die Buecher," ZfG, 32, no. 7 (1984): 603.

11. William J. Bouwsma, *John Calvin: A Sixteenth-Century Portrait* (Oxford, 1988), 2–3, and James M. Kittelson, *Luther the Reformer* (Minneapolis, 1986), 16–17, make the same observations with respect to their subjects.

12. On the nature of conversion, see Marilyn J. Harran, *Luther on Conversion* (Ithaca, 1983), and Bouwsma, *Calvin,* 9–15 and the literature cited there.

13. See Friesen, *Reformation and Utopia,* 127, 209–216.

14. Hans-Juergen Goertz, *Innere und Aeussere Ordnung in der Theologie Thomas Muentzers* (Leiden, 1967).

15. See especially Paul Wappler, *Thomas Muentzer in Zwickau und die "Zwickauer Propheten",* 2d ed. (Guetersloh, 1966), and Walter Elliger, *Thomas Muentzer. Leben und Werk* (Goettingen, 1975).

16. See especially Guenter Vogler, "Thomas Muentzer und die Staedte," in Rainer Postel and Franklin Kopitzsch, eds., *Reformation und Revolution. Beitraege zum politischen Wandel und den sozialen Kraeften am Begin der Neuzeit* (Stuttgart, 1989), pp. 138–154, and Siegfried Braeuer, "Thomas Muentzers Beziehungen zur Braunschweiger Fruehreformation" TL, 109, no. 8 (1984): 636–638.

17. Vogler, "Muentzer und die Staedte," 141.

18. MSB, 537.

19. See Manfred Bensing and Winfried Trillitzsch, "Bernard Dappens 'Articuli . . . contra Lutheranos.' Zur Auseinandersetzung der Jueterboger Franziskaner mit Thomas Muenster und Franz Guenther 1519," *Jahrbuch fuer Regionalgeschichte* 2 (1967): 118.

20. See Eric Gritsch, *Reformer without a Church: The Life and Thought of Thomas Muentzer, 1488[?]–1525* (Philadelphia, 1967), 6.

21. Braeuer, "Muentzers Beziehungen," 637–638.

22. Max Steinmetz, "Thomas Muentzer in der Forschung der Gegenwart," ZfG 23, no. 6 (1975): 676.

23. See the evidence presented in Bensing and Trillitzsch, 117–119.

24. Quoted in Bensing and Trillitzsch, 118.

25. Ibid., 132–137.

26. Ibid., 137.

27. Ibid., 140. A little further on Dappen mentioned 300 as the number of years the Church had been led astray. And still later he said: "Insuper asserebat idem magister Thomas sanctum evangelium plus quam tracentis aut quadragentis annis iacuisse sub scamno et quod opertebit multos colla prebere gladio pro sancti evangelii de sub scamno revocatione" (p. 142).

28. Shinzo Tanaka, "Eine Seite der geistigen Entwicklung Thomas Muentzers in seiner 'lutherischen' Zeit," LJ, 40 (1973), 76.

29. See also Siegfried Braeuer, "Muentzerforschung von 1965 bis 1975," LJ 45 (1978): 108.

30. MSB, 379. All translations of Muentzer's writings are my own. In other

instances I have, wherever possible, used standard translations. These are duly noted in the footnotes.

31. WABr, 1: 389–393.

32. See especially Wappler, *Thomas Muentzer in Zwickau,* 30, and Elliger, *Thomas Muentzer,* 121–122.

33. MSB, 361.

34. Bensing and Trillitzsch, 127.

35. Steinmetz, "Muentzer in der Forschung," 676–677.

36. See especially the essays in Christoph Demke, ed., *Thomas Muentzer: Anfragen an Theologie und Kirche* (Berlin, 1977), and Gordon Rupp, "Programme Notes on the Theme 'Muentzer and Luther,' " in *Vierhundertfuenfzig Jahre lutherische Reformation, 1517–1967. Festschrift fuer Franz Lau.* (Goettingen, 1967).

37. Gordon Leff, "The Making of the Myth of a True Church in the Later Middle Ages," JM&RS 1 (Spring 1971): 1–15.

38. A. G. Dickens and John Tonkin, *The Reformation in Historical Thought* (Oxford, 1985), 1.

1: JOHN TAULER AND THE BAPTISM OF THE HOLY SPIRIT

1. WABr, 1: 359; AE, 48: 114.

2. Bensing and Trillitzsch, 143.

3. MSB, 374.

4. MSB, 558.

5. WABr, 1: 65.

6. Wilhelm Pauck, ed., *Luther: Lectures on Romans,* LCC, vol. 15 (Philadelphia, 1961): 243.

7. See the editorial notes in Pauck, *Romans,* 5, 93, 154, 240, 241, 243, and 288.

8. WA, 9: 95–104.

9. E. G. Rupp and Benjamin Drewery, eds., *Martin Luther* (London, 1970), 172–179.

10. See especially Leif Grane, *Modus Loquendi di Theologicus 1515–1518* (Leiden, 1975), 121–127.

11. See especially Harran, *Luther on Conversion.*

12. WA, 1: 152–153.

13. WA, 1: 153.

14. WABr, 1: 79.

15. WA, 1: 375.

16. WA, 1: 378.

17. WABr, 1: 160.

18. Ibid.

19. WABr, 1: 295.

20. WA, 1: 378–379.

21. WA, 1: 378.

22. Pauck, *Romans,* 243.

23. WA, 1: 557–558.

24. AE, 7: 133.

25. Hartmann Grisar, *Martin Luther: His Life and Work* (London, 1930), 99.

26. See John Headley, *Luther's View of Church History* (New Haven, 1963), p. 171, where the author argues that Luther used the Church Fathers in the same way.

27. See especially the essay by Bernhard Lohse, "Die Bedeutung Augustins fuer den jungen Luther," K&D, 11, no. 2 (April 1965): 116–135, and Hans-Ulrich Delius, *Augustin als Quelle Luthers* (Berlin, 1984).

28. Gordon Rupp, "Programme Notes," observes: "Luther's early marginal notes on Tauler, the indebtedness of his first lectures on the Psalms to the 15th century background, . . . his edition of the 'Theologica Germanica' which he handed over to become the manifesto of the German radicals—his own exploitation of 'Anfechtung' and his early expositions of the 'Theologia Crucis,' brought him at some points nearer to Muentzer than he ever knew" (303).

29. MSB, 356.

30. Elliger, *Muentzer,* 66.

31. Quoted in Elliger, *Muentzer,* 66–67. See also Heinrich Boehmer, *Studien zu Thomas Muentzer* (Leipzig, 1921), p. 17, who observes that as late as the eighteenth century Muentzer's copy of the 1508 Augsburg edition of Tauler's sermons was still to be found in the church library at Gera. The church burned in 1780 and the copy with it.

32. Elliger, *Muentzer,* 66–68.

33. "Luthers Randbemerkungen zu Taulers Predigten," WA, 9: 95.

34. Ibid. James M. Clark, *The Great German Mystics: Eckhart, Tauler and Suso* (Folcroft, PA, 1969), 48 states: "and the story of his conversion, which usually accompanies the sermons. . . ." Heinrich S. Denifle, however, in his "Taulers Bekehrung kritisch Untersucht," *Quellen und Forschungen zur Sprach- und Culturgeschichte der Germanischen Voelker,* 34 (Strassburg, 1879), p. 109, states categorically: "Es ist also wahr: es existiert keine Tradition darueber dass Tauler der Meister der Historie sei. Die Identification beruht auf einen blossen aber falschen Calcul, dessen Resultat zwar in der juengsten Hs., naemlich L, noch reine Muthmassung war,—die Historie selber hat in ihr keine Ueberschrift—die aber schon im ersten Druck 1498 das bescheidene Kleid einer Hypothese ablegte, um von jetzt an als ausgemachte Wahrheit an der Spitze *einer jeden neuen Auflage* der Historie bis herab zur Ausgabe Schmidts zu erscheinen. Dass hierin alle spaetere Drucke von der esten Ausgabe im Jahre 1498 abhaengig sind, bedarf keines weiteren Beweises."

35. I wish to thank James L. Lewis of the Houghton Library, Harvard University, for inspecting Harvard's copy of the 1508 edition to ascertain whether it did indeed contain the *Historia.* And it did. Letter of 3 July 1984.

36. Boehmer, *Studien,* 17. The basic problem with Goertz's study as it relates to Tauler's influence on Muentzer is that he worked from a modern edition of Tauler's sermons which no longer contained the *Historia.* The same is true of Elliger, *Muentzer;* Gritsch, *Reformer without a Church;* and Gordon Rupp,

"Thomas Muentzer: The Reformer as Rebel," *Patterns of Reformation* (Philadelphia, 1969), 157–333.

37. No study of Muentzer that I know of has done so.

38. Denifle, 106.

39. Walter Elliott, ed., *The Sermons and Conferences of John Tauler* (Washington, D.C., 1910), 14–31.

40. Clark, 43.

41. MSB, 495.

42. For a discussion of this problem in the context of the Radical Reformation, see Abraham Friesen, "The Radical Reformation Revisited," JMS, 2 (1984), 124–176.

43. Elliott, *Sermons,* 9–49. I will be quoting from Elliott's excellent translation, but will give the appropriate citations from the *Historia* in the 1498 Leipzig edition entitled: *Sermon des grossgelarten in gnade erlauchtiten doctoris Johannis Thauleri prediger ordens* . . . (Leipzig, 1498), cclxi–cclxxxi.

44. *Sermons,* 14; *Historia,* cclxiij.

45. *Sermons,* 16; *Historia,* cclxiiiij.

46. *Sermons,* 21; *Historia,* cclxvij.

47. *Sermons,* 26; *Historia,* cclxix.

48. *Sermons,* 30; *Historia,* cclxxij.

49. *Sermons,* 30; *Historia,* cclxxij.

50. *Sermons,* 31; *Historia,* cclxxij.

51. MSB, 495.

52. Ibid.

53. Ibid., 496.

54. Ibid., 497.

55. "Die Reformationssehnsucht ist der Grundtenor der apokalyptischen Erwartungen bei den Taboriten wie bei Muentzer . . ." *Die Apokalyptische Theologie Muentzers* (Stuttgart, 1977), 7–8. See also Friesen, *Reformation and Utopia,* 37–43.

56. *Sermons,* 132. Subsequent references to the *Sermons* will appear in parentheses after each citation in the text of Chapter 1.

2: EUSEBIUS AND THE APOSTOLIC CHURCH

1. See Bensing and Trillitzsch, 140.

2. WA, 1: 613, 677; AE, 31: 225.

3. Headley, *Church History,* 179. WA, 2: 226.

4. Bensing and Trillitzsch, 142.

5. WABr, 1: 150.

6. See Rupp and Drewery, *Luther,* 27.

7. WA, 1: 362.

8. AE, 31: 276.

9. Ibid., 282.

10. Ibid., 284.

11. Pauck, *Romans,* 18.

12. E. G. Rupp and Philip S. Watson, eds., *Luther and Erasmus: Free Will and Salvation*, vol. 17, LCC (Philadelphia, 1969), 123–124.

13. WABr, 2: 149. See also Headley, *Church History*, 225–240.

14. WA, 15: 39.

15. The second Invocavit sermon, WA, 10, Pt. 3: 18–19.

16. WA, 10/1/1: 389.

17. WA, 11: 380.

18. WA, 17/1: 389.

19. AE, 31: 281.

20. Headley, *Church History*, 98.

21. Ibid., 99.

22. WAB, 7: 418.

23. Headley, *Church History*, 162–181.

24. For a partial extension of this view among the Radicals, see Friesen, "Radical Reformation Revisited," 124–176.

25. See Luther's enthusiastic remark about Tauler's theology in his preface to the fragmentary writings of Johannes Goch. WA, 10, pt. 2, 329.

26. "Disputation and Defence of Brother Martin Luther against the Accusations of Dr. Johann Eck," AE, 31: 313–331.

27. See also Bensing and Trillitzsch, 127.

28. WA, 2: 226. Eck's accusation is found in WA, 2: 255.

29. WA, 2: 279; 23–30. See also Donald J. Ziegler, ed., *Great Debates of the Reformation* (New York, 1969), 19.

30. WA, 2: 246.

31. WA, 2: 275.

32. WA, 2: 244–245.

33. WA, 2: 275–276.

34. WA, 2: 279.

35. Headley, *Church History*, 225.

36. WA, 2: 247–248 (AE, 51: 57–59).

37. MSB, 352–353: "Relegi D. Augustini libros usque and 6 partem et caetera historiarum volumina revolvi: haec crux mihi in domino Jesus adhuc amara, quodplerosque auctores mihi vlade necessariores consequi non possum." The only other study on Muentzer's view of history is by Wolfgang Ullmann, "Das Geschichtsverstaendnis Thomas Muentzers," in Demke, ed., *Anfragen*, 45–63, but Eusebius hardly plays any role in it at all.

38. This could be inferred from his letter to Achatius Glov of 3 January 1520 where he wrote: "Recepi cronographiam Eusebii disputationis tempore [Leipzig] nescio certe, quante eande, mihi vendideris." And: "Rescribe, quantum debeo pro Eusebii cronographia et quanti precii sint omnia opera Jeronimi et epystole s. Augustini cum sermonibus eiusdem." MSB, 353–354.

39. MSB, 353–354.

40. MSB, 503–504.

41. MSB, 356.

42. MSB, 354, n. 13.

43. See Luther's "Preface to the Revelation of St. John [11], 1546 (1530)," AE, 35: 400, and "On the Babylonian Captivity of the Church," AE, 36: 118.

For the Radicals, see Gunnar Westin and Torsten Bergsten, eds., *Balthasar Hubmaier Schriften*, vol. 9 of *Quellen zur Geschichte der Taeufer* (Guetersloh, 1962), 185, 188, 232, 245–246, as well as *The Complete Works of Menno Simons*, trans. Leonard Verduin, ed. by J. C. Wenger (Scottdale, PA, 1956), 185, 248.

44. Eusebius, *The History of the Church*, trans. G. A. Williamson (Baltimore, 1965), 22. See also Robert Grant, *Eusebius as Church Historian* (Oxford, 1980), 85.

45. MSB, 503–504.

46. MSB, 161.

47. MSB, 243–244.

48. See especially Hugh Jackson Lawlor, "The Hypomnemata of Hegesippus," in *Eusebiana: Essays on the Ecclesiastical History of Eusebius, Bishop of Caesarea* (Oxford, 1912).

49. Eusebius, *Church History*, 181–182.

50. Regarding pseudo-Hegesippus, see Eva Matthew Sanford, "Propaganda and Censorship in the Transmission of Josephus," *Transactions and Proceedings of the American Philological Association*, 66 (1935): 127–145, and M. Karl Mras, "Die Hegesippus-Frage," *Anzeiger der oesterreichischen Akademie der Wissenschaften: Philosophisch-Historische Klasse*, Nr. 8 (1958): 143–153.

51. See Heinz Schreckenburg, *Die Flavius-Josephus-Tradition in Antike und Mittelalter* (Leiden, 1972), 56–59.

52. See Arthur Cushmann McGiffert, "The Life and Writing of Eusebius of Caesarea," in *The Nicene and Post-Nicene Fathers*, vol. 1, 2d Series, *Eusebius*, ed. Philip Schaff and Henry Wace (Reprint: Grand Rapids, 1975), 54.

53. *Hegesippi qui dicitur historiae libri V*, ed. Vincentius Ussani, vol. 66 of the *Corpus Scriptorum Ecclesiasticorum Latinorum* (Vienna and Leipzig, 1932).

54. See Schreckenburg, *Flavius-Josephus-Tradition*, 56–59, and Sanford, "Propaganda and Censorship," 136.

55. For the evolution of the name, see Schreckenburg, *Flavius-Josephus-Tradition*, 56.

56. See the opening sentence of Book 5 of Josephus, *The Jewish War*, trans. G. A. Williamson (Baltimore, 1965), p. 277.

57. MSB, 504.

58. Eusebius, *Church History*, 181–182. Muentzer read from the Rufinus translation of Eusebius, and we shall return to its possible influence for Muentzer's views in a moment. The passage in Rufinus is a faithful rendition of the Hegesippus passage. See *Eusebius Werke*, 2 vols. *Die Kirchengeschichte*, ed. Eduard Schwartz, with the Latin translation of Rufinus prepared by Theodor Mommsen (Leipiz, 1903), 1: 371–373.

59. Eusebius, *Church History*, 143.

60. Lawlor, "The Hypomnemata of Hegesippus," 37–39.

61 Ibid., 39. See also Grant, *Eusebius*, 67.

62. Lawlor, "The Hypomnemata of Hegesippus," 9.

63. Ibid., 38–39.

64. W. Telfer, "Was Hegesippus a Jew?" HThR, 53, no. 2 (January, 1960): 144.

65. See especially K. F. Noesgen, "Der kirchliche Standpunkt Hegesippus," ZfK, 2, no. 2 (1878): 193–233.

66. Grant, *Eusebius*, 85.

67. Socrates Scholasticus, *The Ecclesiastical History*, in *Nicene and Post-Nicene Fathers*, vol. 2, ed. P. Schaff and H. Wace (Reprint: Grand Rapids, 1979), 22–23.

68. Telfer, "Was Hegesippus a Jew?" 146.

69. "Egiosiopus, ein glaubhaftiger schreiber der geschichte, der aposteln schuler, am funften buch der erklerunge . . ." MSB, 161.

70. J. E. L. Oulten, "Rufinus's Translation of the *Church History* of Eusebius," JThS 30 (1929): 153–156. Rufinus was himself strongly attracted to Monasticism and the ascetic ideal that would cause him to accentuate the "pure life." He is generally assumed to have written the *Historia Monachorum* and was a translator from Greek to Latin. In his preface to the translation of Origen's works he discussed his approach to translation, in the manner of Jerome himself: "in making a translation I should follow as far as possible the method of my predecessors, and especially of him [Jerome] of whom I have already made mention. He, after translating into Latin above seventy of the books of Origen which he called Homiletics, and also a certain number of the 'Tomes,' proceeded to purge and pare away in his translation all the causes of stumbling which are to be found in the Greek works; and this he did in such a way that the Latin reader will find nothing in them which jars our faith. In his steps, therefore, I follow, not, indeed, with the power of eloquence which is his, but, as far as may be, in his rules and methods, that is, taking care not to promulgate those things which are found in the books of Origen to be discrepant and contradictory to one another." *Nicene and Post-Nicene Fathers*, 3: 428. It can be assumed that Rufinus proceeded in like fashion in his translation of Eusebius who was suspected of Arian leanings.

71. Eusebius, *Nicene and Post-Nicene Fathers*, 1: 565.

72. *Eusebius Werke*, 2: 957–1040. There is, however, some question as to whether Rufinus even wrote those last two chapters himself. F. Scheidweiler, "Die Kirchengeschichte des Gelasios von Kaisareia," *Byzantinische Zeitschrift*, 46 (1953), 277–301, discusses both past literature on the problem and argues convincingly that Rufinus makes a number of stupid errors that could only come from mindlessly translating the works of another, namely the *Church History* of Galasios of Caesarea of 395. Rufinus's translation with the two new chapters appeared around 401.

73. Eusebius, *Church History*, 328.

74. Ibid., 397.

75. Leff, "Myth of a True Church," 1–15. See also Steinmetz's reference to Muentzer's notes on the Book of Acts, "Muentzer und die Buecher," p. 605.

76. See also Grant, *Eusebius*, 64.

77. Eusebius, *Church History*, 131.

78. Ibid., 177, 194, 196.

79. Ibid., 91. Regarding Eusebius's use of Philo, see Grant, *Eusebius*, 128.

80. Oulton, "Rufinus's Translation," 161.

81. See, for example, Eusebius, *Church History*, 201, 214, and 230.

82. Ibid., 148, 180, 205, 210, 222, etc.

83. Ibid., 151, 205, 209, 248, 268, 336, etc.

84. Ibid., 170, 210, 236, 290, etc. See also Grant, *Eusebius,* especially Chapter 12, entitled "The Final Theme: The Merciful and Gracious Help of Our Saviour," 142–163.

85. Oulton, "Rufinus's Translation," 166–167.

86. Eusebius, *Church History,* 209–210.

87. Ibid., 131.

88. Ibid., 194.

89. Ibid., 205.

90. Cf. ibid., 210: "This will suffice to show that diversity of gifts continued among fit persons till the time I am speaking of." See also p. 198. Cf. ibid., 111: "Furthermore, the members of the Jerusalem Church, by means of an oracle given by revelation to acceptable persons there. . . ."

91. Ibid., 267–268.

92. Ibid., 282–283.

93. Ibid., 399–400.

94. Ibid., 90. See also p. 148.

95. Ibid., 291.

96. Ibid., 291–292.

97. Ibid., 87.

98. Ibid., 143.

99. Ibid., 225, 318, and 328.

100. Goertz, *Innere und Aeussere Ordnung,* 25–28.

101. MSB, 243–244.

102. MSB, 245.

103. MSB, 249.

3: AUGUSTINE AND THE PARABLE OF THE TARES

1. MSB, 261.

2. See also the observation by Erwin Muehlhaupt, *Luther ueber Muentzer* (Witten, 1973), 109, and Werner Krusche, "Zum 450. Todestag von Thomas Muentzer," K&D 21, no. 4 (1975): 315–321. The only other attempt to connect Muentzer to Augustine is A. Zumkeller, "Thomas Muentzer—Augustiner?" *Augustiniana* 9 (1959): 380ff. It is very different from the present chapter.

3. Augustine is cited 64 times; all others together 69 times, with Bernard of Clairveaux second with 20, and St. Gregory third with 14.

4. WA, 1: 378.

5. See especially Augustine's "On the Spirit and the Letter," *Works,* 5: 79–114, and the sections where he treats of the "righteousness of God," discussions that influenced Luther in his lectures on Romans. See especially Luther's letter to Spalatin, 19 October 1516, WABr, 1: 69–72.

6. See Peter Brown, *Augustine of Hippo* (Berkeley and Los Angeles, 1967), 158–181.

7. Ibid., 168.

8. Tauler, *Sermons, 505.*

9. Ibid., 658. Cf. Augustine's "Confessions," *Works,* 1: 107–108.

10. Ibid., 129.

11. The editors of the *Nicene and Post-Nicene Fathers* edition and translation of Augustine's works substituted "aedificari" for "deificari." *Works,* 1: 228. See also Brown, *Augustine,* 132, who reads the passage as "deificari in otio."

12. *The Fathers of the Church,* ed., Ludwig Schopp, et al., vol. 4, *Writings of St. Augustine* (New York, 1947), 146–147.

13. He states as much in his "Confessions," *Works,* 1: 114–115.

14. Brown, *Augustine,* 146–147.

15. Ibid., 147.

16. See especially "On the Spirit and the Letter."

17. Brown, *Augustine,* 177.

18. WA, 2: 255.

19. WA, 2: 274.

20. WA, 2: 273.

21. WA, 2: 279. Cf. Augustine, *Works,* 1: 350.

22. MSB, 354. The sermons were published in Paris in 1516 and the letters in 1517.

23. Augustine, "Letters," *Works,* 1: 239.

24. Ibid., 240. This was the passage that had struck Augustine at the time of his conversion! No wonder he was particularly sensitive here.

25. Augustine, *Works,* 6: 279.

26. For an insight into how this parable was used from the time of the Church Fathers through the Reformation, see Roland H. Bainton, "The Parable of the Tares as Proof Text for Religious Liberty to the End of the Sixteenth Century," CH 1 (June 1932): 67–89.

27. Augustine, *Works,* 6: 244.

28. Augustine, *Works,* 1: 253.

29. Brown, *Augustine,* 212–213.

30. Ibid., 213.

31. Ibid., 214.

32. Ibid., 221–222.

33. Augustine, *Works,* 6: 255–256.

34. Ibid., 302.

35. Ibid.

36. Augustine, *Works,* 1: 255–256.

37. Ibid., 283.

38. Ibid., 283–284.

39. Ibid.

40. Ibid., 258.

41. See ibid., 299, 315, and 318.

42. Ibid., 343. See also a somewhat later letter to the Donatists, ibid., 387.

43. Ibid., 286.

44. We shall have further occasion to note that Augustine never did give up hope of reforming the Church, as his sermons clearly demonstrate.

45. Augustine, *Works*, 6: 334.

46. Ibid.

47. Ibid., 334–335.

48. This is, indeed, how the Donatists interpreted the parable. See W. H. C. Frend, *The Donatist Church* (Oxford, 1950), 166–167. The culmination of this quarrel came at the Conference of Carthage in 411. There some 286 Catholic bishops gathered to discuss these matters with 279 Donatist bishops. Augustine was the main spokesman for the Catholics; Petilian, for the Donatists. See Philip Schaff, *History of the Christian Church* (New York, 1910), 3: 362–366. For a detailed discussion of the two positions, see Serge Lancel, *Actes de la conference de Carthage en 411* (Paris, 1972), 221–273.

49. Augustine, *Works*, 6: 334.

50. MSB, 503.

51. In opposition to what I argued in my 1973 essay on "Thomas Muentzer and the Old Testament," MQR 47, no. 1 (January 1973): 5–19.

52. MSB, 398.

53. See especially Luther's sermon: "The Signs of the Day of Judgment," second Sunday of Advent, 1522. *The Sermons of Martin Luther*, ed. and trans. John Nicholas Lenker (Reprint: Grand Rapids, 1983), 1: 59–86, and Martin Greschat, "Luthers Haltung im Bauernkrieg," ARG, 56 (1965): 31–47, as well as Headley, *Church History*.

54. Augustine, *Works*, 6: 422.

55. Ibid., 423. See also Augustine's commentary on the Gospel of John, *Works*, 7: 107, for exactly the same kind of explanation.

56. Augustine, *Works*, 6: 384.

57. Ibid., 385.

58. Ibid.

59. Ibid.

60. Ibid., 458.

61. Ibid.

62. Ibid., 329.

63. Ibid., 343, 351, 376, 378–383, 458, 491–495; *Works*, 1: 313, 336, 460, 479.

64. Augustine, *Works*, 6: 343.

65. Ibid., 313, 377, 413.

66. Ibid., 335.

67. Ibid., 336.

68. Augustine had himself, however, as Brown observes, criticized the Catholic clergy earlier. *Augustine*, 209.

69. Augustine, *Works*, 6: 335.

70. Brown, *Augustine*, 250.

71. Augustine, *Works*, 1: 284.

72. Ibid., 297. The same is repeated elsewhere, for example, p. 375. See also pp. 242–244, 264, 283, 288.

73. See his discussion in the letter to Boniface of 408, *Works*, 1: 408–409, and pp. 489–492. Also *Works*, 6: 277–278.

74. Augustine, *Works*, 6: 504.

75. Augustine, *Works*, 1: 313.
76. Ibid., 481.
77. Ibid., 483.
78. Eusebius, *Church History*, 181.
79. MSB, 403.
80. MSB, 228.

4: ZWICKAU AND THE PROPHETS

1. See the discussion by Elliger, *Muentzer*, 74–77.
2. On Zwickau see Susan C. Karant–Nunn, *Zwickau in Transition, 1500–1547: The Reformation as an Agent of Change* (Columbus, Ohio, 1987); and from a Marxist perspective: Helmut Braeuer, "Zwickau zur Zeit Thomas Muentzers und des Bauernkrieges," *Saechsische Heimatblaetter* 20, no. 5 (1974): 193–223.
3. See also Steinmetz, "Muentzer und die Buecher."
4. Wappler, *Muentzer*, 30.
5. Elliger, *Muentzer*, 121–122.
6. J. K. Seidemann, *Thomas Muentzer, Eine Biographie* (Dresden and Leipzig, 1842), p. 7. Compare with the first part of Muentzer's letter of 13 July 1520 to Luther.
7. See Elliger, *Muentzer*, 78, who casts some doubt as to its tone.
8. On Muentzer's relations with the city's elite, see Karant-Nunn, *Zwickau in Transition*, 95–115.
9. MSB, 357–358.
10. These are given by Guenther Franz in the footnotes, ibid., 357–358. All biblical citations are taken from the King James version unless otherwise noted, because it gives these a sixteenth-century flavor.
11. MSB, 358.
12. MSB, 359–360.
13. Gordon Leff, *Heresy in the Later Middle Ages* (Manchester and New York, 1967), 2: 288.
14. MSB, 361.
15. See especially Howard Kaminsky, *A History of the Hussite Revolution* (Berkeley and Los Angeles, 1967), 114–119.
16. Quoted in ibid., 116–117.
17. John P. Dolan, ed. and trans., *The Essential Erasmus* (New York, 1964), 74.
18. R. A. B. Mynors and D. F. S. Thomson, trans., *The Correspondence of Erasmus* (Toronto and Buffalo, 1978), 2: 297.
19. MSB, 548.
20. On Muentzer's use of the term, see Michael G. Baylor, "Theology and Politics in the Thought of Thomas Muentzer: The Case of the Elect," ARG 79 (1988): 81–102.
21. Quoted in Elliger, *Muentzer*, 122.
22. See also Rupp, "Programme Notes," 303.
23. Muentzer asserted as much in a letter to the mayor and Council of

Neustadt on 7 January 1521, while still in Zwickau. MSB, 366. See Also Hans Loebe's letter to Muentzer of 15 June 1521. MSB, 370.

24. Wappler, *Muentzer*, 32, n. 127; see also p. 35. According to Seidemann, *Muentzer*, 110ff, there existed a letter entitled "Brieff der 12 Aposteln und 72 Juenger" directed against Egranus, accusing the latter of having changed his theological position and ridiculing those who possessed the Spirit. Apparently Egranus had remarked, with obvious irony, that he would accept twelve apostles and 72 disciples as parallel and equal to the original ones after they had performed miracles and driven out devils. Even Egranus, then, was apparently aware of the attempt on the part of Muentzer and his followers to establish the new Apostolic Church.

25. See also Siegfried Hoyer, "Die Zwickauer Storchianer—Vorlaeufer der Taeufer?" JfRG 13 (1986): 74.

26. Muentzer will make this very argument against Luther later. See Chapter 7 of the present study.

27. MSB, 367–368.

28. See Agricola's letter to Muentzer of 1521, before April (exact date is unknown). MSB, 368–369. Also Elliger, *Muentzer*, 127–131.

29. MSB, 513.

30. See also his reference in the *Hochverursachte Schutzrede*, MSB, 324, and *Auslegung des Unterschieds Daniels*, MSB, 260.

31. See *Elliger*, 149–151.

32. MSB, 514.

33. MSB, 513–515.

34. MSB, 372.

35. See also Erwin Iserloh, "Revolution bei Thomas Muentzer: Durchsetzung des Reiches Gottes oder sociale Aktion?" HJ, 92, no. 2 (1972): 282–299.

36. Hoyer, "Storchianer," 60–78, argues the same thing but from an altogether different perspective and from different motives. Nor does he accept the heretical antecedents of the Prophets' thought. Nonetheless, though the argument is a hazardous one, I do think it makes the best sense of what evidence—and that very problematical—there is.

37. Tauler, *Sermons*, 180.

38. Leff, *Heresy*, 1: 308.

39. Tauler, *Sermons*, 189.

40. Leff, *Heresy*, 1: 308.

41. Ibid., 309.

42. Ibid.

43. Kaminsky, *Hussite Revolution*, 352.

44. Leff, *Heresy*, 1: 314–315. The propositions as quoted in ibid., 315.

45. Ibid., 327.

46. Quoted in Kaminsky, *Hussite Revolution*, 358. However, see Robert E. Lerner, *The Heresy of the Free Spirit in the Later Middle Ages* (Berkeley and Los Angeles, 1972) who denies that the Free Spirit was sexually promiscuous.

47. Kaminsky, *Hussite Revolution*, 350–353.

48. Ibid., 353.

49. Ibid. Especially the rejection of infant baptism.

50. Wappler, *Muentzer*, 18.

51. Whether or not it is a coincidence, there are Nicolaitans mentioned in the Bible, and that twice—both times in the Revelation of John—without indicating what their "sin" was. Church Fathers, however, were virtually unanimous in their assertion that their sin was sexual in nature and constituted gross immorality. See the *Dictionnnaire de Théologie Catholique* (Paris, 1931), 499–508, both for the Church Fathers and the Nicolaitan tradition throughout the Middle Ages.

52. Elliger, *Muentzer*, 122.

53. See Muentzer's letters to Luther of 13 July 1520, MSB, 357ff, and of 27 March 1522, MSB, 379–382.

54. WABr, 2: 345.

55. See Melanchthon's letter to the elector. CR, 1: 533–535.

56. AE, 48: 366, 367–372.

57. See especially his letter of May 1522 to Christoph Hofmann. WABr, 2: 550.

58. See Wappler, *Muentzer*, 73–76.

59. WABr, 2: 515.

60. WABr, 2: 546 (29 May 1522).

61. WABr, 2: 597. See also WA, 37: 176. Wappler, *Muentzer*, 77, seems to agree with Luther that Muentzer is the source of the anti-infant baptism attitude.

62. WATr, 2: 306 (#2060).

63. WA, 38: 213. He repeated this in one of his 1540 Table Talks, WATr, 4: 703 (#5185).

64. MSB, 157–206.

65. Wappler, *Muentzer*, 80–81. Karant-Nunn, *Zwickau in Transition*, writes: "A friend of Storch's described him in his Zwickau years: '. . . But he was an unchaste man' " (107).

66. See above, notes 47 and 51.

67. WATr, 1: 598 (#1204).

68. WATr, 1:257, (#564).

69. WA, 46: 498.

70. See also Karant-Nunn's observation that Muentzer was the more important of the two. *Zwickau in Transition*, 107.

71. MSB, 391. N.I.V. translation. Muentzer's attitude toward the Zwickau Prophets stands in sharp contrast to that of Martin Cellarius who had clearly come under their influence. Cellarius became vehement in his defense of Stuebner in Luther's presence. See WABr, 2: 493. Luther's letter to Spalatin of 12 April 1521.

72. The emphasis on Jeremiah is intriguing. It can be clearly seen in his *Prague Manifesto* as well as in Luther's "Von der Beicht," where both are in vehement opposition to the Catholic Church. Indeed, in his letter to Muentzer of 21 December 1522, Carlstadt notes: ". . . video te in maledictionem maledictionis Hieremie haud dissimilem incidisse, quam ideo non probo, quod et in Hieremia cerno granum frumenti in terram collapsum, nec dum mortuum." MSB, 386.

73. MSB, 398.

74. Friesen, "Thomas Muentzer and the Old Testament," 5–19.

75. Richard Bailey, "The Sixteenth Century's Apocalyptic Heritage and Thomas Muentzer," MQR 57, no. 1 (1983): 27–44. Although Bailey had the good sense not to cite my essay, I at least called the evidence "circumstantial."

76. Kaminsky, *Hussite Revolution,* 358. See also Leff, *Heresy,* 1: 327.

77. Kaminsky, "Chiliasm and the Hussite Revolution," CH, 26, no. 1 (1957): 43–71.

78. See Wappler, *Muentzer,* 42–48.

79. Published in A. Goetze and L. E. Schmitt, eds., *Aus dem Sozialen und Politischen Kampf. Flugschriften aus der Reformationszeit,* 20 (Halle/S., 1953), 53.

80. Kaminsky, *Hussite Revolution,* 358.

5: PRAGUE AND THE NEW APOSTOLIC CHURCH

1. January 3, 1520: "Si acta consiliis Constantiensis [Milan, 1511] mihi miseris, rem gratissimam mihi facies, et acta consiliis Basiliensis simul non ligata." MSB, 354.

2. MSB, 495.

3. MSB, 372.

4. MSB, 370.

5. Letters to Michael Gans, MSB, 371, and to Hausmann, MSB, 372.

6. This is a reference to Isaiah 62:1. He had used the same passage earlier in the above letter to Luther.

7. MSB, 372.

8. MSB, 371.

9. See Matthew Spinka's remark in the introduction to his *John Hus and the Council of Constance* (New York and London, 1965), 85.

10. MSB, 373.

11. Matthew 24:3.

12. MSB, 373. Matthew 24:15 reads: "When ye therefore shall see the abomination of desolation, spoken of by Daniel the prophet, stand in the holy place, (whoso readeth, let him understand:)."

In his letter from Constance during his imprisonment and trial, John Hus also referred to the fulfillment of Christ's prophecies in Matthew 24. *The Letters of John Hus,* ed. and trans. by Matthew Spinka (Manchester, 1972), 100.

Could Muentzer's paraphrase refer to the "Word" as mediated directly through the Holy Spirit, or "the mouth of God," as Muentzer wrote in the *Manifesto?*

13. MSB, 373.

14. When Luther began, in a sermon on the Eucharist prior to Christmas of 1520, to advocate communion in both kinds—the chief demand of the Hussite movement—there was a rush, as Daniel Olivier has said, "to identify his [Luther's] teachings with the Hussite heresy." *The Trial of Luther,* trans. John Tonkin (London and Oxford, 1978), 109. Scores of woodcuts carried the same message.

15. MSB, 504.

16. As translated by Matthew Spinka, *Hus at the Council,* 261–263. See the original Latin in Appendix II of Spinka, *John Hus' Concept of the Church* (Princeton, 1966), 401–409.

17. Ibid., 263.

18. Ibid., 73.

19. Ibid., 73.

20. Ibid., 86.

21. Ibid., 260.

22. Ibid.

23. Ibid., 260–261.

24. See note 9 above.

25. Spinka, *Hus at the Council,* 264.

26. Ibid., 212.

27. Ibid., 261.

28. Ibid., 191.

29. See Friesen, "Radical Reformation Revisited," JMS 2 (1984): 124–176.

30. Vaclav Husa, *Tomáš Muentzer a Čechy* (Prague, 1957), 64–66.

31. J. K. Zeman, *The Anabaptists and the Czech Brethren in Moravia* (The Hague, 1969), 63–64.

32. MSB, 377.

33. See Kaminsky, *Hussite Revolution,* 86.

34. Eberhard Wolfgram, "Der Prager Anschlag Thomas Muentzers in der Handschrift der Leipziger Universitaetsbibliothek," *Wissenschaftliche Zeitschrift der Karl-Marx-Universitaet* 6, no. 1 (1956/57): 297.

35. Heinrich Boehmer and Paul Kirn, eds., *Thomas Muentzers Briefwechsel* (Leipzig and Berlin, 1931), 139.

36. Annemarie Lohman, *Zur geistigen Entwicklung Thomas Muentzers* (Leipzig and Berlin, 1931), 19–21, and Wolfgram, "Der Prager Anschlag," 296–298.

37. MSB, 505.

38. Spinka, *Hus at the Council,* 73.

39. The reference is to Matthew 23, which deals with Christ's condemnation of the scribes and Pharisees, especially verse 4: "For they bind heavy burdens and grievous to be borne, and lay them on men's shoulders; but they themselves will not move them with one of their fingers."

40. The original does not make clear whether it is the abyss of the soul that is emptied by the Holy Spirit, or whether the Holy Spirit works in the emptiness of the abyss of the soul.

41. See, in this regard, Wolfgang Ullmann, "Ordo rerum: Muentzers Randbemerkungen zu Tertullian als Quelle fuer das Verstaendnis seiner Theologie," *Theologische Versuche* 7 (1976): 125–140. The author promises more than he delivers.

42. MSB, 501.

43. Ibid. N.I.V. translation of Jeremiah 23:1–4.

44. Ibid.

45. See Steinmetz, "Muentzer und die Buecher," 605.

46. See G. H. Williams and Angel Mergal, eds., *Spiritual and Anabaptist Writers*, vol. 25, LCC (Philadelphia, 1957), pp. 147–160.

47. MSB, 498.

48. As paraphrased by Muentzer.

49. MSB, 499.

50. Luther to Spalatin, WABr, 3: 120.

51. MSB, 499–500.

52. Ibid., 500.

53. Ibid.

54. Ibid.

55. Ibid., 500–501.

56. Ibid., 502–503.

57. Ibid., 503.

58. Ibid., 504.

59. Ibid., 504–505.

6. ESTRANGEMENT FROM LUTHER

1. Eric W. Gritsch, *Thomas Muentzer: Reformer without a Church*, (Philadelphia, 1967), 60. There are a goodly number of essays on Muentzer and Luther. For the best discussion of the literature, see Eric W. Gritsch, "Thomas Muentzer and Luther: A Tragedy of Errors," in Hans J. Hillerbrand, ed., *Radical Tendencies in the Reformation: Divergent Perspectives*, vol. 9 *Sixteenth-Century Essays & Studies* (Kirksville, MO, 1988): 55–84.

2. MSB, 378.

3. See Elliger, *Muentzer*, 215.

4. WA, 8: 129–185.

5. WA, 8: 132.

6. See the letters and reports in CR, 1: 459–642.

7. CR, 1: 560–563. See also Mark U. Edwards, *Luther and the False Brethren* (Stanford, 1975), 16.

8. WABr, 2: 410, Luther to Spalatin, 5 December 1521. See also Bernard Lohse, "Luther und der Radikalismus," LJ 44 (1977): 11. Lohse implies that Luther, while being pleased with the reforms, was concerned about the turmoil. But his reference to social unrest would appear to be directed elsewhere.

9. See Edwards, *False Brethren*, 16–18.

10. Ibid., 30.

11. See also Ingetraut Ludolphy, *Friedrich der Weise, Kurfuerst von Sachsen 1463–1525* (Goettingen, 1984), 450.

12. See especially Olivier, *Trial of Luther*.

13. WABr, 2: 448–449.

14. See Wilhelm Borth, *Die Luthersache (Causa Lutheri) 1517–1524. Die Anfaenge der Reformation als Frage von Politik und Recht* (Luebeck and Hamburg, 1970).

15. WABr, 2: 126–130, n. 33. See also Ludolphy, *Friedrich der Weise*, 443.

16. WABr, 2: 453–457.

17. WABr, 2: 462. See also Edwards, *False Brethren*, 18.

18. See especially the first of these sermons. Ronald J. Sider, ed., *Karlstadt's Battle with Luther: Documents in a Liberal-Radical Debate* (Philadelphia, 1978), 18–19.

19. The "inner and outer order" in the theology of Muentzer posited by Goertz is simply the result of Muentzer's putting Tauler's mysticism together with the Hegesippus passages in Eusebius. It does not derive solely from Tauler. Furthermore, it is the context derived from Eusebius that makes the cleansing of the external order, the Church within society, truly revolutionary.

20. MSB, 380–382.

21. MSB, 384.

22. MSB, 387.

23. MSB, 382.

24. MSB, 383.

25. See the same argument used in his letter to the people of Muehlhausen after the defeat of the peasants. MSB, 473–474.

26. MSB, 384–385.

27. MSB, 387–388.

28. Elliger, *Muentzer*, 249.

29. It is a letter that has been repeatedly misinterpreted by scholars because they have not taken seriously Muentzer's reference to Luther's "Von der Beicht, ob die der Bapst macht habe zu gepieten," WA, 8: 129–185. All three recent biographers—Elliger, Rupp, and Gritsch—even omit the critical passage of the letter entirely from their discussion. It reads: "Sed quod pestilentissimum Egranum tuis apud me commendasti litteris, mirum modum movebat, dum fermiter in dies expertus presciveram hunc corvum quandoque furto sumptas depositurum plumas asuetumque cadaveribus putridis suis nequaquam appetentem iustitie, prorsus lepidum animal ventris graphice suis seipsum depinxit coloribus in *egregio libro de facienda confessione,* ubi tam erudite reproborum malignantium commendat ecclesiam, quo nihil utilius impiis contulisset. Tu voluisti hominem tam cupidum glorie mihi conciliandum, ne turbatim in te hostes prosilirent; ego ob gloriam nominis Dei me murum immobilem obieci. Ego integra mente contradixi 'superbo oculo et insaciabili corde cum hoc non edam.' " MSB, 389–390.

30. MSB, 389.

31. MSB, 389, n. 5.

32. WA, 8: 129–185.

33. WA, 8: 138–139.

34. WA, 8: 139.

35. WA, 8: 140.

36. WA, 8: 141.

37. WA, 8: 141.

38. "Ye shall not add unto the word which I command you, neither shall ye diminish aught from it, that ye may keep the commandments of the Lord your God which I command you."

39. "Therefore we ought to give the more earnest heed to the things which we have heard, lest at any time we should let them slip. For if the word spoken by

angels was steadfast, and every transgression and disobedience received a just recompense and reward, how shall we escape, if we neglect so great salvation."

40. WA, 8: 143–144.

41. "Auslegung des Unterschieds Daniels," MSB, 244.

42. Proverbs 7:8; 2:16–17; 9:13–18.

43. WA, 8: 146.

44. WA, 8: 147.

45. WA, 8: 148–149.

46. WA, 8: 149: 31.

47. WA, 8: 150.

48. WA, 8: 150.

49. WA, 8: 150–151.

50. WA, 8: 155–160. See also Guenther Muehlpfordt, "Der fruehe Luther als Authoritaet det Radikalen. Zum Luther-Erbe des 'linken Fluegels,' " in *Weltwirkung der Reformation,* Max Steinmetz and Gerhard Brendler, eds. (Berlin, 1969), 1: 205–225, and Hermann Barge, "Luther und Karlstadt in Wittenberg," HZ 99 (1907): 256–324.

51. WA, 8: 160.

52. WA, 8: 162.

53. Leif Grane, "Thomas Muentzer und Martin Luther," in Abraham Friesen and Hans-Juergen Goertz, eds. *Thomas Muentzer,* vol. 491, *Wege der Forschung* (Darmstadt, 1978), pp. 88–89, argues that Luther continues to think in terms of the *corpus christianum.* Indeed, Luther appears caught between the two positions. Against the Roman Catholic Church, as in the above case, he argues for a Church of believers; against the Radicals (Muentzer) he argues for a territorial Church, from a post-Constantinian position. It is probably the logic, or illogic, of his position that determines his argumentation. For, like Augustine, who argued for a pure Church in his congregation at Hippo and for a Church of wheat and tares against the Donatists, Luther argues for a believers' Church against the Catholics, and a Church of wheat and tares against Muentzer.

54. WA, 8: 163.

55. WA, 8: 163.

56. WA, 8: 169.

57. WA, 8: 174.

58. Rupp, *Patterns of Reformation,* 186, for example, calls it his "famous alibi."

59. Ibid.

60. In his "Sendbrief an die Brueder zu Stolberg" of 18 July 1523, Muentzer covered the same material he had in his letter to Luther of 9 July. Cf. MSB, 21–24. The above passage is found in MSB, 390.

61. I John 2: 27.

62. MSB, 390.

63. Luther himself described this conversion experience in his "Von der Beicht" in nearly mystical terms. WA, 8: 178–179.

64. MSB, 391.

65. This may have been the reason why Muentzer is supposed to have kept two dream interpreters with him at all times. See MSB, 427–429.

66. MSB, 391. "Therefore night shall be unto you, that ye shall not have a vision; and it shall be dark unto you, that ye shall not divine; and the sun shall go down over the prophets, and the day shall be dark over them."

67. MSB, 391. There are more parallels in the passage. Paul, the most recent convert (Muentzer?), corrects Peter, who had been with Christ from the beginning (Luther?). Paul recognized them as brothers, and they—Peter, James and John—"saw that I [Paul] had been given the task of preaching the gospel to the Gentiles." Nonetheless, Paul did not hesitate to censure the older Christian, Peter, when he believed him to be in error. N.I.V. translation used because of greater clarity.

68. MSB, 392.

69. See the discussion in Elliger, *Muentzer,* 379.

70. WABr, 3: 120.

71. WABr, 2: 515.

72. He could later recall vividly enough Muentzer's advice about marriage in that letter. See his Table Talk of 1535. WATr, 1: 598 (# 1204).

73. WABr, 3: 120.

7. A FAITH DIFFERENT FROM LUTHER'S

1. Luther's letter to Spalatin, in which he discussed what he told Zeiss, is dated 3 August 1523. WABr, 3: 119–120. On the relationship between Hans Zeiss and Muentzer, see Wieland Held, "Der Allstedter Schosser Hans Zeiss und sein Verhaeltnis zu Thomas Muentzer," ZfG 35, no. 12 (1987): 1073–1091.

2. See Luther's letter to the Dukes of Saxony concerning the revolutionary spirit in Allstedt of August 1524. WA, 15: 210–221. Although I am in disagreement with Siegfried Braeuer on a number of counts, nonetheless see his "Die Vorgeschichte von Luthers 'Ein Brief an die Fuersten zu Sachsen von dem aufruehrerischen Geist,' " LJ 47 (1980): 40–70, for the context of Luther's letter.

3. Elliger, *Muentzer,* 403–404.

4. Ibid., 403.

5. MSB, 240.

6. MSB, 230.

7. MSB, 231.

8. MSB, 231.

9. MSB, 233.

10. MSB, 233–234.

11. MSB, 234.

12. MSB, 234.

13. MSB, 235.

14. MSB, 235.

15. MSB, 235.

16. MSB, 235.

17. MSB, 236.

18. MSB, 237.

19. MSB, 237.
20. MSB, 237.
21. MSB, 237–238.
22. Muentzer had already stated in his *Manifesto* that the priests "have not even had a smell of what the Whole or the Undivided Perfection consists of, which is a measure equalling the sum of its parts." MSB, 496.
23. MSB, 393–397.
24. See, for example, MSB, 217–224, 225–240.
25. MSB, 398. It is in the above context that Muentzer introduced Joachim of Fiore, saying: "You should also know that they ascribe this teaching [concerning salvation?] to the Abbott Joachim and call it, with great sarcasm, an eternal gospel. I hold the witness of Joachim in high regard. I have read him only on Jeremiah. But my teaching is high above; I do not accept it from him but from the very mouth of God, as I will demonstrate at the appropriate time on the basis of a total analysis of Scripture." A number of aspects of the above passage should be noted: First, the context does not suggest even a hint of anything eschatalogical. It is therefore probably safe to conclude that Muentzer did not even think of Joachim in that context. Second, he had read Joachim only on Jeremiah. Aside from the fact that this was pseudo-Joachim, Muentzer probably wished only to see what he had to say about Jeremiah since certain Jeremiah passages held a considerable importance for him. Third, Joachim was a mere witness for Muentzer whose teachings had come directly from God, not Joachim.
26. MSB, 220.
27. MSB, 221.
28. MSB, 222.
29. MSB, 222.
30. WA, 15: 211.
31. WA, 15: 213.
32. WA, 15: 214–215.
33. WA, 15: 215.
34. WA, 15: 217.
35. WA, 15: 217.
36. WA, 15: 217–218.
37. MSB, 389.
38. MSB, 430.
39. MSB, 430.
40. MSB, 430–432.
41. See the parallel columns in MSB, 265–319.
42. See especially "Hochverursachte Schutzrede," MSB, 340–342.
43. MSB, 268.
44. MSB, 268–269.
45. MSB, 269.
46. MSB, 271.
47. MSB, 273.
48. MSB, 274.
49. MSB, 275–276.
50. MSB, 277.

51. Tauler, *Sermons,* 14–21.
52. MSB, 277.
53. MSB, 279.
54. MSB, 280.
55. MSB, 281.
56. MSB, 282.
57. MSB, 283.
58. MSB, 286.
59. MSB, 287.
60. MSB, 289.
61. MSB, 289–290.
62. MSB, 291.
63. MSB, 296–297.
64. MSB, 304.
65. MSB, 306.
66. MSB, 310.
67. MSB, 311.
68. MSB, 322–323.
69. MSB, 323.
70. MSB, 323.
71. MSB, 325.
72. MSB, 326–327.
73. MSB, 328.

8. OF REFORM, "GODLESS" AND "PIOUS CHRISTIAN" PRINCES

1. MSB, 226–227.
2. MSB, 353.
3. MSB, 503–504.
4. MSB, 161.
5. Once again, Goertz's "inner and outer order."
6. MSB, 161.
7. MSB, 161.
8. MSB, 381.
9. On the similarity to Bernard Rothmann, see my "Radical Reformation Revisited," 155–172.
10. Wappler, *Muentzer,* 32, n. 27.
11. MSB, 379–382.
12. MSB, 379–382.
13. MSB, 208. See also p. 211.
14. MSB, 163.
15. MSB, 226.
16. MSB, 226.
17. MSB, 242.
18. See also Erwin Iserloh, "Sakraments-und Taufverstaendnis bei Thomas Muentzer," *Zeichen des Glaudens: Studien zur Taufe und Firmung.* Balthasar

Fischer zum 60. Geburtstag, Hansjoerg auf der Maur & Bruno Kleinheyer, eds. (Zurich and Cologne, 1972), 109–122.

19. MSB, 228.

20. MSB, 228. This interpretation is at least partially dependent on Tauler's sermon on "The Pool of Healing" where the "stirring of the waters" was compared to the descent of the Holy Spirit, with transforming power, into a man's soul. Gritsch leaves out the "not" in the passage: ". . . that John 3 does *not* fit together with John 7 . . ." (*Reformer without a Church*, 88).

21. See also the letter to Christoph Meinhard of 30 May 1524. MSB, 402–403.

22. Muentzer proceeded to show how the entire Gospel of John was to be understood from this perspective. MSB, 229.

23. MSB, 227–230.

24. Christian Meyer, "Der Wiedertaeufer Nikolaus Storch und seine An-haenger in Hof," ZfK 16, no. 1 (1896): 120–121, does indeed argue that Storch baptized adults.

25. MSB, 214. See Muentzer's letter to Zeiss of 25 July 1524 on how baptism was to be understood. MSB, 423.

26. See MSB, 526. Also Iserloh, "Taufverstaendnis," 122.

27. MSB, 501.

28. MSB, 209.

29. MSB, 221.

30. MSB, 308–309.

31. MSB, 341.

32. The similarity of this passage to his statement in the *Manifesto* with respect to his own preparation as the "servus electorum dei" (MSB, 504) is so striking as to leave little doubt that he conformed precisely to this archetype.

33. MSB, 307–308.

34. MSB, 381.

35. MSB, 381.

36. WATr, 1: 598 (# 1204).

37. MSB, 500. The Czech version has "common" inserted.

38. For a definition of the term, "common man," see Robert H. Lutz, *Wer war der gemeine Mann?* (Munich, 1979).

39. MSB, 498.

40. MSB, 501.

41. MSB, 163–164.

42. See Muentzer's letter of 4 October 1523 to Elector Frederick. MSB, 395. See also MSB, 296.

43. *Neues Urkundenbuch*, 229.

44. MSB, 30, 157.

45. "Ueber das alles haet auch keyn billichs vortragen vnd protesteren wollen helfen, das der wolgeborner graf Ernst von Mansfelt den ganczen sommer durch vnd durch ymmer mehr seynen unterthanen hat, *ehe d. h. g. Keysers mandat yhe auszgangen wahr*, vnd. . . ." *Neues Urkundenbuch*, 233.

46. See Ernest of Mansfeld To Zeiss, 21 September 1523. *Neues Urkundenbuch*, 228.

47. See Zeiss and Allstedt Council to Frederick, 11 April 1524. AGBM, 2: 30 (# 144).

48. See Frederick to Ernest of Mansfeld, 24 September 1523. *Neues Urkundenbuch,* 231.

49. Muentzer had used the same argument against the Catholic clergy earlier.

50. MSB, 393–394. Roland H. Bainton, "Thomas Muentzer, Revolutionary Firebrand of the Reformation," SCJ, 13, no. 2 (1982): 14–15, demonstrates how Muentzer translated from the Psalms in his German Mass, accentuating the differences between "godless" and "elect" far beyond what the original text allowed.

51. *Neues Urkundenbuch,* 231.

52. Ibid.

53. Ibid., 232.

54. Cf. the opening lines of his *Manifesto.*

55. The issue of revolt must also be seen in the context of the Imperial edict, for if the count was going counter to the way in which the common people were in fact—and rightly so—interpreting the edict, then he was the one causing them to rebel against a tyrant.

56. MSB, 395–397.

57. See the introduction to Luther's "Wider die Verkehrer und Faelscher kaiserlichs Mandats," WA, 12: 58–59. Frederick apparently had it read from the pulpits of the churches in his lands, so Muentzer would have been quite familiar with its content. See the statement by Johannes Laue, AGBM, 2: 902.

58. See Hans von der Planitz, *Berichte aus dem Reichsregiment in Nuernberg 1521–1523,* ed. E. Wuelker and H. Virck (Hildesheim and New York, 1979), p. 390.

59. See AGBM, 2: 902.

60. On Schwarzenberg, see W. Scheel, *Johann Freiherr von Schwarzenberg* (Berlin, 1905). Leopold von Ranke, *Deutsche Geschichte im Zeitalter der Reformation,* vol. 2 (Hamburg, n.d.), pp. 283–296, is still the best on the edict.

61. Adolf Wrede, ed., *Deutsche Reichstagsakten unter Kaiser Karl V,* (Goettingen, 1963), 3: 149–150.

62. Muentzer observed in his confession: "Ursache das er m. g. h. den landesfursten und graven Ernesten zu Mansfeld beschediget und geschulden, sey dorumb gescheen, dan sich dye underthan beclagt, das in das wort gottes nit geprediget were auch verpoten und hett nit wollen nachgelassen werden dorzu zu gehen. Habe er ine befohlen, solichs yedern seynem obern anzuzeygen. Woe dasselbige alsdann nit geprediget, das sye alsdan zi ime kommen solten. Wolt er in das selber predigen, und sollten sich dorinne nymands vorhindern lassen." MSB, 546.

63. WA, 12: 63. In his letter of 29 May 1523 to Frederick, Luther wrote: "Will aber der starcken zuversicht vun hoffnung zu Gott seyn, weyl das kayserlich mandat itzt ausgangen vnter andern klerlich ynnhelt, *das man alleyn das heylig Evangelion predigen vnd leren vnd die lerer odder prediger bescheydelich vnd der massen weyszen soll,* das daraeus mit nichte verstanden werdem muge, als wolt man die Evangelische warheyt verheyndern odder verdruecken, myr solle auch vnuerbotten vnd vnuerweyszlich seyn, gegen allermenniglich, so

ich mich ynn schrifftlicher veranttworttueng mehr der gottlichen Evangelische warheyt dann meyner vnschuld halben begeben muste" [italics mine]. WABr, 3:77.

64. WABr, 3: 123–124.

65. Martin Bucer, "An ein christlichen Rath und Gemeyn der statt Weissenburg," in Robert Stupperich, ed., *Martin Bucers Deutsche Schriften,* (Guetersloh, 1960), 1: 136.

66. AGBM, 2: 902.

67. The edict played a particularly important role in the free imperial cities, a role contemporary social historians have largely ignored. See, for example, Adolf Baum, *Magistrat und Reformation in Strassburg bis 1529* (Strassburg, 1887), 23ff., as well as other local studies.

68. Felician Gess, ed., *Akten und Briefe zur Kirchenpolitik Herzog Georgs von Sachsen* (Leipzig, 1905), 1: 609.

69. Ibid.

70. MSB, 408–415, Muentzer's letters to his followers in Sangerhausen. That Duke George was basing his actions on the same edict is made clear in a letter to the elector and Duke John of 8 August 1524. There George remarked: "Ist darumb s. f. g. freundlich byt, E. Kfl. G. wolle dieselben boshaftigen propheten *noch inhalt ksl. mandat selber vorjagen,* verfolgen und yren mutwillen nicht gestatten. Denn wo sie lenger s. f. g. also sein volk zu vorfuhren understehen und von E. Kfl. und F. G. nich kann widerkomen werden, so wirdet s. f. g. geursacht, selber sich kegen denselben *laut ksl. mt. ausgegangen mandat* zu bezaygen, domit er solchs von yhne vortrag habe. . . ." Gess, *Akten,* 1: 719.

71. AGBM, 2: 31.

72. MSB, 546.

73. MSB, 403.

74. On Thilo Banse, see Manfred Bensing, "Idee und Praxis des 'Christlichen Verbuendnisses' bei Thomas Muentzer," in Friesen and Goertz, *Muentzer,* 309.

75. MSB, 545–546.

76. MSB, 546.

77. See Andrew W. Drummond, "Thomas Muentzer and the Fear of Man," SCJ, 10, no. 2 (1979): 63–71.

78. MSB, 408–409.

79. See also Duke George's orders as to what to do to the family members of those who had left for Allstedt. Gess, *Akten,* 1: 715–716.

80. "These things have I spoken unto you, that ye should not be offended. They shall put you out of the synagogues; yea, the time cometh, that whosoever killeth you will think that he doeth God service."

81. MSB, 412.

82. MSB, 413.

83. MSB, 413.

84. MSB, 414.

85. Gritsch, *Reformer without a Church,* 91–93.

86. It is impossible to tell, as Bensing ("Christlichen Verbuendnisses," pp. 299–338) would have it, whether or not the *Bund* is a transformation, under

Luther's influence, from a simple revolutionary tool of his early years to an overtly Christian weapon in his fight against godless rulers. Although Bensing's is the most comprehensive study of the *Bund,* it presents a number of problems. First, it seems to me that Bensing accepts too readily the fact of Muentzer's revolutionary past. Second, he fails to see the connection to the Imperial edict of 6 March 1523 with its *mandate* to preach the "holy Gospel," as well as Muentzer's opposition to the "idolatry" of the monks and nuns. Indeed, one would have expected Bensing, as a Marxist, to pay much closer attention to the political context in which Muentzer operated. Lastly—though much more could be said—it seems to me too restricted by Marxist categories of the class conflict, though Bensing does have a real feeling for Muentzer's religious convictions.

87. *Neue Mitteilungen,* 153–154.

88. AGBM, 2: 29–31.

89. *Neue Mitteilungen,* 156.

90. Ibid.

91. Ibid., 155.

92. Ibid., 156.

93. Ibid., 158.

94. MSB, 405.

95. MSB, 406.

96. We shall use the German term throughout.

97. *Neue Mitteilungen,* 158.

98. MSB, 405. See also the letter from Zeiss, the mayor and Council to Frederick. AGBM, 2: 29.

99. WABr, 3: 275.

100. AGBM, 2: 470.

101. See note 87 above.

102. MSB, 545.

103. AGBM, 2: 453.

104. MSB, 421.

105. MSB, 421.

106. Without this, he had said earlier, "it will not be possible for our understanding Father to put aside His gracious rod of punishment."

107. MSB, 422.

108. The unclarity between the "elect" and the "whole congregation" was never satisfactorily worked out by Muentzer.

109. MSB, 423.

110. MSB, 422.

111. MSB, 423.

112. Letter to Jeori, end of July 1524. MSB, 424.

113. See Frederick's letter to the leaders in Wittenberg of 7 August 1523. CR, 1: 621–622.

114. MSB, 405–406.

115. *Neue Mitteilungen,* 158.

116. Frederick to Zeiss, 9 August 1524, observed: "Denn wo dye ler von God vnd rechtgeschaffen ist, darff man nyemants mit keiner bundtnuss, aufrur, noch blutuergiessens bedrawen. . . ." *Neue Mitteilungen,* 190.

117. Ibid., 183–185. In an earlier part of the hearing transcript, Muentzer is to have said: "das er es dafur hielte, sie mochten ein zimlich pundtnus domit Inen vngewert sein mochte, das evangelium zu horen, wol machen" (183).

118. Ibid., 164–165.

119. See the three notes, ibid., 159–160.

120. Ibid., 184.

121. Mayor and Council to Zeiss, 14 June 1524. Ibid., 164.

122. Zeiss to the elector, 26 June 1524. Ibid., 166.

123. Ibid.

124. Ibid., 163.

125. Ibid., 164.

126. Ibid., 167.

127. Ibid., 168.

128. Ibid.

129. See especially W. Borth, *Die Luthersache*.

130. WABr, 3: 307.

131. Ibid.

132. On this general theme, see P. D. L. Avis, "Moses and the Magistrate: A Study in the Rise of Protestant Legalism," JEH, 26, no. 2 (1975): 149–172.

133. WABr, 3: 309. See also Gritsch, *Reformer without a Church*, 99, and John S. Oyer, "The Influence of Jacob Strauss on the Anabaptists," in Marc Lienhard, ed., *The Origin and Characteristics of Anabaptism* (The Hague, 1977), 66–67.

134. MSB, 407.

135. MSB, 414.

136. MSB, 417, 430.

137. MSB, 422.

138. For the historical significance of the book of Daniel, see Klaus Koch, "Spaetisraelitisches Geschichtsdenken am Beispiel des Buches Daniel," HZ 193, no. 1 (1961): 1–32.

139. MSB, 247.

140. MSB, 248.

141. MSB, 248–252.

142. A possible reference to Eusebius's description discussed in Chapter 2.

143. MSB, 252.

144. MSB, 255. The translation is that of Williams, *Spiritual and Anabaptist Writers*, p. 62.

145. MSB, 255. Williams's translation.

146. MSB, 256.

147. MSB, 257.

148. MSB, 257.

149. MSB, 258.

150. MSB, 258.

151. MSB, 259.

152. MSB, 259.

153. MSB, 260.

154. MSB, 261.

155. MSB, 262.

156. MSB, 255.

157. See "Ein nutzlicher Dialogus odder gesprechbuchlein zwischen einem Muentzerischen Schwermer und einem Evangelischen frumen Bawren / Die straff der auffrurischen Schwermer zu Franckenhausen geschlagen / belangende," Ludwig Fischer, ed., *Die lutherischen Pamphlete,* (Tuebingen, 1976), 87–88.

158. *Neue Mitteilungen,* 170.

159. MSB, 407.

160. MSB, 572.

161. AGBM, 2: 941.

162. MSB, 417.

163. AGBM, 2: 38.

164. Gess, *Akten,* 1: 716.

165. MSB, 417.

166. MSB, 417.

167. MSB, 420.

168. MSB, 420.

169. *Neue Mitteilungen,* 179–182.

170. Ibid., 182.

171. Ibid., 185.

172. Ibid., 185–186.

173. AGBM, 2: 39–40.

174. *Neue Mitteilungen ,* 187.

175. Ibid., 187–188.

176. MSB, 430–432.

177. *Neue Mitteilungen,* 190.

178. Ibid., 193.

179. Ibid., 195–196.

180. Ibid., 200.

9: THE TIME OF HARVEST

1. MSB, 431.

2. *Neue Mitteilungen,* 200.

3. Zeiss mentions only the short note of 7 August and the longer letter of 15 August. Foerstemann published the latter in *Neue Mitteilungen,* pp. 196–198, from the Weimar archieves, which must not have contained the drafts.

4. Reichart is repeatedly mentioned as the secretary of the *Bund.* AGBM, 2: 452, 470.

5. MSB, 432–433.

6. MSB, 433–434.

7. MSB, 434–436.

8. Muentzer apparently left Allstedt in the company of a goldsmith from Nordhausen. Letter of Zeiss to Duke John, 25 August 1525. *Neue Mitteilungen,* 202.

9. MSB, 573.

10. Rudolf Enders, "Thueringen," *Der deutsche Bauernkrieg*, Horst Buszello et al., eds. (Paderborn, 1984), 160. Also Elliger, *Muentzer*, 666.

11. Paul Wappler, *Die Taeuferbewegung in Thueringen von 1526–1584* (Jena, 1913), 231.

12. Ibid., 245.

13. See Werner Packull, "Gottfried Seebass on Hans Hut: A Discussion," MQR 49, no. 1 (1975): 58.

14. Franz, *Quellen*, 475. Pfeiffer preached at the suburban church of St. Nicholas.

15. AGBM, 2: 875.

16. Franz, *Quellen*, 475–477.

17. Duke John was a patron and protector of the city. See note 8 above.

18. H. Nebelsieck, ed., "Briefe und Akten zur Reformationsgeschichte der Statdt Muehlhausen i. Th.," *Zeitschrift des Vereins fuer Kirchengeschichte in der Provinz Sachsen* 15 (1919), 420.

19. See also Andreas Osiander, "Gutachten ueber Heinrich Schwertfeger (gen. Pfeiffer)," Gottfried Seebass and Gerhard Mueller, eds., *Andreas Osiander D. Ae. Gesamtausgabe* (Guetersloh, 1975), 1: 255–266.

20. See also Werner Packull, *Mysticism and the Early South German–Austrian Anabaptist Movement 1525–1531* (Scottdale, PA, 1977), 38.

21. The demands placed before the Council by the eight elected representatives of Pfeiffer's faction, on or about 3 July 1523, also contained a number of items dealing with taxes, dues, and interest. Franz, *Quellen*, 477–478.

22. Franz, *Quellen*, 489.

23. Ibid.

24. On the date, see the editors' remarks to the letter. WA, 15: 234–235.

25. WA, 15: 238–240.

26. Franz, *Quellen*, 490–491.

27. Gess, *Akten*, 1: 749.

28. Berlepsch uses the word "obirkeyt," as in "das sy keyner obirkeyt gehorsam." This would seem to imply all authority.

29. This need not, as Bensing asserts, indicate a radicalization of Muentzer's thought. "Christliche Vereinigung," 317.

30. Gess, *Akten*, 1: 748–749. Berlepsch's letter was written on 26 September.

31. Franz, *Quellen*, 490.

32. Packull, "Seebass on Hut," 59.

33. Gess, *Akten*, 1: 750.

34. Obviously Muentzer had no intention of abolishing all authority. The demand for a new Council that would act in the fear of the Lord may therefore strengthen our earlier contention that he merely wished the city of Muehlhausen to reject all authority over it.

35. Franz, *Quellen*, 491–494. The copy in AGBM, 2: 47–48, is addressed to the nearby village of Horsmar, indicating it was also addressed to the surrounding villages under the city's jurisdiction. Dated "around 20 September."

36. In an addendum to the above letter, Berlepsch wrote: "Was Muentzer von Allstedt und Heynrich Pfeyffer, die falschen propheten zu Molhawszen, in icziger ufruhr, als sy vorgangen montags zu Molhawszen erwegkt, fur artickel

erticht und der dorfschaften im Molhawsischen gerichte, auch dem gemeynen pofel zu Molhawszenn uberschigkt hat schreyben laszen, werden E. F. G. inliegender vorzeichnus gnediglich vornehmen. . . ." Gess, *Akten,* 1: 749.

37. MSB, 436.

38. MSB, 448.

39. MSB, 448.

40. Gess, *Akten,* 1: 749.

41. Franz, *Quellen,* 490–491.

42. Packull, "Seebass on Hut," 58.

43. Instead of being a disciple of Muentzer, Hans Hut may have become attached to Pfeiffer in Muehlhausen before Muentzer arrived there, for it was with him that he traveled to Nuremberg later. In any case, it is unlikely that Hut would have been present to add his name to the list without having been fairly conversant with what was happening in Muehlhausen.

44. See. G. Franz's introduction, MSB, 265–266.

45. On Herrgott, see A. Kirchhoff, "Johann Herrgott, Buchfuehrer von Nuremberg und sein tragisches Ende 1527," *Archiv fuer Geschichte des deutschen Buchhandels* 1 (1878): 15–55.

46. Franz, introduction, MSB, 266.

47. Packull, "Seebass on Hut," 58.

48. MSB, 450.

49. Since it would take us too far afield to address anew the question of Muentzer's relationship to the Swiss Anabaptists, see James Stayer and Werner Packull, eds., *The Anabaptists and Thomas Muentzer* (Dubuque and Toronto, 1980).

50. On Carlstadt and the Anabaptists, see Calvin Augustine Pater, *Karlstadt as the Father of the Baptist Movements: The Emergence of Lay Protestantism* (Toronto, 1984).

51. See Friesen, "Martin Cellarius: On the Borders of Heresy," Hans-Juergen Goertz, ed., *Radical Reformers* (Scottdale, PA, 1982), pp. 234–246. English edition by Walter Klaassen.

52. Manfred Krebs and Hans Georg Rott, eds., *Quellen zur Geschichte der Taeufer, VII, Elsass 1. Teil* (Guetersloh, 1959), p. 24.

53. MSB, 544.

54. See Elliger, *Muentzer,* 629–639.

55. MSB, 243–244.

56. Elliger, *Muentzer,* 658ff, and Thomas Scott, "The 'Volksreformation' of Thomas Muentzer in Allstedt and Muehlhausen," JEH 34, no. 2 (1983): 204–205. The document can be found in Franz, *Quellen,* 231–234.

57. Franz, *Quellen,* 235–236.

58. Elliger's argument for a strong influence of Muentzer has been challenged by Peter Blickle, "Thomas Muentzer und der Bauernkrieg in Suedwestdeutschland. Bemerkungen zu Walter Elliger, *Thomas Muentzer, Leben und Werk,"* Zeitschrift fuer Agrargeschichte und Agrarsoziologie 24 (1976): 79–80.

59. AGBM, 2: 865, 872.

60. AGBM, 2: 66.

61. The *Muehlhausen Chronicle* asserted that both Pfeiffer and Muentzer

had returned by this time, but this cannot have been the case. See Franz, *Quellen*, 494.

62. The *Muehlhausen Chronicle* stated that Muentzer was called to the Church of St. Mary on 28 February. How long before that date he had returned is not known. Franz, *Quellen*, 496.

63. AGBM, 2: 67.

64. Berlepsch to Duke George, 9 January 1525. Gess, *Akten*, 2: 6–7.

65. Gess, *Akten*, 2: 87–90.

66. Ibid., 26–28, 29–31.

67. See Berlepsch's report to Duke George, 17 March 1525. Gess, *Akten*, II, 82.

68. Franz, *Quellen*, 496–497.

69. Gess, *Akten*, 2: 79–80.

70. Eusebius, *Church History*, 90, 148.

71. Augustine, *Works*, 6: 343.

72. Franz, *Quellen*, 534.

73. MSB, 464. In his confession Pfeiffer used the same term—"establish a Christian order."

74. AGBM, 2: 911.

75. See Abraham Friesen "Philip Melanchthon (1497–1560), Wilhelm Zimmermann (1807–1878) and the Dilemma of Muentzer Historiography," *Church History* 43 (1974): 170.

76. See the interrogations in AGBM, 2: 762, 904. The authorities seem to have reserved this question for preachers like Laue, Muentzer and Pfeiffer in Muehlhausen.

77. Wappler, *Taeuferbewegung*, 335.

78. Gess, *Akten*, 2: 80–81.

79. Franz, *Quellen*, 497.

80. Franz, *Quellen*, 497; Gess, *Akten*, 2: 82.

81. Gess, *Akten*, 2: 498.

82. AGBM, 2: 67–68, 69–70.

83. AGBM, 2: 73.

84. AGBM, 2: 77–78.

85. AGBM, 2: 85, 111.

86. Gess, *Akten*, 2: 109.

87. AGBM, 2: 95.

88. MSB, 450–451.

89. Gess, *Akten*, 2: 109.

90. Gess, *Akten*, 2: 115.

91. Gess, *Akten*, 2: 117.

92. AGBM, 2: 98; Franz, *Quellen*, 498.

93. Franz, *Quellen* 498.

94. Franz, *Quellen*, 498.

95. AGBM, 2: 98.

96. MSB, 430–431.

97. I hope to publish shortly an essay entitled "Acts 10: The Baptism of Cornelius as Interpreted by Thomas Muentzer and Felix Mantz," which will,

I believe, shed new light on the relationship between Muentzer and the Anabaptists.

98. See the 25 April 1525 report by Reibisch to Potinger. Gess, *Akten,* 2: 128–129.

99. The *Muehlhausen Chronicle* said 400; Reibisch, 500. The latter number may include those who joined the original 400 from Muehlhausen. How many of these were actually from the city is another matter.

100. Gess, *Akten,* 2: 130.

101. MSB, 453. The editor indicates April 16 as the date, but the note says "Datum am 26. tag apprilis [*sic*] anno 1525."

102. AGBM, 2: 130.

103. One would assume that the differences between Muentzer and Luther were known. If that is so, the above can only be interpreted as a clear rejection of Muentzer's and Pfeiffer's attempt to use the Salza uprising for their own purposes.

104. MSB, 454–456.

105. The Black Forest peasants had already been defeated on 14 and 16 April, though the news may not have reached Muentzer as yet since it was only on 1 May that Albrecht of Mainz informed Duke George of their defeat. AGBM, 2: 159.

106. As we have seen in the last chapter, Muentzer had said that not all members of the *Bund* needed to be "friends of God."

107. In a letter of 30 April to Langensalza, Muentzer wrote: "Nachdem ir durch eur verursachunge uns erregt, muszt ihr euch nit also kindisch stellen. . . ." MSB, 453. This event, then, may have been decisive for Muentzer's increasing revolutionary fervor.

108. MSB, 454–456.

109. Franz, *Quellen,* 540. See also Reinhard Jordan, "Pfeiffers und Muentzers Zug in das Eichsfeld und die Verwuestung der Kloester und Schloesser," *Zeitschrift fuer Thueringische Geschichte* 22 (1904): 36.

110. MSB, 462.

111 Jordan, "Zug in das Eichsfeld," 37.

112. Ibid.

113. See the 22 February 1525 letter of Zeiss to Spalatin. AGBM, 2: 66.

114. AGBM, 2: 878. The confession was made on 19 March 1527. See also the confession of Hans Weber. Ibid.

115. AGBM, 2: 878.

116. MSB, 474.

117. AGBM, 2: 529.

118. Gess, *Akten,* 2: 108–109.

119. Other sources make the same point. See Gess, *Akten,* 2: 134, 136, 140.

120. AGBM, 2: 923. In his letter of 5 Mar. 1525 Zeiss wrote to Christoph Meinhard: "Es ist auch nicht, das Muentzer ein rottmeister sei oder solichen haufen furen sole, wie man sagt. Er ist nichts anders dann ein prediger der von Molhausen. So sein sonst im haufen auch vil prediger, die das evangeli nach Luthers auslegung predigen. Sie achten Muentzers nit sonderlich, wiewol er sich selber ins spil mit seim schreiben hierherre gibt." AGBM, 2: 203.

121. Gess, *Akten*, 2: 139, 168, 172, 200, 215, 303; AGBM, 2: 594.

122. AGBM, 2: 558.

123. Jordan, "Zug in das Eichsfeld." See also the report of the city of Muehlhausen of 10 May 1530. AGBM, 2: 925.

124. I believe this to be particularly true of Bensing's article on the *Bund* and Marxist interpretations, with their central emphasis on revolutions as the nodal turning points of history, in general.

125. See Scott, "Volksreformation," 198–199, and the Marxist historians discussed in my *Reformation and Utopia*.

126. MSB, 423.

127. MSB, 501.

128. Franz, *Quellen*, 497.

129. AGBM, 2: 878. In his 14 March 1527 confession Daniel Strutmann of Muehlhausen said that Pfeiffer had commanded them to march to the Eichsfeld. AGBM, 2: 876.

130. Gess, *Akten*, 2: 192–193.

131. Ibid., 6.

132. Ibid., 499.

133. Franz, *Quellen*, 499.

134. MSB, 457.

135. On 6 May Apel von Ebeleben wrote Duke George that he could not supply him with troops because "mir die von Molhauszen heute acht tage alles, was ich gehabt, geplundert, genomen, das haus zuschlagen und zubrochen und vorterbt haben. . . ." Gess, *Akten*, 2: 191.

136. Franz, *Quellen*, 500.

137. Gess, *Akten*, 2: 160, 174, 175.

138. AGBM, 2: 927. See Jordan, 44–48.

139. "Damit sie Muenzern und Pfeiffern bewegt, dasz sie die Spitze gewandt nach dem Eichsfelde." Franz, *Quellen*, 500.

140. AGBM, 2: 926.

141. Jordan, 48–49.

142. Franz, *Quellen*, 501.

143. Gess, *Akten*, 2: 164; MSB, 459. Duderstadt is further from Frankenhausen than Muehlhausen.

144. MSB, 463, 467–470. See his letters to the Dukes of Mansfeld.

145. AGBM, 2: 228. A letter of the Counts of Mansfeld to Duke George of 6 May adds the Count of Gleichen to the list. Gess, *Akten*, 2: 191. See also p. 167 with respect to the Count of Hohnstein.

146. AGBM, 2: 101–105, 106–107.

147. Ibid., 108–128.

148. Ibid., 151, 160–161.

149. Ibid., 194–196.

150. Gess, *Akten*, 2: 175.

151. Ibid., 334–340.

152. Ibid., 335.

153. Ibid., 337, 338.

154. MSB, 459.

155. MSB, 461.

156. MSB, 467.

157. Augustine, *Works*, 4: 640. Here Augustine uses the same argument, and the same examples to substantiate it, as had Muentzer!

158. AGBM, 2: 162.

159. MSB, 461.

160. MSB, 462.

161. MSB, 462–463.

162. MSB, 463.

163. AGBM, 2: 162–163.

164. Ibid., 178. See also the letter of 3 May. AGBM, 2: 181.

165. Ibid., 163.

166. Ibid., 181, 186–187, 210.

167. Ibid., 202–203.

168. Ibid., 229, 230.

169. Ibid., 214.

170. It is intriguing to ask to what extent the peasants themselves were aware of the 6 March 1523 Imperial edict. Nowhere do they mention it specifically, but their reasoning makes it plausible that they were very much aware of it. AGBM, 2: 215.

171. Gess, *Akten*, 2: 189, n. 1.

172. AGBM, 2: 235.

173. Gess, *Akten*, 2: 190, note 1.

174. Ibid., 191.

175. AGBM, 2: 230.

176. WABr, 3: 480–482.

177. AGBM, 2: 258.

178. On Duke George see Hans Becker, "Herzog Georg von Sachsen als kirchlicher und theologischer Schriftsteller," ARG 24 (1927): 161–269.

179. AGBM, 2: 941–942.

180. Gess, *Akten*, 2: 223, n. 1.

181. Ibid., 189, note 1.

182. Ibid., 221–225.

183. AGBM, 2: 235.

184. Ibid., 235.

185. Ibid., 249.

186. Ibid., 254.

187. MSB, 463–464, beginning with his letter to Eisenach, 9 May 1525.

188. AGBM, 2: 278.

189. Ibid., 888. The report by the Frankenhausen Council, written 5 September 1527, accused the people of Artern of complicity in the execution of Matern of Gehofen. Ernest of Mansfeld had apparently exacted a heavy penalty from Frankenhausen because of the execution, and the Council was therefore eager to shift at least some of the blame and part of the penalty to that town as a consequence. Artern responded on 21 November, stating that had Frankenhausen not begged Muentzer to come to their aid, Gehofen would never have

been executed. Even if some of its subjects had participated in the incident, the city shared none of the blame. AGBM, 2: 893–896.

190. Ibid., 888.

191. Letter to Luther of 26 May 1525. Ibid., 379.

192. MSB, 547.

193 MSB, 547, n. 76.

194. MSB, 467–468.

195. MSB, 469–470.

196. Muentzer's letter to Erfurt accompanied Frankenhausen's letter of appeal to the same city. The Erfurt authorities, however, refused to accept it. AGBM, 2: 281–282.

197. MSB, 471–472.

198. MSB, 472.

199. MSB, 472–473.

200. AGBM, 2: 305.

201. Ibid., 897.

202. Ibid., 378, n. 3a, has the following excerpt from the "Kanzlei-Handbuch 1525–38 fol. 2 (Rudolstadt)": "Item auf montag nach Cantate [15 May] haben der landgrave von Hessen etc. und herzog Georg von Sachsen etc. die stat Frankenhausen, dorinne ein prediger von Molhausen, Thomas Montzer gnant, mit 7,000 und sterker gemeins baursvolk und von Molhausen bei sich gehapt, denen geprediget: *sie solten sich vor den fursten nit furchten, dan er wolle alle ire buchsenstein in einem ermel fassen,* und die fursten wurden in sich selbst schissen, also het ime der geist gots offenbar, erobert ane grosse stuermen und gewalt und bei 4500 man und mehr erstochen und entheupten lassen" [italics mine]. See also Ruehel to Luther, 26 May: "Als aber der erste schusz angegangen, der ist zu kurz gewesen, hat er [Muentzer] geschrieen: ich habe euch vor gesagt, kein geschuez wuerde euch schaden." AGBM, 2: 378.

203. AGBM, 2: 378.

204. Ibid., 378. The accounts are virtually unanimous in saying that the peasants offered no, or little, resistance. Ibid., 293, 305, 309.

205. Ibid., 397, 432. One account lists 8,000 dead; another lists 7,000.

206. Ibid., 326.

207. Ibid., 343.

208. Gess, *Akten,* 2: 299.

209. MSB, 550.

210. Boehmer, "Studien zu Thomas Muentzer," p. 2.

211. WABr, 3: 507.

212. WABr, 3: 510.

213. WABr, 3: 515–516.

214. MSB, 473.

215. Muehlhausen had not yet been captured, but would be shortly.

216. MSB, 473–474.

217. MSB, 474.

218. MSB, 454.

219. MSB, 303.

220. MSB, 463.
221. AGBM, 2: 897.
222. AGBM, 2: 897, n. 3a.

CONCLUSION

1. Gritsch, "Muentzer and Luther: A Tragedy of Errors."
2. On Christian revolution see: Robert Banks, "A Christian Revolution-ary Tradition?" *Journal of Ecumenical Studies* 9, no. 2 (1972): 285–299, and Hans Schulze, "Zur Kritik der Revolutionstheologen," K&D 15, no. 3 (1969): 239–257.
3. See Thomas Nipperdey, "Theologie und Revolution bei Thomas Muent-zer," ARG 54 (1963): 145–179, and Hans-Juergen Goertz, "Der Mystiker mit dem Hammer. Die theologische Begruendung der Revolution bei Thomas Muentzer," K&D 20 (1974): 23–53.

Bibliography

PRIMARY SOURCES

Augustine. *Works.* Vols. 1–8, *The Nicene and Post-Nicene Fathers.* Ed. Philip Schaff. Reprint: Grand Rapids, 1958.

Boehmer, Heinrich, and Paul Kirn, eds. *Thomas Muentzers Briefwechsel.* Leipzig and Berlin, 1931.

Bretschneider, C. G., ed. *Philippi Melanthonis Opera Quae Supersunt Omnia,* vol. 1, *Corpus Reformatorum.* Halle/S, 1834.

Dictionnaire de Théologie Catholique. Paris, 1931.

Dolan, John P., ed. and trans. *The Essential Erasmus.* New York, 1974.

Elliott, Walter, ed. *The Sermons and Conferences of John Tauler.* Washington, D. C., 1910.

Erasmus, Desiderius. *The Correspondence of Erasmus,* vol. 2. Trans. R. A. B. Mynors and D. F. S. Thomson. Toronto and Buffalo, 1974.

———. *Literary and Educational Writings,* vol. 1. Ed. Craig R. Thompson. Toronto and Buffalo, 1978.

Eusebius. *The History of the Church From Christ to Constantine.* Trans. G. A. Williamson. Baltimore, 1965.

Eusebius Werke. 2 vols., *Die Kirchengeschichte.* Ed. Eduard Schwarz, with the Latin translation of Rufinus prepared by Theodor Mommsen. Leipzig, 1903.

Fischer, Ludwig, ed. *Die lutherischen Pamphlete gegen Thomas Muentzer.* Tuebingen, 1976.

Foerstemann, Carl E., ed. *Neue Mitteilungen aus dem Gebiet historisch-antiquarischer Forschungen.* 12. Halle/S., 1869.

———. *Neues Urkundenbuch zur Geschichte der evangelischen Kirchen-Reformation.* Hamburg, 1842.

Franz, Guenther, ed. *Quellen zur Geschichte des Bauernkrieges.* Darmstadt, 1963.

————, ed. *Thomas Muentzer: Schriften und Briefe.* Guetersloh, 1968.

Fuchs, W. P., and Guenther Franz, eds. *Akten zur Geschichte des Bauernkrieges in Mitteldeutschland.* 3 vols. Jena, 1942.

Gess, Felician, ed. *Akten und Briefe zur Kirchenpolitik Herzog Georgs von Sachsen.* 2 vols. Leipzig, 1905.

Goetze, A., and L. E. Schmitt, eds. *Aus dem Sozialen und Politischen Kampf. Flugschriften aus der Reformationszeit.* 20. Halle/S., 1953.

Heine, Heinrich. *Werke und Briefe.* 4. Berlin, 1960.

Josephus, Flavius. *The Jewish War.* Trans. G. A. Williamson. Baltimore, 1965.

Krebs, Manfred, and Hans Georg Rott, eds. *Quellen zur Geschichte der Taeufer,* VII, *Elsass.* 2 vols. Guetersloh, 1959.

Lancel, Serge. *Actes de la conference de Carthage en 411.* Paris, 1972.

Lenker, John Nicholas, ed. and trans. *The Sermons of Martin Luther.* 8 vols. Reprint: Grand Rapids, 1983.

Luther, Martin. *D. Martin Luthers Werke.* Weimar, 1833–1948.

————. *D. Martin Luthers Werke. Briefwechsel.* Weimar, 1930–1978.

————. *D. Martin Luthers Werke. Tischreden.* Weimar, 1912–1921.

————. *D. Martin Luthers saemmtliche Schriften.* Ed. J. G. Walch. 23 vols. St. Louis, 1880–1910.

————. *Luther's Works,* American Edition. 55 vols. Eds. Helmut T. Lehmann and Jaroslav J. Pelikan. Philadelphia, 1955.

Muehlhaupt, Erwin, ed. *Luther ueber Muentzer.* Witten, 1973.

Nebelsieck, H., ed. "Briefe und Akten zur Reformationsgeschichte der Stadt Muehlhausen i. Th." *Zeitschrift des Vereins fuer Kirchengeschichte in der Provinz Sachsen* 15 (1919):410–455.

Pauck, Wilhelm, ed. *Luther: Lectures on Romans.* Vol. 15, LCC. Philadelphia, 1961.

Planitz, Hans von der. *Berichte aus dem Reichsregiment in Nuernberg 1521–1523.* Eds. E. Wuelker and H. Virck. Hildesheim and New York, 1979.

Rupp, E. G., and Philip S. Watson, eds. *Luther and Erasmus: Free Will and Salvation.* Vol. 17, LCC. Philadelphia, 1969.

Scholasticus, Socrates. *The Ecclesiastical History.* Vol. 2, *The Nicene and Post-Nicene Fathers.* Eds. Philip Schaff and Henry Wace. Reprint: Grand Rapids, 1979.

Schopp, Ludwig, ed. *Writings of St. Augustine.* Vol. 4, *The Fathers of the Church.* New York, 1947.

Seebass, Gottfried, and Gerhard Mueller, eds. *Andreas Osiander D. Ae. Gesamtausgabe.* Vol. 1, *Schriften und Briefe 1522 bis Maerz 1525.* Guetersloh, 1975.

Sermon des grossgelarten in gnade erlauchtiten doctoris Johannes Thauleri prediger ordens. . . . Leipzig, 1498.

Sider, Ronald J., ed. *Karlstadt's Battle with Luther: Documents in a Liberal-Radical Debate.* Philadelphia, 1978.

Spinka, Matthew, ed. and trans. *The Letters of John Hus.* Manchester, 1972.

Stapulensis, Faber, ed. *Hegesippi qui dicitur historiae libri V.* Paris, 1510.

Stupperich, Robert, ed. *Martin Bucers Deutsche Schriften.* Vol. 1, *Fruehschriften 1520–1524.* Guetersloh, 1960.

Ussani, Vincentius, ed. *Hegesippi qui dicitur historiae libri V.* Vol. 66, *Corpus Scriptorum Ecclesiasticorum Latinorum.* Vienna and Leipzig, 1932.

Verduin, Leonard, trans. *The Complete Writings of Menno Simons.* Ed. John C. Wenger. Scottdale, PA, 1956.

Wappler, Paul. *Die Taeuferbewegung in Thueringen von 1526–1548.* Jena, 1913.

Westin, Gunnar, and Torsten Bergsten, eds. *Balthasar Hubmaier Schriften.* Vol. 9, *Quellen zur Geschichte der Taeufer.* Guetersloh, 1962.

Williams, George H., and Angel Mergal, eds. *Spiritual and Anabaptist Writers.* Vol. 25, LCC. Philadelphia, 1957.

Wrede, Adolf, ed. *Deutsche Reichstagsakten unter Kaiser Karl V.* Vol. 3. Goettingen, 1963.

BIBLIOGRAPHIES

Hillerbrand, Hans J., ed. *A Bibliography of Anabaptism 1520–1630.* Elkhart, IN, 1962.

———, ed. *Thomas Muentzer: A Bibliography.* St. Louis, 1976.

HISTORIOGRAPHY

Berbig, Hans Joachim, "Thomas Muentzer in neuer Sicht." *Archiv fuer Kulturgeschichte* 59, no. 2 (1977): 489–495.

Braeuer, Siegfried. "Muentzerforschung von 1965 bis 1975." *Lutherjahrbuch* 44 (1977): 127–141, and 45 (1978): 102–139.

Dickens, A. G. and John Tonkin. *The Reformation in Historical Thought.* Oxford, 1985.

Friesen, Abraham. "The Intellectual Development of Thomas Muentzer." In *Reformation und Revolution. Beitraege zum politischen Wandel und den sozialen Kraeften am Beginn der Neuzeit,* ed. Rainer Postel and Franklin Kopitzsch, 121–137. Stuttgart, 1989.

———. "The Marxist Interpretation of the Reformation." *Archiv fuer Reformationsgeschichte* 64 (1973): 34–55.

———. "Philip Melanchthon (1497–1560), Wilhelm Zimmermann (1807–1878) and the Dilemma of Muentzer Historiography." *Church History* 43, no. 2 (1974): 164–182.

———. "Thomas Muentzer in Marxist Thought." *Church History* 34, no. 3 (1965): 306–327.

———. *Reformation and Utopia: The Marxist Interpretation of the Reformation and Its Antecedents.* Weisbaden, 1974.

———. "Social Revolution or Religious Reform? Some Salient Aspects of Anabaptist Historiography." In *Umstrittenes Taeufertum 1524–1975. Neue Forschungen,* ed. Hans-Juergen Goertz, 223–243. Goettingen, 1975.

Friesen, Abraham, and Hans-Juergen Goertz, eds. *Thomas Muentzer.* Vol. 491, *Wege der Forschung.* Darmstadt, 1978.

Goertz, Hans-Juergen. *Das Bild Thomas Muentzers in Ost und West.* Hannover, 1988.

Goertz, Hans-Juergen, Barbara Talkenberger, and Gabriele Wohlauf. "Neue Forschungen zum deutschen Bauernkrieg. Ueberblick und Aufgabe." *Mennonitische Geschichtsblaetter* 33 (1976): 24–64.

Koch, Hans-Gerhard. *Luthers Reformation in kommunistischer Sicht.* Stuttgart, 1967.

Lohse, Bernhard. "The Marxist Interpretation of Luther and Muentzer." *The Australian Journal of Politics and History* 19, no. 3 (1973): 343–352.

———. "Thomas Muentzer in marxistischer Sicht." *Luther* 43, no. 2 (1972): 60–73.

Packull, Werner O. "Thomas Muentzer between Marxist–Christian Diatribe and Dialogue." *Historical Reflections* 4, no. 1 (1977): 67–90.

Stayer, James M. "Thomas Muentzer's Theology and Revolution in Recent Non-Marxist Interpretation." *The Mennonite Quarterly Review* 43, no. 2 (1969): 142–152.

Stayer, James M., and Werner O. Packull, eds. *The Anabaptists and Thomas Muentzer.* Dubuque and Toronto, 1980.

Steinmetz, Max. *Das Muentzerbild von Martin Luther bis Friedrich Engels.* Berlin, 1971.

———, ed. *Der deutsche Bauernkrieg und Thomas Muentzer.* Leipzig, 1976.

———. "Thomas Muentzer in der Forschung der Gegenwart." *Zeitschrift fuer Geschichtswissenschaft* 23, no. 6 (1975): 666–685.

SECONDARY SOURCES

Althaus, Paul. *Luthers Haltung im Bauernkrieg.* Basel, 1953.

Avis, P. D. L. "Moses and the Magistrate: A Study in the Rise of Protestant Legalism." *Journal of Ecclesiastical History* 26, no. 2 (1975): 149–172.

Baczko, Leo von. *Thomas Muentzer, dessen Charakter und Schicksale.* Halle and Leipzig, 1812.

Baerwald, Robert. *Die Schlacht bei Frankenhausen 1525.* 2d ed. Muehlhausen, 1925.

Bailey, Richard. "The Sixteenth Century Apocalyptic Heritage and Thomas Muentzer." *The Mennonite Quarterly Review* 57, no. 1 (1983): 27–44.

Bainton, Roland H. *Here I Stand: A Life of Martin Luther.* Nashville, 1952.

———. "The Parable of the Tares as the Proof Text for Religious Liberty to the End of the Sixteenth Century." *Church History* 1, no. 2 (1932): 67–89.

———. "Thomas Muentzer: Revolutionary Firebrand of the Reformation." *Sixteenth Century Journal* 13, no. 2 (1982): 3–16.

Banks, Robert. "A Christian Revolutionary Tradition?" *Journal of Ecumenical Studies* 9, no. 2 (1972): 285–299.

Barge, Hermann, *Andreas Bodenstein von Karlstadt.* 2 vols. Leipzig, 1905.

———. "Luther und Karlstadt in Wittenberg." *Historische Zeitschrift* 99 (1907): 256–324.

Baum, Adolf. *Magistrat und Reformation in Strassburg bis 1529.* Strassburg, 1887.

Bax, E. Belfort. *The Peasants' War in Germany 1525–1526.* London, 1899.

Baylor, Michael G. "Theology and Politics in the Thought of Thomas Muentzer: The Case of the Elect." *Archiv fuer Reformationsgeschichte* 79 (1988): 81–102.

Becker, Hans. "Herzog Georg von Sachsen als kirchlicher und theologischer Schriftsteller." *Archiv fuer Reformationsgeschichte* 24 (1927): 161–269.

Bender, Harold S. "The Zwickau Prophets, Thomas Muentzer and the Anabaptists." *The Mennonite Quarterly Review* 17, no. 1 (1953): 3–16.

Bensen, Wilhelm. *Geschichte des Bauernkrieges in Ostfranken aus den Quellen bearbeitet.* Erlangen, 1840.

Bensing, Manfred. *Thomas Muentzer und der Thueringer Aufstand 1525.* Berlin, 1966.

———. "Idee und Praxis des 'Christlichen Verbuendnisses' bei Thomas Muentzer." *Wissenschaftliche Zeitschrift der Karl-Marx-Universitaet* 14 (1965): 459–471.

Bensing, Manfred, and Winfried Trillitzsch. "Bernard Dappens 'Articuli . . . contra Lutheranos.' Zur Auseinandersetzung der Jueterboger Franziskaner mit Thomas Muentzer und Franz Guenther 1519." *Jahrbuch fuer Regionalgeschichte* 2 (1967): 113–147.

Blickle, Peter, ed. *Revolte und Revolution in Europa.* Beiheft 4, *Historische Zeitschrift.* Munich, 1975.

———. *The Revolution of 1525. The German Peasants' War from a New Perspective.* Trans. Thomas A. Brady and H. C. Erik Middelfort. Baltimore and London, 1977.

———. "Thomas Muentzer und der Bauernkrieg in Suedwestdeutschland. Bemerkungen zu Walter Elliger, *Thomas Muentzer, Leben und Werk.*" *Zeitschrift fuer Agrargeschichte und Agrarsoziologie* 24 (1976): 79–80.

Bloch, Ernst. *Thomas Muentzer als Theologe der Revolution.* Munich, 1921.

Blos, Wilhelm, ed. *Dr. W. Zimmermann's Grosser Deutscher Bauernkrieg.* Stuttgart, 1891.

Boehmer, Heinrich. *Gesammelte Aufsaetze.* Gotha, 1927.

———. *Studien zu Thomas Muentzer.* Leipzig, 1922.

Borth, Wilhelm. *Die Luthersache (Causa Lutheri) 1517–1524. Die Anfaenge der Reformation als Frage von Politik und Recht.* Luebeck and Hamburg, 1970.

Bouwsma, William J. *John Calvin: A Sixteenth-Century Portrait.* Oxford, 1988.

Braeuer, Helmut. "Zur fruehen buergerlichen Geschichtsschreibung in Zwickau im 16. Jahrhundert." *Zeitschrift fuer Geschichtswissenschaft* 20, no. 5 (1972): 565–576.

———. "Zwickau zur Zeit Thomas Muentzers und der Bauernkrieges." *Saechsische Heimatblaetter* 20, no. 5 (1974): 192–223.

Braeuer, Siegfried. "Die erste Gesamtausgabe von Thomas Muentzers Schriften und Briefe." *Lutherjahrbuch* 38 (1971): 120–131.

———. "Die Vorgeschichte von Luthers 'Ein Brief an die Fuersten zu Sachsen von dem aufruehrerischen Geist.' " *Lutherjahrbuch* 47 (1980): 40–70.

———. "Hans Reichart, der angebliche Allstedter Drucker Muentzers." *Zeitschrift fuer Kirchengeschichte* 85, no. 3 (1975): 389–398.

———. "Thomas Muentzers Beziehungen zur Braunschweiger Fruehreformation." *Theologische Literaturzeitung* 109, no. 8 (1984): 636–638.

———. "Thomas Muentzers Liedschaffen." *Lutherjahrbuch* 41 (1974): 45–102.

———. "Vier neue Muentzerausgaben." *Lutherjahrbuch* 39 (1972): 110–120.

———. "Zu Muentzers Geburtsjahr." *Lutherjahrbuch* 36 (1969): 80–84.

Brendler, Gerhard and Adolf Laube, eds. *Der deutsche Bauernkrieg 1524/25: Geschichte—Tradition—Lehren.* Berlin, 1977.

Brown, Peter. *Augustine of Hippo.* Berkeley and Los Angeles, 1967.

Bubenheimer, Ulrich. "Thomas Muentzer." In *Protestantische Profile. Lebensbilder aus fuenf Jahrhunderten,* Klaus Scholder and Dieter Kleinmann, eds., 32–46. Frankfurt a/M., 1983.

Buck, Lawrence P. and Jonathan W. Zophy, eds. *The Social History of the Reformation.* Columbus, Ohio, 1972.

Buecking, Juergen. "Der 'Oberrheinische Revolutionaer' heisst Conrad Stuertzel, seines Zeichens kgl. Hofkanzler." *Archiv fuer Kulturgeschichte* 57, no. 1 (1975): 162–180.

Buszello, Horst. *Der deutsche Bauernkrieg von 1525 als politische Bewegung.* Berlin, 1969.

Buszello, Horst, et al., eds. *Der deutsche Bauernkrieg.* Paderborn, 1984.

Chadwick, Henry. *Augustine.* Oxford, 1986.

Clark, James M. *The Great German Mystics: Eckhart, Tauler and Suso.* Folcroft, PA, 1969.

Clasen, Claus-Peter. *Anabaptism: A Social History.* Ithaca, 1972.

Clemen, Otto. "Das Prager Manifest Thomas Muentzers." *Archiv fuer Reformationsgeschichte* 30 (1933): 73–81.

———. "Zwei Anhaenger Thomas Muentzers." *Archiv fuer Reformationsgeschichte* 26 (1929): 188–193.

Cohn, Norman. *In Pursuit of the Millennium.* New Jersey, 1957.

Cranz, Edward F. *An Essay on the Development of Luther's Thought on Justice, Law and Society.* Cambridge, MA, 1964.

Crofts, Richard A. "Three Renaissance Expressions of Societal Responsibility: Thomas More, Desiderius Erasmus, and Thomas Muentzer." *Sixteenth Century Journal* 3, no. 2 (1972): 10–24.

Delius, Hans-Ulrich. *Augustin als Quelle Luthers.* Berlin, 1984.

Demke, Christoph, ed. *Thomas Muentzer: Anfragen an Theologie und Kirche.* Berlin, 1977.

Denifle, Heinrich. "Taulers Bekehrung kritisch Untersucht." *Quellen und Forschungen zur Sprach—und Culturgeschichte der Germanischen Voelker* 34 (Strassburg, 1879): 1–147.

Dienst, Karl. "Thomas Muentzer—eine Gestalt der Bewusstseinsgeschichte." *Luther* 46, no. 3 (1975): 114–124.

Drummond, Andrew W. "Thomas Muentzer and the Fear of Man." *Sixteenth Century Journal* 10, no. 2 (1979): 63–71.

Duelmen, Richard von. "Muentzers Anhaenger im Oberdeutschen Taeufertum." *Zeitschrift fuer Bayerische Landesgeschichte* 39 (1976): 883–891.

Ebert, Klaus. *Thomas Muentzer. Von Eigensinn und Widerspruch.* Frankfurt a/M., 1987.

Edwards, Mark U. *Luther and the False Brethren.* Stanford, 1975.

Elliger, Walter. *Thomas Muentzer: Leben und Werk.* Goettingen, 1975.

———. "Zum Thema Luther und Thomas Muentzer." *Lutherjahrbuch* 36 (1976): 90–115.

Engels, Friedrich. *Der deutsche Bauernkrieg.* Ed. Franz Mehring. Berlin, 1908.

Federer, Jakob Gottfried. *Didaktik der Befreiung: Eine Studie am Beispiel Thomas Muentzers.* Bonn, 1976.

Forell, George. "Thomas Muentzer: Symbol or Reality." *Dialog* 2 (Winter, 1960): 1–12.

Franke, Kuno. "Medieval German Mysticism." *Harvard Theological Review* 5, no. 1 (1912): 110–120.

Franz, Guenther. *Der deutsche Bauernkrieg.* 2d ed. Munich and Berlin, 1943.

Frend, W. H. C. *The Donatist Church.* Oxford, 1950.

———. *The Rise of Christianity.* Philadelphia, 1984.

Friedmann, Robert. *The Theology of Anabaptism.* Scottdale, PA, 1973.

Friesen, Abraham. "The Radical Reformation Revisited." *Journal of Mennonite Studies* 2 (1984): 124–176.

———. "Thomas Muentzer and Martin Luther." *Archiv fuer Reformationsgeschichte* 80 (1988): 59–80.

———. "Thomas Muentzer and the Anabaptists." *Journal of Mennonite Studies* 4 (1986): 143–161.

———. "Thomas Muentzer and the Old Testament." *The Mennonite Quarterly Review* 47, no. 1 (1973): 5–23.

———. "Wilhelm Zimmermann and the Nemesis of History." *German Studies Review* 4, no. 2 (1981): 195–236.

Gerdes, Hayo. "Thomas Muentzers Kampf gegen die Gottlosen." *Luther* 49, no. 2 (1978): 71–83.

Goertz, Hans-Juergen. "Der Mystiker mit den Hammer. Die theologische Begruendung der Revolution bei Thomas Muentzer." *Kerygma und Dogma* 20 (1974): 23–53.

———. *Innere und Aeussere Ordnung in der Theologie Thomas Muentzers.* Leiden, 1967.

———. " 'Lebendiges Wort' und 'totes Ding.' Zum Schriftverstaendnis Thomas Muentzers im Prager Manifest." *Archiv fuer Reformationsgeschichte* 67 (1976): 153–178.

———, ed. *Radikale Reformatoren: 21 biographische Skizzen von Thomas Muentzer bis Paracelsus.* Munich, 1978. English trans. Walter Klaassen, *Radical Reformers.* Scottdale, PA, 1982.

———, ed. *Umstrittenes Taeufertum 1525–1975. Neue Forschungen.* Goettingen, 1975.

Grane, Leif. *Modus Loquendi di Theologicus 1515–1518.* Leiden, 1975.

———. "Thomas Muentzer und Martin Luther." In *Bauernkriegs-Studien.* Ed. Bernd Moeller. Guetersloh, 1975.

Grant, Robert. *Eusebius as Church Historian.* Oxford, 1980.

Greschat, Martin. "Luthers Haltung im Bauernkrieg." *Archiv fuer Reformationsgeschichte* 56 (1965): 31–47.

———. "Martin Bucers Buecherverzeichnis von 1518." *Archiv fuer Kulturgeschichte* 57, no. 1 (1975): 162–180.

Grisar, Hartman. *Martin Luther: His Life and Work*. London, 1930.

Gritsch, Eric W. "Luther und die Schwaermer: Verworfene Anfechtung?" *Luther* 47, no. 3 (1976): 105–121.

———. *Reformer without a Church: The Life and Thought of Thomas Muentzer 1488[?]–1525*. Philadelphia, 1967.

———. "Thomas Muentzer and Luther: A Tragedy of Errors." In Hans-J. Hillerbrand, ed., 55–84, *Radical Tendencies in the Reformation: Divergent Perspectives*. Vol. 9 of *Sixteenth-Century Essays & Studies*. Kirksville, MO, 1988.

Haile, H. G. *Luther: An Experiment in Biography*. New York, 1980.

Harran, Marilyn J. *Luther on Conversion*. Ithaca, 1983.

Headley, John. *Luther's View of Church Today*. New Haven, 1963.

Held, Wieland. "Der Allstedter Schosser Hans Zeiss und sein Verhaeltnis zu Thomas Muentzer." *Zeitschrift fuer Geschichtswissenschaft* 35, no. 12 (1987): 1073–1091.

Hillerbrand, Hans-J. *A Fellowship of Discontent*. New York, 1967.

———. "Thomas Muentzer's Last Tract against Luther." *The Mennonite Quarterly Review* 33, no. 1 (1964): 20–36.

Hinrichs, Carl. *Luther und Muentzer. Ihre Auseinandersetzung ueber Obrigkeit und Widerstandsrecht*. Berlin, 1962.

Hoess, Irmgard. *Georg Spalatin 1484–1545: Ein Leben in der Zeit des Humanismus und der Reformation*. Weimar, 1956.

Holl, Karl. "Luther und die Schwaermer." *Gesammelte Schriften*. Vol. 1, 420–467. Tuebingen, 1932.

Honemeyer, Karl. "Muentzers Berufung nach Allstedt." *Harz-Zeitschrift* 16 (1964): 103–111.

Hoyer, Siegfried. "Die Zwickauer Storchianer-Vorlaeufer der Taeufer?" *Jahrbuch fuer Regionalgeschichte* 13 (1986): 60–78.

———. "Radikaler Prediger und soziales Umfeld–Bemerkungen zu Thomas Muentzers Taetigkeit in Zwickau." In Rainer Postel and Franklin Kopitzsch, eds., 155–169, *Reformation und Revolution. Beitraege zum politischen Wandel und den sozialen Kraeften am Begin der Neuzeit*. Stuttgart, 1989.

Husa, Vaclav. *Tomáš Muentzer a Čechy*. Prague, 1957.

Iserloh, Erwin. "Revolution bei Thomas Muentzer: Durchsetzung des Reiches Gottes oder soziale Aktion?" *Historisches Jahrbuch* 92, no. 2 (1972): 182–199.

———. "Sakraments–und Taufverstaendnis bei Thomas Muentzer." In Hansjoerg auf der Maur and Bruno Kleinheyer, eds., 109–122, *Zeichen des Glaubens: Studien zur Taufe und Firmung*. Zurich and Cologne, 1972.

———. "Zur Gestalt und Biographie Thomas Muentzers." *Trierer Theologische Zeitschrift* 71, no. 1 (1962): 248–253.

Jordan, Reinhard. "Pfeiffers und Muentzers Zug in das Eichsfeld und die Verwuestung der Kloester und Schloesser." *Zeitschrift fuer Thueringische Geschichte* 22 (1904): 36–96.

Kaminsky, Howard. "Chiliasm and the Hussite Revolution." *Church History* 26, no. 1 (1957): 43–71.

———. *A History of the Hussite Revolution*. Berkeley and Los Angeles, 1967.

Kandler, Karl–Hermann. "Reformation + Bauernkrieg = Fruehbuergerliche Revolution." *Luther* 48, no. 3 (1977): 100–117.

Karant-Nunn, Susan C. *Zwickau in Transition, 1500–1547: The Reformation as an Agent of Change.* Columbus, Ohio, 1987.

Kawerau, Gustav. *Johann Agricola von Eisleben.* Berlin, 1881.

Kieckhefer, Richard. "Meitser Eckhart's Conception of the Union with God." *Harvard Theological Review* 71, no. 3–4 (1978): 203–225.

Kirchhoff, A. "Johann Herrgott, Buchfuehrer von Nuernberg und sein tragisches Ende 1527." *Archiv fuer Geschichte des deutschen Buchhandels* 1 (1878): 15–55.

Kirchner, Hubert. *Luther and the Peasants' War.* Trans. Darrell Jodock. Philadelphia, 1972.

Kirn, Paul. *Friedrich der Weise und die Kirche.* Leipzig and Berlin, 1926.

Kittelson, James M. *Luther the Reformer.* Minneapolis, 1986.

Klaassen, Walter. "Spirtualism in the Reformation." *The Mennonite Quarterly Review* 37, no. 1 (1963), 67–77.

————. "Visions of the End in Reformation Europe." In Harry Loewen and Al Reimer, eds. *Visions and Realities.* Winnipeg, 1985.

Koch, Klaus. "Spaetisraelitisches Geschichtsdenken am Beispiel des Buches Daniel." *Historische Zeitschrift* 193, no. 1 (1961): 1–32.

Koeditz, Hanna. "Die Volksbewegung in Muehlhausen in Thueringen 1523–1573." Unpublished doctoral dissertation, University of Jena, 1959.

Kolde, Theodor. "Aeltester Bericht ueber die Zwickauer Propheten." *Zeitschrift fuer Kirchengeschichte* 5, no. 2 (1882): 323–325.

Kreis, J. G. "Das Leben und die Schicksale des Thurgauers Ulrich Hugwald, gen. Mutius." *Thurgauische Beitraege zue vaterlaendischen Geschichte* 41–42 (1901–1902): 140–169.

Krusche, Werner. "Zum 450. Todestag von Thomas Muentzer." *Kerygma und Dogma* 21, no. 4 (1975): 315–321.

Kuenning, Paul P. "Luther and Muentzer: Contrasting Theologies in Regard to Secular Authority within the Context of the German Peasant Revolt." *Journal of Church and State* 29, no. 2 (1987): 305–321.

Lau, Franz. "Der Bauernkrieg und das angebliche Ende der lutherischen Reformation als spontaner Volksbewegung." *Lutherjahrbuch* 26 (1959): 109–134.

————. "Die prophetische Apokalyptik Thomas Muentzers und Luthers Absage an die Bauernrevolution." In Friedrich Huebner, et al., eds., 163–170, *Beitraege zur historischen und systematischen Theologie.* Berlin, 1955.

Lawlor, Hugh Jackson. "The Hypomnemata of Hegesippus." In *Eusebiana: Essays on the Ecclesiastical History of Eusebius, Bishop of Caesarea,* 1–97. Oxford, 1912.

Lawrence, C. H. *Medieval Monasticism.* London and New York, 1984.

Lefebvre, Joel. "Melanchthon, Thomas Muentzer et les origines saxonnes de l'anabaptisme." *Ethno-Psychologie: Revue de Psychologie des Peuples* 32, no. 2–3 (1977): 237–256.

Leff, Gordon. *Heresy in the Later Middle Ages.* 2 vols. Manchester and New York, 1967.

———. "The Making of the Myth of a True Church in the Later Middle Ages." *Journal of Medieval and Renaissance Studies* 1, no. 1 (1971): 1–15.

Leo, Heinrich. *Thomas Muentzer—Ein Vortrag.* Berlin, 1856.

Lerner, Robert E. *The Heresy of the Free Spirit in the Later Middle Ages.* Berkeley and Los Angeles, 1972.

Loesche, Dietrich. " 'Achtmaenner, Ewiger Bund Gottes und Ewiger Rat.' Zur Geschichte der revolutionaeren Bewegung in Muehlhausen i. Th. 1523–1525." *Jahrbuch fuer Wirtschaftsgeschichte* 1 (1960): 135–160.

Lohmann, Annemarie. *Zur geistigen Entwicklung Thomas Muentzers.* Leipzig and Berlin, 1931.

Lohse, Bernhard. "Auf dem Wege zu einem neuen Muentzer-Bild." *Luther* 41, no. 3 (1970): 120–133.

———. "Die Bedeutung Augustins fuer den jungen Luther." *Kerygma und Dogma* 11, no. 2 (1965): 116–135.

———. "Luther und Muentzer." *Luther* 45, no. 1 (1974): 12–32.

———. "Luther und der Radikalismus." *Lutherjahrbuch* 44 (1977): 7–21.

Ludolphy, Ingetraut. *Friedrich der Weise, Kurfuerst von Sachsen 1463–1525.* Goettingen, 1984.

Lutz, Robert H. *Wer war der gemeine Mann? Der dritte Stand in der Krise des Spaetmittelalters.* Munich, 1979.

Malone, Edward E. "Martyrdom and Monastic Profession as a Second Baptism." In Anton Quasten Meyer and Burkhard Neunheuser, eds. *Vom christlichen Mysterium: Gesammelte Arbeiten zum Gedaechtnis von Odo Casel, O.S.B.* Duesseldorf, 1951.

Maron, Gottfried. "Thomas Muentzer als Theologe des Gerichts." *Zeitschrift fuer Kirchengeschichte* 83 (1972): 195–225.

———. "Thomas Muentzer in der Sicht Martin Luthers." *Jahrbuch der Kirchlichen Hochschule Berlin* 12 (1975): 71–85.

McGiffert, Arthur Cushmann. "The Life and Writings of Eusebius of Caesarea." In *Eusebius.* Vol. 1, 2d Series, *The Nicene and Post-Nicene Fathers.* Ed. Philip Schaff and Henry Wace. Reprint: Grand Rapids, 1975.

Mentz, Georg. *Johann Friedrich der Grossmuetige.* 2 vols. Jena, 1903–1908.

Merz, Otto. *Thomas Muentzer und Heinrich Pfeiffer 1523–1525.* Goettingen, 1889.

Metzer, Wolfgang. "Muentzeriana." *Thueringisch–saechsische Zeitschrift fuer Geschichte und Kunst* 16 (1927): 59–78.

Meusel, Alfred. *Thomas Muentzer und seine Zeit.* Berlin, 1952.

Meyer, Christian. "Der Wiedertaeufer Nikolaus Storch und seine Anhaenger in Hof." *Zeitschrift fuer Kirchengeschichte* 16, no. 1 (1896): 117–124.

Meyer, Manfred. "Zur Haltung des Adels im Bauernkrieg." *Jahrbuch fuer Regionalgeschichte* 4 (1972): 200–224.

Molnar, Amedeo. "Thomas Muentzer in Boehmen." *Communio Viatorum: Theological Quarterly* 4 (1958): 242–245.

Mras, M. Karl. "Die Hegesippus-Frage." *Anzeiger der oesterreichischen Akademie der Wissenschaften: Philosophisch-Historische Klasse,* Nr. 8 (1958): 143–153.

Muehlhaupt, Erwin. "Der Begriff 'Linker Fluegel der Reformation' von Luther her gesehen." *Luther* 48, no. 2 (1977): 76–80.

———. "Die betrogene Forelle, oder: die getruebte Reformationsgeschichte." *Luther* 44, no. 1 (1973): 29–35.

———. "Martin Luther oder Thomas Muentzer,—Wer ist der rechte Prophet?" *Luther* 45, no. 2 (1974): 55–71.

———. "Welche Schriften Luthers hat Muentzer gekannt?" *Luther* 46, no. 3 (1975): 125–137.

Muehlpfordt, Guenther. "Der fruehe Luther als Autoritaet der Radikalen. Zum Luther-Erbe des 'linken Fluegels.' " In *Weltwirkung der Reformation*. Max Steinmetz and Gerhard Brendler, eds. Vol. 1, 205–225. Berlin, 1969.

Mueller, Michael. "Die Gottlosen bei Thomas Muentzer—mit einem Vergleich zu Martin Luther." *Lutherjahrbuch* 46 (1979): 97–119.

Nipperdey, Thomas. "Theologie und Revolution bei Thomas Muentzer." *Archiv fuer Reformationsgeschichte* 54 (1963): 145–179.

Noesgen, K. F. "Der kirchliche Standpunkt Hegesippus." *Zeitschrift fuer Kirchengeschichte* 2, no. 2 (1878): 193–233.

Oberman, H. A. "Thomas Muentzer: van verontrusting tot verzet." *Kerk en Theologie* 24 (1973): 205–214.

Olivier, Daniel. *The Trial of Martin Luther*. Trans. John Tonkin. London and Oxford, 1978.

Oulton, J. E. L. "Rufinus's Translation of the *Church History* of Eusebius." *The Journal of Theological Studies* 30 (1929): 150–175.

Oyer, John S. "The Influence of Jacob Strauss on the Anabaptists: A Problem in Historical Methodology." In Marc Lienhard, ed., 62–82, *The Origins and Characteristics of Anabaptism*. The Hague, 1977.

———. *Lutheran Reformers against Anabaptists*. The Hague, 1964.

Packull, Werner. "Gottfried Seebass on Hans Hut: A Discussion." *The Mennonite Quarterly Review* 49, no. 1 (1975): 56–61.

———. *Mysticism and the Early South German-Austrian Anabaptist Movement 1525–1531*. Scottdale, PA, 1977.

Pater, Calvin Augustine. *Karlstadt as the Father of the Baptist Movements: The Emergence of Lay Protestantism*. Toronto, 1984.

Pianzola, Maurice. *Thomas Munzer ou la Guerre des Paysans*. Paris, 1958.

Postel, Rainer, and Franklin Kopitzsch, eds. *Reformation und Revolution: Beitraege zum politischen Wandel und den sozialen Kraeften am Begin der Neuzeit*. Stuttgart, 1989.

Potter, J. M. "Luther and Political Millennarianism: The Case of the Peasants' War." *Journal of the History of Ideas* 42, no. 3 (1981): 389–406.

Preus, James S. *Carlstadt's Ordinaciones and Luther's Liberty: A Study of the Wittenberg Movement 1521–22*. Vol. 27 of *Harvard Theological Studies*. Cambridge and London, 1974.

Ranke, Leopold von. *Deutsche Geschichte im Zeitalter der Reformation*. 2 vols. Hamburg, n.d.

Rochler, Wolfgang. "Das Ringen um die Gottheit Gottes bei Luther und Muentzer." *Luther* 46, no. 2 (1975): 76–87.

————. "Ordnungsbegriff und Gottesgedanke bei Thomas Muentzer." *Zeitschrift fuer Kirchengeschichte* 85, no. 3 (1974): 367–382.

Rommel, Ludwig. "Die Einwohnerschaft der Stadt Frankenhausen in der Schlacht vom 15. Mai 1525." *Jahrbuch fuer Regionalgeschichte* 10 (1983): 93–107.

Rudolph, Guenther. "Thomas Muentzers sozialoekonomische Konzeption und das Traditionsbewusstsein der sozialistischen Arbeiterbewegung." *Deutsche Zeitschrift fuer Philosophie* 23, no. 4 (1975): 558–569.

Rueger, Hans Peter. "Thomas Muentzers Erklaerung hebraischer Eigennamen und der Liber de interpretatione hebraicorum nominum des Hieronymus." *Zeitschrift fuer Kirchengeschichte* 98, no. 1–2 (1983): 83–87.

Rupp, E. Gordon. *Patterns of Reformation.* Philadelphia, 1969.

————. "Programme notes on the Theme 'Muentzer and Luther.' " In *Vierhundertfuenfzig Jahre lutherische Reformation 1517–1967: Festschrift fuer Franz Lau,* 302–309. Goettingen, 1967.

Rupp, E. Gordon, and Benjamin Drewery, eds. *Martin Luther.* London, 1970.

Sanford, Eva Matthew. "Propaganda and Censorship in the Transmission of Josephus." *Transactions and Proceedings of the American Philological Society* 66 (1935): 127–145.

Schaff, Philip. *History of the Christian Church.* Vol. 3. New York, 1910.

Scheel, W. *Johann Freiherr von Schwarzenberg.* Berlin, 1905.

Scheidweiler, F. "Die Kirchengeschichte des Gelasios von Kaisareia." *Byzantinische Zeitschrift* 46 (1953): 277–301.

Schiff, Otto. "Thomas Muentzer als Prediger in Halle." *Archiv fuer Reformationsgeschichte* 23 (1926): 287–293.

————. "Thomas Muentzer und die Bauernbewegung am Oberrhein." *Historische Zeitschrift* 110 (1913): 67–90.

Schreckenburg, Heinz. *Die Flavius–Josephus–Tradition in Antike und Mittelalter.* Leiden, 1972.

Schulz, Karl. "Thomas Muentzers liturgische Bestrebungen." *Zeitschrift fuer Kirchengeschichte* 47, no. 3 (1928): 369–401.

Schulze, Hans. "Zur Kritik der Revolutionstheologen." *Kerygma und Dogma* 15 no. 3 (1969): 239–257.

Schwarz, Reinhard. *Die Apokalyptische Theologie Thomas Muentzers und der Taboriten.* Stuttgart, 1977.

————. "Luthers Erscheinen auf dem Wormser Reichstag in der Sicht Thomas Muentzers." In *Der Reichstag zu Worms von 1521.* Fritz Reuter, ed., 208–221. Cologne and Vienna, 1981.

Scott, Thomas. "The 'Volksreformation' of Thomas Muentzer in Allstedt and Muehlhausen." *Journal of Ecclesiastical History* 34, no. 2 (1983): 194–230.

Seidemann, J. K. *Thomas Muentzer, Eine Biographie.* Dresden and Leipzig, 1842.

Sider, Ronald J. *Andreas Bodenstein von Karlstadt: The Development of His Thought.* Leiden, 1974.

Smirin, M. M. *Die Volksreformation des Thomas Muentzers und der Grosse Bauernkrieg.* Berlin, 1952.

Spillmann, Hans Otto. *Untersuchungen zum Wortschatz in Thomas Muentzers Deutschen Schriften.* Berlin and New York, 1971.

Spinka, Matthew. *John Hus and the Council of Constance.* New York and London, 1965.

———. *John Hus' Concept of the Church.* Princeton, 1966.

Spitz, Lewis W. *The Protestant Reformation 1517–1559.* New York, 1984.

Stayer, James M. *Anabaptists and the Sword.* Lawrence, KS, 1972.

Steinmetz, Max, et al., eds. *Der deutsche Bauernkrieg und Thomas Muentzer.* Leipzig, 1976.

———. "Thomas Muentzer und die Buecher." *Zeitschrift fuer Geschichtswissenschaft* 32, no. 7 (1984): 602–610.

Streif, Paul. *Thomas Muentzer oder der Thueringische Bauernkrieg.* Leipzig, 1836.

Strobel, G. Th. *Leben, Schriften und Lehren Thome Muentzers.* Nuremberg and Altdorf, 1795.

Tanaka, Shinzo. "Eine Seite der geistigen Entwicklung Thomas Muentzers in seiner 'lutherischen' Zeit." *Lutherjahrbuch* 40 (1973): 76–88.

Telfer, W. "Was Hegesippus a Jew?" *Harvard Theological Review* 53, no. 2 (January 1960): 143–153.

Ullmann, Wolfgang. "Ordo rerum: Muentzers Randbemerkungen zu Tertullian als Quelle fuer das Verstaendnis seiner Theologie." *Theologische Versuche* 7 (1976): 125–140.

Vogler, Guenter. "Thomas Muentzer auf dem Wege zur Bildung—Anmerkungen zur Frankfurter Studienzeit." *Jahrbuch fuer Regionalgeschichte* 11 (1985): 28–35.

———. "Thomas Muentzer und die Staedte." In *Reformation und Revolution. Beitraege zum politischen Wandel und den Kraeften der Neuzeit.* Rainer Postel and Franklin Kopitzsch, eds., 138–154. Stuttgart, 1989.

Waas, Adolf. *Die Bauern im Kampf um Gerechtigkeit.* Munich, 1964.

Wallace-Hadrill, D. S. "Eusebius of Caesarea and the Testimonium Flavianum (Josephus, *Antiquities,* XVIII, 63f.)." *Journal of Ecclesiastical History* 25, no. 4 (1974): 353–362.

Walter, L. G. *Thomas Munzer et Les Luttes Sociales à L'Époque de la Réforme.* Paris, 1927.

Wappler, Paul. *Thomas Muentzer in Zwickau und die "Zwickauer Propheten."* 2d ed. Guetersloh, 1966.

Wehler, Hans-Ulrich, ed. *Der deutsche Bauernkrieg 1524–1526.* Sonderheft 1: Geschichte und Gesellschaft, *Zeitschrift fuer Historische Sozialwissenschaft.* Goettingen, 1975.

Werner, J. "Thomas Muentzers Regenbogenfahne." *Theologische Zeitschrift* 31, no. 1 (1975): 32–37.

Williams, George H. *The Radical Reformation.* Philadelphia, 1962.

Wolfgram, Eberhard. "Det Prager Anschlag Thomas Muentzers in der Handschrift der Leipziger Universitaetsbibliothek." *Wissenschaftliche Zeitschrift der Karl-Marx-Universitaet* 6, no. 1 (1956/1957): 295–308.

Wolgast, Eike. *Thomas Muentzer. Ein Verstoerer der Unglaeubigen.* Goettingen and Zurich, 1981.

Zeman, J. K. *The Anabaptists and the Czech Brethren in Moravia.* The Hague, 1969.

Zimmermann, Joachim. *Thomas Muentzer: Ein deutsches Schicksal.* Berlin, 1925.

Zimmermann, Wilhelm. *Geschichte des grossen Bauernkrieges.* 2d ed. Stuttgart, 1856.

——. *Geschichte des grossen deutschen Bauernkrieges.* 3 vols. Stuttgart, 1841–1843.

Zumkeller, A. "Thomas Muentzer—Augustiner?" *Augustiniana* 9 (1959): 380–385.

Zur Muehlen, Karl-Heinz. "Luther zwischen Tradition und Revolution." *Luther* 47, no. 2 (1976): 61–76.

——. "Zur Erforschung des 'jungen Luthers' seit 1876." *Lutherjahrbuch* 50 (1983): 48–125.

Index

326

Index

to, 179, 181–182; Ernest of
Mansfeld's letter of 24 September
1523 to, 180–181, 183; Luther writes
concerning Imperial edict, 184; 11
April 1524 report of Allstedt Council
to, 185, 190, 194; Muentzer de-
nounces, 192; 22 June 1524 letter of
Duke John to, 200; letter to Zeiss of
27 June 1524, 201; Muentzer sends
exposition of Luke to, 203; wants
Word of God to "do it" alone, 208;
allowed Gospel to be preached, 210,
214, 248; Muentzer's letter of 3 August 1524 to, 215; letter of 9 August
1524 to Zeiss by, 216; letter of 24
August 1524 by Zeiss to, 216; oaths
taken to, 219; George of Saxony
seeks aid against Muehlhausen, 230;
demands Muehlhausen reinstate mayors, 235; Zeiss's letter of 7 May 1525
to, 246, 252, 253; comes to aid of
Naundorf Convent, 251; death of,
255; Muentzer wants to go beyond
Luther and, 271
Free Spirit, heresy of, 90–94, 99, 143
Friends of God: Muentzer calls Luther
"light and example of . . . ," 5–6, 83,
102; as used by Tauler, 21, 24, 26,
30, 31, 32, 78, 255; Muentzer and
Tauler's use of, 46; Muentzer had
counted Luther among, 125, 130,
157; as used by Muentzer, 131, 153,
170, 172, 187; are converted, 142;
highest praise of a Taulerian, 145; Ernest of Mansfeld a harmful enemy of,
257, and active destroyer of, 258
Frohse, 3
Futura ecclesia, 8, 125, 127–129, 151,
157, 170, 176. *See also* New Apostolic Church

Gans, Michael, 101, 102, 121
Gehofen, Matern von, 253, 256
George Duke of Saxony: Allstedt surrounded by lands of, 178; opposes
Muentzer's services and gospel, 179,
206, 210, 228, 248; Luther and, 184;
actions against Muentzer, 185; subjects complain to Muentzer, 186; regarded by Muentzer as a godless
ruler, 189; Luther urges Muentzer to
move to territories, 201; actions of
against Sangerhausen subjects, 212;
offers sanctuary to Muehlhausen mayors, 223, 235; seeks to rally princes
against Muehlhausen, 230; reports of
Berlepsch to, 231, 236, 241; poses

threat to Muehlhausen, 233; writes to
Nuremberg Council, June 1525, 239;
and penalty to Muehlhausen, 240–
241; takes counts who joined
Muentzer's *Bund* to task, 247; pre-
pares for battle, 249; peasants call a
tyrant, 252; Ernest of Mansfeld's re-
port to, 254; peasants seek to intimi-
date, 255, 261; and Muentzer's cap-
ture, 256; and troops before
Frankenhausen, 14 May 1525, 259;
and Muentzer's confession, 263–265,
267
Gideon, 160, 255, 257; sword of, 252,
255, 256, 259, 262
Glatz, Kaspar, 14, 15, 17
Glov, Achactius, 6, 7, 38, 58, 100
Grebel, Conrad, 227
Grisar, Hartmann, 14
Gritsch, Eric, 190
Goermar, 244, 245
Goertz, Hans-Juergen, 2, 50
Gregory, St., 29
Guenther, Franz, 3, 4, 5, 9, 38, 39, 100,
168
Guenther Count of Schwarzburg, 246,
247, 249, 253; father Henry, 246

Haferitz, Simon, 192
Halle, 96, 130, 132
Harmony of Old and New Testaments:
in *Historia*, 19; in Augustine, 71; in
Muentzer, 72, 87–88
Harttenstein, Steffan, 256
Hausmann, Nicholas: writes to Frederick
the Wise, 13 August 1521, 3;
Muentzer's letter of 15 June 1520 to,
89, 101–103, 113, 119, 126, 190,
202; Egranus's "blasphemy" in pres-
ence of, 242
Headley, John, 36
Hegau, 228, 238
Hegesippus: cited by Muentzer, 7, 39,
42, 43, 51, 63, 90, 118, 267; passages
in Eusebius's *Church History*, 41–44,
50, 71; and Egiosiopus or pseudo-
Hegesippus, 42; not an historian, 44;
Memoranda of, 44; Eusebius places
him earlier than he should have, 44–
45; in Rufinus's translation, 46; Hus
does not share view of fall of Church,
107; Muentzer's use of in
Fuerstenpredigt, 210
Heidelberg Disputation, 34
Heine, Heinrich, 1
Heldrungen, 240, 245, 246, 261, 263,
264, 265; tyrant of, 252, 255

Designer: U.C. Press Staff
Compositor: Huron Valley Graphics
Text: 10/13 Sabon
Display: Sabon
Printer: Bookcrafters
Binder: Bookcrafters